Pope Pius XII:
Architect for Peace

Margherita Marchione

PAULIST PRESS
New York/Mahwah, N.J.

Acknowledgments: The author is indebted to the following for their precious assistance: Barbara and Peter Bye for computer direction; William Doino, Jr. for bibliographical references; Sisters Filomena Di Carlo and Helen Sholander for secretarial help; the staff of *Inside the Vatican* for reading the manuscript and offering valuable suggestions. She expresses appreciation and gratitude for financial help received from Robert Budelman, Ralph M. Cestone, Angela and Francesco Crocenzi, David Jurist, Arthur McGinnis, Phyllis and Michael Mondelli, N. Larry Paragano, Frank Visceglia, and other Catholic and Jewish friends. In a special way the author acknowledges the help given by His Eminence Cardinal Agostino Cacciavillan, then Papal Nuncio in Washington, D.C. Thanks to *Civiltà Cattolica* for "The Myth in the Light of the Archives" and Robert A. Graham for "Church, Shoah, and Anti-Semitism."

Cover design by Tim McKeen

Copyright © 2000 by Religious Teachers Filippini

Library of Congress Cataloging-in-Publication Data

Marchione, Margherita.
   Pope Pius XII : architect for peace / by Margherita Marchione.
     p. cm.
   Includes bibliographical references and index.
   ISBN 0-8091-3912-X (alk. paper)
   1. Pius XII, Pope, 1876–1958. 2. Papacy—History—1929–1945. 3. World War, 1939–1945—Catholic Church. I. Title.
BX1378.M37 2000
282′.092—dc21

                         99-058456
                             CIP

Published by Paulist Press
997 Macarthur Boulevard
Mahwah, New Jersey 07430

www.paulistpress.com

Printed and bound in the
United States of America

Pope Pius XII:
Architect for Peace

Also by Margherita Marchione
published by Paulist Press

YOURS IS A PRECIOUS WITNESS:
Memoirs of Jews and Catholics in Wartime Italy

Of related interest from Paulist Press (United States) and Gracewing
(United Kingdom)

PIUS XII AND THE SECOND WORLD WAR
According to the Archives of the Vatican
by Pierre Blet, S.J.
translated by Lawrence J. Johnson

To the Honorable Frank J. Pino—retired Justice of the Supreme Court of the State of New York and former State Senator—an ardent defender of Pope Pius XII and the Magisterium of the Catholic Church, whose friendship and support I shall always treasure.

Contents

PART III
THE POPE AND THE HORROR OF THE HOLOCAUST

PART IV
BACKGROUND DOCUMENTATION

PART V
APPENDIX

PART VI

We have read your Memorandum very carefully, and We have
found it intensely interesting. The issues are so clear-cut; of
the definite, determined stand of the United States government it
leaves no shadow of doubt.

It gave Us great satisfaction to ~~hear~~ *know* from Your Excellency
how united in this hour of national trial are all
~~that~~ /the Catholics of the United States, under the enlightened
leadership of the Bishops, ~~are united,~~ and that ~~there exist~~ between
the Bishops and the President/ *and his Government there exist* such sincere relations of mutual
trust.

It has been a pleasure for Us to hear Your Excellency recall.
~~No one is more keenly aware than We of~~ President Roosevelt's
aim and efforts to bring about a peace that will be worthy of man's
personal dignity and *of* his high destiny. This peace, as We have
constantly repeated, must be based on justice and charity. It must
take into consideration the vital needs of all nations; all must
find it possible of fulfilment; it must bear within itself the
seeds of longevity. Moreover, to Our mind, there is not the
slightest chance of a peace being genuine and lasting, unless, to
begin with, the mutual relations between governments and peoples,
as well as those between individual governments and their own
peoples, are based not on ~~utility,~~ *utilitarianism,* / arbitrary decrees or brute force,
but on ~~the sacred observance~~ *fulfilment:* of contracts made, ~~of~~ *on the sacred observance* justice and law,
tempered by christian charity and brotherly love ,
\ on reverence for the dignity of the human person and respect for
~~a man's~~ religious convictions; and unless the worship of God again
exercises its due influence in the individual and national life
of all peoples.

For this reason, despite what ~~foreign~~ *any* propaganda may say to
the contrary, We have never thought in terms of a peace by compromis

---

This facsimile of a letter from Pope Pius XII to U.S. Ambassador Myron
Taylor, dated September 22, 1942, is edited by the Pope's own hand. It clearly
underscores that he did not want peace to come as a result of compromise.

Foreword

---

*H*istory at times can be rather fickle. During World War II and in the following years, Pope Pius XII was considered universally as having contributed significantly to saving Jewish lives from the Nazi attempt to eliminate the Jewish people from the soil of Europe.

In the document *We Remember: A Reflection on the Shoah,* published by the Holy See's Commission for Religious Relations with the Jews on March 16, 1998, reference is made to representative Jewish organizations and personalities who in 1945 spontaneously expressed thanks to the Pontiff himself and to the Catholic Church for the help given to Jews throughout Europe during the war. Mention is also made of the message sent in 1958 by Golda Meir, the then Foreign Minister and later the Prime Minister of the State of Israel, on the death of Pius XII, which reads:

> We share in the grief of humanity....When fearful martyrdom came to our people, the voice of the Pope was raised for its victims. The life of our times was enriched by a voice speaking out about great moral truths above the tumult of daily conflict. We mourn a great servant of peace.

Yet, only a few years later, especially after the play *The Deputy* by Rolf Hochhuth in 1963, the same Pope is accused of unjustified silence in respect of the crimes committed against the Jewish people, and even of pro-German sympathy.

The Holy See's document, *We Remember: A Reflection on the Shoah,* received its harshest criticism from Jewish organizations specifically for its references to Pope Pius XII. They objected strongly to the statement that the Pope personally or through his representatives had contributed to saving hundreds of thousands of Jewish lives.

It is obvious from all that has been stated and published in the recent months that the pontificate of Pius XII, especially during the years, 1939–45, requires further study and objective research, reflection, and the dissemination of results. It is not our object, by quoting some few statements of approval and appreciation in the document *We Remember,* to indicate that a final and definitive appraisal of Pope Pius XII's pontificate had been reached. Rather, we wish to affirm just the opposite and not leave unchallenged the emotional and unconfirmed presentation of Pius XII as one who failed to respond adequately to the challenges of his time. We could not allow Hochhuth's analysis to remain unchallenged.

Now it is up to the historians to take up the unfinished business. In the period since the publication of *We Remember* there has been an important contribution from Reverend Pierre Blet, S.J., one of the small group of experts who studied every document concerning the Second World War in the Vatican archives and collaborated on the publication of the twelve volumes in which these documents have been made available to historians and to the public in general. This article is included in Sister Margherita Marchione's present volume, *Pope Pius XII: Architect for Peace.*

In another similar article, published in *L'Osservatore Romano* on November 1, 1998, the Honorable Herbert Schambeck, who is president of the Parliament of the Federal Republic of Austria, quotes the following statement made in 1967 by a Jewish writer, Pinchas E. Lapide:

> The total number of Jews who, also thanks to Christian assistance, survived Hitler in that part of Europe occupied by the Nazis, and leaving Russia apart, was about 945,000. Officially the number of Jews to whose salvation the Catholic Church contributed is given as 700,000 but probably their number should be 860,000.

This contradicts those who ridicule the Vatican statement's claim in this connection. Schambeck also quotes impressive Jewish testimony from Rabbi André Ungar and the Chief Rabbi of Rome, Elio Toaff.

Sister Margherita Marchione's present volume is a valuable contribution to the study of Pope Pius XII and his times. The author has shown here how distorted and untrue are the allegations that Pope Pius XII could have done more to avert the consequences of the Nazi design to eliminate the Jewish people from the societies of Europe.

I must state that I find very disturbing the ease with which responsible people today judge those who had to exercise heavy and important international responsibilities during the time of the Nazi occupation of European countries. It is so naïve to claim that Pope Pius XII should have condemned with a louder voice the evils of National Socialism. Of course, I am told, he should have done more to help. Would it have been better really to make more noise? Most of those who brought real help to the Jewish community so severely persecuted did so in silence.

Sister Marchione has done a service to history and to Jewish-Catholic relations in so thoroughly and scientifically researching the situation that existed in that difficult wartime period. In this book she reproduces for audiences today documentary records of the various activities of Pope Pius XII's Roman Curia during the war. In other books she has recorded the witness of those Jews who have lived to tell their stories. They include religious, even cloistered convents, who did not hesitate to go against the strict canonical regulations regarding religious houses and the danger of severe reprisal from German occupation in order to protect the lives of thousands of Jewish men, women, and children from 1943 to 1945. Her own congregation, the Religious Teachers Filippini Sisters in Rome alone cared for 114 Jewish men, women, and children. It was the experience of her Roman religious Sisters that set her on this task. Had Pius XII made the kind of statements now demanded by those who condemn his alleged "silence," one wonders how many of these Jews would have survived to tell their precious story.

Sister Margherita Marchione's research and writing on this question is indeed a valuable contribution to those who wish to know the truth of that tragic period in the long history of the Jewish people. It will surely help to overcome one of the obstacles to better relations between the Jewish people and the Church as we enter the third Christian millennium. I express the thanks of the Holy See's Commission for Religious Relations with the Jews and leave the reader to reflect on the evidence that Sister Margherita has recorded in these pages so as to reach an objective judgment on Pope Pius XII. I am convinced that an unprejudiced reading of these pages will leave the reader with a deep conviction that Pope Pius XII was indeed a true "Architect for Peace."

Edward Idris Cardinal Cassidy, President
Commission for Religious Relations with the Jews
Pontifical Council for Promoting Christian Unity

Prologue

I was truly excited when I came across a reference to the Superior General of the Pontifical Institute of the Religious Teachers Filippini, founded in 1692, in *La Chiesa e la Guerra (The Church and the War)*. This out-of-print book, published in 1944, is indeed a treasury of information about the work of the Vatican during World War II.

Though no name was given for the Superior General, I saw her—Mother Teresa Saccucci—in my mind's eye. I felt once again the strength of her prayerfulness, her humble and dignified appearance, white hair, angelic smile, and heard her maternal and affectionate words, extending an extraordinary peace among us—as it affected me—when I was in the novitiate at Villa Walsh in Morristown, New Jersey, from 1935 to 1939.

Located on a 750-foot elevation, the highest point within a thirty-mile radius of New York City, Villa Walsh commands a breathtaking view described by some visitors as "Little Switzerland." I recall living with Mother Teresa Saccucci in the southern colonial mansion, a beautifully preserved relic of America's gilded age.

Since 1707 the Religious Teachers Filippini were under the jurisdiction and protection of the Secret Almoner of the Pope and, therefore, were listed in the *Annuario Pontificio (Directory of the Holy See)*. This changed with Vatican II. Today the Sisters continue to assist the Vatican at Castelgandolfo, the Pope's summer residence.

In 1920, Pope Benedict XV asked Bishop Thomas Joseph Walsh to guide the Sisters in the United States. I recall the Bishop's frequent visits. We always assembled on the front porch to greet him and his guests. As the entourage drove up the main entrance roadway lined with multicolored trees and slowly passed the six-story huge stone water tower (a panoramic view of New York City and the Brooklyn Bridge is visible from its lookout on cloud-free nights), we were filled with excitement and awe. After Bishop Walsh greeted us individually, we entertained him and his guests with a concert and dinner. These were truly festive occasions.

When Pope Pius XI passed away, Bishop Walsh arranged to have a special liturgy in our beautiful chapel on February 14, 1939. We also celebrated the coronation of Pope Pius XII on March 12. I recall how everyone was bussed to Newark to participate in the official festivities in Saint Patrick's Cathedral. As members of the pontifical family, we were imbued with much love and devotion for the newly elected Pontiff.

Soon after, Mother Teresa Saccucci left for Rome and remained there as Superior General during World War II. I am sure she embraced the 114 Jews (men, women, and children) hidden in three of our convents in Rome for more than a year during the Nazi occupation with the same solicitude and gentleness I experienced as a young Sister. Their thanks to the Sisters who had saved them was expressed by the gift of a five-foot statue of the Madonna, still standing on the fourth floor in the corridor of Arco dei Ginnasi, where sixty Jews once took refuge. In November 1994, I became acquainted with the Sisters who recounted to me the events of the war years and, despite the dangers encountered, had demonstrated heroic Christian solicitude for their Jewish guests.

What I learned from *The Church and the War* was that the Religious Teachers Filippini also helped the Holy Father in the Information Bureau of the Vatican Secretariat of State. According to this rare book, Mother Teresa responded to an interviewer's inquiry: "For this work in the Information Bureau, I had designated five or six Sisters with typewriters. But every day there were other young women and children of the school who wanted to work for the Holy Father and answer the letters of prisoners of war and the needy. I did all I could to satisfy the Pope's wishes. The work had to be kept secret. As followers of Saint Lucy Filippini, the Sisters dedicated themselves to this task. It was a good sign when there was work in the office and the pontifical initiative succeeded. It was a charity that had no bounds in the midst of hatred and destruction."

In consonance with the Pope's wishes, hundreds of thousands of requests for information were answered and appropriate letters were sent to prisoners of war by members of religious orders and volunteers. Throughout the war, under the direction of the Provincial Superior, Mother Ninetta Jonata, the Religious Teachers Filippini in the United States not only visited the Italian prisoners of war and internees sequestered here, but began shipping tons of cases of medicine and clothing to the Vatican to help care for the needy. This charity continued through 1966, when I crossed the Atlantic on the *Michelangelo* and arrived in Naples with many cases of clothing and medicine for the Pope's poor.

Pius XII expressed his appreciation for the help of the Religious Teachers Filippini by personally approving their revised Rules with these words written in his own hand: "Having examined the present Rules of the Pontifical Institute of the Religious Teachers Filippini, We willingly give Our approval. From the Vatican, 13 October 1951, Pius XII."

Obviously the present work will contain facts well known to the generation who lived through World War II. However, some of the victims may have buried their memories or forgotten the past. It is imperative that today's youth learn about those facts. While it is difficult for a new generation to judge the past without having suffered the horrors of war, they must interpret history and discover the way to arrive at historical truth. They must understand the action undertaken by the Church to put an end to the evil committed during this enormous human tragedy, the Holocaust.

I interviewed Lola Rozzi, now a resident of Pennsylvania, who was born in Italy during the Fascist regime. As a young girl, she played a role in a Catholic Action youth group. She recalls that many of her school companions were orphaned or mutilated by bombings; undetected mines left in the city or in the fields of the countryside of Ascoli Piceno also wrought damage on the innocent. She remembers her great fear at seeing the Germans enter her apartment and days when she closed the blinds for protection or ran for safety after the sirens rang. She remembers her mother's anxiety and nervousness when the Germans asked her father—a post-office clerk—to translate or send messages by telegraph. Above all, she remembers when she had the unforgettable honor to meet the Pontiff: "The presence of Pius XII not only inspired us: it was a powerful, mystical experience. From him emanated a love and human warmth that only those who have had the privilege of being near him can feel and relate."

Between 1939 and 1946, Pius XII gave particular attention to the prisoners of war. To them, his Christmas messages, especially the one of 1943, offered great comfort. He sent them gift packages accompanied by a spiritual blessing and words of consolation. One prisoner called the day when the Pope's gift arrived, "the most beautiful day of captivity."

In a foreign land, the only link the prisoners of war had to a voice of friendship was with the Vatican Information Bureau. Their hope for the future was based on the interest expressed by the Pope, as he inspired and comforted them with the visits of his representatives.

In the Vatican, Pius XII maintained not only a diplomatic network throughout the war, but in order to save the lives of Jews and others hunted by the Nazis, he also increased the number of Papal Guards from three hundred men in September 1943 to four thousand within nine months. Members of the Papal Guards protected the Vatican walls and the extraterritorial buildings, but the main reason for the increased number was to assist in hiding the identities of targeted victims, regardless of race or religion. The hunted were given Vatican identification and lived in the Vatican itself or in one of its extraterritorial buildings. When services were no longer needed at the end of the war, the Pope kept these endangered persons in the Papal Guards. Their work was to distribute food and clothing to the needy in Rome and its suburbs.

Pius XII was personally interested in the life of each individual brought to his attention. Young and old appealed to him for help in locating missing relatives. In order to correspond with the families of the prisoners, the Holy Father established the Vatican Information Bureau. Requests for information came from every country in the world. All received his attention. This was the only archive in the world completely dedicated to transmitting news to the families of prisoners of war.

Even today, in the reference room where the research staff worked, beneath a painting of Pius XII with outstretched arms, there is an excerpt from his Christmas message to the prisoners.

My first trip to Italy was in May 1957 as a Columbia University Garibaldi Scholar, where for three months I researched Clemente Rebora's life and poetry. Accompanied by Pius XII's niece, Elena Rossignani Pacelli, I had the opportunity to meet him in the Basilica of Saint Peter. He was extremely interested in Rebora, the poet who had joined the Rosmini Fathers after his conversion in 1929. I asked the Pope to bless my research. The memory of this precious meeting remains with me. I also possess a photograph with the Holy Father and Elena that was taken during the papal audience as we gathered in front of Giovanni Lorenzo Bernini's impressive bronze baldachin beneath the dome.

Pius XII's piercing eyes penetrated my soul and I still see his tall, dignified, and ascetic stature along with his penetrating glance, his loving smile, and animated gestures. He had a magnetic personality full of intelligence and nobility of spirit. When I think of Pius XII, I feel inspired. How can I not dedicate myself to him with the same fervor that impelled me to write about Clemente Rebora, Giovanni Boine, Philip Mazzei, Giuseppe Prezzolini, and other historical figures?

There is great need to eliminate the false interpretations of the so-called "silence" of Pope Pius XII that has circulated for half a century. In his talks, Pius XII does not explicitly mention any specific group of victims. However, everyone understood his reference to "Jews." Pius XII's thoughts were expressed clearly and emphatically. His style was that of a diplomat who pondered over every word he uttered. He used trenchant terms to protest the atrocities: "the wrath of God," "acts which cry to God for vengeance," "woe to those who...oppress and torture the unarmed and the innocent." He expressed his concern for: "all victims of this war," "those expelled from their native land," "those who are suffering on account of nationality or race," "those threatened with extermination."

The Vatican was the one major refuge for thousands of persecuted people, and its Information Bureau was the sole means of communication available to prisoners of war and their families. It is my wish to make clear the role of the Church in this period, to defend Pius XII's actions, and to make the truth known.

Tributes of love and gratitude poured into Rome when Pope Pius XII died on October 9, 1958. Richard Cardinal Cushing of Boston expressed the esteem of the whole world: "Theologian, canonist, scholar, linguist, statesman, diplomat—all of these Pius XII was. For all of them he has been hailed and praised. But more than anything else he was a pastor, a good shepherd of souls, selflessly dedicated to the honest interests of the Church and to the greater glory of God."

It is time to put an end to the calumny—which began in 1963 with the play *The Deputy* by Rolf Hochhuth—regarding Pius XII's "silence." It is time to promote Catholic-Jewish dialogue and reflect upon the well-known truths supported by Vatican documents that some critics have chosen to ignore. It is time to distinguish between fiction and fact established beyond a reasonable doubt: to reject the former and accept the latter.

As we near the close of the twentieth century, may Pope Pius XII's efforts to bring about peace and help all victims of war be seen for what they actually were—a long, dedicated work of mercy and love.

One final organizational note. This book proceeds neither biographically nor chronologically. It considers a variety of criticisms lodged against Pius XII in light of what he actually did and said; the circumstances in which he spoke and acted; and, most importantly, relevant scholarship on the pertinent original documents relating to these matters.

Part I consists of (A) *Overview: Judging Pius XII,* and (B) *The Historical Record. Overview* deals with the new period of Catholic-Jewish dialogue inaugurated by Vatican II, discusses the circumstances in which the negative reactions to Pius began, reviews and briefly comments on the rising tensions in Catholic-Jewish exchanges. *Overview's* final section offers responses to comments in September 1998 by the International Jewish Committee on Interreligious Consultations. *The Historical Record* is the heart of the book. It is primarily an examination of pertinent historical records from the pontificate of Pius XII.

Part II continues with documents and commentary, concentrating mainly on the Vatican efforts on behalf of victims, and concludes with an "Epilogue" that briefly sums up the case for Pius XII. Part III reprints documents from Pius XII's pontificate, as well as analyses and commentaries by leading Catholic experts. Parts IV and V provide a chronology of Pope Pius XII's life and wartime writings with extensive bibliographical information and historical documents.

A reader who is attentive to the narrative and the documents in this volume will find ample evidence to dismiss the allegations of critics such as John Cornwell whose 1999 book, *Hitler's Pope,* mixed facts, errors and speculation in a manner that casts doubts on any claim to be considered a work of serious historical scholarship.

Few speaking or writing about Pope Pius XII today do so from a detached perspective. I am no exception. I am convinced that Pius XII was a wise and saintly man. I hope that the evidence I bring to bear concerning his work on behalf of victims of war, especially Jewish victims, will convince others of his wisdom and holiness. I have not deluded myself that I have made the complete or final case for this dedicated servant of God. I do hope, however, that this book, whatever its strengths or weaknesses, will encourage others to do justice for this mistakenly criticized man. I truly believe that those who charge Pius XII with not doing everything he should have done to foster peace and help all victims of war and oppression "know not what they do."

Margherita Marchione, Ph.D.
Professor Emerita
Fairleigh Dickinson University

Part I
Pope Pius XII in the Maelstrom of World War II

A. OVERVIEW: JUDGING PIUS XII
B. THE HISTORICAL RECORD

A. Overview: Judging Pius XII

---

*D*uring World War II, 1939–45, and for nearly twenty years after, Pope Pius XII was almost universally regarded as a saintly man, a scholar, a man of peace, a tower of strength, and a compassionate defender and protector of all victims of the war and genocide that had drowned Europe in blood for six years. At the end of the war Western nations paid tribute to his steadfast efforts on behalf of the oppressed. Jews heaped praise on him for his help in their darkest hour and, at his death thirteen years later, they were among the first to express sorrow and gratitude for his solicitude for Jews during the Holocaust.

In the 1960s, however, there began a campaign of vilification against the Pope. The sources of these hostile attacks are difficult to pin down precisely, but their overall effect was to replace the judgment of Pius XII as a great and good man with the judgment of him as a weak, cold, church bureaucrat. Today the media, liberal Catholics, academicians, and editorial commentators with few exceptions accept as unquestionably true the claims made by his detractors—that he lacked courage, human compassion, and a deep sense of moral rectitude. Even when no solid evidence is provided to support such demeaning allegations, he is judged guilty of a sin of omission, such as not having personally raged against Hitler or not having excommunicated all Catholics serving under Hitler.

The accusers' strategy is to rewrite history, to ignore the reality of who had the power and the will to destroy mercilessly from 1933 to 1944 and to pretend that Pius XII possessed some kind of extraordinary ability that no one else in the world had—to make Hitler obey him. Their essential logic is this simple; the Holocaust occurred, millions died, and the mighty Pope refused to exercise his incredible authority. Therefore, he is guilty and shares responsibility for the Nazi crimes.

13

Today the principal admirers of Pius XII are devout Catholics, those who have studied his life and actions, the Vatican, and John Paul II. Those who have most carefully reviewed every day of his life and every word that he wrote—select members of the Congregation for the Causes of Saints—are so convinced of his worthiness that they are pushing forward his cause for beatification and possible canonization. But the world that praised him during the war and long afterwards has given way to a world that holds him morally weak. The Jews of the earlier years who expressed gratitude and admiration for his help have been generally replaced by those of the present who repeatedly charge him with "silence" in the face of the Holocaust. What caused this?

There are too many causes to list, but the ones this book will most frequently refer to in reviewing the criticism of Pius XII from 1965 to the present can be briefly stated. It is difficult for a Catholic not to believe that antireligious and anti-Catholic prejudices have played a role. The Church preaches doctrines to bring human beings into eternity, and many in the world hate its preachers "because they do not belong to the world" (Jn 17:14). The 1960s cultural revolution expressed a good deal of this hatred. It devalued all traditional religions, particularly Catholicism. A key expression of that devaluation was Rolf Hochhuth's libelous and shoddy dramatization of Pope Pius XII, *The Deputy.* First produced in 1963, it immediately led thousands to believe that Pius XII had acted on narrow and self-serving motives.

Perhaps stronger than anything behind the attacks on Pius XII are the deep and lasting psychological effects of the Holocaust. That disaster generated, among other things, a compelling longing to uncover the hidden causes and agents of the Nazi genocide. Perhaps even Hochhuth began with a legitimate desire to find hidden Nazi collaborators. Unfortunately, he and scores of other detractors have falsely accused not only an innocent man, but a man totally devoted to helping all victims. Then there is the inevitable selective use of evidence among Pius XII's critics and the failure of these critics to study carefully what Pius XII actually did and said in those nightmarish years. Lastly, there is the difficulty, despite good intentions on both sides, that Christians and Jews face in trying to establish trust and understanding after two thousand years of distrust and misunderstanding.

The Deputy

Revisionists have been at work since the debut in Berlin in February 1963 of *The Deputy,* the purely fictional play by Rolf Hochhuth, in which he portrayed Pius XII as a Nazi collaborator and accused the Pope of "silence." He offers no historical evidence for his claims against Pope Pius XII. Hochhuth's play shows fanatical prejudice clearly related to Stalin's standard anti-Catholic Communist propaganda.

Rolf Hochhuth was a disciple of Erwin Piscator, founder of the German drama school called the "Political Theatre" that advocated putting live politicians or figures recently deceased on stage, for either pillorying or praise.

According to Robert A. Graham, Pius XII became a villain, not on historical grounds, but for psychological reasons. In a lecture delivered at The Catholic University of America on October 10, 1989, this Jesuit historian suggested several hypotheses: "The most important is the timing. The first session of the historic Second Vatican Council had terminated just a few months previously. A new vision dawned not only on the Catholic Church, but also on world opinion. This was also the time when America was deeply troubled in conscience by the drama, the tragedy of the Vietnam War. Also, just two years previously the trial of Adolf Eichmann, the organizer of the Hitlerian program for the extermination of Jews, had taken place." Someone needed to be blamed for the Holocaust.

Revisionists have joined Hochhuth, intent upon discrediting the efforts of Pope Pius XII and the Catholic Church during the Holocaust. They have made baseless, out-of-context statements, along with innuendoes and speculation. Because the secular media have repeated these statements without consulting the sources of truth available to them, Pius XII is perceived by many as anti-Semitic and "silent" during World War II while Jews were rounded up and transported to concentration camps. The hostile critics insist that Pius XII could have done more to save Jewish lives from torture and death, that if he had personally attacked the Nazis, the Holocaust would have been stopped or abated, and that he aided in the escape of war criminals.

To counteract the impact of *The Deputy,* at the request of Pope Paul VI, Vatican documents relating to the activities of Pope Pius XII and the Church's role in World War II were released (1965–82).

Incidentally, as one questions *The Deputy*'s veracity, it is interesting to note that Hochhuth also wrote a play about Churchill. In this play a pilot was said to have sabotaged the plane killing the Polish commander of the volunteers who were allied to the British. According to the play, the pilot was then liquidated by the secret service. Hochhuth was sued and forced to pay considerable damages to the British government and to the pilot, who was found living in California.

Issues may be allowed to subside, but only to emerge once more. For example, *The Deputy* myth was revived in 1983 on its twentieth anniversary by Deborah E. Lipstadt of UCLA, who concluded that "Hochhuth's work has stood the test of time....millions are now aware of the indelible scar of shame borne by the Catholic Church and its leaders."[1]

However, the *Journal of Ecclesiastical History* calls the well-documented book, *German Resistance to Hitler: Ethical and Religious Factors* by Mary Alice Gallin, "the first real effort to discuss the events and motives of those involved from a dispassionate and scholarly viewpoint....There are many new insights, a real sympathy with the subject and a courageous defense of men who faced a terrible dilemma and who gave their lives in a Christian cause."

Gallin concludes: "The history of the Resistance in Germany makes it clear that the Catholic bishops offered straightforward and courageous opposition to the ideology and tactics of the Nazis, but it also attests to the fact that they offered no encouragement or support to any plans for a revolution by which the Nazis would have been removed from power. Revolution was specifically rejected and denounced by them on several occasions."[2]

Based on research in Germany's wartime archives, Gallin's book is a definitive refutation of the myths found in Guenter Lewy's anti-Catholic book, *The Catholic Church and Nazi Germany.*[3]

Lewy's attack on Vatican policy is rejected by Robert A. Graham in the article, "A Return to Theocracy": "In Lewy's book, the Pope is taken at his own estimate as the Vicar of Christ and therefore as a prophet of sorts in a theocracy. But this unexpected acknowledgement is then used as the point of departure for serious accusations of dereliction of duty and blame for the resulting human tragedies of the war.

"Guenter Lewy, forced to leave his native Germany in his teens because of Hitler's racial persecutions, is the Rolf Hochhuth of the academic fraternity. His book is *The Deputy* of nonfiction. Both these writings, characteristically the work of the postwar generation, exemplify the ambivalence that marks present non-Catholic European sentiment in regard to the position of the Vatican and the Church in world affairs. The conclusions of Lewy, like the message of Hochhuth, are unfavorable."

Lewy wants "a return to the politico-ecclesiasticism of the Middle Ages. He wants the Catholic Church, in a burst of clericalism imaginable these days only to someone outside the Church, to wield its supernatural authority to purge every evil, whether it be religious, moral, social or political....Nowhere does he display any awareness that he is dealing with tendentious and mendacious documents. It is hardly scholarly, for instance, to base an exposition of the Vatican's policy on anti-Semitism on an uncritical use of anti-Semitic sources."

On page 305, Lewy writes: "One is inclined to conclude that the Pope and his advisers—influenced by the long tradition of moderate anti-Semitism so widely accepted in Vatican circles—did not view the plight of the Jews with a real sense of urgency and moral outrage. For this assertion no documentation is possible, but it is a conclusion difficult to avoid."

This statement is followed by Graham's comment: "In other words, Pius was 'silent' because he was anti-Semitic. A reviewer may be allowed to object vehemently against this characterization, founded, by the author's own admission, not on the record but on a subjective conviction. This is no way to write the history of these tragic years....This ready acceptance of a Nazi-inspired wartime legend is a measure of Lewy's inability to plumb the motives of Pius XII. It is quite in keeping with his refusal to see in the Church's ideological struggle with the Nazis anything but a banal defense of Church property....There is no proof, in this book or anywhere else, that Pius XII thought Nazism was a 'bulwark' in defense of Christianity."[4]

It is a sad but indisputable fact that the official publications of the Holy See, documents of the Nuremberg Trial Proceedings, state papers of the warring countries, and published Vatican War Documents have been largely ignored by those who would impugn the Pope's integrity. These documents demonstrate the close collaboration among the Holy See, Jewish representative bodies, the international Red Cross, and allied governments. No one can deny that numerous protests were made by Pius XII.

Repeatedly, Pope John Paul II has defended Pope Pius XII, recalling how deeply he felt about the tragedy of the Jewish people and how hard and effectively he worked to assist them during the Second World War.[5]

In the words of the Jewish-Hungarian scholar, Jenö Levai, it is a particularly regrettable irony that the one person (Pope Pius XII) in all of occupied Europe who did more than anyone else to halt the dreadful crime and alleviate its consequences is today made the scapegoat for the failures of others.

In February 1945 Chief Rabbi Isaac Herzog of Palestine stated: "The people of Israel will never forget what His Holiness and his illustrious delegates, inspired by the eternal principles of religion, which form the very foundations of true civilization, are doing for our unfortunate brothers and sisters in the most tragic hour of our history, which is living proof of Divine Providence in this world."

Jewish leaders worldwide recognized the greatness of Pius XII— the Pope who had saved the lives of so many thousands of people without distinction of race, nationality, or religion. *The Jewish Post* reported: "It is understandable why the death of Pope Pius XII should have called forth expressions of sincere grief from practically all sections of American Jewry. For there probably was not a single ruler of our generation who did more to help the Jews in their hour of greatest tragedy, during the Nazi occupation of Europe, than the late Pope."[6]

The Search for Trust: Dialogue and Confrontation

It's clear that Vatican II's 1965 *Nostra Aetate* was a response to the Holocaust. It was in a sense an historic "never again" statement. Never again would Christians and Jews be unaware of their shared roots. When *Nostra Aetate* emphasized "the spiritual patrimony common to Christians and Jews," exonerated the Jewish people of responsibility for the Crucifixion, and condemned "anti-Semitism directed against the Jews at any time and from any source," it initiated a period of unprecedented reconciliation and exchanges. Ten years after *Nostra Aetate,* in its *Guidelines* on the application of the teachings in that document, the Vatican also stated: "The spiritual ties which link the Christian to Judaism….render obligatory a better mutual understanding…." From the outset of his pontificate in 1978, John Paul II sought to broaden these conciliatory efforts and achieve a complete *rapproachment.* On a number of occasions, most notably his historic visit in 1986 to the Synagogue of Rome, he reached out to Jews to heal old wounds. When disputes arose, such as the one at Auschwitz over a Carmelite convent, he quickly acted to defuse them.

But Catholic-Jewish exchanges have been going on at two very different levels. While some were searching for a new understanding of what unites and separates the two communities, others were confronting the Church for past wrongs and in opposition to its contemporary moral stands on sexual practices, abortion, euthanasia, and Church authority.

One kind of exchange occurred at the synagogue and church level. These followed the lead of the Vatican's Commission for Religious Relations with the Jews, which had initiated a wide range of contacts and discussions. Such interactions led dioceses to appoint ecumenical commissions and committees in many places around the world, both at the diocesan and parish levels. Rabbis spoke to Catholic congregations and priests to Jewish institutes concerned with Jewish-Catholic questions. These ecumenical groups, formed to promote friendship and wider intellectual contact among scholars, found homes in universities and colleges. There the most sensitive questions could be asked and answered, fresh reassessments might be reached, and sometimes old suspicions might yield to new awareness and trust.

Another entirely different kind of exchange was taking place on TV and in books, magazines, and newspapers. Charges of Christian anti-Semitism were regularly made. Liberal Catholics, eager to point to past Church failures, culled the tragic history of Christians and Jews and chastised actions of deceased as well as living Church leaders, particularly those of Pope Pius XII; but even John Paul II was not above criticism. Some Jews, as individuals and representatives of organizations, found little in Catholicism to praise and much to attack. Confrontation instead of dialogue grabbed the headlines, feeding the media's insatiable appetite for controversy. Almost without fail the media presented criticism of the Church not as one judgment among many, but as the only sensible judgment for all right-thinking modern people. Those foolhardy enough to oppose anti-Catholic criticism were labeled a remnant, uninformed and obviously wrong. Not only Pius XII, but the Church itself has been harshly judged and dismissed in the post-Vatican II era of open and frank exchanges.

The pitch of hostile criticism has been rising for about ten years. By the final weeks of 1998 some angry rabbis were leveling charges of anti-Semitism and threatening to withdraw from further dialogue. And Vatican officials bristled at what they regarded as unprecedented and unwarranted Jewish interference in internal Church matters—raising the question of whether all the responsibility for the historical antagonism between the two groups rests with Christians, asking whether Jews, too, might not do well to examine their own past actions and words to see if they contributed to anger and bitterness. At the beginning of 1999 it seemed that more than the millennium was coming to an end, that perhaps a generation of unprecedented progress in Christian-Jewish understanding might also be eroding.

What Feeds the New Controversy?

Some blame Pope John Paul II's 1987 decision to beatify Edith Stein, a German-Jewish nun who died at Auschwitz, for igniting wider and more caustic quarrels, which officials of the Israeli government joined at one point. Though outcries greeted the raising of Stein "to the honors of the altar," the protests, on examination, prove to be less concerned with beatification than with unresolved questions about the Holocaust that had cast a shadow over Catholic-Jewish understanding since World War II.

One suspects that if Stein had been a Spanish-Jewish Carmelite in Spain and had been killed by the Communists in that country, her beatification would have hardly raised a murmur of criticism. Only a few devout Catholics and rabbis might have noted the beatification, not the high priests of the media. However, because the event was connected with the Nazi extermination of nearly six million Jews, it was seen through the prism of the tragic past. Stein embodied for some Jews a new threat to their identity and all those differences that continue to exist between Christians and Jews—for example, sanctity, martyrdom, sacrificial death, conversion, and Jesus Christ.

And the expressions of Jewish outrage irritated Christian sensitivity. Some Christians saw Stein being posthumously subjected to unjust criticism. They asked: Who has the right to dismiss her heroic choices, to ignore her holiness, to exalt blood above belief, and to trivialize the very idea of canonization by presenting it as an instance of crass Church politics?

All of this demonstrates that Catholic-Jewish dialogue may well be a more complicated and difficult undertaking than either community realized. The precise elements required for it to succeed—years of cordial relations, a solid backlog of trust and mutual understanding, and tolerance for missteps—are apparently absent at the present time.

Pope Pius XII is at the center of these confrontations because some feel he is the prime example of the Church's failure to defend the Jews during the Holocaust. The case against him is summed up in a single, ill-defined and unproven allegation—his "silence." Even when it is demonstrated from the historical record that he was not silent, what he did say is dismissed or belittled because it is not what his accusers themselves think, fifty and more years after the events, would have been "the heroic" statement! But what they would have had him say would, in all probability, not have saved a single victim and instead could have cost thousands and thousands of additional innocent lives. Pius XII today is all too similar to the victim in a primitive scapegoat ritual. He is denounced for the sins of a wicked age and tribal shamans drive him out of the society of "the righteous."

Can it be that some deep, subliminal prejudice against the papacy is behind this? It is certainly possible. Anti-Catholicism is as alive and popular today as it has been for four centuries. After all, since the Reformation various kinds of anti-Catholicism have been passed down among all social classes. Among enlightened thinkers, burghers, and laborers, the papacy may be seen as the superstitious, wicked foe of enlightened modernism and progress. The comic description of anti-Catholicism attributed to Daniel Defoe masks a hostile attitude toward Catholics: "There were a hundred thousand country fellows...ready to fight to the death against popery, without knowing whether popery was a man or a horse."

It is hard not to sense a connection between the attacks on Pius XII and the colossal cultural changes that swept over the Western world in the 1960s. In his own time the Pope was loved and respected. Jews, who credited Pius XII with being one of their greatest defenders and benefactors in their hour of greatest need, stood in the forefront of those mourning his death in 1958. But five years after his death the cultural revolution was well underway. Revealed religion was mocked, the death of God espoused, change deified, emotion preferred to reason, passion exalted, every text questioned—only the powerful reader could offer an acceptable interpretation, which would quickly be replaced by the next powerful interpretation. Sacred scripture was made relative. The Church was shaken to its foundations. Priests tore off their collars, nuns their habits. Anyone who submitted to religious authority was regarded as childish or stupid or both. Out of this *zeitgeist* came the revisionist attack on the character of Pius XII.

The new culture was ready for a sinister image of the wartime Pope as a "silent," uncaring moral monster. And that is precisely what Hochhuth provided in his propagandistic play, *The Deputy*. Once Hochhuth's imaginary Pope appeared, a depiction without factual support, Pius was almost everywhere reviled, even among Catholics who should have known better. This vilification occurred virtually without new evidence, without damaging facts.

Pius XII embodied much of what the revolution of the sixties attacked. He was a Christian believer, scholar, and mystic bred from youth to the ways of the Church and diplomacy. He was a man of absolute faith, prayer, revelation, tradition, reason, and complete trust in the Providence of God. His diplomatic skills were learned from Benedict XV, the Pope whose policy of strict neutrality in World War I was seen as Christlike leadership. First faith, then reason, then experience taught Pius that provocative declarations beget violent response. Peace must be the first goal. To do anything that would prevent peace would be against reason and conscience. No Pope could endanger human lives; his task was to save them. Politicians, generals, and dictators might gamble with the lives of people; a Pope could not.

In the terrible year of 1942, when it still seemed the Nazis might triumph, Poland, France, England, and the United States all repeatedly urged the Pope to attack Germany directly and specifically. He thought and prayed night and day for Divine guidance. He had repeatedly condemned invasions, killings, treatment of prisoners (including Jewish), but always in terms of Christian and humanitarian principles, never specifically attacking leaders or nations. Everyone knew who was being indicted in his statements—the Germans responded with fury, the Allies with gratification. The *New York Times* and the *Times* of London took note and named names.

Everyone understood he was being the Pastor, working for peace, defending victims, naming sins, warning of the wrath of the Almighty to punish those harming defenseless victims, but leaving the sinner to God. By not attacking the Nazis directly, he was able to protect thousands and thousands threatened by German brutality and to provide shelter in Church buildings.

Almost every churchman in the German-occupied nations who advised him also warned about Hitler's unpredictable and irrational fury. Bishops in Germany said that open defiance would only lead to greater Nazi brutality; Polish Cardinals confided that they could not even publish the Pope's communications of support and broad condemnations among the faithful because these actions would immediately arouse the Germans to additional atrocities.

Still, in the fateful year of 1942, when all of Europe was being squeezed in a Nazi vise of terror and death, Pius XII wondered if he was not being called on to do something more dramatic, more extreme.

All the warring nations wanted words from the Pope to use for their purposes, that is, for propaganda. To become a tool of the Allies would destroy any chance to persuade Italy and Germany to end the slaughter. But increasing accounts of atrocities and reports on the plight of the Jews, still hard to believe in full, made him question his own prayerful efforts for peace. Might not a direct papal attack on Germany shock its leaders and awaken their consciences? Nothing that had happened since the Nazis took power in 1933 suggested that Hitler would deviate from his program of total war and destruction. Still, desperate times demanded that he try to force Hitler to end his mad policy.

Sister Pasqualina Lehnert reported that in the summer of 1942 the Pope drafted a fiery denunciation, gambling that the Nazis might not unleash a blitzkrieg of death on the most immediate victims. Then on July 26, 1942, the Dutch bishops did precisely what Pius XII was planning to do—they openly condemned Nazi deportations of workers and Jews. The German response: fury and expanded deportations. The end result was more victims. If Pius XII had been looking for a sign as to whether to strongly defy the Nazis, Holland gave it to him. Open Catholic defiance would only result in countless additional deaths. Sister Lehnert said the Pope was convinced that the Bishops' protest cost forty thousand lives and a protest by him would mean two hundred thousand innocent lives would be lost.

Still, Pius XII's critics insist that if he had confronted Hitler directly—publicly excommunicating him and all who supported him—that German Catholics might have risen up in revolt. That is the accusation of the *New York Times* of March 18, 1998: "The Pope did not encourage Catholics to defy Nazis' orders." The idea that the Pope could bring about massive German defiance is completely implausible. Nearly ten years of Nazi rule had proved that anyone, Catholic or Communist, brave enough to defy the Nazis was immediately seized and punished. The *Times* first endows the Pope with power he did not possess and then demands that he act on that power. Essentially, it is a demand that he should have accepted the sacrifice of innocent people.

The only certain result of papal moral rage would have been Hitler's immoral rage. Further, the historical record on excommunications is clear. They have been notoriously ineffective over the last four or five centuries. Excommunicating Luther did not slow Protestantism nor did it cow Henry VIII nor any subsequent king or emperor out to humble and loot the Vatican. A pontifical excommunication against the Catholic powers of Venice (1606) only succeeded in demonstrating the uselessness of the act. Those who vest Pius XII's Vatican with the kind of power held for a limited period in the Middle Ages but never demonstrated before or since are being disingenuous. It is unconscionable to malign a brave and good man with such feeble arguments.

To put it as simply as possible: The Pope's dilemma was like that of the pilot of a plane seized by terrorists. Should he encourage his crew to resist? Or should he keep the terrorists talking as long as he can in the hope of saving as many lives as possible? Pius XII's conscience told him he must do all he could to save lives, to speak clearly and strongly against brutality and atrocities, constantly urging an end to the killing and working ceaselessly for peace. To condemn Pius XII for his faith, his pacifism, his "church language," his neutrality and for deciding not to incite a half-mad dictator is to ignore Pius XII's virtues and courage and to overlook the historical circumstances in which he acted.

Before turning to the historical record, it might be useful to look a little more closely, from a Catholic viewpoint, at the 1998 crisis in Catholic-Jewish discussions. Those exchanges tell us a great deal about the present circumstances in which the controversy over Pius XII is being played out.

The "Shoah" Document

Shoah, the Hebrew word for disaster or catastrophe, is the term many Jews now prefer to *Holocaust.* Throughout his papacy John Paul II contemplated an official Church response to the Holocaust and to the failings of Christians then and throughout the centuries. To put such a response in historical and scholarly context, the Pope appointed a pontifical commission to investigate and report on this extraordinarily complex question. On March 16, 1998, after a decade of investigations and hearings, the Commission for Religious Relations with the Jews published its findings. The document was entitled: *We Remember: A Reflection on the Shoah.* The statement was composed by a group headed by

Edward Idris Cardinal Cassidy and prefaced by a letter from John Paul II. It was a considered and balanced report. It expressed deep sorrow and regret. It confessed fault on behalf of Catholics who had not responded courageously and in some cases had actually taken part in the persecution. It also drew distinctions between historical anti-Semitism and anti-Judaism and, more importantly, stressed the uniqueness of Nazi racial hatred—which it insisted was a product of modern paganism rather than Christian teachings. Then came the assertion that many Jews found most disturbing. In a long footnote, the Commission defended Pius XII's actions in the face of the Nazi extermination program.

Some Jewish replies were balanced and appreciative, but the majority were critical. The *New York Times* called the document a rationalization, virtually accusing the Vatican of a cover-up. Along similar lines was the reaction of Jerusalem's Chief Rabbi, Israel Meir Lau, who dismissed the report as "too little and too late," and "not courageous enough." He claimed that among those carrying out the slaughter were a large number of "believing Catholics."

Obviously such reactions stung Catholics, among whom there already existed serious doubts about making any sort of public confession for past offenses. The out-of-hand rejection of what they saw as a sincere and deeply felt confession appeared to confirm their reluctance to expose the Church to insulting comments. Many were convinced that for some critics of the Church, as Professor Mary Ann Glendon put it, "no apology will ever be enough until Catholics apologize themselves into nonexistence."

Even though the Commission's confession of fault for the sins of previous generations was not the same as a private confession before a priest, still its rejection ran counter to the whole Catholic idea of confession—where no sincere, heartfelt confession can be "too late." True, the sooner the better, but *late* is better than *never.* The important action is to confess honestly. Thus rejection of the Shoah confession was equated to calling it a false confession.

A few months later, Rabbi Lau would make another unhappy contribution to Catholic-Jewish understanding. The Italian daily *Il Giornale* of November 13, 1998, reported that Lau, while observing the sixtieth anniversary of *Kristallnacht* (November 9–10, 1938), used the occasion to attack "the silence" of Pius XII. "Where," he asked, "was Pius XII in November of 1938....Why did he not denounce the violence of that night?"

The paper highlighted an obvious error: Pius XII did not exist until Eugenio Cardinal Pacelli became pope on March 2, 1939. Was Lau so anxious to connect Pius XII with an early Nazi crime that he predated Pacelli's papacy by nearly four months?

In 1938 Cardinal Pacelli was serving as Secretary of State for Pius XI, the Pontiff who infuriated the Nazis by openly declaring to a group of pilgrims: "Spiritually we are all Semites." As Secretary of State, Pacelli had drafted Pius XI's encyclical attacking Hitler's racial theories and had thereby already caused the Nazis to rage in their newspapers about "the Jewish God and his Vicar in the Vatican." The Nazis were not confused about who was opposing their policies and when.

Clearly great crimes were committed on *Kristallnacht* and just as clearly Cardinal Pacelli did not cause them nor could he have prevented them or the worse ones to follow. Actually Pacelli was one of the first to recognize the Nazis and speak out against them. On April 28, 1935, addressing 250,000 pilgrims at Lourdes, France, he called the Nazis "miserable plagiarists who dress up old errors in new tinsel." He went on: "It makes no difference whether they march to the banners of social revolution, whether they are guided by a false concept of the world and of life, or whether they are possessed by the superstition of race and blood cult!" Why his ghost should be summoned for blame in 1998 by Lau says more about the current temper of Jewish-Catholic exchanges than about Pius XII.

Much more serious than predating Pius XII's pontificate is Lau's earlier accusation that large numbers of "believing Catholics" were among Hitler's murderers. Surely the Rabbi knows that both Pius XI and Pius XII and the overwhelming majority of German bishops said that Nazism and Catholicism were incompatible. A *believing* Catholic could not be a Nazi. A Catholic with a badly formed conscience, perhaps twisted by fear or ignorance, could well have become seriously involved with the Nazis. But such a person would have been *unbelieving or falsely believing.* Surely we would not say that those frightened and misguided Jews who cooperated with the Nazis were "believing Jews"!

Professor Stephen Aschheim of Jerusalem's Hebrew University, speaking recently in Washington, D.C., touched on a fundamental truth underlying Christian-Jewish relations: The Church never taught Christians to kill Jews. He added that even during severe medieval pogroms, Jews understood this and sought protection from popes and bishops against murderous mobs, sadly sometimes unsuccessfully.

As a matter of historical record, there were a number of popes who issued papal bulls forbidding any Catholic from harming Jews, such as Calixtus II's *Sicut Judaeis* (As for the Jews), issued in 1120. The European record on the treatment of Jews over the centuries is admittedly grim, but it does not include the Church teaching Christians to kill Jews—quite the opposite. The Church wanted to convert Jews and wrongly resorted to harsh and repressive means, but it constantly reiterated that they were not to be harmed and certainly not killed.

Contemporary Catholics, like members of Cardinal Cassidy's Commission, granted that many of their coreligionists were confused and intimidated by Nazi power and failed to act as Christians, but they attribute this to "human weakness," to prejudice, envy, greed, indifference, and omnipresent fear. There is clear evidence, for example, that those "fallen away" Catholics actually involved in murder had already disowned the Church and its teachings. One dramatic instance is the nurse who administered the lethal injection to Father Titus Brandsma, an anti-Nazi activist beatified in 1984 by John Paul II. During proceedings leading to his beatification, the nurse came forward and reported that in her final conversation with the doomed man he tried to persuade her to accept his rosary. She told him that though she had been born Catholic, she had left the Church and no longer considered herself Catholic.

The evidence we have on the role of religious belief in Nazi Germany, which we will touch on later, shows that among those few who heroically resisted Hitler, many did so because of deeply held Christian beliefs. The anti-Nazi students who formed the White Rose Society, for example, made it clear that they found the courage to speak out against Hitler in their religious faith. The entire group was hunted down and executed.

Ironically, it is a judgment by former Mayor Ed Koch of New York, who is Jewish, that expresses in summary form the much criticized position of the Church's Shoah document: "Blaming Christians for the Holocaust would be as unjustified as holding Jews accountable for the death of Jesus. Individuals were responsible in both situations. The bottom line is clear: Blame individuals, not religions for political crimes.

There is new testimony from a Jew who lived the entire war in Germany, in constant fear of deportation and death, recording his observations. The diaries of Victor Klemperer (1881–1960), are just now being published. The first volume, *I Will Bear Witness,* has been hailed as the most thorough record we have by an intelligent, carefully observant victim of Nazi oppression. On January 10, 1939, Klemperer wrote: "Jews and Germans lived and worked together without friction in all spheres of life. The anti-Semitism, which was always present, is not at all evidence to the contrary. Because the friction between Jews and Aryans was not half as great as that between Protestants and Catholics, or between employers and employees, or between East Prussians for example and southern Bavarians or Rhinelanders and Bavarians." Klemperer's distinction between various prejudices and frictions and virulent Nazi race theory approximates the one presented in the Shoah statement.

Cardinal Cassidy Responds

On May 15, 1998, Cardinal Cassidy appeared before Jewish leaders at the ninety-second annual meeting of the American Jewish Committee in Washington, D.C. He strongly defended his Commission's document, flatly rejected the charge that Pope Pius XII did not do enough to help Jews during the Holocaust, and condemned such charges as unjust and false. "It is our conviction," he said, "that in recent years the Pope's memory has been unjustly denigrated by monstrous calumnies" which "have gradually become accepted as facts especially within the Jewish community." He insisted before this deeply involved audience that the "anti-Semitism of the Nazis was the fruit of a thoroughly neopagan regime with its roots outside of Christianity, and in pursuing its aims it did not hesitate to oppose the Church and persecute its members also."

Five months after Cassidy spoke, controversy once more arose over Edith Stein. On October 11, 1998, the canonization of Edith Stein took place. If her beatification raised tempers, her canonization may be said to have caused a firestorm. *The Tablet* of London (November 7, 1998), by implicitly comparing the smooth-sailing Jewish-Catholic dialogue to the unsinkable *Titanic,* saw Stein's canonization as a deadly iceberg. It claimed the effect of the canonization was "disastrous." Among examples of Jewish outrage cited was this: "The Board of Deputies of British Jews condemned the canonization in the strongest terms, after Jewish representatives had made angry speeches calling for the breaking-off of official Jewish-Catholic dialogue."

Emotions had not quieted a month later, when the beatification of Alojizje Cardinal Stepinac, Archbishop of Zagreb, took place in Croatia, preceded and followed by more Israeli protests. Then came a report out of the Congregation for the Causes of Saints to the effect that Pope Pius XII would soon be raised to the honors of the altar. This brought vehement reactions not only from rabbis and leaders of Jewish organizations but from Israel's ambassador to the Vatican, Aharon Lopez, who took the unprecedented step of telling Rome, in effect, that it did not know enough about Pius and should wait until feelings cooled and historians could make a more informed judgment in, say, fifty years. Quipped Vatican journalists: "Why wait only fifty years? Five-hundred years wouldn't be long enough for scholars to agree!"

In the midst of these exchanges Israeli Prime Minster Benjamin Netanyahu threatened to prevent the installation of newly named Greek Catholic Archbishop, Boutros Mualem, which was to take place in Haifa. He called Mualem too pro-Palestinian and demanded the Vatican appoint as archbishop a man he approved. He had conveyed this view to the Pope two months earlier but the Pope had said only the Greek Catholic synod had the right to name bishops—not an Israeli Prime Minister. Netanyahu eventually backed off and Mualem was installed on October 17.

In late October the Vatican's foreign minister, Archbishop Jean-Luis Tauran, went to Israel seeking support for the proposal that sites holy to Christians, Muslims, and Jews be protected by international guarantees. While there, he called Jewish settlements in East Jerusalem "an illegal occupation."

But a priest who lost relatives to Hitler's murderers and who himself had to flee Germany most forcefully expressed the Vatican's shock at the mounting criticisms by Israeli officials and leaders of Jewish groups, particularly at their rejection of the Church's judgment on Pius XII. Father Peter Gumpel, S.J., the member of the Congregation for Saints in charge of Pius XII's cause, a man who has read everything there is to read about the Pope, told journalists: "These attacks and insults are counterproductive. I would not be surprised if it led to a rise of anti-Semitic feeling. Many Catholics feel outraged. The call for such a postponement [of Pope Pius XII's beatification] is nonsense and far removed from the competence of the ambassador. A beatification is strictly an internal affair of the Catholic Church." He also said that he wondered if the attack on Pius were not actually "an attack on the Catholic Church" and if that were the case then "unacceptable Jewish statements against Christianity" would have to be reexamined.

The Chief Rabbi of Vienna, Paul Chaim Eisenberg, was quoted in the European press as saying Gumpel's remarks seemed to him an instance of "crude anti-Semitism."

In spite of such unhelpful events, indeed, because of them, Jewish-Catholic dialogue must continue.

The "Silence" of Pius XII: Some Facts

Though the villainous "silence" of the Pope has been firmly established in the minds of many, numerous records show that he was not silent, that both before and after he became Pope he spoke against the Nazis and, above all, in season and out of season, bravely attempted to help all victims of war. Eugenio Pacelli was almost universally recognized, especially by the Nazis themselves, as an opponent of Hitler, a tireless defender of the faith and seeker of peace, a comforter of the oppressed, a scholarly and saintly man. Before he became Pope, Cardinal Pacelli, as Secretary of State under Pius XI, had the opportunity to observe the Nazis very closely and judged them to be totally anti-Christian. As early as the mid-1920s, Hitler, in his *Mein Kampf* made it clear that he would eliminate any and all who opposed him: the Jews as soon as possible, Christians more slowly.

As Papal Nuncio, Pacelli observed Hitler's efforts to control Christian churches and to make them support National Socialism. The Führer's long-range design was to form his own national church after he had conquered his political enemies. He saw himself as following in Martin Luther's footsteps. By 1934 Hitler was openly attempting to nazify the Protestant churches, saying, "I am convinced that Luther would have done the same thing and would have thought of a unified Germany first and last." He tried to subject all religions to state control: Catholicism particularly angered him because its center of authority was in Rome, not Berlin.

Every Catholic in Germany was keenly aware that the elite SS would not even admit Catholics—only those who repudiated the Church. It was clear that loyal and dedicated Catholics were regularly questioned, intimidated, imprisoned, even killed. In 1934 the SS murdered Dr. Erich Klausner, the head of Catholic Action in Germany. Catholics who would not disown Catholicism—even famous World War I heroes like Catholic Hermann Koehl, an air ace and the first man (with two others) to fly the Atlantic east to west—were fired from their jobs and treated as nonpersons.

On August 11, 1935, the observant Victor Klemperer recorded in his diary: "The Jew-baiting has become so extreme...there are the beginnings of a pogrom here and there and we expect to be beaten to death at any moment. Not by neighbors, but by purgers who are deployed now here, now there as the 'soul of the people'....Almost as wild agitation against 'political' Catholics...." Catholics who lived their religion and resisted Hitler were victims of choice after Jews.

With Cardinal Pacelli's speech at Lourdes in 1935, his contribution to Pius XI's strongly anti-Nazi encyclical *Mit brennender Sorge* (With Burning Anxiety, 1937) needs to be mentioned. Drafted by Pacelli, printed in German, smuggled into Germany, and read in all German Catholic churches, the encyclical infuriated the Nazis and led to the imprisonment of many priests.

On March 3, 1939, correspondent William L. Shirer recorded in his famous *Berlin Diary,* "Eugenio Cardinal Pacelli is the new Pope, elected yesterday, and a very popular choice all around except perhaps in Germany." Nazis knew that the new Pope was a committed opponent.

On October 20, 1939, Pius XII issued the Encyclical *Summi Pontificatus* (On the Unity of the Human Family) that was almost everywhere greeted as a denunciation of the Nazis. On October 28 of that year, the *New York Times* carried a front-page article with the following upper-case headline: "POPE CONDEMNS DICTATORS, TREATY VIOLATORS, RACISM; URGES RESTORING OF POLAND." The *Times* presented the Pope's statement as a powerful attack on totalitarianism and a clear expression of the Pontiff's determination to boldly defend the rights of individuals and families and to fight the enemies of the Church. A *Times* writer saw the Pontiff as an Old Testament prophet "speaking words of fire." The entire encyclical was printed on pages eight and nine of the paper.

After the beginning of the war in 1939, when German Protestant and Catholic churches refused to pray for a Nazi victory, Hitler ordered over seven hundred German monasteries and convents closed. In one month sixty Catholic priests were expelled from their parishes. The work of scores of other priests and pastors halted when they were confined to their homes or forbidden to preach. Protestants, Lutherans, and Catholics resisted to the point of death. Pastor Martin Niemöller and Jesuit Rupert Mayer, among others, steadfastly opposed the Nazis and endured living martyrdoms. From the concentration camp in Sachsenhausen, Niemöller smuggled out his 1940 Advent message: "The Apostles have borne witness....In their strength let us go forward on the way in His footsteps unconcerned with the censure of men, but with the peace of Christ in our hearts and with praise of God on our lips. So help us God!"

Niemöller was Hitler's "personal prisoner." He was later transferred to Dachau, where thousands of the clergy were interned and many exterminated.

When Pastor Niemöller was arrested, his congregation held a prayer service. The police tried to stop it. There was a spontaneous demonstration, and two hundred fifty of his parishioners were arrested. Among them was Pastor Franz Hildebrandt, of Jewish ancestry, who was now in great danger. A friend secured his release and escape to England. That friend was Dietrich Bonhoeffer—a theologian, pastor, and martyr whose courageous resistance against Hitler, imprisonment, and execution dramatize "the cost of discipleship."

The *Times* in London published a letter by the Anglican Bishop of Chichester, in which he sounded one of the earliest unequivocal warnings from abroad about the Nazis: "This is a critical hour. This is not a question of the fate of a single vicar; it is a question concerning the whole attitude of the German state to Christianity" (Anton Gill, *An Honourable Defeat: A History of German Resistance to Hitler, 1933–1945*, New York: Henry Holt, 1994, p. 51).

Again, the *New York Times* of March 14, 1940, stated: "Pope Is Emphatic About Peace: Jews' Rights Defended." Describing Pius XII's confrontational meeting with German Foreign Minister Joachim von Ribbentrop, the story reads: "Twice in two days Pope Pius XII has gone out of his way to speak out for justice as well as for peace, and Vatican circles take this as an emphasis of his stern demand to Joachim von Ribbentrop, that Germany right the injustice she has done before there can be peace....It was also learned today for the first time that the Pontiff, in the burning words he spoke to Herr von Ribbentrop about religious persecution, also came to the defense of the Jews."

In 1940, in a letter to be read in all churches entitled *Opere et Caritate* ("By Work and by Love"), Pope Pius XII instructed the Catholic bishops of Europe to assist all people suffering from racial discrimination at the hands of the Nazis.[3]

The same year Thomas Mann, the exiled 1929 Nobel Prize laureate in literature and no defender of the Catholic Church, stated: "There can be no real peace between the cross and the swastika. National Socialism is essentially unchristian and anti-Christian." On December 23, 1940, *Time* magazine's cover caption, "Martyr of 1940," was followed by the words: "In Germany only the cross has not bowed to the swastika."

In that same *Time* cover story also appeared, from a Jew and an agnostic, one of the best known tributes to the spirit of Germany's Christians. It was a tribute by the renowned physicist Albert Einstein: "Being a lover of freedom, when the Nazi revolution came in Germany, I looked to the universities to defend it, knowing that they had always boasted of their devotion to the cause of truth; but, no, the universities immediately were silenced. Then I looked to the great editors of the newspapers, whose flaming editorials in days gone by had proclaimed their love of freedom; but they, like the universities, were silenced in a few short weeks....Only the Church," Einstein concluded, "stood squarely across the path of Hitler's campaign for suppressing the truth. I never had any special interest in the Church before, but now I feel a great affection and admiration because the Church alone has had the courage and persistence to stand for intellectual truth and moral freedom. I am forced thus to confess that what I once despised, I now praise unreservedly."[7]

On December 25, 1942, the *New York Times* quoted the papal Christmas message and concluded in its editorial: "If a prominent personality who is obligated to the impartial consideration of Nations in both camps condemns the new form of Nation-State as heresy, when he accuses the expulsion and persecution of men for no other reason than their race...then this impartial judgment amounts to the verdict of a Supreme Court....This Christmas more than ever, the Pope is a lonely voice crying out in the silence of a continent." One would hope that the *New York Times* would refer to its wartime reporting and editorials.

It is common knowledge that no broad actions involving Catholic churches in Rome are carried out without the Pope's approval. The historian Renzo DeFelice lists, besides Vatican buildings, one hundred fifty convents and monasteries in Rome alone where Jews were hidden.

Among the twelve volumes of *Actes et documents du Saint-Siège relatifs à la Seconde Guerre Mondiale (Acts and Documents of the Holy See Relative to the Second World War),* published from 1965 to 1982, there are four volumes dealing exclusively with the Vatican's work for the victims of the war, mainly Jewish victims. Included is its correspondence with the world Jewish organizations who were then appealing for help. One of these volumes alone has over five hundred seventy items relating to attempts by the Vatican to assist Jews.

Father Robert Graham, one of the four Jesuits who edited the documents, commented: "In reference to the deportation of the European Jews, nearly every world Jewish rescue organization at work in the field is represented: the World Jewish Congress (both the London and the Geneva centers), the American Jewish Congress, the Jewish Agency for Palestine, Agudas Israel, the Emergency Committee to Save the Jews of Europe, the Union of Orthodox Rabbis of the United States and Canada. Prominent Jewish leaders who recognized the papal role included Rabbi Isaac Herzog of Jerusalem, Chief Rabbi Hertz of England, and the War Refugee Board, created by President Roosevelt to aid the persecuted Jews."[8]

In his final summary at the end of the war (1945) the executive director of the War Refugee Board, John W. Phele says: "The Holy See and the Vatican hierarchy throughout Europe were solicited time and again for special assistance both as a channel of communication to the leaders and people of enemy territory and as a means of rendering direct aid to the suffering victims of Hitler. The Catholic clergy saved and protected many thousands and the Vatican rendered invaluable assistance to the Board and to the persecuted in Nazi hands."

Many times during the horrors that befell Europe after the rise of Nazism in 1933, Pius XII faced agonizing decisions in his position as supreme pastor of the Roman Catholic Church. Guiding all his actions was the determination to serve God and those whose lives he could reach. Chief among the goals that he prayed and labored to achieve was peace. But he was determined to avoid any action that would cause more innocent victims; one role he was totally committed to carrying out was that of universal pastor, of kind and loving father to all victims near and distant.

*   *   *

Responses to the International Committee

The International Jewish Committee on Interreligious Consultations is an umbrella organization consisting of the Reform, Conservative, and Orthodox branches of Judaism as well as the World Jewish Congress, the American Jewish Committee, the Anti-Defamation League, B'nai B'rith, and the Israel Interfaith Committee. In September 1998 the Committee issued its *Response to the Vatican Document "We Remember: A Reflection on the Shoah."*

The Committee's response is important because it provides an opportunity to deal with many of the attitudes underlying today's negative judgment of Pius XII. It begins and ends with an expression of gratitude for Pope John Paul II's many efforts to improve Catholic-Jewish understanding. It claims *We Remember* fails to get history straight, fails to condemn past Church teaching sufficiently, fails to recognize the clear development from Christian anti-Semitism, ignorance, and prejudice to Nazism—that is, fails to say explicitly that Christian teaching prepared the way for the Holocaust, fails to accurately state the widespread absence of Christian help for Jews.

The Committee objects to the document's mention of Pius XII's humanitarian efforts and its praise of Jewish wartime Rabbis and leaders who acknowledge his contribution. It also finds offensive the inclusion of the phrase "the drama of the Middle East" in its list of the century's genocides and human tragedies around the world.

The Committee's final paragraph states: "Our critique of the document is not meant with any negative intent but as a pointer to the guidelines which we think should be adopted in Catholic teaching of the Shoah." It then goes on to call for Catholics and Jews to work together along the lines of Cardinal Cassidy's step-by-step approach and in John Paul II's spirit of cooperating "together for a world of true respect for the life and dignity of every human being."

I share the International Committee's "true respect for the life and dignity of every human being," and, like the Committee, hope the remarks that follow—to paraphrase the Committee—do not seem negative but rather as pointers that might serve as guidelines to Jewish teaching about Pope Pius XII and the Catholic Church.

Cardinal Cassidy has several times counseled: "Throw off all fear of truth. Our journey must continue. What harm can come from a dialogue that enters into the heart of what constitutes our identities as faith communities?" In hopes of serving that truth, we quote and then comment upon some of the committee's observations from an individual Catholic perspective.

The Document and Anti-Semitism

"This document will reach millions in parts of the world....We hope that everything will be done to ensure that the message will quickly reach grass roots level."

Indeed the goal of the Catholic Church is to spread this message. Only through education can this be accomplished. As the message spreads throughout the world, the relationship between Jews and Catholics will be clarified. Pope Pius XII's unmistakably anti-Nazi words and actions will be understood. Through education, it will be known, for example, that the Vatican's Holy Office issued a formal decree on March 25, 1928, explicitly condemning anti-Semitism: "Moved by Christian charity, the Holy See is obligated to protect the Jewish people against unjust vexations and, just as it reprobates all rancour and conflicts between peoples, it particularly condemns unreservedly hatred against the people once chosen by God; the hatred that commonly goes by the name of anti-Semitism." In another statement, on October 11, 1930, the Vatican newspaper *L'Osservatore Romano* declared: "Belonging to the National Socialist Party of Hitler is irreconcilable with the Catholic conscience." In fact, in his book, *Who Voted for Hitler?* (Princeton University Press, 1982), Richard Hamilton proves that in 1932, when the Nazis were beginning their climb to power, German Catholics voted overwhelmingly—more than 85 percent—against Hitler's National Socialism.

The Historical Treatment

"Our disappointments in the historical treatment were accentuated by the great impression made upon us by the series of statements on the subject published by the National Episcopal Conferences...."

What the Interreligious Committee points out is that the statements by German and French bishops were harsher and more outspoken about their fellow Catholics under the Nazis than were those of the authors of *We Remember.* But is it not common for different commissions, with different members, covering different areas to come up with differing reports? One presumes both the bishops' apologies and the Vatican's came from their judgment of the facts in their possession. The Vatican Commission worked longer, very likely with much more information, and had to deal with a much wider area. The bishops were concerned with their own countries, the Vatican with the entire Church. The two groups spoke from different levels of authority.

It is a mistake to think that the statements of the bishops were accepted without correction. Father Pierre Blet, in a piece published in the Italian journal *30 Days,* pointed out that it is inaccurate to say the German and French statements of apology represented all of the bishops in those countries. He went on: "The document put out by the French bishops is a condemnation by a tribunal that had neither jurisdiction nor scholarship: [they lacked] jurisdiction because the bishops today have no jurisdiction over their predecessors; scholarship because these are very delicate things to judge. It is not easy to see one's way through these things and the task is better left to historians....The condemnation did not come from the French Episcopal Conference, even if the public believes so, but only from some of the bishops, 30 out of a total of 120 and without having discussed it with their fellow bishops...."[9]

But even if they had represented national conferences, their authority would have been quite limited. Joseph Cardinal Ratzinger, in *The Ratzinger Report* (pp. 60, 61), states: "We must not forget that the episcopal conferences have no theological basis...they have only a practical, concrete function....It [the limited function] is, moreover, what is confirmed in the new Code of Canon Law, which prescribes the extent of the authority of the conferences, which cannot validly act in the name of all the bishops unless each and every bishop has given his consent." Ratzinger further goes on to say that conferences sometimes depend too much on the opinions of others and can even respond to the pressure to achieve consensus, and then makes the telling point that in Germany in the 1930s the voice of integrity was that of individuals, not groups: "The really powerful documents against National Socialism were those that came from individual courageous bishops. The documents of the conference, on the contrary, were often rather wan and too weak with respect to what the tragedy called for."[10]

To mention but three examples of individual bishops who spoke out: On August 23, 1942, Archbishop (later Cardinal) Jules Gerard Saliège of Toulouse echoed the principles constantly stressed by Pius XII: "The Jews are our brethren. They belong to mankind. No Christian dares forget that!" Bishop Pierre-Marie Thèas sent a letter to the priests of the Diocese of Montauban to be read to their congregations: "I raise my voice in protest, and I assert that all men, Aryans and non-Aryans, are brothers....anti-Semitic pressures flout human dignity and violate the most sacred rights of the human person and family."[11]

On December 12, 1942, Archbishop Joseph Frings of Cologne condemned the tragic persecution of Jews, appealing to the "ultimate principles of justice." These "inherent rights," Frings declared, include "the right to life, to inviolability, to freedom, to property, and to a marriage whose validity does not depend on the arbitrary will of the state." These, he said, must not be denied to someone "who is not of our blood or does not speak our language." The Germans must always remember that "denial of these rights or indeed the inhumane treatment of our fellow human beings is an injustice not only against a foreign people but against our own people as well." On August 8, 1943, the Catholic bishops issued a pastoral letter describing the Ten Commandments as the "Vital Law of Nations" and condemning genocide.[12]

Gerhard Ritter, who lived through the Nazi rule in Germany and who was jailed by them, pays tremendous tribute to the anti-Nazi actions of German bishops in his book, *The German Resistance.*[13] A study of individual pastoral letters demonstrates that the German bishops protested against the arbitrary confiscation of private property, the concentration camps, the methods of police spying, the shooting of innocent hostages or prisoners, the abduction of foreign workers, and the extermination of the mentally afflicted.

As earlier noted in citations from Gallin's *German Resistance to Hitler,* revolution "was specifically rejected and denounced by them on several occasions."[14] There were, however, courageous Germans who sought to overthrow Hitler and they received complete support from Pius XII. The Holy Father did not hesitate to approach the British on behalf of German officers seeking to get rid of him, because these officers offered the only real possibility of achieving peace.

Christianity and Historical Anti-Semitism

Initial Jewish reactions...were deeply concerned by the incorporation of the quotation from the Pope's speech of 31 October 1997 in which he said: "In the Christian world—I do not say on the part of the Church herself—erroneous and unjust interpretations of the New Testament regarding the Jewish people and their alleged culpability have circulated for too long."

The troubling phrase is: "I do not say on the part of the Church herself." Apparently many Jews interpreted this to mean that the Holy Father was absolving individual Catholics, especially the hierarchy, for past misdeeds and this, according to the Committee, led Jews to go *"into great detail concerning the misdeeds of the Church."*

Although many Catholics would have trouble explaining the phrase, they would realize that John Paul II was not exonerating Catholics but referring to the mystical, spiritual, invisible Church. It is understandable that the distinction between the mystical Church and her fallible, sinful members might be misunderstood. Yet, it is not too different from the distinction between Israel, the people of the Covenant, and the actions of individual Jews. When asked by Jewish groups to explain the phrase, Cardinal Cassidy said: "the term *the Church,* refers for Catholics to the inerrant mystical bride of Christ, whereas the term *sons and daughters of the Church* does not exclude members of the Church at any level." *Lumen Gentium* says this in a much expanded fashion, drawing on a dozen biblical metaphors to try to convey the Church that is both mystical and sinful—and the human Church is constantly in need of reform *(Ecclesia semper reformanda).*

It might be useful to reflect for a moment on what, if any, personal meaning the phrase, "the Church herself," when connected to anti-Semitism, might have for John Paul II. For it was through that Church that young Karol Wojtyla early learned to love things Jewish. Tad Szulc's *John Paul II,* which carefully chronicles the Pope's lifelong relations with Jews, connects Wojtyla's intense feelings for them with the central prayer life of the Church. Szulc quotes the Holy Father as saying his feelings for Jews *began* in "my youngest years, when, in the parish church of my native Wadowice, I listened to this psalm [147] sung during evening Mass:" *O Jerusalem, glorify the Lord; Praise Your God, O Zion! For He made the bars of Your gate strong, And blessed Your children within you....*

The Pope went on: "I still have in my ears these words and this melody, which I have remembered all my life. And then came the terrible experience of World War II and the [Nazi] occupation, the Holocaust, which was the extermination of Jews only for the reason that they were Jews. It was a terrible upheaval that has remained in the memory of all the people who were close to these events."

While *We Remember* explicitly said that "erroneous and unjust interpretations" concerning Jews existed for centuries in the Church, while these errors and injustices were evident in Good Friday services, they were not the essence of the Church's teaching nor part of the central rite of her worship. The essential teachings of the Church are charity, justice, and forgiveness. Every day in its prayers and liturgy it has demonstrated a veneration for Jewish piety, enabling devout Catholics, like Karol Wojtyla, to see beyond whatever unjust interpretations they may have encountered.

"We feel it unfortunate that the distinction [between anti-Judaism and anti-Semitism] *was not spelled out in the document...."*

The Vatican document distinguishes between religious prejudice against the Jews, termed anti-Judaism, of which Christians have been guilty, and anti-Semitism as a racial theory that guided Nazism.

A number of times the Committee justifiably complains that *We Remember* was not specific enough, not spelling things out sufficiently. In meeting with Jewish groups following the publication of *We Remember,* Cardinal Cassidy granted that some phrases in the report may not be as clear as they might have been, nor as complete as some reasonable people might have desired. The document's writers had to choose between issuing a thousand pages or the brief summary it did. As members of the Commission for Religious Relations with the Jews, their primary purpose was not scholarly, historical, nor apologetic. It was religious. They wanted to produce a penitential document, a statement of sorrow, a confession rather than an investigative treatise, a reflection that expressed the view of its experts and the Church's Magisterium. *We Remember* explicitly stated that it was leaving detailed historical examination in the hands of the scholarly community. It would summarize, express grief, and accept responsibility for past wrongs and, at the same time, add to the foundation of understanding provided by Vatican II and John Paul II.

We Remember admits Catholics failed and expresses sorrow for that failure, says implicitly that the official Church never preached racial anti-Semitism, and states explicitly that both Pius XI and Pius XIII rejected Nazi ideology and worked against it in every possible way. In an effort to make more clear the unprecedented virulence of Nazism, it distinguishes: "between anti-Semitism, based on theories contrary to the constant teaching of the Church on the unity of the human race and the equal dignity of all races and peoples, and the long-standing sentiments of mistrust and hostility that we call anti-Judaism, of which, unfortunately, Christians have also been guilty."

This distinction points up a fundamental difference between the Vatican Commission and the Jewish International Committee. The Committee sees a direct, causal connection between "the sentiments of mistrust and hostility" that plagued Christian-Jewish relations for centuries and Nazi anti-Semitism. Where the Committee would seem to find only a difference in degree, the Vatican Commission finds a difference in kind as well as in degree. The Committee says Nazi anti-Semitism arose from centuries of Christian hostility; the Vatican says that Nazi racism came out of nineteenth-century anti-Christian scientism, pagan mythological models, and the deification of nationalism—all of which were un-Christian and strongly anti-Catholic. It sees Nazi ideology as one of several nineteenth- and twentieth-century ideologies seeking the destruction of religion itself. Where the International Committee tends to see one continuous form of prejudice and persecution with various shadings, the Vatican sees a radically new and deadly racism coming to a full realization under Hitler.

It is true, as the Committee claims, that *We Remember* does not *"spell out"* this distinction. But scores of books and articles have been written that support the Commission's clearly stated conclusion: "The Shoah was the work of a thoroughly modern neo-pagan regime. Its anti-Semitism had its roots outside of Christianity and, in pursuing its aims, it did not hesitate to oppose the Church and persecute her members also." Actually, many Jewish writers have made the case for the uniqueness of Nazi anti-Semitism and its difference from medieval anti-Judaism/anti-Semitism.

The official Church has never preached "the teaching of contempt for Jews." It teaches that no human being has the right to kill other human beings. The Church during the Middle Ages urged that Jews should be converted and baptized, but not killed. The Nazis decreed that the Jews must be oppressed, quarantined, and exterminated. Time after time, popes intervened against persecutors of Jews. The Nazis were determined to exterminate Jews.

Commenting on Christian legislation against Jews in the Middle Ages, Professor Yosef Yerushalmi states: "Between this and Nazi Germany lies not merely a 'transformation' but a leap into a different dimension. The slaughter of Jews by the State was not part of the medieval Christian world order. It became possible with the breakdown of that order."[15]

"The [Vatican Commission's] statement that...anti-Judaism "was essentially more sociological and political than religious" plays down the fact of the unbroken line of Christian anti-Judaism/anti-Semitism and its impact throughout Europe."

To find "anti-Judaism" "more sociological and political than religious" is an attempt to get away from oversimplifications. It is an appeal for an objective, scholarly look at the multiple causes of prejudices—sociological, political, psychological, and others. Surely all of the world's frightening competitiveness, self-seeking, apparently ineradicable envy and jealousy cannot be blamed on Christianity, pure or perverted? All the Commission does is to suggest that those inevitable tensions, disputes, and hatreds that arise out of "turf warfare," economic competition, and the clash of vested interests must be weighed as causes of "anti-Judaism." Speaking of Europe prior to the eighteenth century, *We Remember* notes that these endemic social and political rivalries often became deadly: "In times of crisis such as famine, war, pestilence, or social tensions, the Jewish minority was sometimes taken as a scapegoat and became the victim of violence, looting, even massacres." Describing Europe at the beginning of the nineteenth century, it observes: "In a climate of eventful social change, Jews were often accused of exercising an influence disproportionate to their numbers."

The Church and the Shoah

"The implication that while Christians have been guilty of anti-Judaism but anti-Semitism is a contradiction of the teaching of the Church is dubious and it is unfortunate that it is put forward in generalities...."

This objection needs to be divided: first, a comment on Christian guilt, then on the Church's teaching about anti-Semitism.

We Remember grants that many in the Church lived and taught anti-Jewish views. It expresses sorrow that these practices contributed to the Jews being held in contempt, ghettoized, victimized, and deported. In naming these actions "anti-Judaism," there is no attempt to deny them or to avoid the burden of responsibility they put on Christians.

But historian Norman Ravitch raises the point that the International Committee reaches in the final page of its appraisal—the need for contemporary Jews to have a better understanding of Christians. He writes: "Too many accept the distorted view that Christianity is pagan, idolatrous, superstitious, morbid, and inhumane. Having the greater guilt by far, Christians have surely the greater need for reconciliation, but when the Jewish authorities had political power they understandably used it in their own interest, including against the nascent Christians. Reconciliation, atonement, forgiveness, and understanding cannot be a one-way street."

Being sins, both anti-Judaism and anti-Semitism are against the teaching of the Church. Both are violations of Jesus' teaching, perhaps most simply stated in his summation of the Commandments: *" 'Thou shalt love the Lord thy God with thy whole heart, and with thy whole soul, and with thy whole mind.'* This is the greatest and the first commandment. And the second is like it: *thou shalt love thy neighbor as thyself.' "*

The Church not only teaches that anti-Semitism is incompatible with Christianity, it teaches that it is as an attack on Christianity. Sixty years ago Jacques Maritain expressed a truth that in one form or another has long been held by Christians: "For a Christian to hate or to despise or to wish to treat degradingly the race from which sprung his God and the Immaculate Mother of God...always turns in the end into a bitter zeal against Christianity itself." The late Father Edward Flannery, a pioneer in Jewish-Catholic relations and the author of *The Anguish of the Jews: Twenty-three Centuries of Anti-Semitism,* stated in a 1967 interview: "The anti-Semite...is the real Christ-killer. He thinks he's religious, but that's a self-delusion. Actually he finds religion so heavy a burden, he develops 'Christophobia.' He's hostile to the faith and has an unconscious hatred of Christ, who is for him, Christ the repressor. He uses anti-Semitism as a safety valve for this hostility and is really trying to strike out at Christ."

These are not pious generalities; they are quite accurate descriptions of Hitler's anti-Semitism. That one was written before the Holocaust and one afterwards only indicates that Maritain clearly sensed in 1939 what Hitler's hatred would lead to. Anti-Semitism and the removal or destruction of Jews was a first step; the second was the destruction of Christians. Flannery remarks on Nazi teachings: "Jewish and Christian biblical spirituality and morality were denounced as a massive alienation of humanity from its true natural condition. Only with their abolition could humankind be free and true to itself....The brunt of the violence emanating from this philosophy was visited upon Jews and Judaism. Christianity, considered an extension and disguise of Semitic spirit, was given a temporary reprieve for tactical reasons. Here was, in sum, an anti-Semitism, a-religious, murderous, and pagan to its core."[16]

As the process of secularization emerged, it passed into the rationalism and skepticism of the French Enlightenment and English

Deists, and finally, with the rise of the scientific ethos, took a materialistic and technological turn. Modern racism's complex parentage finds
forebears in numerous antireligious and radical ideologies: Feuer-
bach's atheism, Fichte and Hegel's statism, social Darwinism, Niet-
zsche's Promethean will to power, to mention a few of the more
conspicuous. From this conglomerate of philosophies the premise
emerged that religion as exemplified by Judaism and Christianity
stands as the last obstacle to a liberated humankind, the last shackle to
be shed for humanity's return to its true instincts and vitality and to the
earth to which it properly belongs.

As for Hitler's intentions about destroying Christianity, there is
indisputable evidence of this. One of the more interesting items is in
Adolf Hitler, Monologe im Füherhauptquartier 1941–1944, edited by
W. Jochmann. Hitler: "The war will come to an end and I shall see my
last task as clearing the church problem. Only then will the German
nation be completely safe....In my youth I had the view: dynamite!
Today I see that one cannot break it over one's knee. It has to be cut off
like a gangrenous limb" (page 150).

In *A Requiem for Hitler and Other New Perspectives on the German Church Struggle* (Trinity International, 1989), Klaus Scholder
states that, for Hitler, Judaism was the root of all disaster. The Jewish
question and the Christian question were closely connected in the Third
Reich. After annihilating the Jews and winning the war, Hitler was
resolved to annihilate Christianity. According to his associates, in his
1941–42 monologues he considered Christianity as a Jewish invention
because it rejected the National Socialist worldview. How to dissolve
the Church was his last great problem. Only the downfall of Hitler prevented Christians from being brutally awakened to this fact.

*"It may be noted that Hitler, Himmler, and the other Nazi leaders were
all baptized Christians who were never excommunicated."*

This is inaccurate. Because of their apostasy and violent actions
against the German clergy, Hitler and the other Nazi leaders who were
born Catholic incurred automatic excommunication under Canons
2332 and 2343, which, in part, state: "Those who, either directly or
indirectly, impede the exercise of ecclesiastical jurisdiction...persons
who lay violent hands on the person of a Patriarch, Archbishop or
Bishop....incur excommunication...*speciali modo.*"[17] One cannot

claim that Hitler and other baptized Nazi leaders were still members of the Catholic Church.

The subject of excommunication is usually brought up to support the idea that if Pius XII had excommunicated Hitler and others, the Holocaust might have been prevented or limited. The least that can be said about this theory is that it was a judgment call, and no one will ever really know what would have resulted. Those familiar with Hitler and his psychology point to his pattern of terroristic murder and conclude that any provocation by the Pope would have resulted in violent retaliation, the loss of many more Jewish lives, especially those then under the protection of the Church, and an intensification of the persecution of Catholics.

Father Vincent Lapomarda, S.J., Coordinator of the Holocaust Collection at Holy Cross College in Worcester, Massachusetts, cites the view of the Chief Rabbi of Denmark, Marcus Melchior, who managed to escape the Nazis. Many years ago Rabbi Melchior said: "If the Pope had spoken out, Hitler would have probably massacred more than six million Jews and perhaps ten times ten million Catholics, if he had the power to do so." Those claiming Pius should have confronted Hitler sometimes seem to be arguing that Pius should have brought about his own martyrdom—for the good of the Church! Others dismiss the argument that additional deaths would have been caused by saying the Jewish suffering was so extreme that it didn't matter how many more might die. Such an argument makes others thankful that Pius was a kind, generous, and moderate leader.

Behavior during the Shoah

"Did Christians give every possible assistance to those being persecuted and in particular to the persecuted Jews?"

This is a question that *We Remember* poses. Its answer: "Many did, but others did not." The International Committee would say: "A few did, but most did not."

That may or may not be a more accurate statement. How does one know what percentage of a population can be expected to be willing, self-sacrificing martyrs? Few or many? Given the incalculable complication of historical and individual circumstances, the almost complete absence of relatively safe ways of protesting, this is a question only to be finally answered by God himself. To say there were too few requires the ability to look into the hearts of individuals. To the writers of *We Remember,* who were apologizing for those "not strong enough to raise their voices in protest," it must have seemed almost a miracle that anyone was courageous enough to brave certain brutality, concentration camps, and possible death to defy the Nazis. How many risked their lives for the thirty million victims of Stalinism? Or in Cambodia? How many today are even concerned enough to write a letter condemning the million and a half deaths in southern Sudan? The Church teaches that abortion is murder of the innocent. How many Catholics accept the teaching, never mind even murmuring publicly against infanticide?

Would that millions all over Europe had risen up against the Holocaust. If they had, it would have been a world long desired but never known. That there was one such heroic person is encouraging; that there were ten is more encouraging; that there were actually thousands that we know of is inspiring and gives hope for the future.

Pope Pius XII, as mentioned previously, was one of those thousands of exceptions. Harold Deutch notes, in *The Conspiracy Against Hitler in the Twilight War,* that the Pope had "the moral courage" to plot with those trying to overthrow Hitler, an act which, if known by the Germans, would unquestionably have led to his death.

Many of those who seem to have been cowardly may seem so only because we know little or nothing about their circumstances. Pius XII left it to the German bishops to decide whether to publish his letter of January 3, 1943, encouraging them to resist Nazism; they elected not to do so out of prudence, not cowardice. Prudence demands that even when one is convinced that a cause is just, he should nevertheless refrain from taking action unless he has a well-grounded expectation that his action will actually improve matters.

Some members of the Church failed to assist their neighbors in occupied Europe. But their infidelity cannot be turned against the Church. Certainly there were individual Catholics who remained passive, not out of infidelity, but rather because of a variety of circumstances that called for prudence. The Book of Deuteronomy clearly established the principle that no one is responsible for the sins of his ancestors (Dt 24:16). The current members of the Church cannot be held accountable for those misdeeds. They can atone, they can combat anti-Semitism, and they can vow to do all in their power so that the Holocaust will never be repeated.

The words of Rabbi Harold M. Schulweis of Valley Beth Shalom in Encino, California, who gathered evidence from Jewish eyewitnesses, should be remembered: "The most important *mitzvah,* or commandment, of the post-Holocaust era should be *hakarat hatov,* the recognition of goodness...."

The Rabbi tells the story of a Polish farmer named Alex Roslan, who was sickened when he saw bodies of Jewish toddlers and teenagers lying dead in a ghetto street. He came upon Jacob Gilat, then ten years old, and two younger brothers, Shalom and David, apparently uncared for. He smuggled the three young strangers out of the ghetto and hid them in his home with his wife, Mila, and their two sons. He knew that this was a capital crime (Twenty-five hundred Christian Poles were executed for helping Jews!).

When Jacob Gilat and his brother Shalom contracted scarlet fever, they infected Alex's own son Yurek. Though only ten years old, in a hospital in Warsaw, Yurek hid half his medicine so his parents could take it home to the Jewish boys. It was not enough, and Alex sold his three-room apartment and took a smaller one to raise money to bribe a friendly doctor's staff and smuggle the brothers into the hospital.

Shalom Gilat died. His brother Jacob, a nuclear chemist who studied at Berkeley, survived. One day, Jacob called Rabbi Schulweis because he wanted to introduce him to Alex Roslan, the Polish farmer who saved him and his brothers from dying in the ghetto.

Rabbi Schulweis estimates that there were at least fifty thousand non-Jewish Rescuers all over Europe, with the possibility that ten times that many took part in acts that involved risk or consciously turned away from reporting or endangering the hidden Jews for personal reward (Informants received brandy, sugar, and cigarettes, as well as money from the Nazis!).

Many took eight or ten people in for as long as necessary. Stefa Krakowska, a Polish peasant, hid fourteen persons in her home, ranging from age three to sixty. The most astonishing fact is that there were at least eleven hundred rescuers in Berlin!

The late Italian writer, Primo Levi, related how a non-Jewish Italian civilian worker brought him a piece of bread and part of his own ration every day for six months in Auschwitz. Levi wrote: "I believe it was really due to Lorenzo that I am alive today. Not so much because of his material aid, as for his having constantly reminded me by his presence, by his natural and plain manner of being good, that there still

existed a just world outside our own, something and someone still pure
and whole, not corrupt and savage. Thanks to Lorenzo, I managed not
to forget that I myself was a man."

Another book by Yad Vashem's director, Mordecai Paldiel, documents that in 1943 a Catholic priest, Father Simon Gallay, saved the five
Paldiel children and their parents by hiding them in his own home until
he was able to guide them through a double barbed-wire fence into
Switzerland. In 1988 Mordecai Paldiel located Father Gallay and
presided over a moving ceremony honoring him as a "righteous Gentile."

Rabbi Schulweis' testimony is significant: "I am chagrined in
speaking to Catholic audiences to find that there is no awareness of
their own heroes....Let the church celebrate its truest heroes and the
synagogue publicize their spirit. Jews need Christian heroes. Christians
need Jewish heroes. For that heroism from the other side helps break
down the vicious polarization."

Among the many Christian heroes, there are thousands of unsung
Catholic bishops, priests, and nuns who, in consonance with Pope Pius
XII, risked their lives to save Jews and other refugees.

*"The question of the role of Pope Pius XII is obviously a contentious
issue with differing views not only between Jews and Catholics but
among Catholic scholars themselves."*

This is quite true. Pius XII may have become the most denigrated
pope since Alexander VI, especially among those who know very little
about him. And, regrettably, that includes some dissenting Catholic
scholars—most notably Father Richard McBrien and Father John
Morley—who disagree with the testimony of survivors, rescuers, and
Jewish leaders. McBrien also finds the Vatican's *We Remember,* "too subtle, too restrained, too diplomatic in its language." But Father McBrien
gives little evidence that he has studied the matter very closely.

Father Morley, in *Vatican Diplomacy and the Jews during the Holocaust, 1939–1943,*[18] accuses the Vatican of "neglecting the needs of the
Jews." But Vatican historian Robert A. Graham, S.J.,[19] has convincingly
demonstrated that Morley was not in possession of essential facts and
misused some facts he did have in his possession. Morley arrived at his
conclusions, for example, without ever having seen the four volumes of
documents detailing, among other things, the Vatican's efforts on behalf
of Jews. Edited by Graham and three other scholars, these volumes clearly

establish that the Vatican was the one major source of refuge and assistance for persecuted Jews during World War II.

It is worth noting that the Committee makes reference to Catholic scholars with differing views about the role of Pius XII, yet ignores scores of Jewish eyewitnesses and scholars who speak and write in support of him and the Shoah document.

Among those Jewish leaders who have reacted favorably to the Shoah document is Michael Horowitz, a Fellow of the Hudson Institute: "I found the Vatican statement quite balanced, accurate, in places moving and, most of all, consistent with the growing scholarly consensus about Jewish-Christian relations that...makes clear, as the Vatican statement did, that there is a sharp discontinuity between Christian anti-Semitism and Nazism."[20]

Rabbi Jack Bemporad, Director of the Center for Interreligious Understanding at Ramapo College, comments in "Bridging The Gap": "Change has taken place. Premature negative reactions work against the ultimate goal of understanding. The Jewish community should concentrate on the numerous constructive statements of Pope John Paul II....It is only when we begin to educate ourselves that we truly begin to span the bridge of religious understanding."[21]

"The statement that the Pope was responsible for saving hundreds of thousands of Jewish lives has not been substantiated by the published documents."

One of the most surprising aspects of Pius XII's efforts on behalf of Jews is that during and right after the war Jewish praise and gratitude was nearly unanimous. But today Jews far removed from the conditions and circumstances are eager to question and criticize his efforts. In 1945, the Chief Rabbi of Israel, Isaac Herzog, stated: "The people of Israel will never forget what His Holiness and his illustrious delegates, inspired by the eternal principles of religion, which form the very foundation of true civilization, are doing for our unfortunate brothers and sisters in the most tragic hour of our history, which is living proof of Divine Providence in this world." Today, in far different circumstances, Chief Rabbi Israel Meir Lau of Jerusalem attacks the long dead pontiff for not issuing a papal denunciation of *Kristallnacht*—which occurred many months *before* he became Pope.

Once we reject the testimony of contemporaries, we must depend on documents. But the interpretation of documents too often invites further disagreements. It seems very unlikely that any documents will ever surface to establish beyond debate the exact number of Jews saved by Catholic efforts. One of the largest estimates of Jewish lives saved by Pius XII is the 700,000 to 860,000 given by Israeli historian and diplomat Pinchas Lapide in his *The Last Three Popes and the Jews.*[22] Four of the Vatican's twelve-volume *Acts and Documents of the Holy See Relative to the Second World War, 1965–1982 (Actes et documents du Saint-Siège relaltifs à la Seconde Guerre Mondiale)* provide detailed documentation of Pius XII's humanitarian efforts.

Documents show that, in their pastoral letters, the German bishops protested against the arbitrary confiscation of private property, the concentration camps, the methods of police spying, the shooting of innocent hostages or prisoners, the abduction of foreign workers, and the extermination of the mentally afflicted.

Typical of American Jewry's postwar appreciation for what Pope Pius XII accomplished for the Jewish people during the Holocaust was expressed in *The Jewish Newsletter* (1945): "It is to the credit of Pope Pius XII that...instead of preaching Christianity, as the Christian Churches had done for centuries, he and the churches practiced its principles and set an example by their acts and lives, as did the Founder of Christianity."[23]

"We are given one generalizing quotation made by Pius XII but no reference to the charge of silence. He never once explicitly mentioned the Jews in his public pronouncements during World War II."

This is a little like criticizing Pius XII for writing ungrammatical documents because he never used the pronoun *I.* It is true, he never did. But, where's the confusion? The papal practice of the time dictated that he use *We.* Everyone knew it was an individual writing and that what he said expressed his own view as well as that of the Church. Pius spoke in the manner of papal diplomacy, but he frequently spoke of the Jews and their tragedy and everyone understood his references to them. The *New York Times* understood his diplomatic reference to Jews in his 1942 Christmas message and praised him in an editorial. SS leader Reinhard Heydrich also understood what the Pope had written and complained: "The Pope is virtually accusing the German people of injustice toward the Jews and makes himself the mouthpiece of the Jewish war criminals."

There is overwhelming evidence that Pius spoke publicly and privately in favor of the Jews. To cite but one of hundreds of possible examples: referring to various of his writings, the London *Times* of October 1, 1942, explicitly praises him for his condemnation of Nazism and support of Jews: "A study of the words which Pope Pius XII has addressed since his accession, in encyclicals and allocutions to the Catholics of various nations, leaves no room for doubt. He condemns the worship of force and its concrete manifestation in the suppression of national liberties and in the persecution of the Jewish race."

In his addresses, Pius XII pleaded for those who, because of their nationality or race, were condemned to death. In doing so, the Pope regularly used the Latin word *stirps,* which means "race" and was a word used throughout Europe for centuries to refer to Jews. In June 1943, the Vatican radio emphatically stated: "He who makes a distinction between Jews and other men is unfaithful to God and is in conflict with God's commands."

Such broadcasts as this were quoted in the *American Jewish Yearbook 1943–1944.*[24] More importantly, these broadcasts directly influenced heroic Catholic rescuers. Ralph Stewart, in his *Pope Pius XII and the Jews,* provides the testimony of Michel Riquet, S.J., a victim of Nazi terror imprisoned in Dachau because of his efforts to save Jewish families. In Israel in 1965 as the head of a delegation of French Catholics, Riquet said: "Throughout those years of horror when we listened to Radio Vatican and the Pope's messages, we felt in communion with the Pope, in helping persecuted Jews and in fighting Nazi violence."[25]

"The Vatican archives....when they are opened, there will doubtless be both positive and negative disclosures."

This remark by the International Committee ignores the twelve volumes already published from the Vatican archives, which have seldom been studied by those most critical of the Church. The International Committee has to be aware of these volumes, so its observation must mean that it believes there are documents which were not included in the twelve volumes. There is always that possibility, of course. But the world was assured by Father Pierre Blet, S.J., the sole survivor of the team of four scholars who edited the Vatican documents, that this was not the case. In an article entitled "Was There a Culpable Silence with Regard to the Holocaust?" he wrote: "We did not deliberately leave out any meaningful document because it seemed to us that it might harm the Pope's image or the Holy See's reputation."[26] Father Blet repeats this message with great emphasis to all who ask him about the files.

What remains in the Vatican archives has not been opened to the general public because it contains confidential documents that must be respected during the lifetime of the persons involved. Except for those documents within the recognized confidentiality classification, the archives have been open since 1982 and apparently ignored. There is no valid basis, only speculation, for the statement that "doubtless" there will be negative disclosures "when they are opened."

"Christians cannot view the Shoah as they do other genocides."

It is not clear whether the International Committee is saying Christians must see the Holocaust as overwhelmingly horrible, or must see it as caused by Christians, or must see their special relation with Jews because their Messiah came from the Jews.

True, the Shoah has a special place in the history of human slaughter because of its magnitude and the cold-blooded deliberation with which it was carried out. Christians, however, cannot ignore the fact that Germany prepared for that great evil by developing an elaborate administrative apparatus to eliminate "the unfit," an end once again very popular in today's world. Health agencies were required to register children born with congenital deformities, who were then isolated and killed. By late 1939 the program included all children with obvious physical or mental handicaps or severe diseases.

It is important to remember the killing of the handicapped because it establishes that atheistic German science, not German or European Christianity, not hatred of the Jews, led Hitler to kill the handicapped first. As James M. Glass establishes in *Life Unworthy of Life: Racial Phobia and Mass Murder in Hitler's Germany,* the Nazis exterminated Jews because they saw them from a scientific Darwinian perspective as sociologically inferior and contaminated, not because they were non-Christian.

Glass writes: "Political purpose defined and rationalized language and 'subordinated it to authority.' The bureaucrats and professionals who organized the mass killings did not live by conventional

Judeo-Christian moral standards. They lived by a different kind of morality, involving the German biomedical vision that justified killing in the interests of preserving the blood and genetic integrity of the *Volk*. In the words of Rudolph Hoess, commandant of Auschwitz: 'National Socialism is nothing but applied biology.'"[27]

Finally, Christians see the Shoah as evil because each taking of innocent life is evil, according to the commandment of God; the taking of millions of innocent lives is a million times evil. Much the same point is made in Dr. Waclaw Zajaczkoski's *Martyrs of Charity,* quoting the Jewish historian Max Dimond: "If the Christian reader dismisses what happened as something which affected a few million Jews only, he has not merely shown his contempt for the millions of Jews murdered by the Nazis, but has betrayed his Christian heritage as well. And if the Jewish reader forgets the millions of Christians murdered by the Nazis, then he has not merely let those millions of Jews die in vain, but has betrayed his Jewish heritage of compassion and justice."[28]

Dimond sets forth an ideal that both Christians and Jews must all strive to follow. Unfortunately, it is an ideal too seldom even given lip service. On the sixtieth anniversary of *Kristallnacht,* Holocaust survivor Amitai Etzioni, a distinguished American professor and scholar, gave a memorial lecture in Saint Paul's Church, Frankfurt, Germany. It was a talk filled with painful memories, good will, intelligence, wisdom, and sound advice for avoiding other acts of murderous prejudice. When he came to name the victims of Hitler, he provided what seems a very inclusive catalogue: "6 million Jews, 200,000 gypsies, 70,000 handicapped and mental patients, 10,000 homosexuals, as well as political dissidents and other German critics of the regime."

Is this really an accurate list of innocent civilians who were Hitler's victims? No, of course not. It mentions nothing of the approximately three million Polish victims, nothing of Christian martyrs throughout Europe—the phrase "other German critics of the regime" certainly cannot refer to them. Why such partial lists of Hitler's victims have actually come to be seen as more acceptable than more exact lists is another puzzling aspect of the way spin is put on historical facts.

A recent *New York Times* film review by Janet Maslin, "Putting the 'Nazi' into Doctors," also depicts a memorial at the psychiatric hospital in Bedburg-Hau, Germany, remembering the patients killed in a Nazi euthanasia program in 1940: "With chilling efficiency, the Israeli documentary *Healing by Killing* chronicles the subversive process that turned German health care professionals into Nazi doctors. In this process it finds the seeds of genocide, as the patients became prisoners and the Hippocratic oath became a travesty. The film shows the steps that evolved into systematic killing, highlighting sterilization, experimentation, etc....The final emphasis is on preventing the roots of such evil from flourishing again."[29]

The Occult Roots of Nazism, by Nicholas Goodrick-Clarke, documents the role of the anti-Christian Occult Movement.[30] As Patrick Glynn notes in *God—The Evidence:* "In addition to his major project of exterminating Jews (along with Gypsies, Jehovah's Witnesses, the mentally retarded, and other groups), Hitler sought to destroy the mainstream churches. Hundreds of priests and nuns were sent to concentration camps."[31]

British researcher Martin Gilbert, Jewish author of *The Holocaust,* writes: "...in addition to the six million Jewish men, women and children who were murdered, at least an equal number of non-Jews were also killed, not in the heat of battle, not by military siege, aerial bombardment or the harsh conditions of war, but by deliberate planned murder."[32]

Why the silence about these dead? Is it because they were mostly Christian? Is it because mentioning them might possibly point up Hitler's hatred of Christianity—which might tend to undercut the theory that Christianity was the source of Nazism? Would mention of Christian victims somehow make it more difficult for leaders to see Nazism as perverted Christianity? The answer to these questions is: quite possibly, but to explain why is beyond the scope of this book.

It is enormously difficult to correct deep-rooted prejudices, ingrained misrepresentations and constantly repeated partial truths. But that is precisely what we must try to do—not so much for the sake of the dead victims, important as that is—but for the sake of future generations.

*   *   *

Charging the Catholic Church with having led to the Holocaust is seriously unjust. The great strides made in Jewish-Christian relations— spiritually, politically, morally, and intellectually—should not be jeopardized by those who are unwilling to learn the truth and are covertly attacking traditional Christian morality. Indeed, such individuals are anti-Jewish because Christian morality is Jewish morality.

B. The Historical Record

1. Background Information

*A*ll the Western world beyond the border of Germany joined as one in its acclaim of the new Pope on March 2, 1939. Pope Pius XII's role as a peacemaker was acknowledged in biographies written during his lifetime, and recent scholarship has since recognized him as an architect for peace.

As Vatican Secretary of State, Eugenio Cardinal Pacelli worked closely with Pope Pius XI in an effort to combat Communism, which was completely incompatible with Christianity. Attempts to penetrate the Communist blockade and bring the presence of the Church into the Soviet Union proved difficult and dangerous. The rise of Nazism in Germany was an equally serious threat. Catholics were warned that Nazism consisted of ideas that no Catholic could accept without denying his faith.

Vatican policy in Germany called for the free exercise of Catholicism. The staunchly anti-Nazi bishops were surprised when Hitler's speeches began to invoke the help of God and to promote respect for family life. Michael Cardinal Faulhaber of Munich went to Rome for consultation. The Vatican acknowledged Hitler's promises to safeguard the inviolability of family life and freedom of religion and encouraged him to become a champion of humanity. This apparent change in policy led up to the Concordat.

In 1933, in accord with the wishes of Pope Pius XI, Eugenio Cardinal Pacelli signed the Concordat with Germany in order to protect the German Catholics and the Church. The Concordat was not a political document; nor did the Catholic Church compromise its principles against racial persecution and genocide—principles that were subsequently expressed forcefully by both Pope Pius XI and Pope Pius XII. Hitler signed this agreement on July 20, 1933, promising freedom of religion; five days later he abolished the Catholic Youth Movement and soon after forbade the publication of Catholic newspapers and religious processions.

Jews were denied not only most of the amenities of life but often even the necessities. Supplementary decrees to the Nuremberg Laws of September 15, 1935, were published on November 14, defining those who belonged to the Jewish religion. In *Nazi Germany and the Jews: The Years of Persecution 1933–1939,* Saul Friedländer states: "The civic rights of Jews were canceled, their voting rights abolished; Jewish civil servants who had kept their positions owing to their veteran or veteran-related status were forced into retirement. On December 21, a second supplementary decree ordered the dismissal of Jewish professors, teachers, physicians, lawyers, and notaries who were state employees and had been granted exemptions."[1]

The Nazis required the blind, deaf, and physically or mentally handicapped to be sterilized and forbade marriages between Christians and Jews. In 1939 the Nazis began a program of "mercy killing," and, toward the end of 1941, Hitler put the "Final Solution" into effect.

Despite Vatican protests, the persecution continued. Jews, Gypsies, Jehovah's Witnesses, the clergy (Catholic and Protestant), nuns, and all who opposed the Nazis or tried to hide Jews were sent to concentration camps. They were surrounded by electrified barbed wires and guard towers, as well as barking dogs and striking guards; they were treated with brutality and starvation. Food was inadequate. The prisoners became walking skeletons. As the war progressed and numbers of prisoners increased, the Nazis cut rations. Conditions worsened. No longer to a name but to a number that might have marked their skin, these victims answered roll call twice a day, standing at attention for hours. The majority did not survive.

Scientifically and deliberately, millions of Jews and non-Jews were murdered in the gas chambers. At the same time millions of others died on the battlefields and in the bombing of cities.

In 1937, the then Eugenio Cardinal Pacelli participated, to a substantial degree, in the drafting of Pope Pius XI's encyclical[2] condemning the "Nazi idolatry of race and blood." It urged German Catholics to resist all appeals to abandon their Catholic faith for the quasi-paganism of Hitlerism and attacked the racism that was a fundamental part of National Socialism. Upon the publication of *Mit brennender Sorge,* the Nazi press carried vulgar cartoons and claims that "Pius XI was half-Jewish and Cardinal Pacelli was all-Jewish."

Two months before the anti-Semitic horrors of *Kristallnacht* on November 9, 1938, Pius XI stated: "Anti-Semitism is inadmissible; spiritually we are all Semites."

The day after Cardinal Pacelli's election to the papacy on March 2, 1939, the Nazi newspaper *Berliner Morgenpost* succinctly stated its position: "The election of Cardinal Pacelli is not accepted with favor in Germany because he was always opposed to Nazism and practically determined the policies of the Vatican under his predecessor."

Pope Pius XII toiled ceaselessly in the attempt to prevent a European war. In his Easter address he denounced Germany's invasions as violations of the solemn pacts upon which nations build a foundation of international peace and foster reciprocal confidence. While Pius XII extended offers of arbitration and support to England, France, Italy, Germany, and Poland, Hitler began negotiations with Benito Mussolini and Josef Stalin.

Within days of the German invasion of Poland on September 1, 1939, Pope Pius ordered the Vatican Radio to begin its broadcasts as an independent, autonomous entity and not as an organ of the Holy See. The British propagandistic versions of the Vatican Radio were bitterly denounced by the Germans in their repeated diplomatic protests. Not only were the "manipulated" broadcasts vilified, censored, and jammed, but the Germans also retaliated. Goebbels swore to reduce Vatican Radio to silence. Catholics and non-Catholics, in Germany and elsewhere, were imprisoned for listening to the "Voice of the Pope."

Pope Pius XII's pontificate was spent in the midst of war. Convinced that peace could be achieved, he continued to encourage world leaders to stop the bombing. But soon the Vatican was cut off from the world as Italy declared war. Foreign journalism ended and little was known abroad about the activity of the Holy See. The Pope insisted that everyone in the Vatican should share the same privations as the people of Rome. In fact, he ordered that the buildings be without heat and that those living in the Vatican have the same ration of food. The Pope was virtually a "prisoner" of the Nazi-Fascist government until the Allies liberated Rome on June 4, 1944.

Herbert L. Matthews, a keen observer of World War II, wrote in tthe *New York Times* of October 15, 1944: "Much could be written on the Pontiff's encouragement of the Vatican's important work for refugees and war prisoners and of the support he gave to the Vatican's campaign to save Italian art and cultural treasures from destruction. No Pope could have done more along the simple lines of charity and help-fulness than Pius XII....

"During the nine months of Nazi occupation the Vatican's popula-tion grew, for in that period under the Pope's direction the Holy See did an extraordinary job of sheltering and championing the victims of the Nazi-Fascist regime. I have spoken to dozens of Italians, both Catholics and Jews who owe their liberty and perhaps their lives to the protection of the church. In some cases anti-Fascists were actually saved from execution through the Pope's intervention.

"The Grand Rabbi of Rome, Professor Anton Israel Zolli, told me recently of the debt of gratitude which the Jewish community owes to the Pope. The Nazis suddenly demanded a large contribution in gold which the Jews tried desperately to raise; but being a poor community they could not reach the total of sixty kilograms. An 'anonymous' dona-tion, which everybody knew came from the Pope, made up that sum."

The *New York Times* correspondent evaluated Pius XII's perform-ance as a spiritual leader and peacemaker. The article continues: "From the beginning of the war the Pope took a stand against the bombing of cities and he reiterated that policy several times. Long before Mussolini declared war on the United States the Pope had already shown clearly that he considered it imperative to adhere strictly to a role of neutrality while working for peace....Through all the worldly strife and the new and diffi-cult burdens laid upon him by this war, the Pope's role has remained what he chose that it should be—that of peacemaker and conciliator.

"Obviously he has failed, since there has been no peace, and only the Germans now want conciliation. However, one cannot say that his influence has been exercised for naught or that in the coming years of the peace settlement he will not find great scope for his ideals, which have not failed for lack of nobility. His failure has been political, while his true mission is spiritual. In that field he may yet rank as one of the few who have triumphed in these terrible years."

These are the words of an eyewitness who was also a respected journalist. How can one accept the judgment of today's media when it is contrary to that of Pius XII's contemporaries?

According to historian Robert A. Graham, a prime source for this era, Hitler's regime was stung by the Vatican Radio's "massive denunciation of persecutions and oppressions in Germany and in territories occupied by German troops." On January 17, 1976, Father Graham discussed this in an article, "La Radio Vaticana tra Londra e Berlino," appearing in *Civiltà Cattolica,* pointing out that Catholic priests and laity often suffered death or imprisonment at the hands of the Nazis as "martyrs of Vatican Radio." Among the martyrs were Father Alfonse Wachsmann, who was tried at Szczecin (then Stettin), condemned to death, and shot. The Austrian priest Father Carl Lampert was executed, and a canon of Munich cathedral, Father Johannes Neuhäusler, was sent to the concentration camp of Dachau with a Franciscan, Father Odilo Gerhardt.

With the start of the war in September 1939, Pius XII urged that "in occupied territory the lives, the property, the honor, the religious convictions of the inhabitants will be respected." The following month, on October 20, he issued *Summi Pontificatus,* the encyclical condemning racism.

In this encyclical, Pope Pius XII stressed that "universal brotherhood, which Christian teaching awakes and keeps alive in our minds, is not opposed to the love of a man's country and of the glorious memories it has for him....But love of country, a thing which in itself has every right to be encouraged, must not interfere with, must not take precedence of, the commandment to show Christian charity towards all men; a commandment which makes our fellow-creatures generally and their interest take a place in the sunlight of our peace-making love."

Referring to the perils that bring suffering to our age, Pius XII insists that "the re-education, the remolding of the human race, if it is to produce the effects expected of it, must be informed first and foremost by a religious inspiration. It must spring from the doctrine of a divine Redeemer, as governed by a wholehearted spirit of justice; charity must be its crowning completion....No effort must be spared to convince the world, and those especially who are involved in the disasters of war, that Christian charity, the cardinal virtue of Christ's kingdom, is not an empty word, but a living truth."

As earlier noted, the front page of the *New York Times* headlined the fact that Pius XII had condemned dictators: It was a powerful attack on totalitarianism, revealing the Pontiff's determination to step forward bravely into "the immense vortex of errors and anti-Christian movements."

The Pontiff was not "silent" during the Holocaust. In his 1939 Christmas message to the Cardinals, Pius XII referred to the invasion of Poland and related events: "We have been forced to witness a series of acts which are irreconcilable, both with the practices of international law and with the principles of natural right that are based on the elementary feelings of humanity: acts which demonstrate in what chaotic and vicious circles we are now living.

"We find," the message continued, "premeditated aggression against a small work-loving, peaceful people on the pretext of a threat which never existed nor was possible. We find atrocities and illicit use of means of destruction against old men, women and children. We also find contempt for freedom and for human life, from which originate acts which cry to God for vengeance."[3]

Pius XII outlined a five-point plan—the requisites for a just and honorable peace:

1. An assurance for all nations, great or small, powerful or weak, of their right to life and independence;

2. That nations be delivered from the slavery imposed upon them by the race for armaments and from the danger that material force, instead of serving to protect the right, may become an overbearing and tyrannical master;

3. In creating or reconstructing international institutions that have so high a mission and such difficult and grave responsibilities, it is important to bear in mind the experience gained from the ineffectiveness or imperfections of previous institutions of the kind;

4. If a better European settlement is to be reached, there is one point in particular that should receive special attention: it is the real needs and the just demands of nations and populations, and of racial minorities;

5. But even the best and most detailed regulations will be imperfect and foredoomed to failure unless the peoples and those who govern them submit willingly to the influence of that spirit which alone can give life, authority, and binding force to the dead letter of international agreements. They must develop that sense of deep and keen responsibility which measures and weighs human statutes according to the sacred and inviolable standards of the law of God.

The record shows that Pope Pius XII, a spiritual leader who condemned Nazi "idolatry of race and blood," wrote and fearlessly spoke about the dangers of Nazism during World War II. On January 27, 1940, Vatican Radio and *L'Osservatore Romano* revealed to the world the dreadful cruelties of uncivilized tyranny that the Nazis were inflicting on the Jewish and Catholic Poles. The German ambassador protested.

In his 1940 Easter homily, Pius XII spoke about the bombardment of defenseless citizens, infirm and aged people, and innocent children. On May 11, he condemned the invasions of Belgium, Holland, and Luxemburg and referred to a world poisoned by lies and disloyalty and wounded by excesses of violence.[4]

In May 1940, when Pius XII came into possession of vital military intelligence concerning when and where the German attacks against Belgium, Holland, and Luxemburg were going to take place, he did not hesitate to communicate with Paris and London, but he was not believed. He had been in contact with German generals who wanted to get rid of Hitler. They informed him that they would be able to prevent the attacks on the three aforementioned countries if, after they removed the Führer, a subsequent peace treaty guaranteed Germany honorable terms. Reports in the British embassy confirm that the Pope passed on this information, but the British mistrusted his disclosure and did nothing.

Pope Pius XII's 1941 Christmas message on the Vatican Radio was editorially described by the *New York Times:* "The voice of Pius XII is a lonely voice in the silence and darkness enveloping Europe this Christmas....In calling for a 'real new order' based on 'liberty, justice and love,' to be attained only by a 'return to social and international principles capable of creating a barrier against the abuse of liberty and the abuse of power,' the Pope put himself squarely against Hitlerism. Recognizing that there is no road open to agreement between belligerents 'whose reciprocal war aims and programs seem to be irreconcilable,' Pius XII left no doubt that the Nazi aims are also irreconcilable with his own conception of a Christian peace."[5]

Six months later, the following appeared in the front-page article, "War News Summarized": "According to reports reaching Berne, Switzerland, from Vichy, Pope Pius has protested through his Nuncio against mass deportation of Jews from occupied France." On the same page another article referred to the Pope's plea for Jews: "The papal Nuncio protested to Marshal Henri Philippe Pétain, French Chief of

State, against the inhuman arrests and deportations of Jews from the French occupied zone to Silesia and occupied parts of Russia."[6]

Pope Pius XII's 1942 Christmas message also drew praise in another editorial of the *New York Times:* "No Christmas sermon reaches a larger congregation than the message Pope Pius XII addresses to a war-torn world at this season. This Christmas more than ever he is a lonely voice crying out of the silence of a continent. The Pulpit whence he speaks is more than ever like the Rock on which the Church was founded, a tiny island lashed and surrounded by a sea of war."

The editorial continued: "The Pope expresses as passionately as any leader on our side the war aims of the struggle for freedom." Everyone understood the meaning of Pius XII's Christmas message which expressed concern for "those hundreds of thousands who, without any fault of their own, sometimes only by reason of their nationality or race, are marked down for death or progressive extinction."

As British scholar Anthony Rhodes documents in his book, *The Vatican in the Age of the Dictators: 1922–1945* (New York: Holt, Rinehart and Winston, 1973, pp. 272–3), the captured wartime documents reveal the furor aroused within Nazi ranks. The Gestapo interpreted the Pope's 1942 Christmas message as follows: "In a manner never known before...the Pope has repudiated the National Socialist New European Order. It is true, the Pope does not refer to the National Socialists in Germany by name, but his speech is one long attack on everything we stand for....God, he says, regards all peoples and races as worthy of the same consideration. Here he is clearly speaking on behalf of the Jews....that this speech is directed exclusively against the New Order in Europe as seen in National Socialism is clear in the Papal statement that mankind owes a debt to 'all who during the war have lost their Fatherland and who, although personally blameless have, simply on account of their nationality and origin, been killed or reduced to utter destitution.' Here he is virtually accusing the German people of injustice toward the Jews, and makes himself the mouthpiece of the Jewish war criminals."

Some critics fail to note the reaction to the Pope's message because it destroys their image of a "silent" Pope. Moreover, it demonstrates that Pius XII's condemnation of the Final Solution was clear to the Nazis. The testimony of Professor Eamon Duffy of Magdalen College, Oxford, in *Saints and Sinners: A History of the Popes* is important: "Both Mussolini and Ambassador Ribbentrop were angered by this [the Pope's December 25, 1942] speech, and Germany considered that the Pope had abandoned any pretence at neutrality. They felt that Pius had unequivocally condemned Nazi action against the Jews."[7]

The critics who accuse Pius XII of "silence" charge that he failed to make sufficiently trenchant and forceful denunciations of the Nazis, which they claim would have halted the atrocities. Their contention fails to consider the brutal realities in the wake of Nazism, as well as the retaliatory consequences sure to follow any condemnatory action. Some of these experiences follow.

After the issuance of Pius XI's encyclical in 1937, the most emphatic form of denunciation open to the Pope, both anti-Catholic activity and the Jewish persecutions taking place in the Third Reich intensified.

When Pius XII learned of Nazi atrocities in Poland, he urged the bishops of Europe to do all they could to save the Jews and other victims of Nazi persecution. Inspired by this message, on April 19, 1942, the bishops of Holland issued a letter that was read in every Catholic church in the country, denouncing "the unmerciful and unjust treatment meted out to Jews by those in power in our country." In response, the Nazis made a special effort to round up 110,000 men, women, and children and deport them to concentration camps. Holland's Jews—the highest percent of any Nazi-occupied nation in Western Europe—were murdered.

The Royal Institute for War Documentation in Amsterdam has communications of the Reich Commissar that provide information on the long telegram sent on July 11, 1942, in the name of almost every Christian church in the country. The Commissar describes it in one sentence: "The churches state that they feel an obligation in the name of right and justice, *to protest the deportation of Jews and the transport of workers to Germany.*"[8]

Among the ninety-three papal communications to German bishops in World War II, a letter from Pius XII to Bishop (later Cardinal) von Preysing of Berlin, dated April 30, 1943, states: "It was for us a great consolation to learn that Catholics, in particular those of your Berlin diocese, have shown such charity towards the sufferings of the Jews. We express our paternal gratitude and profound sympathy for Monsignor Lichtenberg, who asked to share the lot of the Jews in the concentration camps [Dachau] and who spoke up against their persecution in the pulpit.

"As far as Episcopal declarations are concerned, We leave to local bishops the responsibility of deciding what to publish from Our communications. The danger of reprisals and pressures—as well perhaps of other measures due to the length and psychology of the war—counsel reserve. In spite of good reasons for Our open intervention, there are others equally good for avoiding greater evils by not interfering. Our experience in 1942, when We allowed the free publication of certain Pontifical documents addressed to the Faithful, justifies this attitude."

Writing to Pius XII in 1942, Polish Archbishop (later Cardinal) Sapieha stated: "We much deplore that we cannot communicate Your Holiness' letters to the faithful, but [they] would provide a pretext for fresh persecution and we already have those who are victims because they were suspected of being in secret communication with the Holy See."

On June 2, 1943, Pius XII addressed the dilemma of the extermination of the Jews in a communication to the Sacred College of Cardinals. He called attention to "the anxious entreaties of all those who, because of their nationality or their race are being subjected to overwhelming trials and, sometimes, through no fault of their own, are doomed to extermination....Every word We address to the competent authority on this subject, and all Our public utterances, have to be carefully weighed and measured by Us in the interests of the victims themselves, lest, contrary to Our intentions, We make their situation worse and harder to bear....The ameliorations apparently obtained do not match the scope of the Church's maternal solicitude on behalf of the particular groups that are suffering the most appalling fate. The Vicar of Christ, who asked no more than pity and a sincere return to elementary standards of justice and humanity, then found himself facing a door that no key could open."

Among the documents in the archives of the Secretariat of State, a report on the relations with the International Red Cross reveals that, in October 1939, the Apostolic Nuncio in Switzerland was in touch with the president, Mr. Max Huber. The Nuncio was assured that "orders had been given to the Representatives of the International Red Cross to assist the Representatives of the Holy See and of recognized Catholic organizations with a view to overcoming eventual difficulties that these Representatives of the Church might encounter in the work of affording spiritual assistance in the camps: that the lists of the Central Office (not those compiled by the belligerents) were at the disposition of the

Holy See; that the International Red Cross offered its facilities to send correspondence and packages to the camps for the Holy See." The report further states: "It is to be hoped likewise that in the future International Conventions on this matter, the activity of the Holy See may have an adequate juridical recognition."[9]

Both the International Red Cross and the World Council of Churches in Geneva also agreed to avoid making any statement that would obstruct their work or cause an increase in the suffering of the victims in retaliation for public protest.

[For additional information on prisoners of war and other matters, cf. appendix.]

2. U.S. Wartime Correspondence

Pope Pius XII was in direct contact with Franklin Delano Roosevelt, President of the United States of America.

Roosevelt asked the Vatican to help overcome the American Catholics' opposition to his plan to grant Russia, then fighting Hitler, the support already being extended to Great Britain. His request was granted. The Vatican Secretariat of State then asked the Apostolic Delegate in Washington to direct the task of explaining to American bishops that henceforth the encyclical *Divini Redemptoris,* which ordered Catholics to refuse alliances with all the Communist parties, was not to apply to the present situation and did not forbid the American wartime help to Soviet Russia.

President Roosevelt wrote on August 3, 1944, to Myron C. Taylor, his personal representative: "I should like you to take the occasion to express to His Holiness my deeply-felt appreciation of the frequent action which the Holy See has taken on its own initiative in its generous and merciful efforts to render assistance to the victims of racial and religious persecutions."

Earlier, in response to Roosevelt's letter of December 31, 1942, during the most crucial moment in the war, the Pope expressed his readiness to collaborate with him to achieve peace. "While maintaining this prayerful watch...it is Our undeviating program to do everything in Our power to alleviate the countless sufferings arising from this tragic conflict: sufferings of the prisoners and of the wounded, of families in fear and trembling over the fate of their loved ones, of entire peoples subjected to limitless privations and hardships; sufferings of the aged, of women and children who at a moment's notice find themselves deprived of home and possessions."[10]

When the Allies bombed the ancient and priceless papal basilica of St. Lawrence, Pius XII appealed to President Roosevelt: "It is a prayer that everywhere, as far as humanly possible, the civil populations be spared the horrors of war; that the homes of God's poor be not laid in ashes; that the little ones and youth, a nation's hope, be preserved from all harm—how Our heart bleeds when We hear of helpless children made victims of cruel war—that churches dedicated to the worship of God and monuments that enshrine the memory and masterpieces of human genius be protected from destruction."[11]

While maintaining neutrality and impartiality consistent to the Holy See's policy regarding civil antagonisms between states, His Holiness expressed great pleasure that no vindictive motives were evident in the views of the United States and that, in the interest of permanent moral and peaceful relations, the welfare of all peoples would be protected and assured. He believed that the solution of postwar problems must be considered particularly in the light of the principle of the unity of mankind and of the family of peoples.

With the active cooperation of the Vatican, a National Agency for the Distribution of Relief was formed to help millions of displaced peoples, prisoners of war, men and women engaged in forced labor away from their homelands, and civilian internees in all parts of Europe.

His Holiness received the news of Roosevelt's death on April 12, 1945, with the deepest sorrow, as is revealed in telegrams that were sent to Harry S. Truman and to Mrs. Eleanor Roosevelt on April 13, 1945.

3. Postwar Appraisal of Vatican Policies

After the cessation of hostilities, the wisdom of Pius XII's strategy—to avoid public denunciation of Nazi terrorism—was further vindicated.

According to Robert Kempner, the American deputy chief of the Nuremberg war crimes tribunal, "All the arguments and writings eventually used by the Catholic Church only provoked suicide; the execution of Jews was followed by that of Catholic priests."

At the Nuremberg trials, Ernst von Weizsäcker, Germany's Chief Secretary of Foreign Affairs until 1943 and then ambassador to the Holy See, testified: "It was well-known—everybody knew it—that the Jewish question was a sore point as far as Hitler was concerned. To speak of interventions and requests submitted from abroad, requests for moderation of the course taken, the results of these, almost in all cases, caused the measures to be made more aggravated, and more serious even, in effect."

Albrecht von Kessel, aide to Ernst von Weizsäcker in the Roman Embassy, also testified: "I am convinced, therefore, that His Holiness the Pope did, day and night, think of a manner in which he could help the unfortunate Jews in Rome. If he did not lodge a protest, then it was not done because he thought, justifiably, that if he protested, Hitler would go crazy, and that would not help the Jews at all, that would give one the justified fear that they would be killed even more quickly. Apart from that, the SS would probably have been instructed to penetrate into the Vatican and lay hands on the Pope."

On April 6, 1963, in *Die Welt,* von Kessel wrote: "We were convinced that a fiery protest by Pope Pius XII against the persecutions of the Jews would have in all probability put the Pope himself and the Curia into extreme danger but...would certainly not have saved the life of a single Jew. Hitler, like a trapped beast, would react to any menace that he felt directed at him, with cruel violence."

The truth is that Pope Pius XII, through his inspiring actions and moral leadership, saved many thousands of Jews and countless other refugees from being deported to concentration camps, from eventual torture and death. Details of the Vatican's humanitarian work are available to all who seek the truth: in the records of the Vatican's activities during World War II, in the preserved accounts of individuals bearing witness to tragic events, and in newspaper reports of the era.

It is well known that, in obedience to the Pope's direct urging, hundreds of convents, monasteries, and other religious buildings were opened to shelter and to hide thousands of men, women, and children from Nazi cruelties, not only in Italy, but also in Poland, France, Belgium, and Hungary.

Everywhere, no cloak of immunity saved those protecting Jews and other refugees; they were arrested, sent to prison, and treated with brutality and contempt. Acts of reprisal took the lives of many. Countless priests and nuns suffered cruel interrogation, followed by internment in concentration camps and eventual death in the gas chambers.

In his letter to Luigi Cardinal Maglione on August 5, 1943, Pius XII lamented that no heed was paid to his words and exhorted all the faithful to join him in a crusade of prayer: "We who carry in Our heart the sorrows and the anxieties of all, shall not leave anything untried to replace hatred with charity, and struggle for victory with the serenity of peace....

"We desire that this be done in a most especial way on the forthcoming Feast of the Assumption into Heaven of the Blessed Virgin, so that the Mother of God, moved to compassion by the martyrdom of so many of her children, and by so much misery and bitterness, should intercede with her beloved Son for the remission of sins, in order to bring an end to rivalries, and in order that Christian peace may shine again upon the world, upon the victorious and the vanquished who, once more brought together, not in force but in justice and equity, will enjoy lasting tranquillity and prosperity. Let us unite in a holy crusade; let us raise our fervent prayers...and let the powerful instruments of peace, prayer and brotherhood replace the instruments of war."[12]

4. Arrival of the Allies

Pope Pius XII was prepared to face captivity or death at the hands of the Nazis. During the months before the liberation of Rome, the papacy was under a state of siege. Although the Nazis proclaimed respect for the integrity of the Vatican and the personal status of the Pope, no one knew when Berlin would take over physical control of the Vatican and make the Pope prisoner. On June 4, 1944, the arrival of the Allies in Rome brought a sense of relief to the Vatican.

Newspapers throughout the world credited the Roman Catholic Church for helping the Jews and for easing their lot by truly Christian offers of assistance and shelter.

After the liberation of Rome, there was much concern over the fate of Jewish prisoners in Nazi-Fascist hands in Northern Italy and in Germany. Addressing survivors in August 1944, Pope Pius XII made a fervent plea for brotherhood: "For centuries the Jews have been most unjustly treated and despised. It is time they were treated with justice and humanity. God wills it and the Church wills it. St. Paul tells us that the Jews are our brothers. Instead of being treated as strangers, they should be welcomed as friends."

On July 5, 1944, Foreign Secretary Anthony Eden stated in the House of Commons that there were widespread deportations and massacres of Hungarian Jews. The following day the *New York Times* article, "Hungary Deports Jews," made note in its subheading of the Pope's intervention on behalf of Hungarian Jews. According to the article, "...a direct appeal had been made to the Hungarian people to defend the Jews, and that the Pope and the King of Sweden had made representations." Jewish military chaplains and soldiers serving in Italy confirmed that the Italians did all they could to rescue and harbor Jews fleeing from oppression and certain death.

For fear of worsening the plight of the Jews and other victims, Pope Pius XII did not issue a public condemnation. However, he succeeded in mobilizing all the forces of the Church and extended his charity to all war victims, without distinction of nationality, race, or religion.

Could things possibly have been made any worse by a papal protest during the Holocaust? Of course. It is doubtful that a protest would have deflected the Holocaust. It is certain that, in this fickle world, Pope Pius XII would have borne the blame for the death of additional victims.

5. Hitler's Plan

The Holocaust was a slaughter of monstrous proportions, the evil consequence of a demonic mind—that of Adolf Hitler, who planned to dominate the world, destroy Christianity, and foster a new Godless religion.

"Massacre Pius XII with the Entire Vatican" is the message found in a recently discovered document, which proves that Adolf Hitler intended to assassinate the Pope along with all the Vatican Cardinals. The document refers to the plan as "Rabat-Fohn." It names the unit assigned to execute the plan to be the Eighth Division of the SS Cavalry, "Florian Geyer," and the reason to be "The Papal Protest in Favor of the Jews."

This information appeared in the Milan newspaper *Il Giornale* on July 5, 1998, and confirms what some historians have always believed—Hitler intended to kidnap the Pope. Its implications can no longer be denied. The source of the information is a letter to Vincenzo Costa, the Fascist leader in Milan, from Paolo Porta, the Fascist leader in Como. This letter reveals Hitler's plan to kill the Pope and the Cardinals.

According to Porta, his information comes from a high SS official. In December of 1943, Hitler personally chose Heinrich Himmler and Heinrich Müller, the head of the Gestapo, to study and execute a plan that would eliminate the Pope. Porta writes further that "an SS division disguised in Italian uniforms that they had captured on September 8th, along with Italian guns, would launch an attack at night against Vatican City. Appearing as partisans determined to liberate the Pope, they would massacre the clergy."

At this point, the plan continues, new troops of the Panzer Division Hermann Göring and the parachutists would intervene to kill the disguised partisans and thus leave no witnesses to survive.

Porta further explains that if the Pope were miraculously saved, he would then be deported to Germany under the pretext to save him.

One can imagine the consequences: "The persecution of the Catholic Church would begin with mass deportations to Germany of all ecclesiastics in Italy and throughout the world. They are to be considered the cause of ignorance, of domination, of conspiracies...."

Porta did not know if this plan, to be executed in January of 1944, had been "definitely set aside." But he did not doubt that the Pope deserved such treatment. Nor did Porta doubt the reason: Pius XII defended the Jews, he protested. His Holiness continued to raise his voice in favor of the oppressed. Undoubtedly, he was not Hitler's friend. The Rabat-Fohn plan was prepared by Hitler in retaliation.

This plan was found in the archives of the Archdiocese of Milan by Professor Anna Lisa Carlotti with a letter dated September 26, 1944, requesting it "to be kept with the greatest secrecy." This momentous finding led to the discovery of three documents hidden among the papers of Bishop Enrico Assi, a priest-activist of the Italian Resistance. In 1998, they were published in the *Annali di Storia moderna e contemporanea.*

Obviously during the war years, the Vatican, concerned about the Pope's safety, took measures to counter schemes of malice. In fact, Robert A. Graham, one of the four editors of the Vatican documents, wrote a two-part article, "Did Hitler Want to Remove Pius XII from Rome?"[13] References to possible disaster also appear in the memoirs, depositions, and testimonies of diplomats and military leaders such as Ulrich von Hassell, Ernst von Weizsäcker, Robert M. W. Kempner, Eitel Friedrich Moellhausen, and others.

6. Vatican Documents

Of the four Jesuit editors of the Vatican documents, the sole survivor is Father Pierre Blet, who rejects the accusation that Pius XII harbored sympathies for the German regime. He agrees with the late Father Robert A. Graham, coeditor, who recounted the uninterrupted series of appeals that the Pope and the world Jewish leadership exchanged. Never before in history had there been such a cordial relationship. Accordingly, Father Graham writes, "If we persist in reading purely political significance in every papal move, arbitrarily prescinding from that which makes the Pope a Pope, we shall never arrive at that understanding and objectivity that is, or ought to be, the goal of every serious historian and every fair-minded, intelligent person."[14]

Research of the many scholarly studies of the links between the Pope and world Jewish leadership should include: an examination of the twelve volumes of *The Acts and Documents of the Holy See Relative to World War II,* the product of a team of Jesuit scholars commissioned by Pope Paul VI, available in completed form since 1982; the diplomatic archives of governments that maintained embassies at the Vatican during the war era; memoirs and writings of diplomats and others, who were witnesses to the tragic events of the war; testimony at the Nuremberg trials; news reports of the time; and other reliable sources now available.

In their writings, the authors of these research papers are unanimous in refuting the complete falsity of the charges made by contemporary critics: that Pius XII collaborated with the Nazi regime; that he was silent, meaning that he did little or nothing while thousands of Jews in Nazi-occupied countries were being hounded and transported to death camps; that "he could have done more" to save Jewish lives; that if he had stridently and personally attacked the Nazi leaders and threatened them with excommunication, the Holocaust could have been stopped; that Pius XII and the Vatican aided in the escape of war criminals.

To state that the Catholic Church openly collaborated with the Nazis in Germany, idly standing by while six million Jews were exterminated, is a lie. Millions of Christians also died at the hands of the Nazis. Seven hundred Polish priests were shot and 3,000 were sent to camps where 2,600 died. A count when the day of liberation arrived indicated that 2,720 priests, brothers, and seminarians had been incarcerated in Dachau, and over 1,000 of them had perished there. In February 1944, for example, 162 French priests were arrested by the Gestapo; of them, 123 were shot or guillotined.

Four of the above-mentioned twelve volumes recount the "real record of Jewish-Vatican relations," its work to assist the victims of the war and, in particular, a record of its correspondence with the world Jewish organizations who were appealing for help. Assistance was readily given and drew spontaneous appreciation from Jewish leaders in Britain and the United States. Apparently, the Pope was one of the few on the continent from whom these Jewish leaders could expect understanding and help.

7. *The Jewish Community*

At the end of World War II, Dr. Joseph Nathan, representing the Hebrew Commission, addressed the Jewish community, expressing heartfelt gratitude to those who protected and saved Jews during the Nazi-Fascist persecutions. "Above all," he stated, "we acknowledge the Supreme Pontiff and the religious men and women who, executing the directives of the Holy Father, recognized the persecuted as their brothers and, with great abnegation, hastened to help them, disregarding the terrible dangers to which they were exposed."[15]

On April 5, 1946, the Italian Jewish community sent the following message to His Holiness, Pius XII: "The delegates of the Congress of the Italian Jewish Communities, held in Rome for the first time after the Liberation, feel that it is imperative to extend reverent homage to Your Holiness, and to express the most profound gratitude that animates all Jews for your fraternal humanity toward them during the years of persecution when their lives were endangered by Nazi-Fascist barbarism. Many times priests suffered imprisonment and were sent to concentration camps, and offered their lives to assist Jews in every way. This demonstration of goodness and charity that still animates the just, has served to lessen the shame and torture and sadness that afflicted millions of human beings."[16]

An American newspaper carried the story of the Thanksgiving service in Rome's Jewish Temple that was heard over the radio on July 30, 1944. The Jewish chaplain of the Fifth American Army gave a discourse in which, among other things, he said: "If it had not been for the truly substantial assistance and the help given to Jews by the Vatican and by Rome's ecclesiastical authorities, hundreds of refugees and thousands of Jewish refugees would have undoubtedly perished before Rome was liberated."[17]

On April 7, 1944, Chief Rabbi Alexander Safran, of Bucharest, Rumania, made the following statement to Monsignor Andrea Cassulo,

Papal Nuncio to Rumania: "In the most difficult hours which we Jews of Rumania have passed through, the generous assistance of the Holy See was decisive and salutary. It is not easy for us to find the right words to express the warmth and consolation we experience because of the concern of the Supreme Pontiff who offered a large sum to relieve the sufferings of deported Jews—sufferings which had been pointed out to him by you after your visit to Transnistria. The Jews of Rumania will never forget these facts of historic importance."

The following petition was presented to Pope Pius XII in the summer of 1945 by twenty thousand Jewish refugees from Central Europe: "Allow us to ask the great honor of being able to thank, personally, His Holiness for the generosity he has shown us when we were being persecuted during the terrible period of Nazi-Fascism."

Reuben Resnick, American Director of the Committee to Help Jews in Italy, declared that "all the members of the Catholic hierarchy in Italy, from Cardinals to Priests, saved the lives of thousands of Jews, men, women, and children who were hosted and hidden in convents, churches, and other religious institutions" (*L'Osservatore Romano,* January 5, 1946).

At the end of the war there were many demonstrations of thanks and gratitude from the Jews saved through the assistance of Church institutions. Abramo Giacobbe Isaia Levi, a man of renowned intellect and a Senator of the Kingdom of Italy until the promulgation of the racial laws, was hidden in a convent during the Nazi occupation of Rome. He and his wife later converted to Christianity. He died in 1949 and, in his will, left a large sum of money to help elderly and impoverished Italian Jews. His beautiful estate in the center of Rome, Villa Levi, was renamed Villa Giorgina, in memory of his young daughter, who died prematurely. In his will he donated it to Pope Pius XII because he had been "preserved from the dangers of evil racial persecution, overthrower of every relationship of human life" and was "grateful for the protection that was provided me in that turbulent period by the Sisters of the Infant Mary."

8. Death of Pius XII

On May 15, 1956, in preparation for his death, Pope Pius XII wrote his Last Will and Spiritual Testament. It began with the words: *Miserere mei Deus, secundum magnam misericordiam tuam.*

"These words which I, knowing myself to be unworthy of them or equal to them, pronounced when I accepted with trepidation my election to the supreme pontificate, I now repeat with much greater foundation at this time when the realization of the deficiencies, shortcomings and faults of so long a pontificate in an epoch so grave, brings my insufficiencies and unworthiness more clearly to my mind.

"I humbly ask forgiveness of those whom I may have offended, harmed, or scandalized by my words and my actions.

"I beg those to whom it pertains not to occupy themselves with or preoccupy themselves about erecting a monument to my memory. It will suffice that my poor mortal remains be simply deposited in a sacred place, the more obscure the more welcome.

"I need not recommend myself to prayers for my soul. I know how numerous are these which the norms of the Apostolic See provide and the piety of the faithful offer for a deceased Pope.

"Neither do I find need to leave a spiritual testament, as so many praiseworthy prelates normally do. The many acts and discourses decreed and pronounced by me because of my office, suffice to make my thoughts on various religious and moral questions known to anyone who might perhaps wish to know them.

"Having set down this, I name as my universal heir the Holy Apostolic See from which I have received so much, as from a most loving Mother."

Two years later, following a brief illness while at his summer residence in Castelgandolfo, Pope Pius XII prepared for his eternal reward.

When Pius XII died on October 9, 1958, people from every walk of life throughout the world expressed their condolences. Throngs of visitors rushed to Castelgandolfo to pay tribute to Pius XII, the first Pope to die at the papal villa.

The confusion in the town's small streets was increased by groups of pilgrims from abroad who had been waiting in Rome to be received in audience by the Pontiff in the same hall in which his body now lay in state. In the midst of the mass pilgrimage, a deeply emotional experience to many, the consensus of comments tearfully whispered was: "Here lies a saint."

In the room, crowded with chauffeurs, attendants, prelates—everyone who had been in the papal villa—about thirty people stood beside the Pontiff's bedside, responding to the prayers for the dying, being recited by two prelates. The Pope had been listening to a recording of Beethoven's First Symphony shortly before he suffered his final cerebral stroke. From that day onward, the Jesuit Father Francesco Pellegrino of the Vatican Radio station, broadcast an account of Pius XII's last moments from an antechamber of the Pope's bedroom. Only after Cardinal Tisserant, together with an ecclesiastical notary, signed a parchment attesting to the death of Pius XII, could the Pope's chief physician, Dr. Riccardo Galeazzi-Lisi, prepare the body for embalming.

Hearing the news of the Pontiff's death, thousands of the faithful rushed to Castelgandolfo and climbed the marble staircase to pay tribute as he lay in state. The Pontiff's body was clad in a cassock of white silk under an ermine-tipped red velvet shoulder-length cape, and a fur-lined skull cap covered part of his head. His hands, intertwined with a rosary, held a silver crucifix.

Among those who came to pay tribute—a crowd including Jews, other refugees, even Communists—many recalled the tragic days during the last war when battle raged in the hillsides and Pius XII had ordered the extraterritorial papal villa opened to them.

Giovanni Battista Montini, Archbishop of Milan, who as Vatican Pro-Secretary of State had been closely associated with Pius XII, stated: "Now the Holy Father is leaving this earth. The Church is orphaned without its head; without this great man who has been a giant. It will be difficult to find another like him in the history of the Church and possibly, even, in the Church's future." Cardinal Montini would later become Pope Paul VI.

Prominent Jews acknowledging Pope Pius XII's benevolence included Nahum Goldmann, President of the World Jewish Congress, who wrote: "With special gratitude we remember all he has done for the persecuted Jews during one of the darkest periods in their entire history." Elio Toaff, Chief Rabbi of Rome, stated: "More than anyone else, we have had the opportunity to appreciate the great kindness, filled with compassion and magnanimity, that the Pope displayed during the terrible years of persecution and terror."

Also upon the demise of Pope Pius XII, Golda Meir sent the following message of condolence: "We share in the grief of humanity....When fearful martyrdom came to our people in the decade of Nazi terror, the voice of the Pope was raised for the victims. The life of our times was enriched by a voice speaking out on the great moral truths above the tumult of daily conflict. We mourn a great servant of peace."

The *New York Times* issue of October 10, 1958, featured many tributes on the front page. Cardinal Spellman, traveling from Lisbon to Rome, sent this message: "The death of His Holiness Pope Pius XII means the departure among us of the most impartial, most devoted peacemaker in our weary, warring world. During his long laborious life in prayer, sacrifice and action, Pius XII dedicated himself totally to the service of God and to the welfare of all the children of God. In his great paternal pastoral heart, he embraced each individual man, woman and child of every race, color, culture and creed. Pope Pius XII, like his divine master, was friend to every man, and I am sure that all persons of good will join the Catholic world in mourning the loss of a loving and beloved Holy Father."

News of the Pope's death was flashed around the world. President Dwight D. Eisenhower and Vice President Richard Nixon sent their personal condolences. In New York, Pius XII was acclaimed by Governor Harriman, Nelson A. Rockefeller, and Mayor Wagner as they expressed their sorrow, joining Protestant leaders, the National Council of Churches, and the Protestant Council of the City of New York.

Religious and political leaders praised Pope Pius XII:

FORMER PRESIDENT TRUMAN—I'm sorry to hear of the passing of Pope Pius XII, whom I considered the greatest statesman in the Vatican in 200 years.

FORMER PRESIDENT HOOVER—The world has lost a great man. I have reasons to know the breadth of his spiritual leadership. This world has been better for his having lived in it.

SECRETARY OF STATE DULLES—The passing of this great spiritual leader, who has ever been in the forefront of the defense of Christian civilization, is a profound loss for all peoples of the world. His dedicated devotion to the cause of peace and justice has been a truly great inspiration providing hope to all mankind in difficult and troubled times.

ADLAI E. STEVENSON, former Democratic candidate for president—All of mankind feels, with the oneness he helped give it, an overpowering loss at this saintly man's being gone. A great light has been dimmed now—yet, can never, for it was so great, go out.

FRANK S. HOGAN, Democratic candidate for senator—In a world torn by greed and hate he was an apostle of peace, justice and human brotherhood.

SENATOR JACOB K. JAVITS—The world has lost a great leader for peace and brotherhood.

SECRETARY OF LABOR JAMES MITCHELL—He was a leader in the struggle for world peace and freedom for all men.

GOVERNOR THEODORE R. MCKELDIN of Maryland—The world has lost perhaps the most powerful personal force for the maintenance of peace in these troubled decades.

GEORGE MEANY, president of the American Federation of Labor-Congress of Industrial Organizations—The world has lost a great and good man of God. But the world is the richer because of his wisdom, love and compassion for all mankind.

SENATOR CLIFFORD P. CASE of New Jersey—His noble and persistent efforts to promote peace have left their mark on world history. The human race will miss his courageous voice.

BERNARD BARUCH—During a dark generation of war, hate and unspeakable crimes against humanity, he helped keep burning the torch of peace, love and brotherhood. He epitomized the nobility of which the human soul is capable. To men of all faiths he was an inspiration and an example of courage, dedication and selflessness.

DR. LEWIS WEBSTER JONES, president, National Conference of Christians and Jews—The family of man has lost a great soul, a champion of peace and an eloquent spokesman for religious and racial justice.

DR. FRANKLIN CLARK FRY, president of the Lutheran World Federation—In himself an exemplary character, Pope Pius XII was a skillful leader in his communion and an impressive moral force in the world of our day.

DR. THEOPHILUS MILLS TAYLOR, moderator, and DR. EUGENE CARSON BLAKE, chief administrative officer of the United Presbyterian Church in the U.S.A.—The dedicated life of Pope Pius XII is an example that transcends ecclesiastical boundaries...a light to all Christians everywhere.

BISHOP G. BROMLEY OXNAM, president of the Council of Bishops of the Methodist Church—Methodists throughout the world join Christians everywhere in extending love and sympathy to Roman Catholics in every land.

DAVID O. MCKAY, president, STEPHEN L. RICHARDS and J. REUBEN CLARK JR., counselors of the First Presidency of the Latter-day Saints (Mormon) Church—The world has lost a powerful advocate for peace and an avowed opponent of forces seeking to impose upon humanity a godless world.

RABBI THEODORE L. ADAMS, president of the Synagogue Council of America—The late Pontiff, throughout his long career, ceaselessly fought the forces of racism and bigotry and called for equal justice for all and the recognition of the universal dignity of man, irrespective of creed, race or color.

IRVING M. ENGEL, president, and JACOB BLAUSTEIN and JOSEPH M. PROSKAUER, honorary presidents of the New York Board of Rabbis—The Orthodox, Conservative and Reform Rabbis of New York extend their profound sympathy to the Catholic world on their irreparable loss in the passing of Pope Pius XII, who dedicated himself to the welfare of his fellow men everywhere.

MRS. MOISE S. CAHN, president, National Council of Jewish Women—His humanitarian actions brought people of all faiths closer together in a realization of the common aspirations of mankind.

RABBI JACOB P. RUDIN, president, Central Conference of American Rabbis—His broad sympathy for all people, his wise social vision and his compassionate understanding made his a prophetic voice for righteousness everywhere.

DR. EVERETT R. CLINCHY, administrative president, World Brotherhood—Pope Pius XII will go down in history as the "Pope of Brotherhood."

ARCHBISHOP THOMAS A. BOLAND of Newark—The world had come to look instinctively to him for moral leadership.

BISHOP JAMES A. MCNULTY of Paterson—He taught nations how to live together as brothers in a human family.

BISHOP GEORGE W. AHR of Trenton—Future generations will doubtless assign to Pope Pius XII an outstanding place in the history of the Church and of the world.

BISHOP JUSTIN C. MCCARTHY of Camden—During his pontificate, he always had one great purpose in mind. He was most anxious to promote peace among the nations of the world.

DR. CHANNING H. TOBIAS, chairman of the National Association for the Advancement of Colored People—He abhorred racism and rebuked the advocates of racial discrimination and segregation in any country.

CHARLES ABRAMS, chairman, State Commission Against Discrimination—This heroic leader in the struggle for racial equality and for social justice, understanding and amity among all groups bequeaths to all of us the example of his inspired life and his brilliant and inclusive encyclicals on the dignity and rights of all men.

RABBI EMANUEL RACKMAN, president, Rabbinical Council of America—As a passionate defender of peace and human dignity, Pope Pius XII will have a permanent place in the history of mankind.

RABBI JOACHIM PRINZ, national president, American Jewish Congress—Among his many, great contributions to mankind, the Pontiff will be remembered wherever men of good will gather for his profound devotion to the cause of peace and for his earnest efforts in the rescue of thousands of victims of Nazi persecution, including many Jewish men, women and children.

DR. ISRAEL GOLDSTEIN, chairman, Western Hemisphere Executive of World Jewish Congress—In Rome last year, the Jewish community told me of their deep appreciation of the policy which had been set by the Pontiff for the Vatican during the period of the Nazi-Fascist regime, to give shelter and protection to Jews wherever possible.

*   *   *

In the United States, the Jewish community recognized that the Catholic Church rescued thousands of Jewish victims of Nazism during the greatest manifestation of humanitarianism in the twentieth century—a new and effective method of fighting anti-Semitism. They also recognized the fact that Christians of all denominations saved Jews from Nazi extermination, justly dividing the contribution of the Catholic Church into four parts:

1. When the Germans occupied Italy, the grounds of the Vatican as well as the churches in Rome under its jurisdiction, considered neutral territory by international law, were thrown open as sanctuaries to the Jews by order of the Pope. Any Jew from any country who could manage to reach the Vatican was admitted without questions and thereby removed from Nazi jurisdiction.

2. The protection of Jews was effected through the internationally recognized neutrality of the Vatican used by the Papal Nuncios in other countries who freely issued "protective passports" to Jews threatened by the Nazis, thus placing them under the jurisdiction of the Vatican.

3. Catholic monasteries and convents in France, Belgium, Italy, and other countries of Europe opened their doors and became well known as hiding places for entire Jewish families, particularly for children. This was a fundamental policy Pope Pius maintained throughout the Nazi occupation of Europe in the face of great dangers.

4. Thousands of Jewish refugees were smuggled out from Nazi-occupied countries by an underground movement organized for that purpose by members of the Catholic clergy with the knowledge and authority of the Vatican. The various encyclicals and many outspoken statements issued by the Pope himself and by many archbishops and bishops throughout Europe denouncing the inhumanity of specific acts of Nazi persecution of the Jews were the only rays of light in the long, dark night of Nazism.

9. Developments in the Media

An examination of the intensified criticisms of the actions taken by Pope Pius XII during the Holocaust reveals the presence of powerful influences: the production of *The Deputy*, Rolf Hochhuth's unjust political dramatization, a prime example of the nihilism of the 1960s; the complex and continuing psychological effects of the trauma of the Holocaust; and the failure to analyze with care the courageous role of Pius XII during the nightmarish years of the Nazi reign. While the revolution of the '60s challenged traditional authority, beliefs, and judgments, Hochhuth presented to the Western world a diabolically plausible falsification of Pope Pius. Moreover, the psychological impact of Nazi genocide has influenced all interpretations of papal actions and driven many to find hidden villains for this great tragedy. Unfortunately, in their justified zeal, the critics have accused an innocent man, a man who was totally devoted to helping all victims.

The debate over Pius XII has raged so long and the emotional involvement become so deep that lines have hardened and few minds remain open. Traditional Catholics continue to see him as a holy man of goodness who sought to help the terrorized and suffering world about him. Many Jews see him as intimately connected with their colossal suffering under the Nazis. Some have been among Pius XII's defenders, but more would appear to have judged him guilty at least of the sin of omission, usually of not having excommunicated all Catholics supporting Hitler. Repeated half-truths and inaccuracies have painted even a darker picture of the Pontiff to be uncaring, ineffective, and indifferent in the face of cruelties and slaughter. One of the more curious aspects of this denigration is that it happened during a period when Catholic-Jewish relations were more cordial than at any other time in the nearly two thousand years of their coexistence.

The charges that Christianity is responsible for the Holocaust are without rational basis. Kenneth Woodward of *Newsweek* stated: "No one person, Hitler excepted, was responsible for the Holocaust. And no one person, Pius XII included, could have prevented it."[18]

In accord with papal encyclicals, Marc Saperstein, professor of Jewish history and director of the program in Judaic studies at George Washington University, clearly stated in the *Washington Post:* "The suggestion that Christian doctrines or practice led directly to the Nazi death camps is misleading and inappropriate....Yet this discussion should not blur the distinction between the failure of Christian individuals to protest or to resist, and the crimes of the Nazis who conceived and implemented the policy to annihilate the Jews. There were limits to the capacity of the Pope and the Roman Catholic Church to prevent a world power with military domination over a continent, from murdering the civilians it defined as its enemies. The fundamental responsibility for the Holocaust lies with the Nazi perpetrators. Not with Pope Pius XII. Not with the church. Not with the teachings of the Christian faith."[19]

Almost sixty years after Pius XII's first encyclical *Summi Pontificatus,* an editorial in the *New York Times* stated on March 18, 1998: "A full exploration of Pope Pius's conduct is needed. He did not encourage Catholics to defy Nazi orders." Three days later, the paper stated: "The Vatican Document skirts the issue of the Pope's silence"!

On April 18, 1998, New Jersey Channel Thirteen's *News Hour* presented a program of shocking comments. The moderator stated that "the Pope was largely silent about Nazi atrocities. His only public comment came during his Christmas message of 1942." A priest criticized the Vatican document as "too subtle, too restrained, too diplomatic in its language." A historian stated that in 1933 the Nazis signed a concordat with the Vatican which led "to the German regime feeling that it could do what it wanted." Misrepresentations and indecent allegations were expressed throughout the entire program. No one came to the defense of Pope Pius XII.

Repeatedly during the past years, many articles appearing in the media have denigrated the Catholic Church. Relying on flawed books, some critics have shamelessly misused wartime documents. Their statements and charges have been and can be demolished by scholars. Instead of accusing Pope Pius XII of "silence," critics should study his negotiations with the Nazis and his efforts to alleviate the sufferings of persecuted Jews and other refugees. Perhaps critics should also study—in addition to the countless favorable statements of praise and gratitude toward the Holy Father found in the media—what the Axis propagandists were saying about the Pope's protests, as well as the angry reactions to those protests emanating from both the Nazi and the Fascist press.

Commenting in *The Wanderer,*[20] Tibor Baransky stated: "The Papal Nuncios helped the Jews. They got the orders straight from the Pope." Honored by Israel's national Holocaust remembrance authority Yad V'Shem, Baransky is a board member of the U.S. Holocaust Memorial Council. He also recalled that, while working as a special representative of the Papal Nuncio in Hungary at the age of twenty-two, he knew of Jewish leaders who asked the Pope not to raise a public outcry over the Nazi atrocities.

Baransky, working with Papal Nuncio Angelo Rotta, carried blank documents, forged protective passes, and faked baptismal certificates to save war victims. The Nuncio sent him to retrieve Jews who had been dragged off on death marches despite their protection papers. Baransky remarked that the Pope agreed this was the best way to insure the Church's effectiveness in keeping Jews away from the Nazis. The Pope said, "I know the Nazis; they would be angry with me, but take it out on the Jews."

Dr. Erik von Kuehnelt-Leddihn wrote *The Timeless Christian,* published in 1969 by Franciscan Press. In the appendix he speaks of *The Deputy* "as a shameless and inexcusable attack upon a defenseless dead man who, in view of the laws operative in most 'civilized states,' cannot be given protection against the calumny of this theatrical web of lies." He also refers to documentary evidence that the Pope knew nothing specific about the extermination camps. On his return from the United States, in 1947, he was assured by a cardinal that the German bishops knew nothing definite about the extermination camps. They knew "about the gassing of the mentally ill, against which he and the Bishop of Münster (Count Galen) had protested....From 1944 onwards the Vatican was cut off from Central Europe by the Allied Armies. By contrast, the espionage organizations of the Allies, especially of Britain and America, had at their disposal any amount of funds and excellent sources of information. The horror of the death camps came fully to light only after the Soviet occupation of Poland—at a time, that is, when their activities had long been suppressed. We must ask in all honesty: Did Washington and London know of these extermination camps— apart from the ordinary concentration camps—or were they completely in the dark about the whole thing? In contrast to the Vatican, they—like the equally silent Soviet Union—were indeed belligerent powers. If they knew nothing, then we must ask why the Vatican is supposed to have been better informed than they."

In his last book, *The Vatican and Communism during World War II,* Robert A. Graham illustrates what Communism and National Socialism had in common: a radical and venomous hostility to religion. He states: "It is time for cleaning up the fallout of the defunct ideologies of World War II. The perpetrators of this tenacious campaign of anti-Catholic propaganda were not merely men of Moscow but also their Allies and sympathizers abroad. Diplomats and journalists with prepossessions of their own contributed their share."

Father Graham concludes: "Pius XII, more than ever in wartime, was deeply conscious, as Pope, that the Church was founded with a mission given her by Jesus Christ and subject to no earthly power. From this point of view the Church is an 'idea,' an abstraction, intangible, transcending politics. This of course is not understood, much less accepted, by the world's political forces. The Church is in the world but not of it. The implications of this came out forcibly during World War II. The Catholic Church is indebted to Pius XII for having consistently adhered to this fundamental conception, despite the enormous pressure that governments could and did exert on the Papacy."[21]

Pius XII implicitly condemned Nazism and Communism. If he had named the Nazis, he should surely have named the Allies for the immoral bombing of Dresden, Hiroshima, and Nagasaki, and for the surrender of two million prisoners to the Communists.

In *Pius XII: Greatness Dishonoured,* Michael O'Carroll questions: "Why should Catholics with any self-respect tolerate meekly a sustained campaign of denigration, characterized by unscrupulous manifestations of the truth?"

O'Carroll refutes John F. Morley of Seton Hall University, who misuses the Vatican's World War II documents. In his book, *Vatican Diplomacy and the Jews during the Holocaust 1934–1943,* Morley implies that the Nuncios, the Secretary of State and, most of all, the Pope share the responsibility for failure in saving the victims of the Holocaust.[22] In view of the evidence, now apparent and accessible, the charge of modern critics that Pius XII was "silent" is unfair. His secret diplomatic initiatives, solemn warnings, and appeals to peoples and governments were not heeded. Apparently critics have failed to do their research or have refused to acknowledge the evidence regarding the alleged "silence" of Pius XII.

The evidence overwhelmingly favors Pope Pius XII. When the Allies entered Rome on June 4, 1944, the *Jewish News Bulletin* of the British Eighth Army printed the following: "To the everlasting credit of the people of Rome, and the Roman Catholic Church, the lot of the Jews has been made easier by their truly Christian offers of assistance and shelter. Even now, many still remain in places which opened their doors to hide them from the fate of deportation to certain death. The full story of the help given to our people by the Church cannot be told for obvious reasons, until after the war."

Reports were received from Jewish military chaplains serving in Italy and from Palestinian Jewish soldiers of the sympathetic and helpful conduct of the Italian people under the Fascist regime toward persecuted Jewish inhabitants. They confirmed that the Italians did all they could to rescue and harbor Jews fleeing from oppression and certain death, even providing false passports for them under Italian names.

The fact that Pius XII saved thousands of Jews from the gas chambers cannot be obliterated by revisionists. Nor can the fact that the Jewish community praised the Pope's efforts during and after the Holocaust be denied. Apparently, posterity wishes to ignore these facts. This is the real "silence."

Voices of hindsight are judging the Pope's "silence" without considering the consequences of "speaking out." Those critics do not recall that the Pope had been advised by Jewish leaders and by the bishops in occupied countries not to protest publicly against the Nazi atrocities. However, Pius XII frequently invoked "God's vengeance" on the persecutors. His words were the brave words of a diplomat who put focus on "those who are responsible."

Why is it that Pope Pius XII's numerous protests have been and are ignored by the world press? His messages and addresses have been and are available in the records of both the Vatican Radio and the Vatican newspaper, *L'Osservatore Romano.*

And what about the protests of the bishops in Nazi-occupied countries who, in consonance with the Pope, issued powerful condemnations: Cardinal Hinsley, December 1942 and April 1944; the Bishop of Berlin, February 1943; the German bishops, May 1944; the Bavarian Bishops, July 1945; and those of the Dutch bishops throughout the duration of the war?

It is important that the lessons of the Holocaust, although horrible to recall, be retold truthfully and accurately. It is equally important to recognize those who did all in their power to help the victims of Nazism. In fact, throughout Europe Pope Pius XII operated a vast underground railroad. While Italy was being devastated by Allied bombs, the Nazis were killing innocent people. Eighty-five percent of Italian Jews were saved. In occupied Europe, the Nazis killed 67 percent of the Jews. Millions of Christians did not escape Nazi terror during Hitler's attempt to exterminate all Jews.

Among the numerous stories of compassion and love, one in particular is an inspiration. It began in 1939, when 150 German Jews fled from Germany armed with visas for the United States. In order to obtain transportation, they sought refuge in Italy. But not long after their arrival, the war expanded. Jews were immediately arrested and placed in chains.

Entrusted to Father Francesco Sacco, for three years these prisoners were interned in the town of Campagna, near the Bay of Salerno, living in a monastery and gratefully enjoying the loving care of the local residents. When the Allies bombed the monastery, the Jews fled to the mountains. Days after the Nazis took control of the town, they began shooting the Italians.

When the Jews learned that the Italians were without medical assistance, four Jewish surgeons among them returned to the town to care for the many casualties. These Jews knew the Nazis were searching for them; if caught, they would have been shot or deported. Yet, they did not hesitate. Without medical equipment, they performed forty major operations in two days and saved many Italian lives.[23]

Pius XII's voice was heard around the world. It was the "voice" of a tireless world leader whose contribution to humanity during the Holocaust is incontrovertible.

Monsignor John M. Oesterreicher, late founder and director of the Judaeo-Christian studies program at Seton Hall University, evaluated *The Deputy* as early as November 9, 1963, in *America* magazine: "The author's purpose is to 'unmask' the Pope as one who claimed to be Christ's vicar but was really a betrayer of His spirit. What it accomplishes, however, is to reveal the true character of the reader or hearer: whether he considers himself a champion of justice by burdening one man with responsibility, or whether he faces the involvement of the entire West and, not least, his own involvement."

On June 11, 1977, in his review essay "Auschwitz: Beginning of a New Era?" Monsignor Oesterreicher disagreed with writer Irving Greenberg: "My respect and affection for Greenberg notwithstanding, I cannot accept his injunction 'to quarrel with the Gospels themselves for being a source of anti-Semitism.' Nor can I subscribe to the thesis advanced by several contributors that the teaching of contempt culminated in the Holocaust or that it is responsible for all kinds of Jew-baiting. To hold that this teaching is fully, or even largely, responsible for that outburst of moral insanity that culminated in the Holocaust shows a lack of discernment and of historical knowledge....To do so bespeaks prejudice."

In *The Jewish Newsletter* and in a letter sent to major newspapers, William Zukerman called the rescue of thousands of Jewish Nazi victims by the Vatican "one of the greatest manifestations of humanitarianism in the 20th century as well as a new, effective method of fighting anti-Semitism."

Frequently without reflection or investigation, the media and the public in general repeat any rumor or attack against the Catholic Church and Pope Pius XII. However, they fail to produce documentary evidence. In "Pius XII: The Legends and the Truth" (March 28, 1998, *The Tablet* [London]), Sir Owen Chadwick, author of *Britain and the Vatican in the Second World War,* speaks about the reference to Pius XII in the Shoah document: "It says about him nothing that is not true for the historian. It records how he helped many Jews privately, how Italian Jews afterwards respected him and were grateful to him, how wise he was....This document does mark one more step in the Church's postwar condemnation of anti-Semitism, and as such is to be welcomed wholeheartedly."

Pope Pius XII is now blamed for this tragic period. Yet, Jewish newspapers throughout the world paid tribute to Pope Pius XII and warmly eulogized him when he died in 1958: "Adherents of all creeds and parties will recall how Pius XII faced the responsibilities of his exalted office with courage and devotion. Before, during, and after the Second World War, he constantly preached the message of peace. Confronted by the monstrous cruelties of Nazism, Fascism, and Communism, he repeatedly proclaimed the virtues of humanity and compassion" (*Jewish Chronicle,* London, October 10, 1958). How could Jews on five continents have been so wrong about the Holy Father's conduct? Why not ask the thousands of survivors where they would be if the Pontiff had publicly denounced Hitler? Pius XII was sensitive to the sufferings of the Jews, Christians, and other refugees who were persecuted. His decision not to publicly condemn Hitler in no way diminishes his concern: "We have heard of the very serious threat of retaliation...and received urgent recommendations that the Holy See should not take a drastic stand....Perhaps my solemn protest would have earned me praise from the civilized world, but it would have brought more implacable persecution of the Jews."

The attacks on Pius XII started with the play *The Deputy* in the early 1960s, when Judeo-Christian moral and family values declined. In the late 1940s and 1950s, there were no "organized" efforts to undermine morality. Abortion and gay marriage were unthinkable, and there was legal censorship against pornography. Today, the "natural law," which the Creator has inscribed in man himself, is replaced with utilitarian arguments. Think of abortion, of euthanasia, of the manipulation of the very sources of human life. Marriage and the family are collapsing under the joint assault of an emancipation from values and norms based on human nature.

REFUGE DENIED—an ad sponsored by the U.S. Holocaust Memorial Museum in Washington, D.C., appeared in the *New York Times* "Op-Ed Page," April 13, 1999. Before World War II erupted, one of the last ships to leave Nazi Germany from Hamburg was the *St. Louis.* On May 13, 1939, the U.S. Coast Guard prevented some nine hundred Jewish refugees aboard the ship from seeking haven in the United States. Sixty years have passed and their story has not been fully told. Were other shiploads of human beings who attempted to enter the United States denied refuge?

Fortunately, some nations behaved differently. Feri and Zlata Noiman explained how the Italians saved over five hundred Slovak refugees when their ship was sinking. Many fled to the mountains and were later taken to the Ferramonti-Tarsia concentration camp in Calabria. Conditions were "Italian style": Jews held Passover services and children went to school. When the Nazis retreated, they were allowed to leave the camp.

The Foreign Minister of Czechoslovakia asked Jan Mascyk and Cardinal Hinsley of Westminster to intervene with the Holy See in favor of four hundred refugees. These refugees, who left Presbourg, Rhodes, in 1940 aboard the *Pencho,* were in danger of deportation to Poland. Supported by the Vatican, they were interned in Italy in the

Ferramenti-Tarsia concentration camp and survived. (See *Actes,* Vol. 8, n. 1, p. 481 and Vol. 9, p. 140.)

A Polish survivor, Dr. Rubin Pick of Florida, was studying medicine in Italy when the racial laws were passed in 1938. Under these laws, foreign Jews—including those who had become citizens after 1919—had to leave Italy. He explains: "My father left for Palestine. I was living in Trieste and commuting to Padua. I applied for permission to finish my studies, and the authorities let me stay. My sister was a student at the university in Trieste, so she too applied, and again they agreed. The Italian mentality was: How could you let a young girl be by herself, unprotected, in the city? So they told my mother that she could stay too. On hearing this, my brother said. 'You're letting my brother, my sister, my mother stay and making me go alone?' So they said, 'Okay, you can stay too.'"

Dr. Fernando G. Giustini of West Virginia recalls that his grandfather had spent fifteen years in the United States, and often spoke of his childhood in McKees Rocks, Pennsylvania. The Giustini family not only saved the lives of Helen and Oscar Deutsch, a Jewish couple who were interned in Corchiano, but they also rescued about forty prisoners and airmen who were shot down from the skies. His father, a collaborator of Monsignor Hugh O'Flaherty's organization, smuggled them into Rome, and they were sheltered in the Vatican. (See pp. 49–50, 94, 192–4, 224–30 in *Yours Is a Precious Witness.*)

Pius XII was faithful to his goal of "peacemaker and conciliator." His appeals for peace were not heeded. Nor have Pope John Paul II's appeals been heeded. Will posterity consider John Paul II an accomplice of the 1999 genocide in Kosovo? Will he be accused, as was Pope Pius XII, of not doing enough for peace?

Indeed, on May 4, 1999, an article in the *New York Times,* "How Can the Vatican Stay Neutral?" by the sociologist Andrew Greeley is an example of total misunderstanding of the Vatican's position: "Nothing is lost with peace. All can be lost with war" (Pius XII, August 24, 1939). The article not only smears the character of two outstanding pontiffs—John Paul II and Pius XII—but also demonstrates ignorance and prejudice.

Greeley begins by asking: "Who, I wonder, is advising the Pope on the war in Kosovo?" At the very time that Reverend Jesse Jackson and his group of American religious leaders were carrying out an inspiring mission to end the bloodshed in Yugoslavia, the media published Greeley's uninformed criticism of John Paul II for following a very similar peace-making policy in Yugoslavia.

For nearly ten years the Holy Father sought in every possible way to encourage a peaceful resolution for the ethnic warfare that erupted following the death of Tito. During the ethnic cleansing in Bosnia, John Paul repeatedly offered to face bullets in Sarejevo if his presence there would help defuse passions and lead to negotiations. At every step he supported and encouraged actions of the United Nations that led to an end of the conflict there. He saw the Bosnia solution as a model for Kosovo. By January 1999 his secretary of state, Cardinal Angelo Sodano, was calling for disarming the Serbian forces in Kosovo and for the presence of peace-keeping troops.

The Vatican's policy is not only similar to that of Reverend Jackson's group, it closely parallels what religious leaders throughout Europe have been calling for. Bishop Joakim Herbut of Skopje-Prizen, the diocese that straddles Kosovo and Macedonia, said that air strikes would escalate the conflict and cause additional pain and death. Bishop Antun Skvorcevic of Pozega, Croatia, secretary of the Croatian bishops' conference, asked for resolution "through negotiations" not through conflict. The Russian Orthodox Patriarch, Alexei II of Moscow, called the air attacks "international terrorism." Ecumenical Patriarch Bartholomew of Constantinople also voiced his support for negotiations as opposed to air strikes.

Contrary to the charge of anti-Muslim sentiment in John Paul's stand on Kosovo, the Pope's policy is the same there as in countries where Christians are beset, in India, in Indonesia, and in Africa. In Southern Sudan, where 1.5 million Christians have been victims of an anti-Christian fanaticism as uncompromising as Milosevic's fanaticism (which has been condemned by the Vatican), the Pope called for negotiations and nonviolence.

In his article Greeley denied John Paul II a role as a peacemaker by labeling his efforts in behalf of peace as "neutrality." The author found no moral worth, no religious dimension, no Christian pacifism in the Pope's actions. He presented the Holy Father's "neutrality" as calculated, politically inspired, and evidence of moral cowardice—even as a "pretense" covering up crass motives. He underlined his notion of the Holy Father as a political figure by describing him as "above all a European." If John Paul II is above all "a European," then he is not "above all" what most faithful Catholics know him to be: namely, a son of the Church, a priest, a mystic, a preacher of the Crucified Christ, a man of God.

In the conclusion of his editorial Greeley does refer to the Pope as "the most important [politically powerful] religious leader in the world." He shows no interest in how the Pope's deep, living faith informs and determines his entire response to violence and oppression around the world.

It is faith, not "neutralitiy," that is clear in every word the Holy Father has uttered on Kosovo. On Palm Sunday (March 28) he declared to a crowd in St. Peter's Square: "The Pope stands with the people who suffer, and cries out to all: it is always time for peace! It is never too late to meet and negotiate!" The next day he told UN representatives: "Violence leads to more violence...the extreme violence unfolding on our doorstep will wound the whole of Europe." That night he urged the President of Italy, Oscar Luigi Scalfaro, to work for peace. Two days later he sent Archbishop Jean-Louis Tauran to Belgrade to urge Milosevic to return to the peace table. Hardly a day passed when the Pope did not plead for courageous workers willing to serve and suffer, in the footsteps of Christ, for peace. On May 3, the Pope stated: "I raise my voice again, in the name of God, that this attack of man against man come to an end, that the instruments of destruction and death be stopped, that all channels of aid be activated to help those who are forced to flee their land amid unspeakable atrocities..." "Christ," he says over and over, "is our only hope. Any other promise of salvation is deceptive, since it does not resolve the fundamental human problem of good and evil." This is the Holy Father's "neutrality" that Father Greeley finds immoral.

According to Greeley, the Vatican is guilty of being anti-NATO, anti-American, anti-Muslim, and indifferent to the rape of Kosovar women. He combines an old falsehood and a new one to make his final accusation—that John Paul II's "silence" in the face of genocide compares to Pius XII's! His accusations of Pius XII's "silence" are based on the same kind of prejudices and half-truths as his attack on John Paul II. Evidence for the serious scholar is a brief passage from the October 1, 1942 editorial page of the *Times* of London: "A study of the words which Pope Pius XII has addressed since his accession in encyclicals and allocutions to the Catholics of various nations leaves no room for doubt. He condemns the worship of force and its concrete manifestation in the suppression of national liberties and in the persecution of the Jewish race."

In his 1999 Easter message Pope John Paul II pleaded: "Peace is possible, peace is a duty, peace is a prime responsibility of everyone!"

Speaking of the initiatives that the Holy See has taken in favor of peace, Joaquin Navarro-Valls, director of the Vatican press office, stated on May 8, 1999 in the *New York Times:* "The Holy See is not neutral nor partisan nor anti-American. Instead John Paul II has done and is doing all that is possible so that dialogue based on the respect for law and history can begin once again and without delay."

10. Conclusion

Regarding World War II's concentration camps and systematic extermination, Pope John Paul II wrote: "First and foremost, the sons and daughters of the Jewish nation were condemned for no other reason than that they were Jewish. Even if only indirectly, whoever lived in Poland at that time came into contact with this reality.

"Therefore, this was also a personal experience of mine, an experience I carry with me even today. Auschwitz, perhaps the most meaningful symbol of the Holocaust of the Jewish people, shows to what lengths a system constructed on principles of racial hatred and greed for power can go. To this day, Auschwitz does not cease to admonish, reminding us that anti-Semitism is a great sin against humanity, that all racial hatred inevitably leads to the trampling of human dignity."[24]

That the Church supported Nazism, as contended by a Milan newspaper on January 6, 1998, is a lie. The fifth volume of documents disproves entirely the idea that the Holy See supported the Third Reich out of fear of Soviet Russia. In the article, "The Accusations Against Pius XII," Father Pierre Blet, S.J., answers the rehashed, speculative statements that the Vatican aided, or quietly consented to helping, the escape of war criminals and that it possesses or distributed gold belonging to the victims of the Holocaust. There exists no documentary evidence of such defamatory charges.[25]

There is no evidence of a pro-German attitude on the part of Pius XII. It would be a delusion to think that a confrontation by the Pope's Swiss Guard or the threat of excommunication could have stopped the *Wehrmacht's* tanks. For evidence to the contrary, critics should read Pius XII's efforts to keep Italy out of the conflict; his telegrams, May 10, 1940, to the sovereigns of Belgium, Holland, and Luxemburg after the invasion by the Germans; his courageous advice to Mussolini and to King Vittorio Emanuele III to explore a separate peace.

It is incomprehensible that, today, the unfair portrayal of Pope Pius XII should be given credibility among Jewish leaders and be accepted as fact in a large part of the Jewish community. Fortunately, some historians have challenged critics and proven that these stories were obviously concocted, statements out of context, claims made from forged notes, misleading interview transcripts, as well as other false documents.

Consistently, the Church has taught respect for every human being. To charge that anti-Semitism is part of Church teaching is without foundation. Generalizations that anti-Judaism is also deeply imbedded in the teachings and practices of the Church is lacking in truth. Attacking Christianity and charging the Church as having led to the Holocaust is seriously unjust. From a veritable mountain of sources, no reliable evidence has been produced supporting the defamatory charges against Pope Pius XII that relate to the events of the Holocaust.

In gratitude and unanimity, the Jews of the generation so affected praised the Pope's heroic efforts on their behalf, during and after the Holocaust.

Recent assertions that hold the Catholic Church responsible for the Holocaust require a response. In the words of Pope John Paul II: "Anti-Semitism has no justification and should be absolutely condemned. In the Christian world—I do not say the Church itself—erroneous and unjust interpretations of the New Testament regarding the Jewish people and their alleged culpability, have circulated for too long, engendering sentiments, combined with pagan themes, to fuel the racism that racked Europe under the Nazi regime." He points out that it would be a distortion of the historical record to suggest that the Nazi racial ideology was based on Christianity. The Catholic Church recognizes that for centuries Jews had been marginalized in Europe, repudiates anti-Semitism, and acknowledges the Judaic roots of Christianity.

Repeatedly, John Paul II has defended Pope Pius XII, recalling how deeply his predecessor felt about the tragedy of the Jewish people and how effectively he assisted them. Citing the papal encyclicals, the Pontiff stated: "The Church firmly condemns all forms of genocide, as well as the racist theories that inspire them and give them the pretense of justification."

Archbishop Elden F. Curtiss, in the July/August 1998 issue of *Social Justice Review,* speaks about the pattern of unwarranted media attacks upon the Catholic Church: "The same media which criticize the present Pope John Paul II for interfering in political processes around the world by promoting moral values regarding the sacredness of human life and the fundamental rights of human beings to life and freedom and to the basic necessities of life are the very media which now criticize Pope Pius XII for not taking more decisive action against the Nazi government of Germany. Pius reminded the Allies who wanted him to sign a condemnation of Nazi atrocities against Jews and Christians that they must also sign a condemnation of Stalin's atrocities against Jews and Christians, which they refused to do since the Soviet Union was then an ally of the United States and Britain."

Communists and Nazis shared a deep-seated hatred for Christians. Not only Jews, but non-Jews suffered persecution and death for their national origins and religious beliefs. The lessons learned should help lessen today's racial strife and ethnic prejudice that undermine our solidarity as human beings. Only by becoming more sensitive to each other can Jews and Catholics improve their relationship and achieve reconciliation and peace.

It is time to place the blame for the Holocaust where it belongs. Pope Pius XII warned the world about the consequences of Nazi policies and responded as best he could to the suffering people throughout Europe.

Pius XII was a modern-day leader. In the book *Papal Teachings* one finds his writings applicable in today's world. His pronouncements on the subject of womanhood are unprecedented. On October 21, 1945, his call was for Catholic women to enter public life: "She must compete with man for the good of civic life, in which she is, in dignity, equal to him." In an address to the Federation of Italian Women on October 14, 1956, Pius XII stated that, in virtue of a "common destiny here on earth, there is no field of human activity that must remain closed to women. Her horizons reach out to the regions of politics, work, the arts, sports—but always in subordination to the primary functions fixed by nature itself." No Pope had ever spoken in this fashion.

During the war, Pope Pius XII did not neglect the clarification and advancement of Catholic doctrine. A profoundly important development followed his 1943 encyclical, *Divino Afflante Spiritu,* which allowed scholars to use critical methods to study the sources and historical contexts of the Bible's books. About his encyclical

Humani Generis (1950) Pope John Paul II wrote: "My predecessor Pius XII had already stated that there was no opposition between evolution and the doctrine of the faith about man and his vocation, on condition that one did not lose sight of several indisputable points....

"Today, almost half a century after the publication of the encyclical, new knowledge has led to the recognition of the theory of evolution as more than a hypothesis. It is indeed remarkable that this theory has been progressively accepted by researchers, following a series of discoveries in various fields of knowledge...."

Among the first Catholic scholars to take advantage of this new openness within the Church was the well-known researcher Father Raymond E. Brown, who, in a career of four decades produced forty books. Thanks to his extensive contribution to scholarship, at his death in August 1998, recognition was given to Father Brown for his impact on other denominations.

Any assessment of Pius XII's reputation must include his many contributions not only during the twenty years of his pontificate but also in the period before his election. As Cardinal Pacelli he had a hand in writing the encyclical *Non Abbiamo Bisogno,* which condemned Italian Fascist doctrine, as well as *Divini Redemptoris,* which opposed Soviet Communism and the massacres and starvation that were being perpetrated in its name in Russia (e.g., ten million peasants starved to death in the Ukraine). Cardinal Pacelli was a zealous opponent of totalitarianism and oppression. When the German Roman Catholic hierarchy thanked Pius XI for issuing the encyclical *Mit brennender Sorge* in 1937, the Pope pointed to Cardinal Pacelli, saying it was he who had been responsible for its message. After Pius XII's first encyclical in 1939, *Summi Pontificatus,* repeated the theme, the Gestapo were immediately under orders from the Nazi leadership to prevent its distribution.[26]

When the Church reaches out in a statement of sincere repentance, let it be a two-way street. Attacking Christianity because of the human weakness and personal failure of some to meet the difficult demands of the Catholic faith and charging the Church with such failure for having led to the Holocaust is seriously unjust. That there are bad Christians is no more an indictment of Christianity than that there are bad Jews is an indictment of Judaism.

Our Jewish brethren should join Catholics, in the interests of historic truth and community harmony, to rectify calumnies that malign the Catholic Church and the memory of Pope Pius XII, whom Golda Meir eulogized as "a great servant of peace."

This is a call for justice toward the memory of Pope Pius XII. In light of the documentation that has been ignored, it is a prayer for the restoration of the true historical record of the activities of the Catholic Church during World War II. Finally, it is plea for love and understanding, a plea for Jews and Catholics to build together a human bridge of brotherhood and peace.

Part II
The Pope and His Concern for Prisoners of War

A. Prisoners of War
B. Pope Pius XII to the Prisoners of War
C. Vatican Information Bureau
D. Tributes to Pius XII's Humanitarian Work
E. Epilogue

A. *Prisoners of War*

---

*N*o chronicle of World War II would be authentic without acknowledging the suffering of the thousands of military personnel taken prisoner by the Nazis. Here too the focus of history points to the heroism of the Vatican.

William Simpson, in his *A Vatican Lifeline '44,* published in 1996 (New York, Sarpedon), gives a dramatic account of how Allied fugitives, aided by the Italian Resistance, foiled the Gestapo in Nazi-occupied Rome. In his memoir of real-life exploits, Simpson, a Presbyterian and a highly decorated British prisoner of war (POW), recounts how he collaborated in the Vatican underground with Monsignor Hugh O'Flaherty of the Vatican's Holy Office. He was among the thousands of American, British, and South African POWs imprisoned in Italy who had been captured by the Nazis during two years of desert warfare ranging from Egypt to Morocco.

Seventy thousand extraordinarily brave Italian civilians emerged to help the countless Allied POWs turned loose when Italy surrendered to the Allies in September 1943. They became self-appointed guardians and spontaneously aided these prisoners, who would have fallen prey to the Nazis.

Simpson relates that, going far beyond charity, Italians performed extraordinary acts of courage. Bishops, priests, nuns, artisans, farmers, or aristocrats who were the champions, not only aided the hundreds of thousands of Jews saved from the concentration camps, but also took in the many POWs stranded at their door or exposed in their fields. The people who were there—the people who know best—credit Pope Pius XII for this moral victory.

Transcending politics, religion, and race, Pius XII preached and practiced charity and compassion for all. And in the midst of this

105

human tragedy, the Catholic Church carried on a vast program of assistance and rescue on behalf of the populations at the mercy of the Nazis. Coordinated by the Vatican, there were forces at work striving to reduce human suffering, to rescue the innocent and the weak, to succor the sick, the dying, the prisoner.

When Rome was liberated in June 1944, Jewish leaders, officers, and soldiers of all faiths crowded into the Vatican halls for a papal audience to thank Pope Pius XII for all he had done. The world at large lavished expressions of admiration and gratitude.

Administrator Hedly of the International Committee of the Red Cross, based in Geneva, had the duty of caring for prisoners of war. The Committee was to visit camps, observe procedures, send packages, and supervise communication with families. But their work and that of the international Jewish rescue organizations had to be carried on with extreme discretion so as not to jeopardize the hoped-for results by premature publicity that would generate Nazi reaction and retaliation. Vigilant in the face of risk—one misstep could be fatal—the Vatican's moves were not always apparent.

In a television interview, former Italian Prime Minister Giulio Andreotti recalled "the great charitable activity carried out by Pius XII not only here in Rome, but through a network created in the world for the support of prisoners of war" (*National Catholic Register,* October 29, 1978).

The final year and a half of World War II was highly destructive in Italy. This was the time of the German occupation of Rome, the slow Allied advance from Anzio, and the bombing of Montecassino. As the Germans retreated to northern Italy, hostages were shot in reprisal for acts of resistance. The number of prisoners multiplied; hundreds of thousands became "military internees."

The victims were diverse: In addition to the wounded soldiers who were prisoners of war, they included civilians subjected to bombardments and serious injuries, individuals taken as hostages or threatened with reprisals for actions deemed unlawful, whole populations facing starvation.

A visible sign of Pius XII's paternal solicitude for all victims of war was the work of the Vatican Information Service. It served the humanitarian role of transmitting the names of persons taken prisoner or interned regardless of their nationality, race, or religion. One way in which Pius XII could demonstrate his concern was to send anxious families information about their loved ones in the theatre of war.

The Vatican Information Bureau, as Pius XII's first communication office was called, struggled to obtain recognition and cooperation. Russia would not cooperate and, notwithstanding Vatican efforts, refused to release information. In Germany the Foreign Minister advised German priests not to make any announcements from the pulpit. When the Holy See received twelve hundred requests for information about Australian soldiers who were prisoners, Germany refused to respond.

In the United States, radio transmissions of lists of prisoners and internees were also unavailable. On June 14, 1944, the Apostolic Delegate in Washington, D.C. explained that the matter could not be discussed for "security reasons." Other documents indicate that on March 18, 1944, the Secretariat of State submitted a verbal note to the British Legation at the Vatican regretting the delays and obstacles.

Apparently the Americans were favorable to the exchange of names of internees. Monsignor Carroll assured the Vatican Information Bureau that the American authorities would consent to these radio communications of messages regarding civilians and prisoners in short sentences agreed upon by common consent. The British authorities, on the other hand, did not consent. Thus, after long delays, the lists and messages had to be forwarded by way of Spain.

B. Pope Pius XII to the Prisoners of War

*P*ope Pius XII's Radio discourse of December 24, 1940, addressed prisoners of war and refugees: "Among the most terrible disasters of the inhuman conflict that weighs so heavily on Our heart is that of the prisoners of war. It has become more acute and the possibility for Our paternal solicitude to help has diminished wherever misery and need for Our assistance has increased.

"We recall how, in the name of His Holiness Benedict XV, of happy memory, We were able during the previous war to alleviate the material and spiritual needs of numerous prisoners, and We had hoped that this time the road for the religious and charitable initiatives of the Church would remain open.

"However, if in some countries Our intentions have been frustrating, all Our efforts have not been in vain, since We have been able to reach, at least in part, the Polish prisoners; more frequently the Italian prisoners and those who are interned, especially in Egypt, in Australia, in Canada.

"Nor did We want Christmas Day to dawn without Our wishes, through Our representatives, to reach English and French prisoners in Italy, Germans in England, Greeks in Albania, and Italians spread in many regions of the British Empire, especially in Egypt, in Palestine, in India, wherever We could make known Our encouragement and blessing.

"We were most anxious to inform the families about the destiny of their relatives, so We have initiated an enterprise that is by no means small and We are actively implementing and developing it in order to request and transmit news, wherever it is possible to perform this work, not only for many prisoners, but also for refugees and all those whom the present calamity sadly has separated from their country and from their hearth.

"We have in this way felt the palpitations of thousands of hearts with the emotional tumult of their most intimate affections or in the intense yearnings and the nightmare of uncertainty in the exultant joy of recuperated assurance or in the deep pain and serene resignation to the fate of their loved ones."

Pius XII condemned the conduct of the war and pleaded for relief "to those poor people who are overcome by the sorrows and tribulations of war's calamities, to exiles, to refugees, to unknown wanderers, to prisoners, and to the wounded."

Pius XII's Easter message of April 19, 1941, was broadcast three times to Germany, protesting "atrocious forms" of the fighting, pleading for the safety of the defenseless, affirming his concern for "all the victims of this war," including "prisoners" and "refugees," and reminding the occupying powers that "the treatment of prisoners and civilians in occupied areas is the surest indication and proof of the civilization of individuals and nations. But above all, remember, that upon the manner in which you deal with those whom the fortunes of war place in your hands may depend the blessing or curse of God upon your own Fatherland."

In his 1941 Christmas Eve address, Pius XII condemned the "open or secret oppression of the cultural and linguistic characteristics of national minorities" and pleaded for "those expelled from their native land" and "those deported to foreign lands."

The 1942 Christmas Eve allocution speaks about a "sad succession of acts at variance with the human and Christian sense." Pius XII invited "magnanimous and upright people" to gather together "in a solemn vow not to rest" until society is brought back to its "center of gravity, which is the Law of God."

Vatican Radio's comment on the allocution was given in German on December 28: "It is the Pope's task to appeal to the world's conscience and to recall ethical principles. He has done this very clearly. No man of good will can say that the Pope remained silent....He does not condemn individuals, but wrong and injustice. He condemns false systems, wherever they may be, if they contradict the law of God."

Speaking in French, Vatican Radio on February 19, 1943, condemned forced labor, invoking "the curse of God" on whomever abuses the liberty of men in this respect. Broadcasting in German in April 1943, Vatican Radio protested a long list of horrors, including "an unprecedented enslavement of human freedom, the deportation of thousands for forced labor, and the killing of innocent and guilty alike."

In his June 2, 1943, allocution to the Cardinals, Pius XII clearly referred to the Jews: "Do not be astonished....There are those who, because of their nationality or their descent, are pursued by mounting misfortune and increasing suffering [and] extermination." The Germans and Italians were so astonished that they suppressed this section from all their reports of what the Pope had said. But the Vatican wireless broadcasted it to Germany.

C. Vatican Information Bureau

A closer look at the papal communication service known as the Vatican Information Office or Bureau reveals it to be a living testimonial to goodness in the face of evil: twenty million messages were transmitted. Obstacles abounded—Russia would not respond to the requests for information; in Germany the Foreign Minister forbade priests to mention the Vatican from the pulpit. The Office personnel had begun with two; soon after, the number increased to 885.

This enormous task was undertaken by the Vatican Office in an effort to alleviate, at least in part, the sorrow and the desperation experienced during the war by so many families throughout the world. This work was initiated by Pope Pius XII. The Secretariat of State organized and implemented it amidst infinite difficulties and opposition. In fact, it is incredible and disconcerting to review the difficulties encountered, aside from technical problems, by the refusal on the part of various governments to assist the Vatican in this noble endeavor.

The work began in September 1939. For example, as the German army conquered Polish villages, millions were engulfed in misery, and many did not return home. The family of one missing man did not know to whom they could appeal. With the desperate hope of learning about his whereabouts, his relatives sent a letter from their Polish village to the Vatican. It was the first letter asking for help. By the end of the conflict, 9,891,497 other requests would follow: letters of sorrow and of despair, letters of gratitude and of love.

With that first missive, the Vatican Information Office was initiated, and two clerks were directly responsible to the Secretariat. Rarely has an office been organized so rapidly and in such an impressive manner. After the first office was found to be inadequate, it moved to the Palazzo San Carlo in 1941. But soon this office was also inadequate, both for the space needed by the employees and for the long lines of applicants who came to ask for news. It was necessary to open a new location in the Museo Petriano.

The Vatican Information Bureau closed officially on October 31, 1947. In addition to its 885 staff members in Rome, the thousands of auxiliary personnel who participated, not only in Italy but also throughout the entire Catholic world, must be added. The number of requests seeking response reached almost ten million, and the returning communications surpassed that figure: 11,293,511. To this number must be added the number of messages related to the research and to communication with prisoners and refugees, transmitted via Vatican Radio from June 1940 to May 1945—a total of 1,240,720 and requiring 12,105 hours.

Nonetheless, the Vatican's network grew day by day, depending upon Turkey for the Orient and upon Lisbon for the Western world. Radio, telegraph, and messengers worked together in search of men about whom no information existed. Wherever there was fighting, the network reached thirty-three European countries, twenty-four African, fourteen American, fourteen Asian, and all of Australia. It was a network of incomprehensible dimensions: from Venezuela to Japan, from Australia to Canada, from Kenya to Algiers, from the United States to England, from Palestine to Brazil, and elsewhere.

Filled with desperation and sorrow, trusting in the work of the Church, the requests betrayed the anxiety and sadness with which they were written, so much so that at times the sender's name was omitted or the necessary details for the Vatican to initiate the research were omitted.

Not one letter, even those bearing no names, was discarded. For the "difficult" letters, a specific group of nuns (specialists in deciphering and having much patience) was assigned. They had received orders not to give up, regardless of the difficulty. Some letters were addressed to "My son" and signed "Your mother."

Often, people not of the Catholic faith sent letters to "His Holiness Pope Leo XIII," or "Honorable Father of Christianity" or even "To the Reverend Don Pio XII," and finally there was one "To Miss Secretary of State."

An article in *L'Osservatore Romano* on August 6, 1967, observed: "Who can count the languages of the Vatican Information Service? Every living, universal, local language (some known only to bishops and missionaries), even dead languages. Also Latin, the language of the Church, a language that became fire as a perpetual Pentecost warming the will and the heart of individuals in the midst of warfare. *Tu es Petrus,* in sixty-two languages."

Issuing forth from its Information Office was the Church's language of love during the devastations of war, while mankind ignored cries for peace.

1. Vatican Secretariat of State

The Supreme Pontiff usually conducts business of the universal Church by means of the Roman Curia, which fulfills its duty in his name and by his authority; it consists of the Secretariat of State or the Papal Secretariat, congregations, tribunals, and other institutions, whose structure and competency are defined in special law (can. 360).

The Roman Curia, a complex of departments and institutes, assists the Roman Pontiff in the exercise of his supreme pastoral function for the good and service of the universal Church and of the particular churches, by which the unity of faith and the communion of the people of God are strengthened and the mission that is proper to the Church in the world is promoted.

The Cardinal Secretary of State presides over the Secretariat of State for His Holiness. It includes two sections. The section for General Affairs handles anything entrusted to it by the Holy Father, as well as matters of daily business that do not fall within the competence of other departments. It fosters relations with these departments and with the bishops. The second section is for Relations with States. It handles all matters pertaining to civil governments, fostering diplomatic relations with nations, and maintaining contact with all the diplomatic missions of the Holy See. It also takes care of those matters relevant to the presence and activity of the Holy See in international institutes.

During World War II, the offices of the Secretariat were filled with various groups of people. There was a constant coming and going on the third floor of the Loggias, which in normal times were little frequented. Everyone asked for the Secretariat because, they said, if there is a way to help, the Holy Father will find it. The consensus was that, among the leaders of the world, only Pope Pius XII could offer effective help for prisoners.

Together with ambassadors and prelates in the hallways and in the waiting rooms, there were persons of every age and social condition:

the wife of the sailor who had disappeared, the sister of the infantryman who was missing, the father of the pilot who did not return from his flight. All hoped, perhaps, by the special grace of the Madonna to whom they prayed, that their loved ones were still alive.

The supplicants spoke of investigations that were beginning, of the bombings that were devastating the world, of the persons to whom they should give and from whom they would receive news, of how to leave the country because Italy's borders were now closed.

Among the thousands of requests received by the Holy Father came a letter from a French soldier who, in 1940, on the shores of Dunkerque, while leaning on the knapsack of his fallen companion, was able to write his last letter to the Pope confirming his faith as a believer and entrusting to him the legacy of educating his children and protecting his wife back in France.

Almost always, the Pope would write back a few words in his own hand suggesting a remedy or indicating how to help Jews or Poles, persecuted or missing people. Working with the Holy Father were young and old, priests and cardinals, nuns and laypersons. All wrote words of comfort; some sent financial assistance or recommended a particular case to the proper authority. Radio messages, cablegrams, letters, and packages by postal service departed from the Vatican regularly.

2. Founding of the Information Bureau

In founding the Vatican Information Bureau, Pope Pius XII wanted to give this office the prestige associated with the Secretariat of State, attaching it to the Ordinary Affairs Section. Those assigned to this work were: prelates, religious and secular priests, laypeople, and young members of Catholic Action. There was indeed the precious collaboration of groups of nuns and women of Catholic Action, as well as many other volunteers.

To gather and transmit news and messages, the liaison—between the Holy See and the various countries of the world—was arranged with the pontifical representatives: Nuncios, Delegates, and Apostolic Vicars, with the collaboration, in some countries, of the local Ordinary.

The services were divided into various sectors: Applications for His Holiness, New Correspondence, Postal Service and Relative Sorting, Shopping and Mailing Departures, Radio, Repatriation, Prisoners of the English language, Prisoners of the German and Slovak Language, Navy and Air Force, Studies, Delivery by Hand, Statistics, Foreign Radio Auditions, Archives. For research and messages, the means for transmission used were ordinary correspondence, correspondence by postal service and by air, radio, and telegraph services.

In Palazzo San Carlo, the Information Bureau was located in the center of a large, bright hall where rectangular files were placed. At the end of the hall, where formerly an altar had stood, a large frame held a portrait of the Holy Father extending his arms to man and to God while all around him the tense hands of hundreds of people were raised in supplication.

Correspondence arrived from East Africa, Algeria, Argentina, Australia, Belgium, Brazil, Canada, Chile, China, Belgian Congo, Egypt and Palestine, Finland, France, Japan, Greece, Hungary, India, England, Iraq, Iran, Italy, Kenya, Malta, Mozambique, Peru, Rumania, Syria, United States of America, South Africa, Sudan, Switzerland, Thailand, Venezuela. It arrived in different ways: by mail or by radio, from people who used the applications distributed by the Office, by residents of Rome, or by pilgrims. Others came directly from the Pontiff, from persons who personally placed their requests in the hands of the Holy Father, along with their sorrow and their hope.

A very special component of the arriving correspondence was the delivery of the messages of prisoners, which were usually written on special forms and packed by the hundreds and often thousands. Each letter was scrupulously connected with the Central Index bearing the family name of the "missing person." All necessary information was noted on the file card.

3. Organization of Work

In the catalogue, file cards listed several notations: first name of the person, surname, date of birth, parents, profession, rank, domicile.

Each card had its own history. If the addressee was a prisoner, an internee, or an exiled person who sent news to his family, the research was relatively simple; but it was a difficult task, sometimes a desperate task, when relatives had received no news from the addressee for a month or a year or more.

The work had to proceed expeditiously without waste of time. A prisoner's life was at stake. Following accurate indicators, the name of the prisoner would be linked with the family, the information conveyed, and the case thus happily concluded. At this point a card in red ink was attached to the first card in black that contained the new data, which would soon bring more news from the concentration camp. But often and tragically the addressee was no longer alive.

4. Letters from Prisoners of War

It is remarkable to note the degree of trust that prisoners of war placed in the Holy Father; many made known their innermost desires, convinced that they would be heard and possibly their wishes fulfilled.

One asked for a harmonica, others for religious medals; some wanted authorization to be transferred to another camp, or merely a fatherly word and a papal blessing. All received an appropriate answer graced by the personal interest of His Holiness, as is demonstrated by the many emotional expressions of gratitude that arrived afterward.

Writing to his family, a prisoner added this line: "I am grateful for the interest of the Holy Church, that through the Holy Father it permits us to communicate." Another, a young lieutenant, wrote: "The Vatican has worked diligently to alleviate the sufferings of so many of us and deserves to be commended." A wife wrote to her husband, a prisoner in Australia: "I am happy to know that you are well; we are all fine, also your parents. As you see, through the Holy Father I have received news about you and you can tell me what you are doing and what the Holy Father is doing for the prisoners. I pray to Jesus Christ to bless him for all the good he is doing."

News of the charity of the Pope spread rapidly. Those who cooperated with him—Nuncios, Apostolic Delegates, Bishops, Pastors, and Priests—offered their assistance and comfort to prisoners, to internees, to families.

One prisoner, writing to the Information Bureau, could not forget the benefits received: "My heart cannot find adequate words to thank you for the work that is done by the Apostolic Delegation, with so much goodness and understanding of our needs, especially giving me news about my adorable parents. Your charity will always remain in my poor prisoner's heart."

The mother of a large family turned directly to the Holy Father: "I wish I could find words," she wrote, "to express the grateful sentiments of my heart for your help in sending my beloved child Mauro home where he is slowly regaining his health. Thank you! Thank you! I pray so much for you and I also ask your blessing for my husband who is still in a concentration camp."

A grandmother, advanced in age, pondered how best to express the sentiments of joy that filled her heart: "With great joy," she wrote from her village in Trentino, "I received the good news about my dear family, my beloved nephews, after a year of silence and anxiety, that only a mother, a grandmother can possibly imagine. To whom am I indebted? To the most worthy and most charitable Head of the Church. I cannot find adequate words to manifest my gratitude....Nothing can be a sufficient exchange for such goodness except the offering of fervent and devout prayers that the Lord preserve the Holy Father for a long time...."

There was much sad news also. Yet, amid the bitterness of human sorrow, there emerged an echo of divine consolations: "I desire to thank you wholeheartedly," wrote the surviving sister of one of the soldiers, "for the photograph of my brother's tomb and for the letter sent by the head Chaplain, who speaks about his death and attaches a design of the cemetery. It will be of great help when we do the research necessary in order to transport his body to his native land. The many testimonials assure us that our dear one was assisted by the comforts of his faith and this satisfies our sorrow. How can we express our gratitude?"

"When, after a year of tormented silence, there finally arrived a letter from a young internee in New York," writes his brother in the name of the family, "our first thought was an enthusiastic acknowledgment of the truly unique and universal influence of the Holy Father and of his immense goodness, because no one else in the world, in contrast to all the Nations, could have helped us who are so terribly afflicted and among the least important people."

A soldier who was in prison wanted to express himself with a single statement, conveying his filial devotion by these simply written words: "To His Holiness, Pius XII—Oh, Holy Father, pray for me to the Lord Almighty!"

At times only a brief message embodied the strong passion and hope of all for this fatherly hand on earth, the image and minister of the Fatherhood "who is in heaven."

"I am not a Catholic," wrote an Australian mother, "but I am certain that you who are so good will endeavor to help me find my son."

A prisoner, anxious about his aged mother who was ill, asked for news as soon as possible...but how could he obtain information about her while confined in Johannesburg and thousands of kilometers separated them? Only the Pope could bridge the distance...and then, in just about ten days, the prisoner received the long-awaited response (from the Vatican), assuring him that his mother was fine.

Voices of gratitude gave the Church the strength to continue its mission of love, its very life.

Letters addressed to the Holy Father arrived from every part of the world. Here is letter no. 004225091, undated, from a little girl: "Dear Pope, I am the little girl who sent you Christmas greetings last year. Now I am sending you greetings for this Christmas. I am seeking news about my uncle, my mother's brother, Tonino Mangano, who is in America on Avenue Gremponti [Greenpoint Avenue], Brooklyn, and I want to know how he is and send him many kisses. I pray every evening to the Baby Jesus that all my uncles will return, and also that Jesus will bless you."

In letter no. 00425088, from Bari, Italy, dated December 12, 1942, Marina writes: "I am a poor mother, whose heart is pierced by a terrible sorrow and, as I kneel before you, I beg you to have pity on me. Here is my son: Cannoniere Armaiolo Donato Fortunato, Motonave Tabarca F.N.S. 861 Ministero Marina, Roma. He has been missing since November 30th. I am sure you will take care of the matter, because your holy heart cannot ignore my fervent prayer. I am waiting...."

Letter no. 00425090, dated December 16, 1942 (answered on January 30, 1943): "To His Holiness—My mother is sick and is sixty-eight years old and already sixty-five days have passed and she has no news about her son. She prays and hopes that with God's help she will have news that he is alive and is a prisoner. He belonged to Reggimento Artiglieria Contraerea Vercelli; and for the last eight months he has been in A.J. This is his last address: Francesco Davide 4, Gruppo Artiglieria Terzo Comando Testa M.N. 96—A. J. Freda Erzano; his mother: Bertolero Geraldina Vedova Davide, Vico Farinata I/11, Genova. If you have bad news, write to me—I am his brother, Davide Trento, Vico Farinata I/4, Genova. God bless our Holy Father."

Letter no. 00425088: "To His Holiness, Pope Pius XII, Vatican City, from the undersigned widow, Assunta Barretta, wife of the

Papal Nuncio Eugenio Pacelli, the future Pope Pius XII, distributes packages
to prisoners of war in Germany during World War I.

Pacelli participates in a
church procession in Rottenburg
in the period between the wars.

SEGRETERIA DI STATO

DI SUA SANTITÀ

UFFICIO CIFRA

№ 335

Telegramma *da* Berlino

Ricevuto *il* 26 agosto 1939

Portato al Santo Padre il 26-8-39 alle 13.

Ricevetti Cifrato.

Hitler accennava;nota conversazione esi= ganza vitale Germania et specialmente provoca= zione per eccidi di tedeschi.

Giornali et radio riferiscono oggi nuovi eccidi.

Impressione generale è che Germania iscena minacce guerra imminente per ottenere Polonia venga trattative e cooperare a questo sarebbe far giuoco Germania.

Forse però Polonia potrebbe dietro invito Santa Sede dichiararsi pronta evitare eccidi purché Germania assuma uguale impegno.

Non mi è possibile indagare se Germania accetterebbe:probabilmente farà richiesta inizio trattative;Santa Sede se crede potrà trasmet tere richiesta e eventualmente raccomandarla.

Si ritiene che anche in caso di insuccesso gesto sarà apprezzato perché di carattere neutra le.

Orsenigo

Mi sembra che si potrebbe comunicare al Nunzio di Varsavia questa proposta, — affinché ne dia notizia e la raccomandi al Governo polacco, in quanto sia possibile e opportuno.

6013/39

Vatican diplomats worked mightily for peace to the eve of World War II. This transcript of a telegram from Cesare Orsenigo, Nuncio in Berlin, asks the Pope to intervene between Germany and Poland but warns that German intentions are unpredictable.

Pius XII visits San Lorenzo Church in Rome after it was damaged by
allied bombs in July of 1943.

The Pope meets with wounded Italian soldiers at the Vatican in August, 1942.

The Vatican received thousands of requests for news of missing servicemen during the war and was often able to supply information to worried families. Right, a closer view of some letters.

deceased Raphael, with residence in Naples, Via Stadera a Poggioreale. My son is a prisoner of war in Egypt, and from February 8, 1942, I have had no news about him. I am a poor widow with a large family, I cry day and night, I am reduced to a skeleton. I turn to Your Excellency for news of my son whose name is Major Corporal Mario Migliaccio, No. 334760 Camp 307, p.f. War Chief Postal Center MEF, Egypt. He is the only male child and the others are all very young and I hope Your Holiness will have compassion on a poor woman who has no bread, and that you will send news to No. 12. Trusting you and kissing your feet, Assunta Barretta, Via Stadera, Naples, December 12, 1942."

Between 1939 and 1946, with special devotion to the prisoners of war, Pope Pius XII dedicated his time and efforts. Federico Cardinal Tedeschini stated: "Who has not read in periodicals and magazines letters written by prisoners or by their families to the Pope? There have been rescues and resurrections; mitigations of pain and comfort; news and messages; spiritual and material help; visits and recommendations. The soul that suffers and is consoled, is a noble one. And the soul that knows how to enjoy such an august intervention, is noble and, at times, sublime! But this is not what is dear to the Pope's heart; because even if everyone were forgetful and everyone were ungrateful, the Pope would bless them; it is his mission, it is a necessity, it is his life."

5. Postal Service

Glancing at the forty files where information was distributed daily, one finds records of transcontinental itineraries, every longitude, every latitude. Twice a week the "Corriere" circled the globe with hundreds of packages that traversed seas and mountains, even oceans and fabulous mountain ranges to reach a prisoner or internee.

The precious cargo of these packages was correspondence linking prisoners and internees to their families. Restrictions limited the letters to family news to be transcribed on particular forms. Censorship dictated the use of words, and if the stationery was not the authorized form specified by the Information Office, the letter was transferred ("translated") to the permitted form. Both the original and its new form were then delegated to the Postal Service for departure.

When these sad requests were difficult to fulfill, the Information Office referred them to the Pontifical Representatives in the various countries. Unfortunately, often the requests roamed the world, and the results were negative. The Office communicated with families, even if no response was forthcoming, and assured them that the search would continue, that the desired information would soon arrive.

Twice a week, sometimes by air mail, tens of thousands of packages were sent through this department. The staff worked with alacrity and reaped much good. Animated by the serene and persevering power of charity, this department regularly performed its duty both satisfactorily and expediently.

6. Vatican Radio

Communication with Papal Representatives throughout the world had been difficult until the Italian physicist, Guglielmo Marconi, overcame the obstacles of geography by his development of wireless telegraphy.

Inaugurated in 1931, the Holy See radio station broadcasted an average of 60 hours a day, on five channels and in five continents. The programs are broadcast on short- and medium-wave frequencies by twenty-four transmitters with a total power of nearly four thousand kilowatts to reach millions of listeners in thirty-seven different languages.

Vatican Radio's origins precede those of Vatican State itself. As early as 1925, the future first director, Jesuit physicist Giuseppe Gianfranceschi (President of the Pontifical Academy of Sciences and Rector of the Pontifical Gregorian University), wrote a letter recommending the creation of a Vatican broadcasting center. In June 1929, only four days after the Lateran Concordat entered into force, Pius XI entrusted the setting up of Vatican Radio to Marconi. On November 8, 1929, a Vatican-Italy accord stipulated the regulations for Holy See communications. Its inauguration took place in the Vatican Gardens on February 12, 1931.

Guglielmo Marconi introduced Pope Pius XI: "I have the great honor to announce that, in a few instants the Holy Father Pope Pius XI will inaugurate the new radio station of Vatican City State. Electronic airwaves will carry his words of peace and benediction through space across the world. For almost 20 centuries the Roman Pontiff has spoken the Divine Magisterium throughout the world. But this is the first time that this live voice will be heard simultaneously across the planet." The first papal message was broadcast for Christmas in 1936.

Confronted with increasing appeals from Germany and Latin America to respond to Nazi and Soviet propaganda, the next Jesuit director, Father Filippo Soccorso, augmented the radio's transmissions in German and other languages besides Italian. At the same time, the Radio's equipment was updated with a new transmission tower, which German technicians nicknamed the "Papstfinger" (Pope's Finger). When Pope Pius XI passed away on February 10, 1939, Vatican Radio was the first to announce the news. On March 2, it announced Pius XII's election to the papal throne. The "Pope's Voice" was to play a significant role throughout World War II.

On August 24, 1939, before war commenced, Pope Pius XII made an urgent appeal for peace via Vatican Radio: "Nothing is lost by peace; everything can be lost by war." The following January 21, the Radio denounced Nazi atrocities in Poland, and on January 23 condemned the existence of concentration camps.

In Germany, reactions to Vatican Radio were so severe that several persons were condemned to death for listening to its transmissions. In Italy, the government refused the Radio the right to broadcast Pius XII's messages, while in occupied France, the French Resistance transcribed and circulated Vatican Radio bulletins.

The Vatican Radio station was not only adequate and modern, but it was also considered second to none. From June 1940 on, the Vatican Radio compensated for the lack of normal communication. It offered a service of assistance for tracing mission persons, both civil and military. Between 1940 and 1946, as the bells of the Basilica of Saint Peter resounded, they penetrated everywhere, uniting the faithful so that the voice of Pope Pius XII reached hundreds of thousands of listeners. His were words of comfort, encouragement, and hope.

The Information Bureau had access to the radio station and thereby facilitated its appeals for help. By locating missing persons and transmitting brief messages, it raised the hopes of tortured families, albeit the process was slow.

To avoid misunderstandings, names were spelled out with the letters of each name given the initial of famous Italian cities, since it was neither possible to repeat nor to clarify a conversation. This major scientific breakthrough announced names regardless of race or religion in response to the sighs and prayers of countless grieving mothers and wives.

In his radio message for Christmas Eve 1942, the Holy Father expressed hope for peace among men and spoke about a "sad succession of acts at variance with the human and Christian sense."

Pius XII invited "magnanimous and upright people to gather together in a solemn vow not to rest" until society is brought back to its "center of gravity, which is the Law of God." He stated: "Humanity owes this vow to the innumerable exiles, torn from their motherland by the hurricane of war and scattered on foreign soil, who might join in the lament of the prophet: 'Our inheritance is turned to aliens, our houses to strangers.'

"Humanity owes this vow to the hundreds of thousands of people who, through no fault of their own, sometimes only owing to nationality or descent, are doomed to death or to slow decline. Humanity owes this vow to the many thousands of non-combatants....

"Humanity owes this vow to the endless stream of tears and bitterness, to the mountains of suffering and torment, which are the results of the destructive madness of the widespread conflict which cry out to heaven, invoking the descent of the Spirit for the liberation of the world from the spreading of violence and terror."

D. Tributes to Pius XII's Humanitarian Work

---

*T*hroughout its long history, the people of Europe have suffered and endured many perils—terrible deprivation and destruction—but the heartless deportation of thousands for reasons of "race" further demonstrates the unimagined evils of war.

Despite allegations and misrepresentations to the contrary, Pope Pius XII insisted on the Church's humanitarian role and saved hundreds of thousands of Jews and other refugees.

There is indisputable evidence of the appreciation of the Jewish community for Pius XII's determined efforts on its behalf in the German sphere of occupation during the Second World War.

Rabbi Israel Zolli

Among those saved in the Vatican was Israel Zolli,[1] Chief Rabbi in Rome during the war. He caused a sensation when he entered the Church at the end of the war—at great personal sacrifice. Though Pius XII's charity toward all, especially Jews, no doubt moved Zolli—who took the name Eugenio at his baptism), he had been growing more and more convinced over a period of twelve years that Jesus was the promised Messiah.

Eugenio Israel Zolli's tribute in defense of Pope Pius XII is almost never quoted and has been, for all practical purposes, silenced. Yet, who is a better witness to the Pope's actions during the war?

In his memoirs, the former Chief Rabbi of Rome states at the end of his account of wartime events: "Volumes could be written on the many efforts of Pius XII and of the countless priests, religious and laity throughout the world who stood with him during the war....No hero in

123

all of history was more militant, more fought against, none more heroic than Pius XII in pursuing the work of true charity!...and this on behalf of all the suffering children of God."

"Of Pius XII, one might say that he was inspired by the words of the prophet Isaiah: "Peace is harmony, peace is salvation, to those near, to those afar off. I want to heal them all."

Israel Zolli's prayerful testimony gratefully recognizes Pope Pius XII's contribution: "The Catholic Church loves all souls. She suffers with all and for all; she awaits her children on the sacred threshold of Peter with love, and her children are all mankind. Wisdom, in the Proverbs of Solomon, invites all to her table. The Church, through her visible Head, offers her love and truth and freedom to all. You shall know the truth and the truth shall make you free. (John viii, 32)....The Vicar of Christ wants all men to be within the sphere of human and divine charity. Only charity makes men free. At the very hour in which the terrible sacrificial rite of blood was initiated, the destruction en masse in the name of race, of nation, of the state, concentrating the three into one factor: blood—precisely then, in the midst of so many fanatics, the great Pontiff, unique, serene and wise, exclaims: But the legitimate and just love towards one's own country must not close the eyes to the universality of Christian charity which also considers others and their prosperity in the pacifying light of love!

"There is no place of sorrow where the spirit of love of Pius XII has not reached. Volumes could be written on the multiform works of succor of Pius XII. The Catholic priesthood throughout the whole world, religious men and women and the Catholic laity, stand behind the great Pontiff. Who could ever tell what has been done? The rule of severe enclosure falls everywhere and all things are at the service of charity. As the sufferings grow, so grows the light from the heart of Christ and from His Vicar; more vigilant and ready are his sons and daughters in Christ. Young Levites and white-haired priests, religious of all orders, in all lands, dedicated Sisters, all in quest of good works and ready for sacrifice. There are no barriers, no distinctions. All sufferers are children of God in the eyes of the Church, children in Christ, for them and with them all suffer and die. No hero in history has commanded such an army, none is more militant, more fought against, none more heroic than that conducted by Pius XII in the name of Christian charity.

"At the first hour of his pontificate Pius XII said: 'Exactly in times like these, he who remains firm in his faith and strong in his heart, knows that Christ the King is never so near as in trial, which is the hour of fidelity. With a heart broken by the suffering of so many of her children, but with the courage and firmness that come from faith in the Lord's promises, the spouse of Christ [the Church], advances towards the approaching storm. She knows that the truth she announces, the charity she teaches, and its practice will be the unique counselors and collaborators of men of good will in the reconstruction of a new world, in justice and love, after humanity, weary of running in the way of error, will have tasted the bitter fruit of hatred and violence....'

"I did not hesitate to give a negative answer to the question whether I was converted in gratitude to Pius XII for his numberless acts of charity. Nevertheless, I do feel the duty of rendering homage and of affirming that the charity of the Gospel was the light that showed the way to my old and weary heart. It is the charity that so often shines in the history of the Church and which radiated fully in the actions of the reigning Pontiff."[2] No doubt the vicious attack on Rabbi Zolli by authors Robert G. Weisbord and Wallace P. Sillanpoa, in *The Chief Rabbi, the Pope, and the Holocaust: An Era in Vatican-Jewish Relations,* was prompted by his conversion and support of Pope Pius XII.

Pope Paul VI

In 1963, Giovanni Battista Montini, who served as Vatican Pro-Secretary of State during World War II, was elected to the Papacy and took the name of Pope Paul VI. On March 12, 1964, for the unveiling of Pope Pius XII's monument in the Vatican Basilica, Paul VI recalled the great Pontiff: "More than anyone else could possibly be, We were blessed that We had the good fortune and honor of many years of intimate and daily conversations, while offering him our humble and faithful service. We, though inadequate in our discipleship, enjoyed his confidence, trust, and affability, witnessing with admiration his absolute dedication to his apostolic office, which he understood and constantly reflected on with untiring awareness. We can testify to the meekness of his soul, firm, of complex depth, often restored by his own solitary meditations, which revealed the purity of his religious piety. In all candor, he was not inclined toward external religious ceremonies, but rather drew his strength from private prayers and personal devotions. We can still vividly recall the incomparable vigor of his intelligence, the exceptional power of his memory, the admirable versatility of his spirit, his phenomenal capacity for work—in spite of his slender body and delicate health. We witnessed his rare capacity to pay attention and take care of little things in the course of perfectly carrying out the substantial formal tasks of his work, while simultaneously and ever-vigilantly attending to great concerns which were ceaselessly engaging him.

"We were able to observe the delicate manifestations of his fearless sense of responsibility, evident in all the affairs that crowded in on his shining awareness—in study, research, or striving to perceive all things in light of eternity, in light of the divine will. With rigorous respect for his apostolic mandate, with profound love for the Church, with careful consideration how not to offend anyone, and possibly to edify everyone, he often embarked on a difficult, arduous at first almost incomprehensible course, which gradually became an unmistakably clear and unalterable starting point for carrying out his sacred duty....

"One cannot blame the Pope for indifference, cowardice, or egoism because countless evils devastated humanity. Whoever says otherwise would mock truth and justice. Even if the results Pius XII achieved by his studies, trials, prayers and humanitarian-peacemaking efforts did not match what he hoped to accomplish and the needs of others, he was not mistaken in entering into the tragedy of iniquity, sorrow and blood of a world tortured by war and engulfed by the fury of oppression and totalitarianism.

"To remember him is mercy, to acknowledge him is justice. To follow his teachings and his example will be a comfort, and to think of him being close to us, still a friend, still teacher, still father, in the communion of Saints, will give us all unfailing hope...."

In a discourse given in Jerusalem,[3] Pope Paul VI stated: "We nurture only benevolent thoughts toward all peoples as did Our predecessor Pius XII, sentiments that he manifested at various times during the world conflict, something that all have been able to witness and above all those who have been helped by him. We are pleased to have the occasion to dissipate the misunderstanding in this regard, having been close to and having known this venerable Man, whose delicacy of soul was appreciated by all those who, after the war, visited him in order to thank him for having saved their lives."

Belgium

According to Minister Paul von Zeeland, Pope Pius XII was considered the defender of the poor, the oppressed, the persecuted. He recalled that only the Supreme Pontiff protested Germany's aggression in Belgium, Luxemburg, and Holland. Count Moens de Fernig stated: "Pope Pius XII was, during this period of darkness, a ray of light that permitted us to hope in the return of freedom."

On May 12, 1940, King Leopold of Belgium sent the following telegram to His Holiness, Pope Pius XII: "Grateful for the telegram that Your Holiness addressed to me, following the terrible aggression that we have endured. Thank you profoundly in my name and in the name of all the people of Belgium."

Bulgaria

Archbishop Angelo Giuseppe Roncalli, Apostolic Delegate of the Holy See at Istanbul and the future Pope John XXIII, was a man of lofty spiritual stature, truly concerned about the people who were suffering. He spared no effort on behalf of the Jews of Central Europe and the Balkans.

While in Bulgaria, Archbishop Roncalli, who developed a warm friendship with King Boris II and Queen Giovanna (daughter of the King of Italy), reacted with horror and indignation upon hearing about the deportations and other atrocities committed by the Nazis. In consonance with Pius XII's directives, he sent thousands of immigration certificates, including Palestine immigration papers that he had obtained from the British, to Monsignor Angelo Rotta, the Papal Nuncio in Budapest. Roncalli declared that he was happy to do anything of a nonpolitical nature to assist him. As an emergency measure to guarantee safety, within months hundreds of Jews were "baptized" in the air-raid shelters of Budapest. Others escaped to Palestine, thanks to the immigration certificates forwarded by the Archbishop. Because of the "safe-conduct" passes issued by Monsignor Rotta, many Jews survived the Holocaust in Budapest.

Denmark

The Lutheran Bishop, Dr. Fuglsang-Damgaard, affirmed the need to preserve the freedom of the Jews in the democratic and peaceful country of Denmark. Until October 1943, when the exodus of seven thousand Jews was organized, the Danish Jews were independent. With the greatest secrecy, they all arrived safely in Sweden.

According to Raul Hilberg in the book, *Perpetrators Victims Bystanders: The Jewish Catastrophe 1933–1945:* "The relatively small number was manageable, but the operation was nevertheless unique, because it had been assembled by all sorts of people spontaneously in haste, and because there were neither Danish police upon whom the Germans could rely for help nor an appreciable number of informers who were prepared to betray the undertaking."[4]

Denmark shares with Italy the distinction of having saved the highest percentage of Jews.

Finland

In 1943, the government of Helsinki gratefully acknowledged the help received from Pope Pius XII, who had delegated the Apostolic Vicar, Monsignor William Gobben, to distribute 450,000 marks among the poor children, internees, and Russian prisoners of war. The people of Finland did not consider this act of His Holiness a matter of diplomacy, but rather an expression of his profound understanding and concern.

France

Jews who claimed citizenship of either the United States or Latin American nations were confined in the German concentration camp at Vittel, France. They had been transferred from Germany to France with the hope that they could be exchanged for Germans interned in the Western hemisphere. However, because in many cases their documents appeared to have been illegally obtained, the Latin American governments withdrew recognition of the passports. The Vatican urged that this rejection of the documents be suspended and sent circular instructions to the nunciatures, directing them to solicit from the respective governments continued recognition of the passports, "no matter how illegally obtained." The Jews were transferred to Drancy.

Ralph Stewart, a Canadian Catholic diplomat and scholar, speaks about Father Michel Riquet, S.J., and his efforts to save Jewish families in France in his book, *Pope Pius XII and the Jews.*[5] The priest was imprisoned in Dachau, where he continued to help persecuted Jews and fight Nazi violence.

In his memoirs (1940–1944), *Christian Resistance to Anti-Semitism,*[6] Henri Cardinal de Lubac, a great anti-Nazi theologian, discussed Pius XII's influence on Catholic rescuers of Jews. He recalled how Grand Rabbi Kaplan, after Cardinal Gerlier's death, concluded in a broadcast of *Ecoute Israel:* "Justice, according to our Sacred Book, is more than justice. The Just One, for us, is as much a man of goodness as one of equity, a man of piety as one of charity. In the same spirit, Judaism, in numerous texts, mentions the 'just from among the nations.' Cardinal Gerlier was one of those. He occupied a place of honor among them. This is why his memory will always remain present in our community. As we read in the Talmud: 'The just, after their death, continue to exist in thoughts and in hearts.'"[7]

Germany

"The Church did not submit to Germany," wrote Paolo Vincentin in an article that appeared in *L'Osservatore Romano* in 1965. "We who were members of the German Embassy, although we judged the situation differently, were in complete accord on one point: a solemn protest by Pius XII against the persecution of the Jews, probably would have exposed him and the Roman Curia to great danger and certainly then, in the autumn of 1943, he would not have been able to save the life of a single Jew."

Holland

Wilhelmina, Queen of Holland, answered Pius XII's telegram on May 11, 1940: "I sincerely thank Your Holiness for your message of concern about our welfare and for your prayers that justice and freedom will be re-established. Confiding in God, my people are resolved to contribute with all their strength to the accomplishment of final triumph."

Hungary

"Remain in Hungary to perform a work of Charity" were the words of Pius XII to Archbishop Angelo Rotta, who hid Jews in the

Nunciature in Budapest, distributing over five-hundred passes per day. He did not leave his post until the arrival of the Russians in Budapest. The Nunciature had been bombed and half of it destroyed. When the German general departed, he bequeathed ten thousand wounded German soldiers to this church official saying, "Take care of them, the way you cared for the others."

Archbishop Rotta's records give no indication that he or the Jewish community in Budapest knew the real significance of the wholesale expulsion of the Hungarian Jews. On the theme of deportation, Rotta wrote: "It is said that it is not a question of deportation, but of compulsory labor. It is possible to discuss about the words; but the reality is the same. When old men of over seventy and even over eighty, old women, children and sick persons are taken away, one wonders for what work these human beings can be used?"

Luxemburg

On May 14, 1940, Charlotte, the Grand Duchess of Luxemburg, wrote to Pope Pius XII: "Profoundly moved by the affectionate and comforting testimonial that Your Holiness sent me in the midst of the tragedy that has befallen Luxemburg, I express to Your Holiness our most filial acknowledgment. Confiding in the protection of the Patroness of my dear Country and in the generous help of the Allied Powers, we unite ourselves in prayer with Your Holiness and hope that my Country and my People will soon obtain independence and freedom."

Poland

Monsignor Walerian Meystowicz, President of the Institute of Polish Historical Studies, was able to experience the solicitude and the concern with which the Holy See worked in favor of the persecuted Jews. "The Nazis persecuted the Jews in Poland with great brutality. The number exterminated was enormous: perhaps three million. But the Nazis also persecuted Catholics and the number killed was greater. Jews and Catholics were in the same situation, with one difference: Catholic resistance was active especially in the first phase, while many Jews had a passive attitude."

Sweden

Gunnar Hagglof stated that he never met another person who was able to predict developments over the next ten to fifteen years as Pius XII had done. Some of his predictions were verified only during the pontificates of his successors. However, it was not his political perspicacity that impressed Hagglof, who wrote: "It was his manner of discussion, his passionate nature and the fire in his eyes. He was an ascetic, an intellectual, a hermit, a person who lives only for his ideas, for his religious ideas. Purity of heart is the appropriate expression that describes him."

[For additional documents that testify to the work of Pius XII in favor of the persecuted Jews, as well as documents from Jewish organizations acknowledging his accomplishments in saving the lives of thousands of Jews and other refugees, cf. appendix.]

E. Epilogue

Although this book celebrates Pope Pius XII as the personification of faith in a terror-torn world and as a bulwark of peace, I feel compelled to address one particular point of contention that has emerged in recent times.

Allegations that Pope Pius XII could have done more to avert the consequences of the Nazis' atrocities by "confrontation" rather than by "diplomacy" are distorted and untrue. Correspondence reveals that world Jewish organizations knew from bitter experience that such "confrontation" had ill effects. Pius XII was one of the best friends the Jews had during World War II. Explicit condemnations or even a public rebuke would have sabotaged rescue operations and provoked more brutal reprisals.

That the documentary record of the humanitarian work of the Holy See addresses every means of protesting—as is learned by reviewing thousands of available documents, including the efforts of the Papal Information Bureau—cannot be denied.

Before the war, the Pope sent an appeal to the American bishops urging them to receive and help the refugees, many of whom were scholars of repute, driven out of Germany on racial or political grounds. In 1941, however, the Gestapo assumed absolute authority in its resolution of the Jewish question, and a new form of man's inhumanity to man emerged: the liquidation of European Jews.

Nazi Germany also considered the Catholic Church to be a serious threat to its domestic security and its international ambitions. Hitler's agents recruited informants to report back the political views and activities of bishops and priests. The Nazis systematically intercepted, decoded, and read secret communications between the Pope and his representatives worldwide. In Rome, however, German attempts to penetrate the Papacy were not often successful.

Since the Holocaust, many books have been written about the six million Jewish victims; less attention has been given to the almost equal number of non-Jews who were killed by the Nazis: a total of over eleven million victims.

No concerned human being could question the enormity of the pain inflicted on the Jews by the Holocaust. But that great loss should not rule out just commemoration of all victims of Nazis and Communists, and other innocent victims of brutality and ethnic cleansing past, present, and future around the world.

It is time to right the injustice toward Pope Pius XII, who saved more Jews than any other person, including Oskar Schindler and Raoul Wallenberg. Through public discourses, appeals to governments, and secret diplomacy, the Pope more than any other person in his era sought to curb the war and rebuild peace.

From early 1939, Pius XII's fatherly concern was extended to all victims. He consistently pursued his goal, and the Vatican became a beam of hope as he alleviated suffering and protected human life and human rights. His diplomacy and humanitarian works made him a champion of peace, of compassion, and of human dignity.

In the past, the Israelis defended the name of Pope Pius XII according to the *Jewish Chronicle* (London) on October 11, 1963. A former member of the British Eighth Army's Jewish Refugee Committee in Italy from 1943 to 1945, Jewish historian Pinchas E. Lapide, later Israeli Consul General in Milan, collected documents for more than twenty years. In his book, *Three Popes and the Jews,* Lapide concluded: "The Catholic Church, under the pontificate of Pius XII, was instrumental in saving as many as 860,000 Jews from certain death at Nazi hands....This figure exceeds by far those saved by all other rescue organizations combined. Moreover, this achievement stands in startling contrast to the unpardonable foot-dragging and hypocritical lip-service of those outside Hitler's reach, who certainly disposed of far greater means to rescue Jews including the International Red Cross and the Western democracies in general."[1]

Who can dispute what he said about Pius XII? "Unable to cure the sickness of an entire civilization and unwilling to bear the brunt of Hitler's fury, the Pope, unlike many far mightier than he, alleviated, relieved, retrieved, appealed, petitioned, and saved as best he could by his own lights. Who, but a prophet or a martyr, could have done much more?"

Among the many letters to Pope Pius XII from representatives of a Jewish refugee camp at Ferramonti-Tarsia, in southern Italy, is the following written on October 29, 1944, after the Allied liberation of Italy: "While we have been persecuted and threatened in nearly all European countries, Your Holiness, through His Eminence the Apostolic Nuncio, Cardinal Borgongini-Duca, has not only sent generous gifts to our camp but also shows lively and fatherly interest in our physical, spiritual, and moral well-being....When we were threatened with deportation to Poland in 1942, Your Holiness extended a protective, fatherly hand and foiled the deportation of the Jews interned in Italy, thus saving us from almost certain death."

C. L. Sulzberger, a Pulitzer Prize–winning journalist and a scion of the family who owns the *New York Times,* underscores the inappropriate charges being addressed to Pius XII when he writes in his book, *Go Gentle into the Night,* that "Pope Pius XII the one pontiff with whom I was truly acquainted, was an interesting man who, after 1945, came in for what almost surely is an unfair amount of criticism because he didn't stop the conflict Hitler started and because he didn't do more to save Europe's Jews from Nazi extermination."[2]

On November 30, 1988, Timothy T. O'Donnell made a private tour of the gardens of Castelgandolfo and visited the ruins of the palace of the Emperor Tiberius under the papal residence. He learned that, during the Second World War, in those hidden chambers, Pope Pius XII hid thousands of Jews who were to be deported to German concentration camps. On the walls one can still see the darkened ash where these fugitives from the Nazis lit fires to cook food and keep warm.

In the dark stillness of this subterranean vault stands an enormous wooden cross, beautifully decorated. This Christian symbol of suffering love was given to Pius XII at the end of the war by the Jews who lived there during those terrifying days. It was their way of expressing their deep gratitude and veneration for this Pope who had heroically defied the Gestapo and had saved their lives. Such heroism and such gratitude must not be dishonored.

No better tribute can be paid to Pope Pius XII than the fact that in the encyclical *Pacem in Terris,* Pope John XXIII repeated the words of his predecessor: *"Nothing is lost by peace; everything may be lost by war* [italics added]."[3]

In the same encyclical John XXIII reminded the world about the statement that Pius XII had made in his radio broadcast on Christmas Eve in 1941, that "in the field of a new order founded on moral principles, there is no room for violation of freedom, integrity and security."

Pope Pius XII's words were reported in *The Tablet* of London and may well be applied to present-day media: "That which seems to us not only the greatest evil but the root of all evil is this—often the lie is substituted for the truth and is then used as an instrument of dispute."

The Pope's role was recognized by his contemporaries. On October 15, 1944, John W. Pehle[4] delivered a very important speech in Boston. He explained that the purpose of the War Refugee Board was to strengthen agencies by giving them the support of a statement of sympathetic policy from the government and by using the diplomatic, licensing, and communication facilities of the United States government to help them achieve their welfare ends.

Pehle paid tribute to many non-Jewish groups and individuals who had shown a true Christian spirit in their friendly reaction in support of the helpless of Europe. He stated: "The record of the Catholic Church in this regard has been inspiring. All over Europe, Catholic priests have furnished hiding places and protection to the persecuted. His Holiness, Pope Pius XII, has interceded on many occasions in behalf of refugees in danger."

Indeed, there appears to be a concerted effort to undermine the Church, the Vatican, and the canonization of Pope Pius XII. What more effective way to smear the Catholic Church than to accuse it of condoning or being apathetic to the Nazi Holocaust?

New and violent attacks constantly continue to falsify history and well-known facts. Richard Cohen's syndicated column dealing with canonization—an internal Catholic rite—is neither appropriate nor informed.[5] His charge is that Pope John Paul II is seeking to "shrink" the importance of the Holocaust by his "questionable choices for sainthood" and that this Pontiff's effort to apply historic truth to the wartime role of Pius XII toward the Jews and to promote his cause for sainthood "seems an attempt to pardon the wartime church for its thundering silence as the Jews of Europe were being slaughtered." Such attacks are irresponsible and based on falsehoods. No doubt, such false statements can engender the same hateful feelings that in the past have led to both anti-Catholicism and anti-Semitism.

The canonization process of the Catholic Church is a long, pains-taking search for truth, relating to whether the candidate had the unblemished character and led the highly exemplary Christian life required for sainthood.

At a press conference in Rome on November 3, 1998, the Ambas-sador of Israel to the Holy See, Aharon Lopez demanded that the Cause of Pope Pius XII be delayed. Archbishop Jean-Louis Tauran, the Vati-can's chief foreign-affairs officer, cautioned that the process of beatifi-cation is an internal Church affair, not subject to political influences. He also reiterated that all of the archival material relating directly to the Holocaust had already been made public.

In a letter to Margherita Marchione, dated December 26, 1998, Michael Bobrow, an American Jew and foreign correspondent in the Holy Land in the late 1960s, stated that "the canonization of Pope Pius XII would be an act of supreme justice, charity, and truth....The increasing slanderous attacks on Pope Pius XII by both Jews and Gen-tiles (including some renegade "Catholics") have nothing really to do with Holocaust history, but have everything to do with the present cul-tural war: A determined effort to discredit the Church because of its leading role in the abortion and euthanasia issues, as well as its opposi-tion to pornography and its defense of traditional family values."

In the late 1940s and 1950s, there were no "organized" efforts to undermine morality (abortion and gay marriage were unthinkable, and there was legal censorship against pornography). The attacks on Pius XII, starting with the play *The Deputy,* began in the early 1960s, when Judeo-Christian moral and family values declined.

During World War II, Pope Pius XII was universally praised for his humanitarian efforts. While we can readily forgive the misin-formed, we obviously cannot exonerate the secularist, liberal leaders who are fomenting this defamation of the Catholic Church.

On October 15, 1944, the *New York Times* published an article by Herbert L. Matthews, "Happier Days for Pope Pius: Shadows of war are lifting for a Pontiff whose greatest interest is world peace." In it the well-known journalist summarized the Pope's peace plan based upon the five points he first put forth in his Christmas speech of 1939: "These proposals contained, among other things, the defense of small nations, the right to live, disarmament, some new kind of league of nations and a plea for the moral principles of justice and love. The same themes were re-emphasized in the Pontiff's first important pronouncement after the

United States was at war—his Christmas speech of 1941—and to this day they remain the basis of the Vatican's program."

It is consoling to know that there are countless courageous Jewish survivors who acknowledge the help received from the Catholic Church. Marianne Sann of New Rochelle, New York, a Jewish survivor of Auschwitz, was disturbed by the feud over the crosses there and expressed her thoughts in a letter to the *New York Times*.[6] She vigorously defended the Catholic Church and maintained that Roman Catholic Poles "felt the icy winds of doom" just as acutely as she did and deserve a cross of remembrance and a place of honor among their fellow Jewish victims.

As a Jewish survivor, she attested to the fact that she was saved by Catholic fellow prisoners, at their great personal risk in Auschwitz and again in Mauthausen, Austria; she suggested finding bridges to better understanding, rather than continuing such "mean-spirited bickering" that will only "promote anti-Semitism."

During an interview, Kaz J. Dyner of St. Davids, Pennsylvania, related his experience of love and brotherhood: "Pope Pius XII and the Catholic Church indeed helped Jews and other people during World War II, and saved lives. I was one of them. As an escapee from a POW camp in Germany, with the help of an 'underground army' and the Catholic Church, I found a hiding place in the Vatican. I spent about one year there....The Chief Rabbi of Rome [Israel Zolli] was also hiding in the Vatican."

Indeed, it is time to right the injustice toward Pope Pius XII and to promote the truth about his role with respect to the Holocaust. Vatican documents show that Pope Pius XII not only condemned Nazi atrocities but also aided the persecuted Jews by operating an underground railroad, rescuing European Jews from the Holocaust.

The Holocaust was both anti-Jewish and anti-Christian, and far from being Christian in origin, Nazism was pagan and racist.

Many times during the horrors of the Holocaust, Pius XII faced agonizing decisions. He made judgments based on his knowledge of the conditions of the times and after intense prayer and reflection. Guiding his actions was the determination to serve God and to avoid anything that would cause more innocent victims. He was totally committed as a kind and loving father to all, regardless of race or religion. Chief among the goals that he prayed and labored to achieve was peace.

How does one explain the vicious attack on the Pontiff several years after his death in 1958? Was anti-Catholicism revived by the cultural changes that took place in the 1960s? Apparently, the Church was perceived as an instrument of repression against the freedom of individuals. Television, with a few sound bites, a careful selection of images, and the comments of "experts" generally hostile to the Pope, established in the younger generation's imagination the notion of a "silent" Pope in the midst of the human tragedy of the Shoah. Did centuries-old Western prejudice play a role in the negative reevaluation of Pius XII?

Pius XII, with great courage and compassion, led bishops, nuncios, priests, religious, and laity in saving hundreds of thousands of Jewish lives during the World War II era. This truth is supported by overwhelming evidence provided by historians, including reputable Jewish writers, as well as the many messages of unanimous praise and deep gratitude from worldwide Jewish leaders toward Pope Pius XII.

It is time to put an end to the calumny—which began in 1963 with the play *The Deputy* by Rolf Hochhuth—regarding Pius XII's alleged "silence." It is time to distinguish between fiction and fact established beyond a reasonable doubt: to reject the former and accept the latter.

The recent *We Remember: A Reflection on the Shoah* of the Catholic Church is the most significant and timely statement in support of the truth of the enormity of the Holocaust that resulted in the extermination of millions of Jews, only because they were Jews, as well as an almost equal number of non-Jews.

In accepting the Nobel Peace Prize (1986), Elie Wiesel—who was a child when he was sent to Auschwitz—reaffirmed his commitment to humankind: "I believe that we must have hope for one another also because of one another....I believe that because of our children and their children we should be worthy of that hope, of that redemption and of some measure of peace." He added: "Not all victims were Jews, but all Jews were victims....They were doomed not because of something they had done or proclaimed or acquired but because of who they were."[7]

Primo Levi, another Jewish author and a survivor, was convinced that the lessons of the Holocaust would be lost among the routine atrocities of history. Jews and Catholics pray this will not be so. Their prayer is for understanding and peace as they seek the ideal of one world, regardless of different races and ethnic groups, with love for one another, with hope in the integrity of future generations, and with faith in the Almighty Father of all.

Time is the unfolding of truth. One reads in Ecclesiasticus (3:1–8) that "there is an appointed time for everything, and a time for every affair."

It is time to stop the cruel attacks and to celebrate Pope Pius XII's eternal goodness.

Part III
The Pope and the Horror of the Holocaust

A. *Pope Pius XII's Appeal for World Peace*

(The following is the Pope's message of June 2, 1945, to the Cardinals on the condition of the Church after the surrender of Germany.)

A s we very gratefully acknowledge, venerable brethren, the good wishes which the venerable and beloved dean of the Sacred College has offered to us on your behalf, our thoughts bring us back to this day six years ago when you offered your congratulations on our feast day for the first time after we, though unworthy, had been raised to the See of Peter.

The world was then still at peace: but what a peace and how very precarious!

With a heart full of anguish, perplexed, praying, we bent over that peace like one that assists a dying man and fights obstinately to save him from death even when all hope is gone.

The message which we then addressed to you reflected our sorrowful apprehension that the conflict which was ever growing more menacing would break out—a conflict whose extent and duration nobody could foresee. The subsequent march of events has not only justified all too clearly our saddest premonitions but has far surpassed them.

Today, after six years, the fratricidal struggle has ended in one section of this war-torn world. It is a peace—if you can call it such—as yet very fragile, which cannot endure or be consolidated except by expending on it the most assiduous care; a peace whose maintenance imposes on the whole church, both pastor and faithful, grave and very delicate duties; patient prudence, courageous fidelity, the spirit of sacrifice!

All are called upon to devote themselves to it, each in his own office and at his own place. Nobody can bring to this task too much anxiety or zeal. As to us and our apostolic ministry, we well know, venerable brethren, that we can safely count on your sage collaboration, your unceasing prayers, your steadfast devotion.

I. The Church and National Socialism

In Europe the war is over; but what wounds has it not inflicted! Our Divine Master has said: "All that take the sword shall perish with the sword" (Matthew 26, 52).

Now what do you see? You see what is the result of a concept of the State reduced to practice which takes no heed of the most sacred ideals of mankind, which overthrows the inviolable principles of the Christian faith. The whole world today contemplates with stupefaction the ruins that it has left behind it. These ruins we had seen when they were still in the distant future, and few, we believe, have followed with greater anxiety the process leading to the inevitable crash.

For over twelve years—twelve of the best years of our mature age—we had lived in the midst of the German people, fulfilling the duties of the office committed to us. During that time, in the atmosphere of liberty which the political and social conditions of that time allowed, we worked for consolidation of the status of the Catholic Church in Germany.

We thus had occasion to learn the great qualities of the people and we were personally in close contact with its most representative men. For that reason we cherish the hope that it can rise to the new dignity and new life when once it has laid the satanic specter raised by National Socialism and the guilty (as we have already at other times had occasion to expound) have expiated the crimes they have committed.

While there was still some faint glimmer of hope that that movement could take another and less disastrous course either through the disillusionment of its more moderate members or through effective opposition from that section of the German people which opposed it, the church did everything possible to set up a formidable barrier to the spread of ideas at once subversive and violent.

In the spring of 1933 the German Government asked the Holy See to conclude a concordat with the Reich: the proposal had the approval of the Episcopate and of at least the greater number of the German Catholics.

In fact, they thought that neither the concordats up to then negotiated with some individual German states nor the Weimar Constitution gave adequate guarantee or assurance of respect for their convictions, for their faith, rights or liberty of action.

In such conditions the guarantees could not be secured except through a settlement having the solemn form of a concordat with the Central Government of the Reich.

It should be added that, since it was the Government that made the proposal, the responsibility for all regrettable consequences would have fallen on the Holy See if it had refused the proposed concordat.

Concordat Helpful

It was not that the church, for her part, had any illusions built on excessive optimism or that, in concluding the concordat, she had the intention of giving any form of approval to the teachings or tendencies of National Socialism; this was expressly declared and explained at the time (Cf. *L'Osservatore Romano,* No. 174, July 2, 1933). It must, however, be recognized that the concordat in the years that followed brought some advantages or at least prevented worse evils.

In fact, in spite of all the violations to which it was subjected, it gave Catholics a juridical basis for their defense, a stronghold behind which to shield themselves in their opposition—as long as this was possible—to the ever growing campaign of religious persecution.

The struggle against the church did, in fact, become ever more bitter; there was the dissolution of Catholic organizations; the gradual suppression of the flourishing Catholic schools, both public and private; the enforced weaning of youth from family and church; the pressure brought to bear on the conscience of citizens and especially of civil servants; the systematic defamation, by means of a clever, closely organized propaganda, of the church, the clergy, the faithful, the church's institutions, teaching and history; the closing, dissolution and confiscation of religious houses and other ecclesiastical institutions; the complete suppression of the Catholic press and publishing houses.

Nazism Decried

To resist such attacks millions of courageous Catholics, men and women, closed their ranks around their Bishops, whose valiant and severe pronouncements never failed to resound even in these last years of war. These Catholics gathered around their priests to help them adapt their ministry to the ever changing needs and conditions. And right up to the end they set up against the forces of impiety and pride their forces of faith, prayer and openly Catholic behavior and education.

In these critical years, joining the alert vigilance of a pastor in the long suffering patience of a father, our great predecessor, Pius XI, fulfilled his mission as Supreme Pontiff with intrepid courage. But when, after he had tried all means of persuasion in vain, he saw himself clearly faced with deliberate violations of solemn pact, with a religious persecution masked or open but always rigorously organized, he proclaimed to the world on Passion Sunday, 1937, in his encyclical *Mit brennender Sorge* what National Socialism really was: the arrogant apostasy from Jesus Christ, the denial of His doctrine and of His work of redemption, the cult of violence, the idolatry of race and blood, the overthrow of human liberty and dignity.

Papal Call

Like a clarion call that sounds the alarm, the Papal document with its vigorous terms—too vigorous, thought more than one at the time—startled the minds and hearts of men. Many—even beyond the frontiers of Germany—who up to then had closed their eyes to the incompatibility of the National Socialist viewpoint with the teachings of Christ had to recognize and confess their mistake. Many—but not all! Some even among the faithful themselves were too blinded by their prejudices or allured by political advantage.

The evidence of the facts brought forward by our predecessor did not convince them, much less induce them to change their ways. Is it mere chance that some regions, which later suffered more from the National Socialist system, were precisely those where the encyclical *Mit brennender Sorge* was less or not at all heeded?

Would it then have been possible, by opportune and timely political action, to block once and for all the outbreak of brutal violence and to put the German people in the position to shake off the tentacles that were strangling it? Would it have been possible thus to have saved Europe and the world from this immense inundation of blood? Nobody would dare to give an unqualified judgment.

But in any case nobody could accuse the church of not having denounced and exposed in time the true nature of the National Socialist movement and the danger to which it exposed Christian civilization.

"Whoever sets up race or the people or the state or a particular form of state or the depositaries' power or any other fundamental value of the human community to be the supreme norm of all, even of religious values, and divinizes them to an idolatrous level distorts and perverts an order of the world planned and created by God" (Cf. *Acta Apostolica Sedis,* Vol. XXIX, 1937, pages 149 and 171).

The radical opposition of the National Socialist State to the Catholic Church is summed up in this declaration of the encyclical. When things had reached this point the church could not without foregoing her mission any longer refuse to take her stand before the whole world.

But by doing so she became once again "a sign which shall be contradicted" (Luke 2, 34), in the presence of which contrasting opinions divided off into two opposed camps.

German Catholics were, one may say, as one in recognizing that the encyclical *Mit brennender Sorge* had brought light, direction, consolation and comfort to all those who seriously meditated and conscientiously practiced the religion of Christ. But the reaction of those who had been inculpated was inevitable, and, in fact, that very year, 1937, was for the Catholic Church in Germany a year of indescribable bitterness and terrible outbreaks.

Opposition Intensified

The important political events which marked the two following years and then the war did not bring any attenuation to the hostility of National Socialism toward the church, an hostility which was manifest up to these last months, when National Socialists still flattered themselves with the idea that once they had secured victory in arms they could do away with the church forever.

Authoritative and absolutely trustworthy witnesses kept us informed of these plans—they unfolded themselves actually in the reiterated and ever more intense activity against the church in Austria, Alsace-Lorraine and, above all, in those parts of Poland which had already been incorporated in the old Reich during the war: there everything was attacked and destroyed; that is, everything that could be reached by external violence.

Continuing the work of our predecessor, we ourselves have during the war and especially in our radio messages constantly set forth the demands and perennial laws of humanity and of the Christian faith in modern scientific methods to torture or eliminate people who were often innocent.

This was for us the most opportune—and we might even say the only—efficacious way of proclaiming before the world the immutable principles of the moral law and of confirming, in the midst of so much error and violence, the minds and hearts of German Catholics, in the higher ideals of truth and justice. And our solicitude was not without its effect. Indeed, we know that our messages and especially that of Christmas, 1942, despite every prohibition and obstacle, were studied in the diocesan clergy conferences in Germany and then expounded and explained to the Catholic population.

If the rulers of Germany had decided to destroy the Catholic Church even in the old Reich, Providence had decided otherwise. The tribulations inflicted on the church by National Socialism have been brought to an end through the sudden and tragic end of the persecution! From the prisons, concentration camps and fortresses are now pouring out, together with the political prisoners, also the crowds of those whether clergy or laymen, whose only crime was their fidelity to Christ and to the faith of their fathers or the dauntless fulfillment of their duties as priests.

For them all of us have prayed and have seized every opportunity, whenever the occasion offered, to send them a word of comfort and blessing from our paternal heart.

Polish Priests Suffered Worst

Indeed, the more the veils are drawn which up to now hid the sorrowful passion of the church under the National Socialist regime, the more apparent becomes the strength, often steadfast unto death, of numberless Catholics and the glorious share in that noble contest which belonged to the clergy.

Although as yet not in possession of the complete statistics, we cannot refrain from recalling here, by way of example, some details from the abundant accounts which have reached us from priests and laymen who were interned in the concentration camp of Dachau and were accounted worthy to suffer reproach for the name of Jesus (Acts 5, 41).

In the forefront, for the number and harshness of the treatment meted out to them, are the Polish priests. From 1940 to 1945, 2,800 Polish ecclesiastics and religious were imprisoned in that camp; among them was a Polish auxiliary bishop who died there of typhus. In April last there were left only 816, all the others being dead except for two or three transferred to another camp.

In the summer of 1942, 480 German-speaking ministers of religion were known to be gathered there; of these, forty-five were Protestants, all the others Catholic priests. In spite of the continuous inflow of new internees, especially from some dioceses of Bavaria, the Rhineland and Westphalia, their number, as a result of the high rate of mortality, at the beginning of this year did not surpass 350.

Nor should we pass over in silence those belonging to occupied territories, Holland, Belgium, France—among whom the Bishop of Clermont), Luxemburg, Slovenia, Italy.

Many of those priests and laymen endured indescribable sufferings for their faith and for their vocation.

In one case the hatred of the impious against Christ reached the point of parodying on the person of an interned priest, with barbed wire, the scourging and the crowning with thorns of our Redeemer.

The generous victims who during the twelve years since 1933 have in Germany sacrificed for Christ and his church their possessions, their freedom, their lives, are raising their hands to God in expiatory sacrifice. May the just Judge accept it in reparation for the many crimes committed against mankind no less than against the present and future generation and especially against the unfortunate youth of Germany, and may He at last stay the arm of the exterminating angel.

With ever-increasing persistence National Socialism strove to denounce the church as the enemy of the German people. The manifest injustice of the accusation would have deeply offended the sentiment of German Catholics and our own if it had come from other lips. But on the lips of such accusers, so far from being a grievance, the accusation is the clearest and most honorable testimony to the strong, incessant opposition maintained by the church to such disastrous doctrines and methods in the interest of true civilization and of the German people; to that people we offer the wish that, freed now from the error which plunged it into chaos, it may find again its own salvation at the pure fountains of true peace and true happiness, at the fountains of truth, humility and charity flowing with the church from the heart of Christ.

II. Looking to the Future

A hard-learnt lesson surely, that of these past years! God grant at least, that it may have been understood and be profitable to other nations!

"Receive instruction, you that judge the earth!" (Psalm 2, 10).

That is the most ardent wish of all who sincerely love mankind. For mankind, now the victim of an impious process of exhaustion, of cynical disregard for the life and rights of men, has but one aspiration: to lead a tranquil and pacific life in dignity and honest toil. And to this purpose it hopes that an end will be put to that insolence with which the family and the domestic hearth have been abused and profaned during the war years.

For that insolence cries to heaven and has evolved into one of the gravest perils not only for religion and morality but also for harmonious relations between men. It has, above all, created those mobs of dispossessed, disillusioned, disappointed and hopeless men who are going to swell the ranks of revolution and disorder, in the pay of a tyranny no less despotic than those for whose overthrow men planned.

The nations, and notably the medium and small nations, claim the right to take their destinies into their own hands. They can be led to assume, with their full and willing consent, the interest of common progress, obligations which will modify their sovereign rights.

End to War Game

But after having sustained their share—their large share—of suffering in order to overthrow a system of brutal violence, they are entitled to refuse to accept a new political or cultural system which is decisively rejected by the great majority of their people. They maintain, and with reason, that the primary task of the peace-framers is to put an end to the criminal war game and to safeguard vital rights and mutual obligations as between the great and small, powerful and weak.

Deep in their hearts the peoples feel that their rule would be discredited if they did not succeed in supplanting the mad folly of the rule of violence by the victory of the right.

The thought of a new peace organization is inspired—nobody could doubt it—by the most sincere and loyal good will. The whole of mankind follows the progress of this noble enterprise with anxious interest. What a bitter disillusionment it would be if it were to fail, if so many years of suffering and self-sacrifice were to be made vain, by permitting again to prevail that spirit of oppression from which the world hoped to see itself at last freed once and for all!

Poor world, to which then might be applied the words of Christ: "And the last state of that man becomes worse than the first" (Luke 11, 24–26).

The present political and social situation suggests these words of warning to us. We have had, alas, to deplore in more than one region the murder of priests, deportations of civilians, the killing of citizens without trial or in personal vendetta. No less sad is the news that has reached us from Slovenia and Croatia.

But we will not lose heart. The speeches made by competent and responsible men in the course of the last few weeks made it clear that they are aiming at the triumph of right, not merely as a political goal but even more as a moral duty.

Accordingly, we confidently issue an ardent appeal for prayers to our sons and daughters of the whole world. May it reach all those who recognize in God the beloved Father of all men created to his image and likeness, to all who know that in the breast of Christ there beats a divine heart rich in mercy, deep and inexhaustible fountain of all good and all love, of all peace and all reconciliation.

From the cessation of hostilities to true and genuine peace, as we warned not long ago, the road will be long and arduous, too long for the pent-up aspiration of mankind starving for order and calm. But it is inevitable that it should be so.

It is even perhaps better thus. It is essential that the tempest of overexcited passions be first let subside: *Motos praestat componere fluctus (Virgil, Aeneid* 1, 135).

It is essential that the hate, the diffidence, the stimuli of an extreme nationalism should give way to the growth of wise counsels, the flowering of peaceful designs, to serenity in the interchange of views and to mutual brotherly comprehension.

May the Holy Spirit, light of intellects, gentle ruler of hearts, deign to hear the prayers of His church and guide in their arduous work those who in accordance with their mandate are striving sincerely despite obstacles and contradictions to reach the goal so universally, so ardently, desired: peace, a peace worthy of the name; a peace built and consolidated in sincerity and loyalty, in justice and reality; a peace of loyal and resolute force to overcome or preclude those economic and social conditions which might, as they did in the past, easily lead to new conflicts; a peace that can be approved by all right-minded men of every people and every nation; a peace which future generations may regard gratefully as the happy outcome of a sad period; a peace that may stand out in the centuries as a resolute advance in the affirmation of human dignity and of ordered liberty; a peace that may be like the *Magna Charta* which closed the dark age of violence; a peace that under the merciful guidance of God may let us so pass through temporal prosperity that we may not lose eternal happiness (Cf. *Collect,* Third Sunday after Pentecost).

But before reaching this peace it still remains true that millions of men at their own fireside or in battle, in prison or in exile must still drink their bitter chalice. How we long to see the end of their sufferings and anguish, the realization of their hopes! For them, too, and for all mankind that suffers with them and in them may our humble and ardent prayer ascend to Almighty God.

Meanwhile, venerable brethren, we are immensely comforted by the thought that you share our anxieties, our prayers, our hopes; and that throughout the world Bishops, priests and faithful are joining their supplications to ours in the great chorus of the universal church.

In testimony of our deep gratitude and as a pledge of infinite mercies and Divine favors, with sincere affection we impart to you, to them, to all who join us in desiring and working for peace, our apostolic benediction.

Pope Pius XII

B. Interview with Peter Gumpel, S.J.

Although the relations between the Holy See and the world Jewish community, including the State of Israel, have arguably never been more cordial than they are today, a number of historians and representatives of Jewish groups continue at every opportunity to launch accusations against the Catholic Church regarding the Church's alleged silence during the Nazi persecution of the Jews in the 1930s and 1940s.

Our reconstruction of events, based on voluminous and diverse historical sources, in fact, suggests that no other head of state or religious leader during this period did as much as Pius XII to save Jews fleeing from Nazi persecution.

Indeed, during and after the Second World War, this was the commonly held view of the Pope, as Pius XII received thanks and honors from the highest authorities of the international Jewish community. The great Jewish physicist Albert Einstein was only one among many when he testified to his appreciation of Pius XII's actions during the 1930s in an article published in *Time* magazine on December 23, 1940. It is not an exaggeration to say that no pontiff in history received as many manifestations of affection from the Jewish community as Pope Pius XII.

Within the Church, the merits of Pope Pius XII are so well known that his cause of beatification has been introduced to canonize his heroic virtue and sanctity. Can this square with the vision of the Pope as a quivering, duplicitous coward?

To clarify such a controversial question and comprehend a historical reality so different from the one presented today in the mass media, *Inside the Vatican* decided to interview Father Peter Gumpel, S.J., relator for the cause of Pius XII at the Vatican's Congregation for the Causes of the Saints.

Gumpel is a quiet, distinguished, thoughtful, immensely learned Jesuit of the old school and one of the Catholic Church's leading authorities on the beatification and canonization processes.

Antonio Gaspari, interviewed Reverend Peter Gumpel, S.J., for *Inside the Vatican:*

Father Gumpel, you are the relator of the cause of beatification of Pope Pius XII. Yet Pius XII has been criticized by many, particularly representatives of Jewish groups, for his conduct before, during, and after World War II. Given such serious criticism, can he really still remain under consideration for beatification by the Church?

FATHER GUMPEL: What I am about to say will perhaps not please the critics of Pius XII. I know very well that some of these critics are in the habit of accusing anyone who says a single word in defense of Pope Pius XII of being Fascist or of having Nazi sympathies. So I would like to preface my remarks by specifying some things: I have many Jewish friends; my family suffered tremendously under Hitler; many members of my family were killed; my mother was imprisoned; I was sent abroad twice so that I, too, would not be a victim of the Nazis. Even if I am going to say something which will not please some Jews, it is not because I and my family were Fascists or Nazis, but simply because I want to honor the truth.

That said, it is in fact true that there are many Jews who today accuse Pius XII, but these accusations were never made when he was alive. There are a very great number of Jews, including many rabbis and representatives of many different Jewish organizations, especially in the United States, who have praised Pius XII and thanked him for what he did during his pontificate. These are people who lived through that period of history, while many of those who today attack Pius XII were very young or even not yet born when Nazism was committing its crimes.

Above and beyond considerations and criticisms of a "political" nature, what were the "heroic virtues" of Pius XII which would argue for his beatification?

FATHER GUMPEL: After having studied all the depositions of all the witnesses in Pius XII's cause, I can say that very rarely have I found evidence so persuasive of heroic virtue. Above all, the theological virtues: faith, hope and charity. Pius XII was a man of very deep faith.

He prayed much, hoped much. He was a man of extraordinary charity, laboring ceaselessly not only for the Jews but for all those who suffered from persecution. Up until the final days of the war and beyond he sought to help the victims of Nazism and Fascism. How many trains loaded with food, clothing, shoes and medical supplies did he send to help the victims of the war?

In keeping with the virtues that he practiced, Pius XII was an extremely sober man. He ate very little, slept only a few hours per night, often working until one or two in the morning before taking a brief nap and rising at six in the morning. He was tireless—just look at the twenty volumes of his writings. Out of solidarity with the miserable conditions of the people he did not drink even a single cup of coffee, knowing the people had no coffee. He knew that heating fuel was in short supply, and he ordered the Papal Apartment to be kept without heat even during the winter. During the war he did not take any vacations and did not go to Castelgandolfo. Sister Pasqualina, his assistant, has said that even his linen was tattered. When Papa Pacelli began his pontificate, he possessed a considerable family patrimony. He spent it all in works of charity.

At the end of the war, his patrimony no longer existed. The sole possessions he had were the household furniture that had been given him as a gift when he left the Nunciature in Germany and his books; other than that he did not have a penny. He never stopped instilling hope in others, even in the most difficult moments, inviting everyone to have faith in the work of the Holy Spirit. Pius XII was a man of profound strength and also of great friendliness.

At what point is Pius XII's cause of beatification?

FATHER GUMPEL: Pius XII's cause of beatification is going quite well. There have been a series of investigations and processes (trials). The principal process has been in Rome; supplementary processes have been held in Genoa, Munich, Berlin, Warsaw, Madrid, Lisbon and Montevideo. More than 100 depositions have been gathered from persons who knew Pope Pius XII personally and represent the entire spectrum of the faithful: many ex-ambassadors who were in the Vatican during the Second World War, some of whom later became Foreign Ministers of their countries. There are cardinals, close collaborators of

Pius XII in the Secretariat of State and in other posts, and ordinary, simple people whom he had met in various countries.

All of this material has been gathered, transcribed and is ready to be printed. In the *positio* that we must submit to the Congregation for the Causes of the Saints, we must also include all the documents that in any way refer to the person, life, activity and reputation for holiness of the servant of God. This is a monumental work, considering that Pius XII even before he was Pope for twenty years was for more than two decades Nuncio and Secretary of State in a particularly confused period of history. In this sense, the cause of Pius XII is at a disadvantage in comparison with other causes, like that of John XXIII, who led the Church for only five years in a much more tranquil period.

From this perspective, our job is extremely complicated and above all we have had to wait for the opening of the archives of various states to find documents relative to the work and activity of Pius XII. We have already visited the Foreign Office of London and there are underway investigations at the State Department in the United States, and what is still more complicated, in the archives of Russia and of the countries occupied by the Russians until a short time ago.

These archives have been open for only a short time, and this explains why we have not yet finished our research.

Despite all this, I can say that the work is going forward rapidly, and in my view and in the view of those who know the status of the cause, the more documents we find, the more the cause of Pius XII is strengthened, and the greater grows our conviction that he was an extraordinary man who faced terrible situations with courage and great wisdom, and who was in his personal life an exemplary Christian, priest, bishop, cardinal and Pope.

In sum, the cause is going forward and the prospects of Pope Pius XII's beatification are excellent.

C. Church, Shoah, and Anti-Semitism

by
Robert A. Graham, S.J.

THE HOLY SEE
FACING THE TRAGEDY OF THE JEWISH PEOPLE

(This unpublished manuscript was written several years ago by Robert A. Graham, S.J., for the Vatican Commission on Religious Relations with the Jews. Copies were distributed at a meeting of Jews and Catholics in Baltimore.)

I. Introduction

1. Examining the Holy See's position and action facing modern Anti-Semitism and the Shoah, one should take into account the recent researches and publications on this theme. From the Catholic side, we may recall Cardinal Willebrands' articles, "The Church Facing Modern Anti-Semitism" (Christian-Jewish Relations, 22.1 [1989]: 5–17) and "The Impact of the Shoah and Catholic-Jewish Relations" (in: *The Church and the Jewish People: New Considerations,* Paulist Press). The International Catholic-Jewish Liaison Committee, established in 1970, at the end of its Prague meeting (September 6, 1990), delivered a joint statement (*Information Service* N. 75 [1990]: 173–178), and most of the papers delivered there are now published in French in *Istina* XXXVI (1991): 225–352.2.

2. The theologian, the biblicist, the philosopher, even the poet has his contribution to make to advance the theme that engages us. The historian has also much to contribute within the limits of the genre. We

do not propose to set forth two thousand years of history but to bring
out certain neglected aspects of the relatively few years during which
the tragedy of the Jews was accomplished. We are still searching for
understanding of these years. At that time, what was happening had no
name. Even today we are trying, not too satisfactorily, to find the most
apt way of describing what is evidently proving indescribable.

3. Pope John Paul II, in his historic address to Jewish representatives at Miami, on September 11, 1987, provided a text which can be, I
think, profitably adopted as a point of departure at this moment. The
Pope declared: "I am convinced that history will reveal even more
clearly and even more convincingly how profoundly Pius XII felt the
tragedy of the Jewish people, and how intensely and effectively he
applied himself to assist them in the Second World War." Is it so difficult to evaluate the Pacelli pontificate, over forty years since the end of
the war and thirty years after his death? Evidently it is so. Religion is a
subtle and delicate force in human affairs and never perhaps more than
in the greatest war in the history of a Europe used to war. Pius XII was
only too conscious of this. And we, today, are witness likewise, as the
debate continues over half a century.

4. It would be vain to pretend or assume that all the elements can
be assembled in one short paper. There are special features making historical judgments elusive to define. In our time, the Holy See, the
Papacy, has been catapulted into world consciousness in an entirely
new perspective. It is suggestive that the polemics over Pius XII and
his role in World War II were triggered by a drama or play produced in
Berlin in February 1963, a bare few months after the stirring first session of Vatican Council II. Horizons expanded. "New worlds" opened.
Walls came crumbling down. World opinion watched, fascinated, and
began to identify with what was going on, in both secular and religious
circles. Now it is understood that what the Pope of Rome says, or does
not say, does or does not do, can in important instances transcend,
exceed, the boundaries of purely religious or confessional concerns.
This awareness was not always in evidence before that.

With this, we already have the outline of this paper: 1. What Pius
XII did (or did not do). 2. What he said (or did not say). 3. Why? For
there are two distinguishable aspects of the wartime pontificate of Pius
XII; two sides, so to speak, of the same coin. And they need to be studied in reference to each other, not as if they were mutually unrelated.

II. What Pius XII Did or Did Not Do

5. From the outbreak of World War II on September 1, 1939 (the invasion of Poland), Pius XII set as his goal to alleviate as much as possible the sufferings brought on by the war he had tried by every means to prevent. There followed a multiplicity of demarches, initiatives, projects, etc. directed to keep to a minimum, if not to prevent, the moral and material destruction that accompanies the state of war. In this striving the Pope had in mind his own personal experiences in the First World War, as the representative of Pope Benedict XV, caring for the wounded and the prisoners of war. Pius XII prided himself that his work went forward without distinction of religion, race, nationality, or politics. This was, after all, the model proposed by Jesus Christ to his followers in the parable of the Good Samaritan.

6. The Holy See left an impressive record of humanitarian work during the war. Four volumes of the twelve-volume official documentary *Actes et documents du Saint-Siège relatifs à la Seconde Guerre Mondiale* carry the diplomatic and other correspondence of the Vatican on the theme "War Victims." These papers demonstrate the wide scope, the disinterestedness, the persistence and perseverance of the Pontiff in the pursuit of his goal. The efforts were often not crowned with success, the effects often far short of the need, misunderstandings of motives and positive opposition almost a daily diet. But of the concern on the part of Pius XII for stricken humanity during World War II even the failures remain a striking witness.

7. Throughout the above-mentioned four volumes, the concern of the Holy See for the special predicament of the Jews of Europe stands out in increasing degree. Both individual Jews in jeopardy and the local or world leadership addressed themselves to the Pope with hope and confidence. In the course of the war, as the situation became more and more desperate, these appeals multiplied, particularly on the part of the world rescue agencies outside the danger zone and in a position to know and to act. They acted on the basis of their known readiness of the Pope to respond to their urgings. And the Holy See did not have to wait for outside signals before moving on its own initiative to intervene where intervention stood some chance of success.

8. The degree of communication between the Holy See and the Jewish community in these years can be said to have no parallel in history. On the local scene community leaders approached the papal

representatives for their support. These reported to Rome for instructions and in many cases did not wait before making the needed
demarches to the authorities for the thousands who stood at their
mercy. In their turn, the major world rescue organizations repeatedly
made their needs known to the Vatican and encountered, as is evident
in the record, immediate corresponding action. In the latter years of
the war, the U.S. Refugee Board, amalgamating Jewish efforts hith-
erto dispersed among sometimes competing agencies, kept up the
existing tradition of confident relationships with the Holy See.

9. The greatest setbacks and disappointment were in the Nazi
Reich itself. Should this be surprising? Hitler built his power on disregard for world opinion, on intransigence, in the face of fierce political,
economic, and moral pressure from abroad. Relations between the
Holy See and Germany were at a standstill since Pius XI's encyclical
Mit brennender Sorge of March 1937. The encyclical of Pius XII in the
first month of the war, *Summi Pontificatus,* repeated the strictures of
the earlier encyclical against racism. It was read in the churches but
copies were seized and the printers had their presses confiscated. The
French Air Force dropped thousands of miniature copies over Germany, a significant gesture but of limited effect.

With the fall of France in 1940 and the resulting absolute hege-
mony of the European continent by the Axis, thousands were trapped.
But there remained the possibility of diplomatic intervention, that is,
through the Berlin ministry of Foreign Affairs. But repeated Vatican
appeals were returned—if returned at all—with the notation that nothing could be done for the persons concerned, "on police grounds." This
meant that the fate of these Jews was in the hands of the Gestapo and
the SS. On these papal interventions, the archives of the foreign ministry are not reliable or representative. The State Secretary, Ernst von
Weizsäcker, solved his personal dilemma by choosing to meet the Nunciature representative—the nuncio himself, Archbishop Cesare Orsenigo, or his aide—outside the ministry. In this way the papal initiative
could be downgraded to a "private" or "unofficial" demarche, of which
he did not have to leave a written record. The Nunciature then turned
directly to the police, to Himmler. Of these encounters with the
Gestapo and the Jewish bureau headed by Adolf Eichmann there is also
no record, except by implication. Nothing was ever accomplished, if it
were not to exemplify to the Gestapo that the Vatican was interfering in
things that were none of its business. Contributing to the Vatican's lack

of success in Berlin was the fact that Marshall Göring's famous interception service regularly deciphered the Vatican's telegrams to Orsenigo. The appropriate Nazi officers were thus informed in advance of the papal demand about to reach them.

In 1942 there were still 40,000 Jews left in Berlin, judged indispensable for the war effort in munitions works. But in May a bomb attack on a Goebbels-sponsored anti-Bolshevik exhibit in the Lustgarten provoked a fearful reprisal. Five Jews were implicated and the order went out for executions at the rate of 100 for each of the five Jews. On the same day 250 Jews were shot, and the other 250 deported. Nothing was published in the press but Adolf Eichmann summoned Jewish leaders to inform them, and to warn them. At such a time what effect could an appeal from the Vatican for a single family in distress have on those who, even in normal days, had long since learned to ignore the Pope?

10. In the initial years of the war, when emigration was still possible, the appeals took the form of requests for Vatican influence in favor of those needing exit or transit visas, whether for individuals or for groups. Spain and Portugal were key countries in this respect, for instance, and it was thought that Vatican pressure or recommendations could have some effect. After 1940 and with 1942, the possibilities of emigration evaporated and instead the specter of deportation loomed. Though the ultimate destination, or fate, of the deportees could not be ascertained, the circumstances of the transportation—violent, inhumane, with pitiless disregard for the sick, the aged, women and children—already gave the operation a macabre, grim significance in the Vatican.

At the first major indication, the deportation of 80,000 Slovak Jews in March 1942, the reaction of the Vatican was immediate. The warning came simultaneously from the papal representative in Bratislava and from Jewish officials in the Swiss Agudat Israel. Soon after came another anguished appeal from the Papal Nuncio in Hungary. The Vatican official in Slovakia, reporting on March 9, described the deportation as "an atrocious plan." He wrote: "The deportation of 80,000 persons to Poland, at the mercy of the Germans, is equivalent to condemn them to certain death." In reply to the protests of Cardinal Maglione, Secretary of State, the Slovak official explanation was that these Jews were going to "work." Their treatment, it was said, would be "humane." A year later the government in Slovakia announced a new wave of deportations against which, as before, the Vatican protested.

11. In the years from 1942 onwards, there was hardly a country or a point in Europe where the papal intervention was not solicited, and acted upon. The papal involvement necessarily took various forms according to the circumstances and the Vatican's real possibilities of action. The 1942 deportation of Jews from France was the subject of exchanges by the papal Nunciature of Vichy, with Pierre Laval. In Italy the interventions took, first, the form of recommendations for exemptions from the anti-Semitic laws and, in particular, for the foreign Jews, in the sense of dissuading the Fascist government from handing over refugee Jews to the Germans. In the end, no foreign Jews were ever handed over to the Germans at this time by the Fascist government. It is not necessary to claim that this perhaps surprising denouement was attributed solely to Vatican efforts. But it remains true that the Holy See was constantly present in the unfolding drama. With the fall of Fascism and the German occupation of the country, the danger reappeared.

12. On October 16, 1943, in a rapidly executed raid, special SS squads acting on Hitler's orders, seized over a thousand Roman Jews for dispatch to "Poland," from which few ever returned. The same morning, on the Pope's orders, Cardinal Maglione, Secretary of State, summoned the Reich ambassador Ernst von Weizsäcker to protest. "It is painful, painful beyond telling," said Maglione to the embarrassed German ambassador, "that precisely in Rome, under the eyes of the Common Father, so many persons are being made to suffer solely because they belong to a certain race...." In the aftermath, those Jews who had escaped the Nazi fury in Rome found secret shelter by the hundreds in the convents and religious houses of the Eternal City for the agonizing nine months of the German occupation.

13. In the several Balkan states there were different possibilities of intervention. In Croatia, the papal representative, who was in fact only an "Apostolic Visitator" and hence without any diplomatic status before the new-born Croatian state, made frequent demarches, both with the government and with the local hierarchy, naturally on instructions from the Holy See. In Rumania (predominantly Orthodox Christians), already in 1941 thousands of Jews were deported by the Rumanians themselves, not to Poland but into the newly occupied former Russian zones of Moldavia (Transistria, beyond the Bug River) where many died. In this period the Nuncio Cassulo, on Vatican instructions, was in close touch with Rabbi Alexander Safran and with the famous lay leader William Fildermann. In Bulgaria, also predominantly Orthodox Christian, the

papal representative had only the status of an Apostolic Delegate, that is, without diplomatic standing. But some influence could be exercised, despite the small number of Catholics. As is well known, the Papal Delegate in Turkey, Angelo Roncalli, the future Pope John XXIII, addressed a personal letter to King Boris (June 30, 1943) imploring him to spare the Jews from deportation.

14. In far-off Salonika, a Greek city, where there was a notable concentration of Jews long resident, an easy target for the Nazis, the interest of the Holy See was also manifest. The appeals from the Jewish leadership came to the Pope through the papal representative in Athens, Giacomo Testa, Apostolic Delegate. The region was partially occupied by Italian troops and the Holy See could in this instance address itself to the drama through this channel.

15. In Hungary, prior to the German takeover, the Jewish community enjoyed some measure of toleration, despite anti-Semitic laws. In March 1944 they came into immediate mortal danger. Pius XII, warned by his own Nuncio Angelo Rotta in Budapest, on June 25, sent a famous "open telegram" to the Hungarian Regent, Admiral Horthy, on behalf of those suffering, "because of their nationality or their race." An allusion whose meaning could not be misunderstood. There followed a rain of telegrams from the Jewish organizations and a succession of diplomatic protests of the Nuncio to the anti-Semitic, German-supported successors of Horthy.

16. In Slovakia at this time, the situation became almost identical. The papal representative at Bratislava reported that the chase after Jews was continuing and, in general, the government and the President (Dr. Josef Tiso, a priest) were servile executors of the orders of the occupation. The telegram of reply was signed by Monsignor Domenico Tardini of the Secretariat of State (Cardinal Maglione had died in August) on date of October 29, 1944 (the original draft bearing the handwritten corrections of Pius XII): "Your Excellency shall go at once to President Tiso and, informing him of the profound distress of His Holiness for the sufferings to which so many persons are subjected against the laws of humanity and justice—because of their nationality or race, summon him, in the name of the August Pontiff, to sentiments and resolutions conformable to his dignity and conscience as a priest. Let him know also that these injustices committed under his Government damage the prestige of his country and that the adversary exploit them to discredit the clergy and the Church in the whole world."

17. The case of the Latin American passports, in the spring of 1944, illustrates in a particularly graphic way how Vatican diplomatic intervention could serve the Jewish organizations in their relentless struggle to save what could be saved. Some several hundred refugees were still in France, under German control, but spared deportation because they had passports of a number of Latin American countries.

In fact, many of these passports were manifestly illegal. Under pressure from Berlin some of these countries formally denounced them as invalid, thus leaving the holders liable to deportation. There followed desperate appeals representing that lives were in danger if the passports were repudiated. On the prayers of, for instance, among others, the Union of Orthodox Rabbis of the United States and Canada, the Vatican sent instructions, in a circular telegram, to its representatives in half a dozen of the Latin American republics in this sense. The D-Day landing on June 6 put an end to this crisis but not before many of the persons concerned had already been transferred.

18. This is only a skeleton outline of the interventions on behalf of the beleaguered Jews in World War II, on the part of the Holy See. Is its significance to be measured only by its degree of success, and not rather by the evidence it offers of the continuing and consistent papal concern also for this specially tormented category of "War's Victims"? The action of the Holy See stemmed from its conception of its own humanitarian mission in time of war. But it was also in harmony with the needs and prayers of the Jewish organizations dedicated to the saving of their own people. The concerns of the Holy See, on the humanitarian level, coincided with those of the Jewish community. The Holy See and the world organizations were united at the same points of crisis in the unfolding tragedy.

19. On June 2, 1943, Pius XII lifted the veil momentarily on activities for the Jews pursued so fanatically and murderously by the National Socialists. He first said that he regarded all peoples with equal good will. He continued: "But don't be surprised, Venerable Brothers and beloved sons, if our soul reacts with particular emotion and pressing concern, to the prayers of those who turn to us with anxious eyes of pleading, in travail because of their nationality or their race, before greater catastrophes and ever more acute and serious sorrows, and destined sometimes, even without any fault of their own, to exterminating harassments." "Let the rulers of nations not forget," he went on, "that they cannot dispose of the life and death of men at their will." At the

time the contemporary reader, if he even saw the text, could be possibly excused for not completely understanding what Pius XII meant. Today, with the knowledge, documented and published, of the continuing efforts of the Holy See for the afflicted Jews of Europe, these words ought to have profound meaning for any fair-minded observer.

20. A year later, June 2, 1944, on the same occasion of his name-day, St. Eugenio, Pius XII alluded in similar terms to his continuing preoccupation for the safety of the Jews under Nazism. "To one sole goal, Our thoughts are turned day and night: how it may be possible to abolish such acute suffering, coming to the relief of all, without distinction of nationality or race." More, the Pope could not say and few understood what these words implied at the time. There is no excuse, however, for not understanding them today. The innumerable messages to governments and other correspondents emanating from the Holy See on his personal authority and under his personal supervision eloquently substantiate what the Pontiff declared cryptically in 1943 and 1944.

III. What Pius XII Said or Did Not Say

21. Pius XII was not "silent" during World War II. He was not even "neutral." His public statements, from the first encyclical, were clearly directed against the National Socialist regime, and were so understood on both sides. They were commented on with enthusiasm by the British, and confiscated with equal zeal by the Nazi police. But the Pope's style was not, and could not be, that of the warring belligerents. He spoke, and wrote, instead, in generic phrases, in allusions, with judgments marked by indirectness, naming no names and no country. From the start, before the war had taken on such a horrendous aspect, Pius XII refused systematically to pronounce special express condemnations. This tantalizing restraint was a disappointment to the Allies, who thought they had more than a good case. They sought to elicit from the Holy See some specific denunciation of Nazi aggression and Nazi atrocities, which they themselves stigmatized. They encountered resolute resistance from Pius XII to the end. He considered his public statements were already perfectly clear to those who wished to listen, and he remained determined not to descend into particular details which might please the belligerents at a given moment but would run counter to the concept that the Holy See had of its own proper role in time of a great war.

22. The refusal of the Pope to pass specific moral judgments against offenders during the war has never been appropriately or adequately analyzed. But an effort of clarification is necessary because this policy, particularly as applied to the fate of the Jews in the course of the war, has lent a prejudicial hue to his whole pontificate. Yet Pius XII had a right and a duty to define for himself the dimensions of his own work, in the light of his own situation and mission. He also was entitled to have his own viewpoint fairly considered. For his self-restraint was identical with the precedent set earlier in World War I by Pope Benedict XV. From 1914 onward, after some damaging mistakes, the policy was adopted by the Vatican not to venture on the terrain of specific condemnations but to condemn atrocities in general terms, "wherever they may be committed." The young Pacelli, who was at the center of papal diplomacy in those years, learned this lesson at first hand. Later, as Pope, he was able to convince himself that he had no alternative but to follow the same line of conduct, on the penalty of involving himself in an endless series of fruitless moralizings. In the end, the real moral authority of the Papacy would be compromised in all eyes, rather than enhanced.

23. The traditional papal policy had to undergo severe challenges on many occasions during World War II. The British and the French could not understand why the Pope had not excommunicated their enemies. In the crisis of war both of these countries forgot their long years of "No Popery," or anticlericalism, to revert to medieval conceptions, certainly anachronistic, of a Boniface VIII launching the curse of Rome on malefactors. The Vatican was not impressed by this belated deference to the "moral authority" of the head of the Catholic Church. Its essentially political motivations and its limited terms were too obvious. They were probably not even meant seriously but served as an excellent propaganda platform. The invitation to the Pope to condemn Nazi crimes in the name of his religious authority did not include a like invitation to stigmatize crimes outside of the narrow terms set unilaterally by the petitioners.

24. In the first month of the war the French Premier Édouard Daladier lectured the Vatican for not having condemned the invasion of Poland by the Germans (and the Soviets). The Pope's silence seemed, he said, to give sanction to the cynical violations of the principles that the Pope himself had emphasized, on the higher principles of morality. The fact that the Soviet Union was also guilty, said Daladier, ought to persuade the Pope to come out with a condemnation of Poland's fate.

This was to misjudge the Vatican's alleged obsession, so popular in the minds of the diplomats, with atheistic Communism. About this same time (September 30) Pius XII addressed a group of Polish refugees, among whom was the Primate himself, Cardinal Hlond. They were profoundly disappointed that the Pope did not utter words of condemnation of the German invasion of their country, though he did express his confidence in the eventual rebirth of Poland.

25. It was in 1942 that calls for the Pope to denounce Nazi atrocities reached a peak. Individually and jointly, the coalition centered in London and in the United States urged the Pope to condemn Nazi actions with clear and express words. The leader in this drive was the Polish government-in-exile which felt it had a particular claim to the Holy See's support. The atrocities in question were the occupation policy in general, with emphasis on the taking and shooting of hostages, reprisals on the civilian population, on the principle of "collective responsibility," the plundering of material goods, the deportation of youth, particularly of young girls.

In mid-1942 the nine governments-in-exile then in London addressed an appeal to the major powers (Great Britain, the United States and the Soviet Union), calling to their attention the ruthlessness of the German occupation of their respective countries. This initiative was therefore mainly directed at the three powers. But an additional message, of the same tenor, was directed also to the Holy See. It was delivered to the Vatican on September 12. The ambassadors of Poland and Belgium divided the reading of the document in a formal session before Monsignor Tardini. The two diplomats, after enumerating the Nazi atrocities in their respective countries, expressed the hope that the Holy Father, "sensible to so many horrors in the present and those which threaten in the future, would raise his voice, in order to help to save countless innocent victims."

26. In the meantime, the Brazilian ambassador to the Holy See, Ildebrando Accioly, took a parallel initiative, for which he solicited and got the support of the British and American representatives living with him in Vatican City. Speaking on September 14 in the name and under the instructions of his government, he urged a formal stand by the Holy See on German atrocities. "It is necessary that the authorized and respected voice of the Vicar of Christ be heard against these atrocities." On the same day, duly alerted and authorized by their home governments, d'Arcy Osborne for the British and Harold H. Tittmann Jr. for

the United States, pressed the Vatican for a "public and specific denunciation of Nazi treatment of the populations of the countries under German occupation." A few days later the representatives of Cuba, Uruguay, and Peru had followed suit. It was a concerted demarche.

27. The German war crimes and crimes against humanity, to use terms then coming into use instead of "atrocities," as mentioned in the various documents, did not include the treatment of the Jews of Europe. Only Osborne mentioned this latter manifestation of Nazi brutality. The concerted appeal therefore envisaged the ensemble of Nazi occupation policy, in which doubtless the Jewish travail was implicit. To these different appeals coming to him at this time, the Pope did not give an immediate answer. An inkling of the reaction felt in the Vatican was provided in a few days by d'Arcy Osborne in a report to the Foreign Office of October 9. He said he had asked Monsignor Domenico Tardini if the Pope was going to speak. The Vatican official said he did not know. "He went on to say that collective pressure in which even South American countries had participated looked like an attempt to involve the Pope in political and partisan action. I said that the Catholic Latin American countries, although not victims of the Nazi tyranny, were entitled to express surprise at the Pope's silence. He offered the strange argument that no neutral country had urged the Pope to speak...I think the reference is that the Vatican is embarrassed and the Pope himself resentful, both of [the] criticism and of [the] painful prospect of taking action which will expose him to Axis counter-criticism."

28. But the pressure continued. On September 17, Myron C. Taylor, personal representative of President Roosevelt, arrived in Rome, passing from the airport to Vatican City despite the state of war between the United States and Italy. He bore with him a bundle of memoranda for long and repeated discussions with Pius XII. But, in the Vatican, he acquired another memorandum which Taylor said later in his report to the President, he had been urged by Osborne and Tittmann and others, to submit to the Pope. In this paper Taylor said that it was thought that a word of condemnation from the Pope would encourage all those who were working to save these thousands of persons from suffering and death. He referred globally in these words to the victimization of prisoners of war, of Catholics and Jews, of the civilian populations, especially the shooting of hostages, estimated at 200,000.

Taylor told President Roosevelt he had the impression that at the right moment the Pope would make a public statement in line with his recommendation. In the Vatican, continued Taylor, there was small inclination to condemn individuals or persons by name, but a general condemnation of these inhumanities, such as the Pope had already uttered on different occasions, could be repeated. What Taylor meant is illustrated by the memorandum of the same day, 22 September, recorded by Monsignor Tardini after his own talk with Taylor. The presidential Envoy raised the question of the "opportuneness and necessity" of a word from the Holy Father against so many atrocities committed by the Germans, and how this desire was felt on all sides, in different circles. Tardini recorded this exchange: "I answered that the Pope has already spoken, many times, condemning crimes, by whomsoever committed and I added that some people want the Pope to condemn and name explicitly Hitler and Germany, which is impossible. His Excellency Mr. Taylor answered me: 'I did not ask that. I did not ask to name Hitler.' And then I repeated the Pope had already spoken, Mr. Taylor said, 'He can repeat.' To which I could not but assent."

29. A few days later, September 25, Taylor had an exchange with Cardinal Maglione, the papal Secretary of State. He brought up again the question of refugees, of the imprisonment and execution of hostages, and the transfer of populations. He insisted anew, as already with the Pope, that "a further condemnation of this system would be welcomed in the United States." Maglione told him that a declaration would be issued at the first opportune moment, in the beginning of October, but in general terms. More detailed is the record of this conversation recorded by the American Monsignor Walter Carroll, who was present.

IV. Condemnation to Be Made by Pius XII on the Maltreatment of Refugees and Hostages of Occupied Nations

30. "Ambassador Taylor says there is a general impression—in America as in Europe—an impression that His Excellency, Mr. Taylor cites personally as without any question—that it is now necessary that His Holiness denounce again the inhuman treatment of refugees, of the hostages and in particular of the Jews in the occupied territories. This condemnation is sought not only by Catholics but also by Protestants. His Eminence replies that the Holy See works incessantly to assist the suffering populations. The Secretary of State, and other pontifical institutions, are constantly engaged and with all solicitude with this grave

problem. The representatives of the Church in the various countries have openly denounced the maltreatment of peoples and have sought by every means to aid the oppressed.

"His Holiness has often condemned the oppressors of peoples and of individuals and has said that the blessing or the malediction of God would fall upon rulers, according to the way they treat the occupied countries. This, continues His Eminence, is rather a strong declaration, as strong as it was possible to make without getting into political discussions, asking for documentation, reports, and so forth. Evidently the Pope cannot do this. Mr. Taylor signifies his agreement but insists on the opportuneness of an appeal of a higher character. The previous declarations having been made some time ago, it would seem that the moment has arrived to make another. Certainly it would be well received by everybody. Unfortunately both individuals as well as peoples have a short memory. Many would desire that His Holiness should make a denunciation of these evils every day. His Eminence assures Mr. Taylor that in his opinion, the Holy Father will not fail to express anew and clearly his thought at the first occasion that presents itself."

31. At a last moment, September 27, Taylor received from Washington a notice received in turn by the U.S. State Department from the Jewish Agency of Palestine (Geneva), giving details of the liquidation of the Warsaw ghetto, as brought by two recent escapees from Poland. Among other details, it was said that the Jews deported from Germany, Belgium, Holland, France, and Slovakia were sent to their deaths, to be massacred. The non-Jews from France and Holland were put to work. On behalf of the U.S. Secretary of State, Taylor was instructed to ask: (1) If the Vatican could confirm this information, and, (2) if the Vatican had any recommendations how to mobilize public opinion. As it turned out, information of this kind had just come to the Vatican from an Italian government official returned from a mission in Poland. According to him, there were "incredible massacres" every day. "The massacre of Jews had reached shocking and fearful proportions and forms." Maglione accordingly replied to the U.S. query, that the Holy See had received information of severe treatment of Jews but had not yet been able to verify the information. Maglione added that "the Holy See has not failed to intervene in behalf of Jews every time the possibility is offered."

32. In 1942, during the month of September, what could only be described as unprecedented pressure was put on Pius XII to make a formal and explicit condemnation of Nazi atrocities, not simply maltreatment

and killing of Jews, but a wide range of inhuman actions against the weak and the innocent. Had the time come for the Holy See to change or attenuate its established position? No doubt this was one of the gravest decisions Pius XII had to face in his entire wartime pontificate. Weeks went by without any indication whether and how the Pope would react to the urgings of the Allies. The two diplomats following the affair closest, Osborne and Tittmann, did not expect any change.

33. The Pope, in his Christmas Eve address, they thought, would stick to his policy of not naming specific atrocities or particular countries. In fact, in this discourse, under the heading "Considerations on the World War and the Renewal of Society," Pius XII gave what obviously was his answer to the appeals made to him in September. He spoke of the horrors of war, striking every category of society: families bereft of support, refugees expelled from their homeland. Also, "the hundreds of thousands of persons who, without any fault of their own, sometimes only by reason of their nationality or race, are destined to death or a progressive destruction."

The Pope added, at the close of this listing, the weight of which fell on the German side, what could be, at that moment, and was, taken as a denunciation of the Allied aerial bombardment of German cities, allegedly indiscriminately. The Pope alluded to the "many thousands of noncombatants, women, children, the ailing and the old, whom the aerial war—whose horrors, from the very beginning We have many times denounced—without discrimination and without sufficient carefulness, have been deprived of life, goods, health, homes and places of succor and prayer."

34. The last-cited condemnation—implied, that is, nonspecific—of obliteration bombing as practiced by the RAF at this time over Germany, was no doubt displeasing to the Allies, particularly the British. But it would have been awkward for them to make an issue of this "allusion," after having spent so much effort to prove to the Vatican that only specific condemnations had any meaning. Or, to put it in another way, did the demands that the Pope "speak out" mean, in their minds, that the Pope was expected to condemn and denounce only crimes committed by the Germans, while the Allies must at all times be considered as beyond reproach?

35. The English Minister d'Arcy Osborne had the opportunity to talk with the Pope at year's end. He reported to the Foreign Office: "It is clear that the Pope regards his broadcast as having satisfied all

demands for stigmatization of Nazi crimes in the occupied countries. The reaction of some at least of my colleagues was anything but enthusiastic. To me he claimed that he had condemned the Jewish persecution. I could not dissent from this, though the condemnation is inferential and not specific, and comes at the end of a long dissertation on social problems. As a matter of fact his criticism of the totalitarian systems was unmistakable and, given his temperament, I think he deserves much credit for much of what he said." Osborne repeated his impressions in a later report of January 5, 1943. The British minister had on December 29 given the Pope the joint Allied memorandum on anti-Jewish atrocities issued on December 17. "The Pope," he wrote, "promised that he would do whatever was possible on behalf of the Jews. I doubt there will be any public statement, particularly since [the] passage in his Christmas broadcast clearly applied to Jewish persecution. I impressed on him that Hitler's policy of extermination was a crime without precedent in history."

36. Osborne's colleague among the Allied diplomats living in Vatican City, Harold H. Tittmann Jr. of the United States, had his own audience with the Pope on December 29. The U.S. Chargé d'Affaires reported to Washington: "...the Pope gave me the impression that he was sincere in believing that he had spoken therein clearly enough to satisfy all those who had been insisting in the past that he utter some word of condemnation of the Nazi atrocities and he seemed surprised when I told him that I thought there were some who did not share his belief. He said that it was plain to everyone that he was referring to Poles, Jews, and hostages when he declared that hundreds of thousands of persons had been killed or tortured through no fault of their own, sometimes only because of their race or nationality." Tittmann said the Pope added he could not specifically name the Nazis for their atrocities without at the same time naming the Bolsheviks, which would not be welcomed by the Allies. Tittmann did not comment on the Pope's denunciation of Allied indiscriminate bombing of German cities.

37. If the Christmas Eve broadcast was a disappointment to the Americans and the British, which they could absorb, it was a bitter delusion for the Polish government-in-exile. The Poles were the main movers in the campaign for an explicit papal condemnation of Nazi atrocities. A solemn letter, signed by the President of Poland, Wladislaw Raczkiewicz, under date of January 2, 1943, was brought to the Pope by Ambassador Casimir Papée on January 21. It made no mention of the

Christmas message and insisted anew, as if the Pope had not spoken, for "a word that would clearly and distinctly indicate where the evil is and which would scourge its ministers." In an audience that lasted forty-five minutes, Pius XII expressed his displeasure at the message which, he said, displayed no recognition of all that the Pope had done, and was doing, for the benefit of the Poles in Poland and outside of Poland, for whom the London government claimed to stand up. Ambassador Papée described to his superiors the tense moments he had to experience in the presence of the Pope: "When I had finished, the Pope who had been before smiling and benevolent, said to me, clearly irritated: 'In the first place I ask myself if the President has read my Christmas message. I am astonished. I am also saddened. Yes, saddened. Not one word of gratitude or recognition, of acknowledgment and yet I said everything, everything. I was clear and precise.' At this point the Pope began to cite various passages from his Christmas discourse, dwelling, in particular, on the condemnation pronounced by him, of the persecutions because of nationality or race, of the executions, deportations and plunderings. He cited entire passages by memory."

Papée defended his chief, emphasizing the dire straits of the Polish nation. He ended his dispatch with this observation: "Going away from the audience I felt reinforced in my conviction that Pius XII is sincerely and profoundly convinced to have said clearly and distinctly all that was possible to say in the defense of our country and that they are demanding the impossible of him."

38. New circumstances in 1943 entered into play to bring this pressure on the Pope to an end. The military situation of the Allies which in 1942 was grave, took a progressively better turn with the successes in North Africa and the *Wehrmacht* defeat at Stalingrad. The suppositions as to how much "declarations" really contributed to an amelioration of the bad situation were redimensioned. The British themselves soon took the line that they had said enough in the December 1942 statement and that so far from helping the Jews it did not frighten the Germans and raised false hopes that more could be done for the Jews in Europe. When the foreign ministers of the three major Allied powers met in Moscow in October 1943 they did issue a statement on atrocities but did not mention a word about the situation of the Jews. The Dutch government had objected to singling out the Jews for special notice: they had already experienced the spiteful reprisals of the Nazis in their own country.

V. What International Institutions Brought

39. The Holy See was not the only international institution brought face to face with the problem of the Nazi "war crimes and crimes against humanity." In the crucial months of the war the World Council of Churches ("in process of formation," to use its self-designation at this time) also had to answer the question of its attitude to the war and the conduct of hostilities. The simplest, formal answer consisted in the declaration that, after all, the Council did not "exist" apart from its individual and separate member churches, found among all the belligerents. These were able to make their own declarations, on their own responsibility, and it was not the mission of the Council, which had received no mandate. In fact, as the moving power in the world body was Visser 't Hooft, the Secretariat of the Council was actively anti-Nazi. It had, like the Vatican, opened an office for refugees and was keenly interested in the fate of Jews. But it knew better than to compromise this work by public statements. During the war its ecumenical news service was rich in information on ecumenical developments in the Nazi-occupied countries—with little or no mention of the plight of Jews.

40. The drama within the International Committee of the Red Cross, based also in Geneva, took an even more precise form, but with the same conclusion: this was the time for action and not for "protests." The pressure on the Vatican in 1942 recorded in the foregoing was felt, and keenly, in the leadership of the Geneva Committee. The agency had a recognized and functioning competence for prisoners of war; it could visit camps for the military personnel and it employed ships from overseas that passed through the British blockade, loaded with relief materials. But it could not enter concentration camps and its right even to inquire about civilian refugees, above all Jews, was challenged by the Reich authorities of occupation. The category of civilian prisoners loomed ever large, for those whose assistance the Committee had no legal basis of intervention. It had to resort to stratagems and various circuitous routes, with some satisfactory results, even to the point of being able to send relief packages to concentration camps.

41. But the sentiment for a "public" protest brought a dilemma and division within the Committee. Other relief organizations were consulted, including the papal Nunciature in Switzerland, to whom it was explained that the great fear was that, in making public statements,

which in all likelihood would change nothing, the Committee would only compromise what was already possible and in the end cut themselves off from the Nazi power zone entirely. But Red Cross personnel got to work drafting a statement, under the direction of President Dr. Max Huber. The fourth draft was ready for presentation on September 16, 1942. It was entitled, "Appeal in favor of the application of the essential principles of the law of nations relative to the conduct of hostilities." It was addressed to all the signatories of the Geneva Conventions but was meant really for Nazi Germany. The draft, however, circled ambiguously around the main objective in view, the tragic lot of deportees. The allusion to Jews was put in a subordinate place and nearly lost in circumlocutions. The draft alluded to the fact that "alongside of civil internees properly so-called, certain categories of civilians of various nationalities have been, for reasons depending on the state of war, deprived of their liberty, deported or taken as hostages and are liable by this fact to risks to their lives for acts of which they are often not the authors." The draft was presented on October 24, 1942, to the full session of the International Committee of the Red Cross, and rejected. It was never issued.

42. Relevant to this decision of the Red Cross is the meeting of Carl Burckhardt of the Committee, on November 17, with Gerhart Riegner, the local representative of the "World Jewish Congress." Burckhardt revealed that the Committee had thought very seriously to publish an official protest on the subject of the treatment of the civilian population and of the Jewish question and he wanted Riegner's ideas. Burckhardt said that he himself thought that such a protest would have no positive result and on the contrary the whole activity of the International Committee could be put in jeopardy, especially as at this moment they had barely averted the denunciation of the Geneva Conventions by Germany.

43. What could the answer be, under the circumstances? Riegner declared he saw that a protest was still necessary, but it need not be envisaged until one was convinced that there was nothing more to hope. At the time that it was learned that Hitler had ordered the extermination of all the Jews of Europe it indeed appeared that nothing remained to be done to save them. But recent political developments had apparently modified the situation. Riegner further declared in conclusion, according to his own record, "I believe a protest is necessary only in the case where there is really nothing more to be done at the

time. But if one can still exercise some influence and if one wishes to refrain from a protest, it is necessary to act and not to satisfy oneself with passively recording news of deportees."

VI. Conclusions

44. Is it possible to apply this line of reasoning also to the problem as it presented itself to the Holy See? The Vatican, too, had to face the possibility, even the probability, that a formal and explicit protest, even in the indirect form [rejected] of the Red Cross draft, would destroy at once the meager possibilities existing, on which human lives depended. The difference between the Holy See and the Red Cross, however, consisted in the fact that the Vatican did find a way of going on the record with a public protest, however indirectly phrased. Those engaged in humanitarian work were agreed that the results in terms of human lives were more important and urgent than the manifestation of public indignation that might quiet consciences but would have no real effect and be positively disadvantageous to the persons one is anxious to help.

45. "They are demanding the impossible of the Pope." These words of the Polish ambassador Casimir Papée, to his own government, summed up his analysis of what he had been instructed to get from the Pontiff. He, more than others, having bombarded the Holy See in all these months with accounts of Nazi oppression, and the treatment of Jews in his homeland, knew that the Pope felt himself responsible for the consequences. That the Polish government-in-exile thought otherwise, for reasons satisfactory to itself, did not mean that the Pope had to agree with them, launching on a course which went against his own better judgment. It was not weakness but courage, not passivity but concern, that dominated the papal motivation at this point.

46. The Allies, led by the Poles, asked for and would be satisfied with nothing less than a provocation, regardless of the consequences. This was a reckless attitude that the Pope could not accept, the more so that his own statement would be on his own authority, for the aftermath of which he would have to bear personal responsibility. He was being asked to open a Pandora's box with tragic impact.

47. We can surmise some of the considerations on the practical level that entered into the Pope's reflections during these autumn months of 1942, fixing papal policy on atrocities. The Germans would

in the first place deny the charges, which the Vatican itself had no means of proving. Some of the acknowledged Nazi reprisals, such as the razing of the Czech village of Lidice, would be defended with ferocity. The Vatican would be accused of being in the hands of the British and the American enemies of Germany. The alleged "moral message" would be reduced to a mere political action, especially when the inevitable enthusiastic use of the papal statement became a top theme of Allied propaganda. (The British themselves used the annihilating accusation of "pressure," when the Vatican did something that did not please them.) The Pope would be assailed as having joined the campaign of lies of which Germany had been the victim for long.

48. In short, in Germany, the papal statement would be cut down to nothingness. In the occupied countries, where the Nazi machine was already organized for oppression, the screw would be turned even more tightly, except that this time the Pope would be blamed for it. In the satellite governments, the access of the Vatican would be cut off by German pressure. And the war still had a long way to go. In the coming years, the interventions of the Holy See, above all for the Jews, continued, with good effect. Of this the Jewish organizations were themselves first-hand witnesses, and they gave voice to their recognition and gratitude.

[Notes and references should be consulted for study of the documentary evidence on which Father Robert Graham's monograph is based. Cf. pp. 336–38.]

D. The Myth in the Light of the Archives

by

Pierre Blet, S.J.

(On March 21, 1998, the Civiltà Cattolica *published an article on Pope Pius XII's "silence" during the Holocaust. On the plane to Nigeria a journalist asked Pope John Paul II about Pius XII's "silence." The Pope replied: "Read Father Blet's article.")*

When Pope Pius XII died on October 9, 1958, he was the object of unanimous admiration and gratitude. "The world," President Eisenhower declared, "is now poorer following the death of Pope Pius XII." And Golda Meir, Foreign Secretary for the State of Israel, said: "Life in our time was enriched by a voice which expressed the great moral truths over the tumult of daily conflicts. We lament the loss of a great servant of peace."[1]

But just a few years later, starting in 1963, Pius had come to be viewed by many in an entirely different light: During the war, either due to political calculation or faintheartedness, he was said to have remained unmoved and silent before crimes against humanity that his intervention, it was said, would have prevented.

When accusations are based on documents, it is possible to discuss the interpretation of the texts, to verify if they have been misunderstood, accepted acritically, distorted, or selected on the basis of biased criteria. But when a legend is simply constructed out of disparate elements and elaborated on the basis of imagination, there is no point to such a discussion. The only thing one can do is to set against the myth the historical reality, proved through incontestable documents.

178

That is why Pope Paul VI—who, as Pro-Secretary of State, had been one of Pius XII's closest collaborators—in 1964 authorized the publication of the documents of the Holy See relating to the Second World War.

The Purpose and Scope of Actes et Documents

The archives of the Vatican's Secretariat of State, in fact, conserve the dossiers through which it is possible to follow, often day by day, sometimes hour by hour, the activities of the Pope and the papal offices. One finds there the messages and speeches of Pius XII; the letters exchanged between the Pope and the civil and ecclesiastical authorities; the records of the Secretariat of State, including office notes from subordinate staff members to their superiors to communicate information and make proposals and also private notes, particularly those of Monsignor Domenico Tardini, who had the habit, happily for the historian, of reflecting on events with pen in hand; the correspondence of the Secretariat of State with representatives of the Holy See abroad (Nuncios, Internuncios, and Apostolic Delegates), and the diplomatic notes exchanged between the Secretariat of State and the Ambassadors or Ministers accredited to the Holy See. These documents are normally sent under the name and signature of the Secretary of State or the Secretary of the First Section of the Secretariat of State, but this does not mean that they do not express the Pope's intentions.

Starting with these documents, it would have been possible to write a work describing the attitude and the policies of the Pope during World War II. Or, one could have composed a "White Book" to show the groundlessness of the attacks on Pius XII, all the more so since the main imputation was one of silence; it was easy, starting with these documents, to make clear the action of the Holy See in favor of the victims of the war and, especially, of the victims of the racial persecutions. It seemed more convenient to undertake the full publication of the documents related to the war.

Several collections of diplomatic documents already existed, many volumes of which dealt with World War II: *Documenti diplomatici italiani, Documents on British Foreign Policy: 1919–1939, Foreign Relations of the United States, Diplomatic Papers, Akten zur deutschen auswärtigen Politik 1918–1945.*

In view of the existence of such collections, and following their lead, it seemed useful to let historians study, on the basis of the documents, the role and activity of the Holy See during the war. It was in this context that the publication of the collection of *Actes et documents du Saint-Siège relatifs à la Seconde Guerre Mondiale* was begun.[2]

The difficulty lay in the fact that for this period the archives—both those of the Vatican and those of other states—were closed to the public and also to historians. The peculiar interest in the events of the Second World War, the desire to write the history of those events on the basis of documents, and not only on the basis of more or less direct recollections or testimonies, had induced the states involved in the conflict to publish documents from archives still inaccessible to the public. Those who are entrusted to carry out such a confidential task are subject to a number of rules: they cannot publish documents that concern people still alive or which, once revealed, could hinder negotiations in process. The volumes of the Foreign Relations of the United States for the 1940s were published according to those criteria, and the same criteria were followed in the publication of the Holy See's documents.

The task of publishing the documents of the Holy See relating to the war was assigned by the Secretariat of State to three Jesuit Fathers: Angelo Martini, editor of this journal *[Civiltà Cattolica],* who already had access to the secret Vatican archives, Burkhart Schneider and this writer, both of us lecturers in the Faculty of Church History at the Pontificia Università Gregoriana. The work began in the first days of January 1965 in an office located near the storeroom for the archives of what at that time was the Congregation for Extraordinary Ecclesiastical Affairs and the First Section of the Secretariat of State; the documents connected with the war were stored there.

Under those conditions, our work presented special difficulties but we also enjoyed special privileges. The difficulty was that, since the archive was not open to the public, there were no systematic inventories aimed at assisting research; the documents were not classified either in a strictly chronological or in a strictly geographical order. Those of political interest, and therefore related to the war, were sometimes found together with documents of a religious, canonical, or even personal nature. All the papers were kept in boxes of a quite manageable size, but the contents could be very disparate. Documents concerning Great Britain could be found inside dossiers on France, if the piece of information had been forwarded via the Nuncio in France. Likewise, interventions in favor of Belgian hostages could be found in the boxes of the Nuncio in Berlin. It was thus necessary to examine every box and to skim through all the contents to identify the documents referring to the war. The research was nevertheless made easier thanks to an old rule of the Secretariat of State, in force since the time of Urban VIII (1623–1644), that Nuncios had to deal with only one topic per letter.

To face these difficulties, we enjoyed some special privileges. Working in an office of the Secretariat of State and on its assignment, we were not subject to the limits imposed on scholarly researchers admitted into the reading rooms of the public archives; one of us could take the boxes of documents directly from the shelves of the storeroom. Another important facility was that most of the documents we had to deal with had been typed and were still in the state of separate documents (hand-written papers to be typed for printing were rare); therefore, as soon as a document was recognized as related to the war, all we had to do was take it out, photocopy it, and give the photocopy to the printer along with the appropriate footnotes, as a scholarly work requires.

Although during the winter of 1965 the work was proceeding quite fast, we decided to ask for Father Robert Leiber's help. He had retired to the German College after being for more than thirty years the private Secretary of Eugenio Pacelli, first Nuncio in Germany, then Secretary of State, and finally Pope Pius XII. He had followed German affairs very closely and it was he who told us about the existence of the rough drafts of the letters of Pius XII to the German bishops, which were published in the second volume of the collection and are the documents that best disclose the thought of the Pope.

The Individual Volumes

The first volume, issued in December 1965, and generally well received, covers the first seventeen months of the pontificate (March 1939–July 1940), and reveals the efforts of Pius XII to avert the war. During 1966, while Father Schneider was actively preparing the volume of the letters to the German bishops, Father Robert A. Graham, an American Jesuit collaborating with the journal *America,* who had already published a work on the Holy See's diplomacy *(Vatican Diplomacy),* asked for information about the period which was the object of our research. As an answer, he was invited to join our group, especially in light of the fact that we had become aware of the ever more frequent contacts between Pius XII and Roosevelt and the number of English documents we were coming up against. He immediately set to work with us on the third volume, focusing on Poland, which was conceived on the model of the second (dealing with the relations between the Holy See and the bishops). But the direct exchange of letters with the other episcopates turned out to be much less intense, so that volumes 2 and 3 (in two tomes) ended up being the only ones of this kind.

Thus, we decided to divide the remaining documents into two parts: one, which continued the first volume, for predominantly diplomatic questions, with the title *Le Saint-Siège et la guerre en Europe, Le Saint-Siège et la guerre mondiale:* these were volumes 4, 5, 7, and 11. The other volumes, entitled *Le Saint-Siège et les victimes de la guerre* (volumes 6, 8, 9, and 10), gathered in chronological order the documents regarding the efforts made by the Holy See to come to the aid of all those who were suffering, either in body or in spirit, because of the war: prisoners separated from their families and exiled far from their loved ones, populations undergoing the ruin of the war, victims of racial persecution.

The work lasted more than fifteen years; the various tasks were assigned within the group according to the volumes planned and the time each of us had to dedicate to the work.

Father Leiber, whose help had been so precious to us, was taken away by death on February 18, 1967. Father Schneider, still continuing to teach Modern History at the Pontificia Università Gregoriana, after publishing the letters to the German bishops, devoted himself to the part involving the victims of the war and prepared—with the help of Father Graham—volumes 6, 8, and 9, completed by Christmas, 1975; but in the summer of that year he started suffering from the disease from which he would die the next May.

Father Martini, who had devoted himself to this job full-time and had a role to some extent in all the volumes, did not have the satisfaction of seeing the work completed. He could only, at the beginning of the summer of 1981, see the page proofs of the last volume before he too left us. This volume was issued toward the end of 1981, under the responsibility of Father Graham and myself.

Although he was the oldest of us all, Father Graham was able to work until the completion of the project and then, during the following fifteen years, to continue supplementary research, most of which appeared in the form of articles in *Civiltà Cattolica.* These articles represent an additional source of information that historians of World War II can consult with profit. Father Graham left Rome on July 24, 1996, to return to his native California, where he ended his days on February 11, 1997.

In the beginning of 1982, I for my part, had recommenced my research on the 1600s in France and on Vatican diplomacy. But seeing that, after fifteen years, our work had remained unknown even to many historians, I dedicated the years 1996 and 1997 to summarize the essential facts and conclusions of our work in a volume of modest dimensions but as dense as I could make it.[3]

An objective consultation of the documentation shows the true attitude and behavior of Pius XII during the conflict and, consequently, the groundlessness of the accusations against his memory. The documents show that his diplomatic efforts to avoid the war, to dissuade Germany from attacking Poland and to persuade Mussolini's Italy to dissociate itself from Hitler, went to the limit of his possibilities.

There is no evidence of the supposed "pro-German" attitude he is said to have absorbed during his years as Nuncio to that country. His efforts, together with those of Roosevelt, to keep Italy out of the conflict, the May 10, 1940, telegrams to the sovereigns of Belgium, Holland, and Luxemburg after the invasion by the *Wehrmacht,* his courageous advice to Mussolini and to King Vittorio Emanuele III to explore a separate peace, surely do not suggest such an attitude. It would be a delusion to think that, with the halberds of his Swiss Guard or by threatening excommunication, he could have stopped the *Wehrmacht*'s tanks.

But the recurrent accusation is that he remained silent before the racial persecutions against the Jews until their extreme consequences and that he thus left the way open for the Nazi barbarism. Now, the documents show the firm and continuous efforts of the Pope to oppose the deportations, regarding the end result of which suspicions were continually growing.

The apparent silence hid a secret action conducted through the nunciatures and the bishops to avoid, or at least limit, the deportations, the violence, the persecutions. The reasons for this discretion are clearly explained by the Pope himself in many speeches, in his letters to the German bishops, and in the deliberations of the Secretariat of State: a public declaration would not have been of any help; it would

have accomplished nothing except to aggravate the situation of the victims and multiply their number.

Recurring Accusations

With the intent of obscuring this evidence, the detractors of Pius
XII have called into question the reliability of our work.

Especially peculiar was an article in a Parisian newspaper on the
evening of December 3, 1997: "Those four Jesuits produced [!] in
Actes et Documents texts which have absolved Pius XII of the omissions he is accused of [...]. But those *Actes et Documents* are far from
complete." The idea is that we left out documents embarrassing to the
memory of Pius XII and the Holy See.

First, it is not easy to understand how the "omission" of documents would help to absolve Pius XII of the "omissions" he is continu-
ously accused of. On the other hand, to assert peremptorily that our
collection is not complete is to assert something impossible to prove: a
proof would require comparing our publication with the archives and
showing that some documents are present there which are lacking in
our collection. Though the archive in question is still not accessible to
the public, some have gone so far as to claim they have evidence of
such omissions in *Actes et Documents*. In so doing, they have shown
their narrow vision with regard to the exploration of archives, some of
which they demand be opened.

Picking up a charge first made in a Roman newspaper on September 11, 1997, the article of December 3, 1997, says a correspondence
between Pius XII and Hitler is "missing" in our publication.

Let us note first of all that the letter by means of which the Pope
notified the Chief of State of the *Reich* [Hitler] of his [Pius XII's] election is the last document published in the second volume of *Actes et
Documents*. Beyond that, if we did not publish a correspondence
between Pius XII and Hitler, it is because such a correspondence exists
only in the fantasy of the journalist's mind. The journalist speaks of
"contacts" between Pacelli, Nuncio in Germany, and Hitler, but he
should have checked the dates: Hitler came to power in 1933, and so he
could have had the opportunity to meet the Nuncio only after that date.
But Monsignor Pacelli had come back to Rome in December 1929;
Pius XI had appointed him cardinal on December 16 and Secretary of

State on January 16, 1930. And, above all, if such a correspondence had ever taken place, the Pope's letters would be conserved in Germany's archives, normally in the archives of the Foreign Affairs Ministry of the *Reich*. Hitler's letters would be in the Vatican, but they would also be mentioned in the instructions to the German ambassadors, Bergen and Weizsäcker, charged with delivering them, and in the dispatches of those diplomats saying they had handed them over to the Pope or to the Secretary of State. There is no trace of any of this. Lacking such references, it can be said that the reliability of our publication has been called into question without a shred of evidence.

These observations about the presumed correspondence between the Pope and the Führer hold for the documents that actually exist. Very often, the Vatican documents are supported by other archives, for example, the notes exchanged with ambassadors. One would imagine that many of the telegrams of the Vatican were intercepted and decoded by the intelligence services of the warring powers, and therefore that it might be possible to find copies of them in their archives; consequently, if we had tried to conceal some documents, it should be possible to know of their existence and so to have a basis to question the reliability of our research.

The same Parisian newspaper article, after imagining relations between Hitler and Nuncio Pacelli, mentions a report in the *Sunday Telegraph* of July 1997, which accuses the Holy See of using Nazi gold to help a number of war criminals to escape to South America, especially the Croatian Ante Pavelic, and says: "Some studies support this charge [!]."

The lack of rigor journalists can display in making statements without any documentary evidence is astonishing. Historians, who often need to toil for hours to verify a reference, will be envious. Evidently, a journalist trusts a colleague above all when the English title of the newspaper gives it the appearance of respectability. But there are two more statements that merit separate examinations, that is, the coming into the Vatican of Nazi gold or, more specifically, of the gold of Jews seized by the Nazis, and its use to facilitate the escape of Nazi war criminals to South America.

Some American newspapers, in fact, have produced a document of the Department of the Treasury in which the Department was informed that the Vatican had received Nazi gold of Jewish origin via Croatia.

This "document" of the "Department of the Treasury" may be impressive; but one must read what is written under the title, and there one finds that it is a note stemming from the "communication of a trustworthy Roman informant." Those who genuinely trust such statements should read what Father Graham wrote about the exploits of the informant Scattolini, who made a living by circulating "information" made up in his own mind that he transmitted to all the Roman embassies, including that of the USA, which duly transmitted the "information" to the State Department.[4]

During our research in the archives of the Secretariat of State, we found no mention of gold taken from the Jews coming into the Vatican's vaults. It is up to those who make these charges to support them with documentary evidence, a receipt for example, which, like the letters of Pius XII to Hitler, would not have remained in the Vatican archives. On the other hand, we did find a record of the prompt intervention of Pius XII when the Jewish community in Rome was blackmailed by the SS, who demanded fifty kilograms of gold from them. The Chief Rabbi turned to the Pope to ask him for fifteen kilograms that were lacking, and Pius XII immediately gave instructions to do whatever was necessary.[5]

A recent check has turned up nothing more. The claim that the Vatican helped Nazi criminals escape to South America is not a new one. Of course, we cannot exclude the possibility that some Roman ecclesiastic used his position to aid the flight of a Nazi. The sympathies of the Rector of the German National Church in Rome, Bishop Hudal, for the Reich are known; but to imagine that the Vatican organized the escape of Nazis on a vast scale means one must ascribe to the Roman clergy a truly heroic charity. In Rome, the Nazi plans regarding the Church and the Holy See were known. Pius XII touched on these plans in his consistorial allocution of June 2, 1945, recalling how the Nazi persecution of the Church had become worse during the war, "when its followers still flattered themselves that, as soon as they won the war, they would make an end to the Church forever."[6] The authors our journalist refers to have a rather lofty idea of the forgiveness practiced by the Pope's entourage if they imagine a large number of Nazis were received into the Vatican and from there conducted to Argentina, protected by Peron's dictatorship, and from there sent to Brazil, to Chile, to Paraguay, to save what could be saved of the Third Reich in the hope of bringing about a Fourth Reich in the *pampas*.

In such charges, it is difficult to distinguish between history and fiction. To fiction fans we may suggest reading Ladislao Farago's *À la recherche de Martin Bormann et des rescapés nazis d'Amérique du Sud.* The English title *Aftermath: Martin Bormann and the Fourth Reich* says it all. The author takes us from Rome and the Vatican to Argentina, Paraguay, and Chile on the trail of the Reichsleiter and the other fleeing Nazi chiefs. With the precision of Agatha Christie, he describes the exact position of every character at the moment of the crime, the number of the hotel rooms used by the escaping Nazis and by their pursuers, even introducing the green Volkswagen transporting them. One is struck by the modesty of the author, who says his book is a "French-style investigation," a "serious study, but without any pretense of pure erudition[!]"

Conclusion

The reader will rightly think that the Vatican archives contain nothing of that kind, even should any portion of it prove true. If Bishop Hudal helped some Nazi big shot to flee, he surely did not ask for the Pope's permission. And if, having done so, he had confided in the Pope, we would know no more about it. Among the things the archive will never reveal are the conversations between the Pope and his visitors, except for those with ambassadors who refer what was said to their governments, or with someone like de Gaulle who mentions them in his *Memoirs.*

This does not mean that, when serious historians want to enter an archive personally to verify for themselves the originals of published documents, their desire is not proper and commendable; even after the publication, as accurate as possible, of a document, the consultation of the archives and direct contact with the document helps historical understanding. It is one thing to question the reliability of our research, another to wonder whether we overlooked anything.

We did not deliberately leave out any meaningful document because it seemed to us that it might harm the Pope's image or the Holy See's reputation.

But those who engage in such an undertaking are the first to wonder if anything has been forgotten. Without Father Leiber, we would not have been aware of the existence of the rough drafts of Pius XII's letters to the German bishops and the collection would have been deprived of perhaps the most precious texts to understand the Pope's mind.[7] But all of those texts taken together do not contradict at all what we learn from the diplomatic notes and correspondence. In these letters, we see better the concern of Pius XII to stress to the bishops the necessity of warning German Catholics against the perverse flatteries of National Socialism, more dangerous than ever in time of war. This correspondence, published in the second volume of *Actes et Documents,* confirms, then, the stern opposition of the Church to National Socialism; but we already knew of the warnings of the German Bishops, of Faulhaber and von Galen, and of many religious and clergymen and, finally, the encyclical *Mit brennender Sorge,* read in all the German churches on Palm Sunday 1937 in spite of the Gestapo.

Therefore, we may only consider the assertion that the Church supported Nazism, as maintained by a Milan newspaper on January 6, 1998, a pure and simple lie. Furthermore, the texts published in the fifth volume of *Actes et Documents* disprove entirely the idea that the Holy See supported the Third Reich out of fear of Soviet Russia. When Roosevelt asked the Vatican to help overcome the American Catholics' opposition to his plan to extend to Russia, fighting against the Reich, the support already being given to Great Britain, he was listened to. The Secretariat of State charged the Apostolic Delegate in Washington to entrust to an American bishop the task of explaining that the encyclical *Divini Redemptoris*—which ordered Catholics to refuse alliances with all the Communist parties—was not to apply to the present situation and did not forbid the USA from helping Soviet Russia in its war against the Third Reich. These conclusions are incontestable.

For this reason, though not wishing to discourage future researchers, I am quite doubtful that the opening of the Vatican archives of the war period will modify our knowledge of those times. In that archive, as we already said, diplomatic and administrative documents are together with documents of a strictly confidential kind; this requires a longer postponement of the opening than for the archives of the Foreign Affairs Ministries of the different secular states. Anyone who, not wishing to wait, would like to go deeper into the history of that troubled period can already profitably work in the archives of the Foreign Office, of the Quai d'Orsay, of the Département d'Etat and of the other states represented at the Holy See. The dispatches of the English Minister Osborne show more vividly than the notes of the

Vatican Secretary of State the situation of the Holy See, surrounded in Fascist Rome, later fallen under the control of the German army and police.[8]

By devoting themselves to such researches without demanding a premature opening of the Vatican archives, they will show that their real desire is to seek the truth.

Part IV
Background Documentation

A. CHRONOLOGY OF POPE PIUS XII
B. ANNOTATED BIBLIOGRAPHY

A. Chronology of Pope Pius XII

Part I:
Major Biographical Dates

1876   Born in Rome of Virginia Graziosi, wife of Filippo Pacelli, March 2.
      Baptized Eugenio Maria Giuseppe Giovanni, March 4.

1880   Eugenio Pacelli entered kindergarten, and then attended elementary school.

1886   Received First Holy Communion.

1891   Studied at the Ennio Quirino Visconti Lyceum.

1894   Entered the Capranica Seminary in October; enrolled also at Gregorian University.

1895   Suffered a physical setback, requiring him to live at home, while continuing his studies.
      Registered in the Sapienza School of Philosophy and Letters and at the Papal Athenaum of St. Apollinaris for Theology. He received the Baccalaureate and Licentiate degrees *summa cum laude*.

1899   Ordained a priest, April 2.
      Assigned as curate to the Chiesa Nuova.
      Continued studies for a doctorate in Canon Law and Civil Law at the Apollinaris.

1901   Served as a research aide in the Office of the Congregation of Extraordinary Ecclesiastical Affairs.

1904   Became a Papal Chamberlain with the title of Monsignor.

1905   Became a Domestic Prelate.

1910   Represented the Holy See at the Coronation of King George V in London.

1911   Appointed Assistant Secretary of the Congregation of Extraordinary Ecclesiastical Affairs, March 7.

1912   Became Pro-Secretary of State, June 20.

1914   Became Secretary of the Congregation of Extraordinary Ecclesiastical Affairs, February 1.

1917   Appointed Nuncio to Bavaria, Germany, April 20.
Consecrated Bishop and elevated to the rank of Archbishop, May 13.
Presented his credentials to Ludwig III, King of Bavaria, May 28.

1920   Appointed First Apostolic Nuncio of Germany, June 22.

1924   Signed a Concordat with Bavaria, March 29, ratified by the Bavarian Parliament on January 15, 1925.

1925   Left Munich for residence in Berlin.

1929   Concluded a Concordat with Prussia, June 14, ratified August 14.
Recalled to Rome and received a Cardinal's hat on December 16.

1930   Appointed Secretary of State, February 7.
Became archpriest of the Vatican Basilica, March 25.

1934   Presided as Papal Legate at the International Eucharistic Congress in Buenos Aires, Argentina, October 10–14.

1935   Spoke at Lourdes, April 25–28, as Pope Pius XI's delegate to France for the closing days of the jubilee year honoring the nineteenth centenary of Redemption.

1936   Arrived in the United States of America on the *Conte di Savoia,* October 8, for an "unofficial" trip covering some eight thousand miles chiefly by plane, as he made an in-depth study of the American Church.
Invited to a luncheon at Hyde Park the day after President Franklin D. Roosevelt's reelection.

1937   Traveled to France in July as Cardinal-Legate to consecrate and dedicate the new basilica in Lisieux during the Eucharistic Congress.

1938   Presided at the International Eucharistic Congress in Budapest, May 25–30.

1939   Elected Pope, on March 2, taking the name of Pius XII.
Received the papal tiara, March 12. Issued his first encyclical,

Summi Pontificatus (On the Unity of Human Society—an attack on totalitarianism—October 20, after the Nazis' invasion of Poland, September 1).

1943   Issued *Mystici Corporis Christi,* June 29.

Comforted the injured, administered the Last Rites, distributed money to those in need of food and clothing when American bombers dropped hundreds of tons of explosives on Rome, July 19.

Issued *Divino Afflante Spiritu* (Biblical Studies), September 30.

1947   Issued *Fulgens Radiatur* (fourteenth centenary of St. Benedict), March 21.

Issued *Mediator Dei* (Liturgy of the Church), November 20.

1950   Defined dogma of the Assumption of the Virgin Mary, November 1, with a Papal Bull *(Munificentissimus Deus).*

Issued *Humani Generis,* August 12.

1953   Signed a Concordat with Spain, August 27.

1956   Reformed the Holy Week Liturgy.

1957   Issued *Fidei Donum* (Future of Africa).

1958   Death of Pope Pius XII, October 9.

Part II:
Wartime Messages

1939–1945

Much has been said and printed about Pope Pius XII's "alleged silence" over Nazi atrocities. On the other hand little appears to reveal what he did say through the Vatican Radio and what was printed in the Vatican newspaper, L'Osservatore Romano, *as well as in newspapers worldwide. The following is a partial listing of the Holy Father's messages:*

1939

August 24:   Pope Pius XII pleaded for the preservation of peace among nations.

August 31:   The Holy Father sent a message appealing for peace to the French, German, and Polish Ambassadors and to the British Minister.

November 10: Pius XII spoke about true peace and harmony among peoples during an audience with the Minister of Haiti.

December 24: In his Christmas Eve allocution to the Cardinals, Pius XII referred to the invasion of Poland and related events.

1940

January 2:   Renewing the papal plea for peace, Pius XII sent a message to the President of the United States.

April 15:   Letter to the Cardinal Secretary of State requesting that he announce publicly special prayers for the month of May.

May 11: The Pope referred to a world "poisoned by lies and disloyalty and wounded by excesses of violence," as he condemned the invasions of Belgium, Holland, and Luxemburg.

June 2: On his onomastic day Pius XII addressed the Cardinals of the Curia about the world conflict.

July 10: Pius XII spoke against the overvaluation of blood and race.

December 21: The Holy Father appealed for prayers and action to alleviate, especially among children, the sufferings caused by the war.

December 26: The Pope mentioned the work of the Holy See and pleaded for relief "to those poor people who are overcome by the sorrows and tribulations of war's calamities."

1941

March 30: Vatican Radio denounced Fascist racial theory and alluded to "the wickedness of Hitler."

April 13: In his Easter message, the Holy Father protested "atrocious forms of fighting...and treatment of prisoners and civilians."

April 20: The Pope urged the faithful to pray for peace, especially during the month of May.

June 2: On his onomastic day, the Holy Father again manifested his concern for suffering humanity.

September 21: His Holiness announced publicly that prayers be said in honor of Our Lady of the Rosary in October.

December 24: Pius XII pleaded for the safety of "those expelled from their native land and deported to foreign lands." He stated that in the interests of the common good the rights of the smaller states should be respected—"rights to political freedom, to economic development and to the adequate use of that neutrality which is theirs according to the natural, as well as international, law. In this way, and in

this way only, will they be able to obtain a fitting
share of the common good, and assure the material
and spiritual welfare of their people."

1942

April 15:   Pope Pius XII invited all to join him in a "crusade of
              prayer" to stop the massacre.

May 12:   On the twenty-fifth anniversary of his episcopal con-
              secration, he addressed the world by radio, reaffirm-
              ing his hope for peace.

December 24: Pius XII spoke about the "sad succession of acts at
              variance with the human and Christian sense." On
              Christmas Eve he denounced the war and emphasized
              reconciliation and a new internal order among the
              various nations.

1943

January 25:   Regarding the hardships affecting the faithful, the
              Pope sent a letter expressing his sorrow to the Cardi-
              nal Archbishop of Palermo, as he had already done
              for those of Genoa, Turin, Milan, and Naples.

June 2:   Vatican Radio stated: "He who makes a distinction
              between Jews and other men is unfaithful to God and
              is in conflict with God's commands." The Pope
              referred to "those who, because of their nationality or
              their descent, are pursued by mounting misfortune
              and increasing suffering....Those who guide the fate
              of nations should not forget that, in the words of the
              Scriptures, he who bears the sword is not therefore
              the master over the life and death of men, unless it be
              according to the divine law, from whence all power
              derives." He also mentioned his unsuccessful negoti-
              ations on behalf of the persecuted victims.

June 21:   Vatican Radio broadcasted in German a long text on
              the rights of Jews under natural law and, a few days
              later, a defense of Yugoslav Jews: "Every man bears
              the stamp of God."

July 20:	Pius XII wrote a letter to the Cardinal Vicar of Rome expressing his sorrow over the devastation of the Basilica of San Lorenzo during the bombing of Rome.
August 5:	The Pope wrote to Cardinal Maglione, Vatican Secretary of State, complaining that no heed was paid to his words and his efforts to replace hatred with charity.
September 1:	Four years after the beginning of the war, Pius XII's broadcast was entitled "Blessed Are the Peacemakers," in which he invoked blessings for those ready to make peace, together with a warning against giving "new life to the fire of hatred."
December 24:	In his 1943 Christmas message, Pius XII stated: "We see, indeed, only a conflict which is degenerating into that form of warfare which excludes all restriction and restraint....It is a form of warfare which proceeds without intermission on its terrible way, and piles up slaughter of such a kind that the most bloodstained pages of history pale in comparison with it....Every human sentiment is crushed and the light of reason eclipsed so that the words of wisdom are fulfilled: 'They were all found together with one chain of darkness.'"

1944

March 8:	In an address to the Romans, Pius XII spoke about "an air war that knows no law or restraint." He described his frustration at being unable to stop the deportations and exile of even the sick: "We recognize with bitterness of spirit how inadequate is all human help. There are misfortunes which even the most generous help of man cannot alleviate."
June 2:	Two days before the Allies entered Rome, the Pope referred to "the indigence on every side and the calls for help....For our thoughts, day and night, are bent on our own great problem: how we may be able to meet this bitter trial, helping all without distinction of nationality or race, and how we may help towards restoring peace at last to tortured mankind."

December 24:   In his Christmas broadcast to the world, Pius XII
stated: "If ever a generation has had to appreciate in
the depths of its heart the cry of 'War on war!', it is
certainly the present generation. Having passed
through an ocean of blood and tears in a form perhaps
never experienced in past ages, it has lived through
the inexorable atrocities with such intensity that the
recollection of so many horrors must remain stamped
on its memory, and even in the deepest recesses of its
soul, like a picture of Hell, against which anyone who
cherishes a sense of humanity desires more than anything else to close the door forever."

1945

March 19:   On Passion Sunday, His Holiness spoke about the
deepest cause of the terrible conflict and stated that it
"is the spirit of evil which sets itself up against the
spirit of God." And he continued: "For those who
have allowed themselves to be seduced by the advocates of violence, there is but one road to salvation: to
repudiate once and for all the idolatry of absolute
nationalism, the pride in origin, race and blood."

May 9:   In a short speech, Pius XII commented: "Kneeling in
spirit before the graves and the rivers red with blood
where lie the countless remains of those who fell
fighting, and of the victims of massacres, hunger or
misery, we commend them all in our prayers...."

June 2:   In this message to the Cardinals, Pius XII is truly an
"Architect for Peace." (Cf. Part III, Pope Pius XII's
Appeal for World Peace, pp. 143–52, for the entire
speech of June 2, 1945.)

B. Annotated Bibliography

*T*his annotated bibliography of selected works consists mainly of books and articles by scholars who support the role of Pope Pius XII. Most of them confirm the truth about (1) the commendable record of the Church; (2) the humanity and compassion of Pope Pius XII; and (3) the rescue by Catholics of countless European Jews and other targeted victims of the Nazis.

The Vatican's wartime documents have been published over a sixteen-year period (1965–1981) in *Actes et documents du Saint-Siège relatifs à la Seconde Guerre Mondiale.* One of its editors, Robert A. Graham, S.J., stated: "A study of the Vatican documents is the only way to understand the truth and to do justice to those who stretched a helping hand to the Jews in those tragic days."

The work began in 1964 at the request of Pope Paul VI when Rolf Hochhuth's antihistorical play, *The Deputy,* slandered Pius XII as a cold, "silent" Pope who allegedly placed the Church's interests ahead of those of the victims of Nazi atrocities. Numerous books added to this "black legend," by repeating falsehoods regarding Pius XII's wartime record.

At times, the legend expanded into a direct attack against the Pope, as well as against the entire Roman Catholic Church, particularly the German Catholic community. Notwithstanding the abundance of incontestable evidence, some Holocaust scholars repeat every myth about the Pope and the wartime Catholic Church. Yet, many books support, defend, and vindicate Pope Pius XII.

Actes et documents du Saint-Siège relatifs à la Seconde Guerre Mondiale. Vatican City: Libreria Editrice Vaticana, 1965–81, Tomes I–XI (Tome III in 2 vols.), edited by Pierre Blet, Robert A. Graham, Angelo Martini, and Burkhart Schneider.

Alexander, Edgar. *Hitler and the Pope: Pius XII and the Jews.* New York: Thomas Nelson, 1964. An excellent defense of Pius XII by a noted historian and sociologist who wrote the European best-seller, *The Hitler Myth* (1937).

———. "Rolf Hochhuth: Equivocal Deputy." *America,* October 12, 1963, pp. 416–18, 423. In this article, Alexander effectively eviscerates Hochhuth's play, and reveals "the anti-Semitic and anti-Catholic mental baggage" of a misguided playwright.

Alzinger, Joseph Adolphe. *A Dangerous Little Friar.* Translated by the Earl of Wicklow. Dublin: Clonmore and Reynolds, 1957.

Andreotti, Giulio. "Christians and Anti-Judaism." Editorial in *30 Days,* 1998, No. 10, pp. 4–9. Andreotti explains that Pius XI condemned *Action Française* for its anti-Semitism in 1926. The clearest condemnation of anti-Semitism is found in a decree of March 25, 1928: "The Holy See…condemns unreservedly hatred against the people once chosen by God; the hatred that commonly goes by the name of anti-Semitism."

Balling, Adalbert Ludwig. *Martyr of Brotherly Love.* New York: Crossroad, 1992.

Bentley, Eric. *The Storm Over* The Deputy. New York: Grove Press, Inc., 1964. A collection of materials about Rolf Hochhuth's anti-Catholic play.

Berenbaum, Michael, ed. *A Mosaic of Victims: Non-Jews Persecuted and Murdered by the Nazis.* New York: New York University Press, 1990.

Binchy, Daniel A. *Church and State in Fascist Italy.* London: Oxford University Press, 1970, revised edition.

Blet, Pierre. *Pie XII et la Seconde Guerre Mondiale d'après les archives du Vatican.* Paris: Perrin, 1997. Translated by Lawrence J. Johnson. *Pius XII and the Second World War: According to the Archives of the Vatican.* Mahwah, N.J.: Paulist Press/Leominster: Gracewing Publishing, 1999. This book summarizes Pius XII's assistance to all Nazi victims, demolishes the accusations launched at Pope Pius XII, establishes the historical record of his compassion and heroism, and documents his opposition to all totalitarian movements, especially Nazism.

———. "Controversy: Pius XII. Was There a Culpable Silence with Regard to the Holocaust?" *Inside the Vatican,* May 1998, pp. 52–57.

Bracher, Karl Dietrich. *The German Dictatorship: The Origins, Structure, and Effects of National Socialism.* Translated from the German by Jean Steinberg. New York: Holt, Rinehart and Winston, 1970. This is an important study by an eminent German historian who documents the resistance of many German Catholics and points out that Catholics voted against Hitler by and large.

Breitman, Richard. *Official Secrets: What the Nazis Planned, What the British and Americans Knew.* New York: Hill and Wang, 1998. This book is a broad effort to grasp the relationship between Nazi decisions, German behavior, and Western responses.

Bullock, Alan. *Hitler: A Study in Tyranny.* New York: Harper and Row, 1964. This study reveals Hitler's warped, anti-Christian life. It also explains the seven major plots to overthrow Hitler. For two of them, Pope Pius XII was an active mediator.

Carroll-Abbing, John Patrick. *But for the Grace of God.* Rome: O.N.C.R. and New Jersey: Delacorte Press, 1965.

Chadwick, William Owen. "The Pope and the Jews in 1942." In *Persecution and Toleration, Studies in Church History*, Vol. 21, edited by W. J. Sheils, Ecclesiastical History Society. Oxford: Blackwell, 1984.

———. *Britain and the Vatican during the Second World War.* Cambridge: Cambridge University Press, 1986.

Chélini, Jean. *L'Eglise sous Pie XII.* Paris: Libraire Fayard, 1983. Chélini concludes the first of two volumes by stating that the Pope saw the Nazis as criminals working for the destruction of the Church and civilization: "To accuse Pius XII of sympathy for the Nazis appears, in the light of the preceding pages, a dishonest absurdity."

"Christ in Buchenwald." *Catholic World*, February 1947, pp. 443–47.

Church in History Information Center (21 Elm Road North, Birkenhead, L42 9PB, United Kingdom). This is an invaluable resource center of historical information on the Catholic Church. These highly documented monographs defending the Church's wartime record are essential reading for an accurate account of the Church and Nazism: *The Roots of Nazism, Hitler's Rise to Power, Father Tiso, Slovakia and Hitler, Croatia 1941–46, Three Sermons against Racism by Archbishop Stepinac in 1943, Three Sermons by Bishop von Galen, Mit brennender Sorge.*

Cianfarra, Camille M. *The Vatican and the War.* New York: E. P. Dutton, 1944. A balanced, well-informed account by a *New York Times* journalist who covered the Vatican during the war years. It describes the Pope's relentless struggle against evil.

Cornwell, John. *Hitler's Pope: The Secret History of Pius XII.* New York: The Viking Press, 1999. This controversial work by British author John Cornwell is not a "secret history" at all but a miscellany of facts and speculation, little of which is new and some of which had been discredited before the book was written. The book harshly attacks Pope Pius XII via criticisms, misrepresentations and exaggerations. In distorting the truth about the efforts of the Catholic Church to save the Jews during World War II, it depicts Pius XII as an authoritarian, traditional Pope, claims that he collaborated with the Nazis and omits the real record of Jewish-Vatican relations that earned the appreciation of Jewish leaders of that generation throughout the world.

Courtois, Stephane et al. *The Black Book of Communism.* New York: Harvard University Press, 1997. This book caused a sensation when it appeared in Europe and has now been translated. It demonstrates that Communism was as evil as Nazism. Pius XII was not "obsessed" with Communism but was legitimately horrified by this appalling evil and—unlike so many who chose one or the other—fought vigorously against both.

Craughwell, Thomas J. "The Gentile Holocaust." In *Sursum Corda*, Summer 1998, pp. 28–30, 47–49. This article describes the suffering of non-Jews and documents that both Jews and Christians in Poland were systematically murdered by the Nazis.

Cunningham, Francis A. *The War upon Religion.* Boston: The Pilot Publishing Company, 1911. A cultural survey of the anti-Christian movements which paved the way for the twentieth century totalitarian ideologies.

Daniel-Rops, H. *A Fight for God, 1870–1939.* New York: E. P. Dutton and Company, Inc., 1965. This book documents the opposition of the Catholic Church to Fascism and Nazism and corrects many erroneous views about the Church's record.

De Felice, Renzo. *Storia degli ebrei italiani sotto il fascismo.* Torino: Giulio Einaudi editore, 1961.

Delp, Alfred. *Prison Meditations.* New York: Macmillan, 1966.

De Lubac, Henri. *Christian Resistance to Anti-Semitism: Memories from 1940–1944*. San Francisco: Ignatius Press, 1990. This book reveals the profound influence Pius XII had on the heroic French Catholics who rescued Jews.

Deuel, Wallace R. *People Under Hitler*. New York: Harcourt, Brace and Company, 1942.

Deutsch, Harold C. *The Conspiracy Against Hitler in the Twilight War.* Minneapolis: The University of Minnesota Press, 1970. This book reveals the various plots to overthrow Adolf Hitler from power with documents on Pius XII's mediation of and support for these efforts.

Dinneen, Joseph. *Pius XII: Pope of Peace*. New York: Robert McBride and Company, 1939.

Donahue, James. *Hitler's Conservative Opponents in Bavaria, 1930–1945*. Leiden: E. J. Brill, 1961. This is a description of German conservatives—both Catholic and Protestant—who resisted the Nazis during their rise and reign. There is a section on the White Rose student peace movement.

Doyle, Charles Hugo. *The Life of Pope Pius XII*. New York: Didier Publishing Company, 1945.

Duclos, Paul. *Le Vatican et la Seconde Guerre Mondiale*. Paris: Pedone, 1955.

Duffy, Eamon. *Saints and Sinners*. New Haven: Yale University Press, 1997. A modern history of the Papacy that provides an overall assessment of the Vatican during the Nazi era. Professor Duffy states that Pope Pius XII "did everything in his power to protect the Jews" and that the Vatican's wartime documents establish "the falsehood of Hochhuth's specific allegations" against him.

Duncan-Jones, Arthur. *The Struggle for Religious Freedom in Germany*. London: V. Gollancz, Ltd., 1938. Useful for the many documents appended to the text.

Encyclopedia of German Resistance to the Nazi Movement. Edited by Wolfgang Benz and Walter H. Pehle and translated by Lance W. Garmer. New York: Continuum Publishing, 1997.

Falconi, Carlo. *The Silence of Pius XII*. Boston: Little, Brown and Company, 1970. This book was reviewed by Graham in an essay published in the *Pilot*, Archdiocese of Boston, October 31, 1970, pp. 1, 16. As Graham shows, contrary to Falconi's assertions, there was no papal "silence" regarding Nazi atrocities. Falconi repeats Hochhuth's calumnies. When the English translation

appeared, six volumes of the Vatican's wartime documents had
been published. Falconi made no reference to these documents.

Faulhaber, Michael von. *Judaism, Christianity and Germany.* Translated by G. D. Smith. New York: Macmillan, 1935. Delivered
after the Nazis seized power, Cardinal Faulhaber's four Advent
sermons were a courageous defense of Christianity's Jewish
roots. He insisted: "The God of the New Testament is not a different God from the God of the Old Testament."

Fisher, Eugene J. "Jews, Catholics and the Holocaust." In *The Priest.*
Our Sunday Visitor Press. Part I: August 1995, pp. 10–15. Part II:
September 1995, pp. 34–38.

Flannery, Edward H. *The Anguish of the Jews: Twenty-Three Centuries
of Antisemitism.* New York/Mahwah, N.J.: A Stimulus Book published by Paulist Press, 1985. The late Father Flannery was an
ecumenical leader and pioneer. This revised edition is an important review of Jewish-Christian relations.

Fraenkel, Heinrich. *The German People versus Hitler.* London: Allen
and Unwin, 1939. After four months of war, Fraenkel emphasizes
the lack of enthusiasm of the German people for the victories over
Poland; a general resentment of the existing scarcity, restrictions
and severity, directed against the British blockade and the Nazis,
and a real apprehension about the future.

Friedländer, Henry. *The Origins of Nazi Genocide: From Euthanasia to
the Final Solution.* Chapel Hill: The University of North Carolina
Press, 1995. This book establishes how new "enlightened" science and medicine—not Christian theology—laid the ground-
work for the biological racial program of the Nazis, which led to
the euthanasia program of 1939–41, that murdered seventy thousand "defective" Germans and Austrians and led to the Nazi
Holocaust. Based on extensive research in American, German,
and Austrian archives as well as Allied and German court records,
the book also analyzes the involvement of the German bureaucracy and judiciary, the participation of physicians and scientists,
the motives of the killers, and the nature of popular opposition.

Friedländer, Saul. *Pius XII and the Third Reich.* New York: Alfred A.
Knopf, 1966. Graham's excellent critique and refutation of Saul
Friedländer's book was published in *America*, May 21, 1966, pp.
733–36.

————. *Nazi Germany and the Jews: The Years of Persecution 1933–1939*. New York: Harper-Collins, 1997.

Frossard, André. *Forget Not Love*. San Francisco: Ignatius Press, 1991.

Gallin, Mary Alice, O.S.U. *German Resistance to Hitler: Ethical and Religious Factors*. Washington, D.C.: The Catholic University of America Press, 1961. This is a highly documented book based upon research in Germany's wartime archives. It is the definitive refutation of Guenter Lewy's anti-Catholic statements.

Gasman, Daniel. *The Scientific Origins of National Socialism*. New York: American Elsevier Publishing Company, 1971. This book reveals that an atheistic worldview—not Christianity—inspired Nazism.

Gaspari, Antonio. "Justice for Pius XII!" In *Inside the Vatican*, June 1997, pp. 20–26. This article is an interview with Father Peter Gumpel, S.J., relator of the cause for beatification of Pius XII.

Gay, Peter. *My German Question*. New Haven: Yale University Press, 1998. Professor Gay is a Jewish scholar who grew up in Nazi Germany and barely escaped death with his family. He asserts that the Christian churches did protest both in Germany and throughout Europe.

"German Martyrs." In *Time*, December 23, 1940, pp. 38–40.

Gilbert, Martin. *Auschwitz and the Allies*. New York: Holt and Company, 1981. This book documents how Allies knew of the extermination of Jews but did little directly to stop it. Also documents Pius XII's condemnation of the Final Solution in his 1942 Christmas message on the Vatican Radio.

————. *The Holocaust: A History of the Jews of Europe during the Second World War*. New York: Holt, Rinehart and Winston, 1985. An outstanding history of the Holocaust by a Jewish historian crediting Pius XII for saving Jews. He is also Winston Churchill's official biographer.

Glass, James M. *Life Unworthy of Life; Racial Phobia and Mass Murder in Hitler's Germany*. New York: Basic Books, 1997.

Godden, G. M. *Poland: Yesterday, Today, and Tomorrow*. London: Burns, Oates and Washbourne, 1940. A succinct and powerful account of the Nazi invasion of Poland on September 1, 1939, and its horrifying aftermath for both Polish Catholics and Jews. Miss Godden includes important testimony from the world's press and from Vatican Radio on the atrocities in Poland.

Goebbels Diaries, The. Edited by Louis P. Lochner. London: Hamish
    Hamilton, Ltd., 1948. These volumes document the Nazi Propa-
    ganda Minister's hatred for Christianity, the Catholic Church, and
    the Pope. The July 27, 1943, entry explicitly attacks Pius XII for
    his assistance to the victims: "Again and again reports reached us
    that the Pope is feverishly at work during this entire crisis."

Gonella, Guido. *The Papacy and World Peace: A Study of the Christ-
    mas Messages of Pope Pius XII*. London: Helles and Carter, 1945.
    Gonella, an Italian humanist and scholar (who was arrested by
    Mussolini), examines the Pontiff's Christmas messages, which
    unequivocally condemned the evils of Fascism, Nazism, and anti-
    Semitism. This book is a powerful antidote to those who assert
    that Pius XII was "silent" during the war. Professor Gonella
    proves that the Pontiff was an outspoken champion of human
    rights and freedom for all.

Goodrick-Clarke, Nicholas. *The Occult Roots of Nazism*. New York: New
    York University Press, 1992. The historical oversight that ignores
    the role of the anti-Christian Occult Movement on the Nazis has
    been corrected in this book. Utilizing this book's excellent research,
    the Discovery Channel's television documentary, *Nazis: The Occult
    Conspiracy*, explains how the Third Reich created a reign of terror
    using ancient myths, pagan lore, and the occult.

Graham, Robert A. *Vatican Diplomacy*. Princeton: Princeton Univer-
    sity Press, 1959. This book received the John Gilmary Shea Prize
    of the American Catholic Historical Association. It is an outstand-
    ing study of Vatican diplomatic policy and is indispensable for
    understanding the Holy See's relations with world governments.
    This excellent, balanced presentation vindicates the Papacy.

————. "Pius XII and the Nazis: An Analysis of the Latest Charges That
    the Pope Was a 'Friend' of the Axis." In this article, published in
    America, December 5, 1964, pp. 742–43, the author responds to
    the accusation that Pius XII sympathized with the Axis: (1) Pius
    XII willingly aided the anti-Nazi German resistance, which plot-
    ted to abolish Hitler and his regime; (2) despite Axis pressure, the
    Pope sturdily refused to hail the mid-1941 Nazi attack on Russia
    as a "crusade"; (3) Pius XII supported Roosevelt's desire to
    extend Lend-lease to Russia.

————. *Pius XII's Defense of Jews and Others*. Milwaukee: Catholic
    League for Religious and Civil Rights, 1987.

———. *The Vatican and Communism in World War II. What Really Happened?* San Francisco: Ignatius Press, 1996. This book demolishes the allegation that Pius XII harbored secret sympathy for Nazism because he saw it as a "bulwark" against Communism. In fact, Pius XII regarded Nazism just as diabolical as Soviet Communism. He saw them as twin evils dedicated to the destruction of Judeo-Christian civilization. The Pope was aware of the infamous Nazi-Soviet Pact of 1939 to carve up Roman Catholic Poland. In his view, Nazism and Communism both had to be defeated.

———. *Nothing Sacred: Nazi Espionage Against the Vatican, 1939–1945.* London: Frank Cass, 1997. David Alvarez coauthored this book, which shows that the Nazis considered the Catholic Church an archenemy beyond any hope of accommodation, let alone collaboration.

Groppe, Lothar, S.J. "The Church's Struggle with the Third Reich." In *Fidelity Magazine*, October 1983, Part I, pp. 12–15, 23–27. "The Church and the Jews in the Third Reich," November 1983, Part II, pp. 18–26. This two-part essay contains translations of often neglected pastorals of German Catholic bishops. Written by one of Germany's top Church historians, these articles show the Church's fierce opposition to Nazism and anti-Semitism, as well as its assistance to European Jewry.

———. *Hitler and the Christians.* Translated by E. F. Peeler. New York: Sheed and Ward, 1936.

Gurian, Waldemar. "Hitler's Undeclared War on the Catholic Church." *Foreign Affairs*, XVI, 1938, pp. 260–71.

Haecker, Theodor. *Journal in the Night.* Translated by Alexander Dru. New York: Pantheon Books, 1950. Haecker, a convert to the Catholic Church, was associated with Karl Muth, editor of *Hochland*, and knew the *Scholl* group. His diary expresses strong anti-Nazi sentiments.

Halecki, Oscar, and James F. Murray, Jr. *Pius XII: Eugenio Pacelli, Pope of Peace.* New York: Farrar, Straus and Young, Inc., 1951.

Hales, E. E.Y. *The Catholic Church in the Modern World: A Survey from the French Revolution to the Present.* New York: Hanover House, 1958. It includes a chapter on the papacy's vigorous opposition to Communism, Fascism, and Nazism.

Hamerow, T. S. *On the Road to the Wolf's Lair: German Resistance to Hitler.* Boston: Harvard University Press, 1997.

Hamilton, Richard. *Who Voted for Hitler?* Princeton: Princeton University Press, 1982. This book is an analysis of the voting patterns of German citizens during the rise of Hitler and proves that German Catholics voted overwhelmingly against him. Hamilton writes: "Unlike the situation in Protestant communities, where some elites or notables, if not actively supporting the National Socialists, at least vouched for them as worthy allies in the national struggle, in Catholic communities, the leaders, both lay and clerical, were overwhelmingly opposed to their aspirations." In the 1932 elections, when the Nazis gained their greatest electoral successes, more than half the non-Catholic Germans voted National Socialist; fewer than fifteen percent of Catholic Germans voted National Socialist.

Hatch, Alden and Seamus Walshe. *Crown of Glory: The Life of Pope Pius XII.* New York: Hawthorne Books, Inc., 1957.

Herzer, Ivo, Klaus Voight, and James Burgwyn. *The Italian Refuge: Rescue of Jews During the Holocaust.* Washington, D.C.: The Catholic University of America, 1989.

Hilberg, Raul. *Perpetrators, Victims, Bystanders.* New York: Harper-Collins, 1992. This book is an attack on Pius XII.

Hitler's Secret Conversations 1941–1944. Introduction by H. R. Trevor-Roper. New York: Farrar, Straus and Young, 1953. Hitler reveals his hatred for both Judaism and Christianity.

Hitler Speaks: A Series of Political Conversations with Adolf Hitler on His Real Aims. London, 1939. (See Rauschning, *The Voice of Destruction.*)

Hoffman, Peter. *The History of the German Resistance, 1933–1945.* Cambridge: MIT Press, 1977. Hoffman is considered an authority on the anti-Nazi German Resistance. He maintains that the churches were the only effective forces to resist Nazism. Of the Catholic Church, he writes: "It could not silently accept the general persecution, regimentation or oppression....Over the years until the outbreak of war Catholic resistance stiffened until finally its most eminent spokesman was the Pope himself (Pius XI) with his encyclical *Mit brennender Sorge* of March 14, 1937, read from all German Catholic pulpits. Clemens August Graf von Galen, Bishop of Muenster, was typical of the many fearless Catholic speakers." Hoffman states that "the churches achieved a certain success, for even during the war the Nazi rulers did not think that they could risk complete destruction of the churches. They were confronted here with barriers they could not understand—the fortitude and integrity of religious conviction, conscience and a sense of responsibility for one's fellow men which were not to be extinguished by regulations and prohibitions."

Holmes, J. Derek. *The Papacy in the Modern World 1914–1978*. New York: Crossroad, 1981.

Is the Catholic Church Anti-Social? A Debate Between G. G. Coulton and Arnold Lunn. London: Catholic Book Club, 1947. Lunn, a Catholic scholar and apologist, debates Coulton, an anti-Catholic historian, on the historical wartime record of the Church. Following Albert Einstein's tribute to the Church, Lunn quotes Countess Waldeck, daughter of a Jewish banker in Mannheim: "There exist opponents to Hitler whose strength of soul and integrity is so great that, notwithstanding the calumnies with which the Nazis have tried to smear them, the Germans know that these men risk their lives and liberty, not for selfish interest, but for the spiritual protection of the Fatherland. For these men are Churchmen. Their every sermon and every pastoral letter is a political event in the Germany of today and no word by them is ever lost." In her book, *Excellenx*, the Countess pays tribute to the Catholic Bishops, "whose utterances are a remarkably frank denunciation of Nazi treatment of the Jews and conquered people and their contempt for individual rights....To all practical intents and purposes Catholic opposition to Nazism has been much more important and articulate than Protestant opposition."

John Paul II, Pope. *Crossing the Threshold of Hope*. New York: Knopf, 1994.

"Judging Pope Pius XII." Lead story in *Inside The Vatican*, June 1997, pp. 12–19.

Kempner, Benedicta Maria. *Priester vor Hitlers Tribunalen*. Munich: Rutten und Loening, 1966.

Kershaw, Ian. *Hitler: 1889–1936: Hubris*. New York: W. W. Norton and Company, 1999. The first of a two-volume biography reveals Hitler's hatred of Judaism and Christianity and his plans to annihilate both. It also documents the Catholic Church's resistance to Nazism.

Klaas, Augustine, S.J. "The Apostle of Munich." In *Catholic Mind*, 1953, pp. 599–602.

Klemperer, Victor. *I Will Bear Witness: A Diary of the Nazi Years, 1933–1941*. New York: Random House, 1998. Translated with a preface by Martin Chalmers, this is the first of two diaries in which Klemperer recorded the day-to-day experience of living as a Jew in Germany under Hitler. It is an unvarnished account of his life and full of observations on the nature of the Nazi regime. It demonstrates how Catholic friends resisted the Nazis.

Kluz, Ladislaus. *Kolbe and the Kommandant*. Translated by M. Angela Santor. Steubenville: DeSmet Foundation, 1984.

Krieg, Robert Anthony. *Karl Adam: Catholicism in German Culture*. London: University of Notre Dame, 1992. An excellent biography of Germany's leading Catholic theologian during the Nazi era, with several chapters on the confrontation with Nazism.

Kuehnelt-Leddihn, Erik von. *The Timeless Christian*. Chicago: Franciscan Herald Press, 1969. A political scientist, the author was an opponent of Hitler and the Nazis. His book contains an appendix that dismantles and refutes Rolf Hochhuth's play, *The Deputy*.

Lamb, Richard. *War in Italy 1943–1945*. New York: St. Martin's Press, 1993. This is an excellent study by one of Great Britain's leading military historians who is himself a World War II veteran. It contains an important chapter on the Nazi occupation of Rome and Pius XII's rescue efforts that "saved the lives of a great number of Roman Jews." In conclusion Lamb states: "Pius XII's record of opposition to Hitler throughout the war is impressive."

Lapide, Pinchas. *Three Popes and the Jews*. New York: Hawthorn Books, 1967. This book responds to Rolf Hochhuth's play *The Deputy* and Saul Friedländer's *Pius XII and the Third Reich*, which condemned the Papacy for allegedly placing its own interests over those of Jewish lives. In a country-by-country analysis of wartime Europe, Lapide responds by documenting the exceptional relief and rescue program conducted by the Pope and his diplomats. Lapide reports statements of appreciation from many prominent Jewish people after the death of Pius XII and adds: "No pope in history has been thanked more heartily by Jews."

Lapin, Daniel. *America's Real War*. Sisters, Oregon: Multnomah Publishers, 1999. Rabbi Lapin includes a chapter on "Christians and the Holocaust," defends the Jewish-Christian alliance, condemns the attempt to blame Christianity for Nazism, and praises Pius XII.

Lapomarda, Vincent A. *The Jesuits and the Third Reich (Texts and Studies in Religion, Vol. 39)*. New York: Edwin Mellen Press, 1989. Contains an outstanding bibliography on the Church's opposition to Nazism, including recent German scholarship that anti-Pius XII historians fail to consult. It focuses on Jesuit efforts in defense of human rights, particularly those of Jews. It is a highly documented volume on how the Jesuits—under the inspiration and direction of Pope Pius XI and Pope Pius XII—fought Nazism and anti-Semitism. It helps one to better understand the dimensions of the Holocaust, which took its toll on Jews and Gentiles alike.

Lehnert, Pascalina. *Pio XII. Il privilegio di servirlo*. Milan: Rusconi, 1984.

Lenz, Johann Maria. *Christ in Dachau*. Translated by Barbara Waldstein. Vienna: Missionsdruckerei St. Gabriel, 1960.

Lewy, Guenter. *The Catholic Church and Nazi Germany*. New York: McGraw-Hill, 1964. Though it was published over thirty years ago, Lewy's book continues to have an extraordinary influence upon authors who have not the knowledge to recognize its errors. Graham's review, "A Return to Theocracy," is a brilliant, point-by-point refutation of Lewy's assertions, published in *America*, July 18, 1964, pp. 70–72.

Levai, Jenö. *Hungarian Jewry and the Papacy*. London: Sands and Company, 1968. Levai, an eminent Jewish historian, is the foremost authority on the Holocaust in Hungary and an outspoken champion of Pope Pius XII. He has publicly rebuked other historians for maligning the Pope. In this book, he documents how the Hungarian Nuncio and the bishops of the Catholic Church "intervened again and again on the instructions of the Pope," and explains that because of these directives "in the autumn and winter of 1944 there was practically no Catholic Church institution in Budapest where persecuted Jews did not find refuge." The book contains an important preface by Robert M. Kempner, deputy chief U.S. Prosecutor at the Nuremberg war trials, who categorically rejected Rolf Hochhuth's malicious thesis against Pope Pius XII.

Lichten, Joseph. *A Question of Judgment: Pius XII and the Jews*. Washington, D.C.: U.S. Catholic Conference, 1963.

———. *Pius XII and the Holocaust. A Reader*. Milwaukee: Catholic League for Religious and Civil Rights, 1988.

Lipschitz, Chaim. *Franco, Spain and the Jews*. New York: KTAV Publishing, 1984. Revealing Catholic rescue efforts, Rabbi Lipschitz concludes: "The pattern of unmistakable humanitarian aid by the Spanish government during the war remains unmatched among Western and neutral governments, many of whom were in much more fortunate political and economic circumstances."

Lukas, John. *The Hitler of History*. New York: Alfred A. Knopf, 1997. An important study which examines previous biographies of Hitler and concludes that, far from being the product of a traditionalist conservative Catholic background, Hitler was a revolutionary who wanted to overturn and annihilate Judeo-Christian civilization.

Lukas, Richard C. *The Forgotten Holocaust: The Poles Under German Occupation, 1939–1945*. University Press of Kentucky, 1986; revised edition, New York: Hippocrene Books, Inc., 1997. The genocidal policies of the Nazis resulted in the deaths of about as many Polish Gentiles as Polish Jews. This book focuses on how the Poles responded to the German occupation and how they, as covictims of the Holocaust, got along with the Jews during this tragic era. It refutes "Polish anti-Semitism accusations."

Marchione, Margherita. *Yours Is a Precious Witness: Memoirs of Jews and Catholics in Wartime Italy*. New York/Mahwah, N.J.: Paulist Press, 1997. This book traces both documentary and anecdotal evidence of Pope Pius XII's efforts. His example inspired Italians to respond with countless acts of individual heroism. Convents, monasteries, and papal buildings in Italy became havens for refugees.

——. "Jews, Catholics and Pope Pius XII." In *The Catholic Answer*, September/October 1998, pp. 36–43.

——. "Pius XII and the Jews." In *Culture Wars*, South Bend, Ind., September 1998, pp. 14–17.

——. "Silence? Choosing Diplomacy Over Protest." In *Sisters Today*, Collegeville, Minn., September 1998, pp. 367–74.

——. "The Truth About Pope Pius XII." In *Catalyst, Journal of the Catholic League for Religious and Civil Rights*. New York, March 1998, pp. 8–9.

——. "The Silence of Pope Pius XII." In *Social Justice Review*, St. Louis, Mo., July/August 1998, pp. 100–105.

————. "Answering Questions and Charges." In *Inside the Vatican,* New Hope, Ky., January 1999, pp. 68–74. Part Two, "Questions About Catholics and the Holocaust," March 1999, pp. 70–78.

————. *Pius XII: Architect for Peace.* New York/Mahwah, N.J.: Paulist Press, 2000.

Marrus, Michael. *The Holocaust in History.* Hanover: University Press of New England, 1987. It is an attack on Pius XII and repeats the calumnies of Hochhuth, Lewy, et al.

Mason, John Brown. *Hitler's First Foes.* Minneapolis: Burgess, 1936.

Meltzer, Milton. *Rescue: The Story of How Gentiles Saved Jews in the Holocaust.* New York: Harper and Row, 1988. The various stories about rescue offer reasons for hope and for the belief in the goodness of men, women, and children who risked their lives to save Jews. These heroes and heroines made moral choices and by their courageous actions, defying the Nazi plan for extermination, they show us that one need not be passive or silent in the face of evil.

Micklem, Nathaniel. *National Socialism and Christianity.* Oxford: Clarendon Press, 1939.

————. *National Socialism and the Roman Catholic Church, 1933–1938.* New York: Oxford University Press, 1939.

Mignault, R. P. Albert-Marie, O.P. *La résistance aux lois injuste et la doctrine catholique.* Montreal: Bibliothèque de l'Action Française, 1921.

Mlodozeniec, Juventyn M. L. *I Knew Blessed Maximilian.* AMI Press, 1979.

Morley, John F. *Vatican Diplomacy and the Jews during the Holocaust: 1939–1943.* New York: KTAV Publishing House, 1980. Father Morley's book has become the "Bible" of anti-Pius XII commentators who conclude that the Pope failed to adequately assist European Jewry. In a review/critique in *America*, August 9, 1980, Father Robert Graham described Morley's work as "a grotesque anti-historical and in the end self-defeating incrimination." A more comprehensive review in the *Long Island Catholic* (August 14, 1980, pp. 1–2) is titled "Father Morley's Book Is Strange and Unfair." Graham demonstrates Morley's misunderstanding of papal diplomacy and misinterpretation of wartime documents. Morley does not include important documents found in the last volumes of *Actes...,* published in 1980 and 1981.

Murphy, Paul I. and R. René Arlington. *La Popessa*. New York: Warner Books, 1983. This book about Sister Pascalina (Pius XII's housekeeper) claims incorrectly that before becoming Pope, Eugenio Pacelli gave money to Adolf Hitler (The two never met!), and that after the Nazi invasion of Russia, Pius XII prayed for a Nazi victory. In fact, the opposite was the case: Pius XII took active measures to assist the Allies, as his correspondence with President Roosevelt amply reveals.

Neuhäusler, Johann Bapt. *Kreuz und Hakenkreuz*. Munich: Katholische Kirche Bayerns, 1946. The two volumes document the Catholic Church's bitter struggle against the Nazi regime. Monsignor Neuhäusler was a Dachau prisoner for four years.

———. *What Was It Like in a Concentration Camp at Dachau?* Translated from the German. 7th edition. Munich: Manz, 1960, 1973.

Neumann, Franz. *Behemoth: The Structure and Practice of National Socialism 1933–1944*. New York: Oxford University Press, 1944.

O'Carroll, Michael. *Pius XII: Greatness Dishonoured*. Dublin: Laetare Press, 1980. In this extraordinarily well-documented volume on the life and legacy of Pope Pius XII, O'Carroll makes ample use of the Vatican wartime archives and other source material to systematically demolish the accusations against Pius XII. Objective scholars will concur with Father O'Carroll's conclusion: "The criticism of the Pope is, to borrow Father Robert Graham's phrase, 'a fabricated scandal.' Pius XII is the greatest benefactor of the Jewish race in modern times."

Oesterreicher, John. *The New Encounter Between Christians and Jews*. New York: Philosophical Library, 1985. Monsignor Oesterreicher, founder of the Institute of Judeo-Christian Studies, Seton Hall University (1953), presents an outstanding collection of essays on Jewish-Catholic Relations, which refute the charge that Christianity is responsible for the Holocaust.

———. "The Deputy." In *America*, November 9, 1963, pp. 570–82.

———. "The Challenge of the Holocaust" (Review/essay *of Auschwitz: Beginning of a New Era?*). In *America*, June 11, 1977, pp. 525–27.

———. "A Night to Be Burned into Our Hearts: A Meditation on the 50th anniversary of the *Kristallnacht*." In *America*, November 5, 1988, pp. 332–33.

———. "Anatomy of Contempt: A Critique of R. R. Ruether's *Faith and Fratricide*" (Teshuvah Paper #4). South Orange, N.J.: Institute of Judaeo-Christian Studies.

———. "The Brotherhood of Christians and Jews." South Orange, N.J.: Institute of Judaeo-Christian Studies.

Padellaro, Nazareno. *Portrait of Pius XII*. Translated by Michael Derrick. London: Catholic Book Club, 1956.

Palazzini, Pietro. *Il clero e l'occupazione di Roma*. Rome: Apes, 1995.

Papeleux, Leon. *Les Silences de Pie XII*. Brussels: Nouvelles Editions Vokaer, 1980.

Pawlikowski, John. "Pius XII and the Jews—Further Research, Please." In *Commonweal*, July 17, 1998. Father Pawlikowski calls Pope Pius XII an "enigmatic figure," and comments that the term "silent" may be appropriate. Obviously, he has not consulted the twelve volumes of documents nor the countless books of testimonials by witnesses and contemporaries who were saved because of the Pope's prudent diplomacy. Yet, he justly states that the Christmas messages show the Pope calling for "an entirely new social order in Europe and in the world-at-large, an order that would enhance justice and peace for all."

Perrin, Henri. *Priest-Workman in Germany*. New York: Sheed and Ward, 1948.

Persecution of the Catholic Church in German-Occupied Poland, The. London: Burns & Oates, 1941. Reports by Cardinal Hlond of Poland as well as translated material from Vatican Radio and *L'Osservatore Romano* that included documentary evidence on the Nazi assault against the Polish Church.

Persecution of the Catholic Church in the Third Reich, The. London: Burns & Oates, 1940. Edited by W. Mariaux and published with the approval of Pope Pius XII. This is a compilation of primary source material from Nazi Germany, translated into English.

Phayer, M. "Pope Pius XII, the Holocaust, and the Cold War." In *Holocaust and Genocide Studies*, Vol. 12, No. 2, Fall 1990, pp. 203–50. The argument, that the Pope was sympathetic to the Germans because of his fear of the Bolsheviks, has been rejected by Father Robert Graham in *The Vatican and Communism in World War II. What Really Happened?* (Ignatius Press, 1996).

Phillips, Peter. *The Tragedy of Nazi Germany.* New York: Frederick A. Praeger, 1969. A former British prisoner of war who survived a

Nazi concentration camp and later became a distinguished professor of history. This book strongly praises Pope Pius XII's wartime
activities on behalf of Jews and other Nazi victims.

Pies, Otto. *The Victory of Father Karl*. New York: Farrar, Straus and
Cudahy, 1957.

Pinson, Koppel J., ed. *Essays on Antisemitism*. 2nd edition, revised and
enlarged. New York: Conference on Jewish Relations, 1946.

Pollard, J. F. *The Vatican and Italian Fascism 1929–1932*. Cambridge:
Cambridge University Press, 1985.

The Pontifical Commission for Justice and Peace. *The Church and
Racism: Towards a More Fraternal Society*. Vatican City, 1988.

The Pope Speaks: The Teachings of Pope Pius XII. Compiled and
edited by Michael Chinigo with the assistance of the Vatican
archives. New York: Pantheon Books, 1957. The manuscript was
submitted to the Holy Father for approval and represents the
essence of his message to the world.

Power, Michael. *Religion in the Reich*. London: Longmans, 1939. This
is an eyewitness account of Nazi persecution of Christianity.

Rauschning, Hermann. *Die Revolution des Nihilismus*, 1938. Published
in English as *The Revolution of Nihilism*. London: Heinemann,
1939; New York: Longmans, Green and Company; Garden City
Publishing Co., 1940.

———. *Gespräche mit Hitler*. Zurich and Vienna, 1940. Published in
the United States as *The Voice of Destruction*. New York: G. P.
Putnam's Sons, 1940. Published in England as *Hitler Speaks: A
Series of Political Conversations with Hitler on His Real Aims*.
London: Butterworth, 1939. An early associate of Hitler, later a
critic, Rauschning soon turned against him. In a series of books
the author revealed the ruthless character of Hitler, his hatred of
the Christian churches, and his plans to destroy them.

"Records and Documents of the Holy See Relating to the Second
World War," in *Yad Vashem Studies* 15, 1983, 327–45.

Rhodes, Anthony. *The Vatican in the Age of the Dictators 1922–1945*.
New York: Holt, Rinehart and Winston, 1973. This book by a distinguished scholar is one of the first works to make use of the Vatican
archives, as well as the largely unexamined state papers of the warring countries. Rhodes not only establishes the true wartime record
of Pope Pius XII, but also refutes unfounded allegations that the
Papacy harbored sympathy for Fascism and Nazism.

Ritter, Gerhard. "The German Opposition to Hitler." In *Contemporary Review*, CLXXVII, 1950, pp. 339–45.

——. *The German Resistance*. London: Ruskin House, 1958. Translated by R. T. Clark and published in America by Praeger. Ritter, a well-known German historian who was jailed by the Nazis, pays tribute to the anti-Nazi convictions of German Catholic bishops. On page 56: "They [the bishops] declared expressly that they were obliged to enter the lists on behalf not only of religious and ecclesiastical rights but of 'human rights as such' without which culture must collapse. They therefore never shrank from an even stronger protest than that of the Evangelicals against the arbitrary confiscation of private property, against the concentration camp, against the methods of police spying, against the shooting of innocent hostages or prisoners and the abduction of foreign workers and, of course, against the extermination of the mentally afflicted."

Roche, Georges and Saint-Germain, Philippe. *Pie XII devant l'histoire*. Paris: Laffont, 1972. This book reports that, on Vatican orders, an estimated one million Jews were being housed in convents and monasteries throughout Europe. He also states that the Catholic Refugee Committee in Rome enabled thousands of European Jews to enter the United States as "Catholics," providing them with documentation, including baptismal certificates, financial aid, and other transnational arrangements.

Rothfels, Hans. *The German Opposition to Hitler*. Hinsdale, Ill.: Henry Regnery Company, 1948. This publication shows convincing insight into the reality of a continuous anti-Nazi movement within Germany and its basic ethical motivation.

Schafer, Peter. *The Ancient World*. Boston: Harvard University Press, 1997. This distinguished scholar clearly demonstrates that anti-Semitism did not begin with the birth of Christianity.

Schwartz, Michael. *The Persistent Prejudice: Anti-Catholicism in America*. Bloomington, Ind.: Our Sunday Visitor, 1984. This book reveals how and why anti-Catholic bigotry develops. Contains an excellent chapter on anti-Catholicism provoked by Rolf Hochhuth's play *The Deputy*.

Scrivener, Jane. *Inside Rome with the Germans*. New York: Macmillian, 1945. In her diary, Jesse Lynch, an American citizen known as Mother Mary St. Luke, uses the pen name of Jane Scrivener. She depicts the role of Pope Pius XII and the Vatican with great spontaneity in an authentic eyewitness account about rescue efforts the Pope was directing and coordinating. She describes the months of suspense, hope, and despair as food was scarce and the city of Rome was overcrowded with refugees and escaped war prisoners. Many details about the Allied bombings and other historic events taking place in Rome are also included.

Simpson, William C. *A Vatican Lifeline '44.* New York: Sarpedon, 1996. A Glasgow gunner, Simpson was taken prisoner in June 1942 and transported to Italy. He escaped and joined the underground Vatican network directed by Monsignor Hugh O'Flaherty of the Vatican's Holy Office. This is a well-deserved tribute to the heroism of Vatican clergy and Italian citizens.

Shirer, William L. *The Rise and Fall of the Third Reich, A History of Nazi Germany.* New York: Simon and Schuster, 1960. This is a balanced, well-informed book that shows the anti-Christian, pagan roots of Nazism.

Smith, Howard K. *Last Train from Berlin.* New York: Alfred Knopf, 1942. An eyewitness account by famed reporter of activities inside Nazi Germany, revealing the heroism of anti-Nazi Catholic Germans, who were inspired by Pius XII.

"Speaking of the Jews." In *The Bible Today*, April 12, 1964, pp. 864–68.

Stasiewski, Bernhard and Volk, Ludwig. *Akten Deutscher Bischofe über die Lage der Dirche, 1933–1945.* Mainz: Matthias-Grünewald, 1968–1985. This publication in six volumes contains the formal statements of the German Bishops who were inspired by Pope Pius XII and Church teachings in defense of human rights and against Nazi racism and anti-Semitism.

Stehle, Hansjakob. *Eastern Politics of the Vatican, 1917–1979.* Translated by Sandra Smith. Athens: Ohio University Press, 1979. A hostile and prejudiced book that repeats all the errors about Pius XII, unaware of the evidence that vindicates him.

Stewart, Ralph. *Pope Pius XII and the Jews.* New Hope, Ky.: St. Joseph Canonical Foundation, 1990.

Taylor, Telford. *Sword and Swastika.* New York: Simon and Schuster, 1952.

"The Church and the Holocaust, As John Paul II Defends Pius XII." In *Inside the Vatican*, April 1998, pp. 28–32.

The Tablet (London). During the 1930s and 1940s many articles document the life and death struggle between the Catholic Church and the Nazis, as well as the Church's extraordinary assistance to victims in Germany, Czechoslovakia, Rumania, Poland, Russia, Yugoslavia, Latvia, Holland, France, Hungary, Lithuania, Germany, etc.

Tolstoy, Nikolai. *Stalin's Secret War*. New York: Holt, Rinehart and Winston, 1981. The author, a descendant of Leo Tolstoy, demonstrates that at least half of the estimated thirty million Russians who died during World War II were killed because of Joseph Stalin's murderous practices. The Western Allies were indifferent to these practices. Pope Pius XII was the only morally consistent force in world politics at the time who opposed Communism as strongly as he opposed Nazism.

"Vatican Document, *We Remember: A Reflection on the Shoah.*" The Holy See's Commission for Religious Relations with the Jews. *Inside the Vatican*, April 1998, pp. 2–7.

Von Hassell, Ulrich. *The Von Hassell Diaries: The Story of the Forces Against Hitler Inside Germany, 1938–1944*. San Francisco: Westview Press, 1947; reprinted 1994. The day-by-day testament of a leader of the anti-Nazi German resistance. It documents Pius XII's active assistance to the anti-Nazi cause within Germany and the esteem in which the Pontiff was held. Talks were arranged through the Pope for the purpose of laying a foundation for the discussion of peace terms after a change in the German regime. The confidential agent for Operation X was Dr. Josef Müller. Omitted in the translation are many valuable notes and appendices.

Waller, John H. *The Unseen War in Europe: Espionage and Conspiracy in the Second World War*. New York: Random House, 1996. This book picks up and expands upon Harold Deutsch's book, *The Conspiracy Against Hitler in the Twilight War*. Waller unveils recent revelations concerning espionage activities against Hitler. Included is a chapter entitled, "Operation X: The Vatican Connection," which describes Pius XII's daring efforts to remove Hitler from power.

Weiss, John. *Ideology of Death: Why the Holocaust Happened in Germany*. Chicago: Ivan R. Dee Company, 1997. This is a virulent attack on Christianity and Pius XII.

Wohl, Louis de. *Pope Pius XII: The World's Shepherd.* New York: Vision Books, published by Farrar, Strauss and Cudahy, 1961.

Woodruff, Douglas. "Pius XII and the Jews." In *The Tablet*, May 11, 1963, pp. 504–6; June 29, 1963, pp. 714–15.

Woodward, Kenneth L. "In Defense of Pius XII," in *Newsweek*, March 30, 1998, p. 35.

Yerushalmi, Yosef Hayim. "Response to Rosemary Ruether." In Eva Fleischner, ed., *Auschwitz: Beginning of a New Era?* New York: KTAV/ADL/St. John the Divine Cathedral, 1977, pp. 97–107.

Yla, Stasys. *A Priest in Stutthof.* New York: Manyland Books, 1971.

Zahn, Gordon. *German Catholics and Hitler's Wars: A Study in Social Control.* London: Sheed and Ward, 1962. Zahn, a Catholic scholar with a pacifist outlook, published this book in an attempt to indict Germany's Catholic bishops during the Nazi era and alleges that they supported the Nazi war effort. Contrary to Zahn's assertions, these bishops were strongly opposed to Nazi ideology and war aims. In a devastating rebuttal, Father Robert Graham exposes Zahn's book as a simplistic, superficial lack of analysis that grossly distorts the true record of the German bishops. The review was published in *America*, April 28, 1962, pp. 145–46.

Zajaczkowski, Waclaw. *Martyrs of Charity (A Christian and Jewish Response to the Holocaust).* Washington, D.C.: St. Maximilian Kolbe Foundation, 1988. This book was written by a Polish Catholic survivor whose family was honored by Israel for rescuing wartime Jews from the Nazis. The Introduction refutes the lie that Christianity provoked the Nazi campaign against the Jews and describes the suffering of approximately three million Polish Catholics.

Zolli, Eugenio. *Before the Dawn.* New York: Sheed and Ward, 1954. Reprinted with the title, *Why I Became a Catholic.* New York: Roman Catholic Books, 1997.

Part V
Appendix

A. INTRODUCTION
B. DOCUMENTS

A. Introduction

Documents regarding the extraordinary peace efforts and the humanitarian work of the Holy See have been published in the twelve-volume series, *Actes et documents du Saint-Siège relatifs à la Seconde Guerre Mondiale* (1939–1945), Rome: Libreria Editrice Vaticana, 1965–1981. The following documents in English have been selected from Volume 1, *Le Saint-Siège et la guerre en Europe;* Volumes 5 and 7, *Le Saint-Siège et la guerre mondiale;* and Volumes 6, 8, 9, and 10, *Le Saint-Siège et les victimes de la guerre:*

1. Peace Efforts of Pope Pius XII

Volume 1, *Le Saint-Siège et la guerre en Europe (The Holy See and the War in Europe, March 1939–August 1940)* 1970, 558 pages, consists of a 94-page Introduction and includes 379 documents in English, French, German, Italian, or Latin, with Footnotes and an Index. There are five Appendices: 1. Letters of Pope Pius XII to King Leopold of Belgium; 2. List of members of the Secretariat of State; 3. List of Vatican Representatives throughout the world; 4. Diplomatic Corps as of January 1, 1940; 5. Correspondence between Cardinal Luigi Maglione and Nuncio Filippo Cortesi in Warsaw.

2. World War II

Volume 5, *Le Saint-Siège et la guerre mondiale (The Holy See and the World War, July 1941–October 1942)* 1969, 795 pages, consists of a 63-page Introduction and includes 511 documents in English, French, Italian, and Latin, with Footnotes and an Index.

3. Jewish Leaders and Organizations

Volume 6, *Le Saint-Siège et les victimes de la guerre (The Holy See and the Victims of the War, March 1939–December 1940]* 1972, 559 pages, consists of a 37-page Introduction and includes 519 documents in English, French, German, Italian, and Latin, with Footnotes and an Index.

4. World War II

Volume 7, *Le Saint-Siège et la guerre mondiale (The Holy See and the World War, November 1942–December 1943)* 1973, 767 pages, consists of a 70-page Introduction and includes 505 documents in English, French, Italian, and Latin, with Footnotes and an Index.

5. Assistance to Prisoners of War

Volume 8, *Le Saint-Siège et les victimes de la guerre (The Holy See and Victims of the War, January 1941–December 1942),* 1974, 807 pages, consists of a 67-page Introduction and includes 581 documents in English, French, German, Italian, and Latin, a List of 644 unpublished documents in abridged form or mentioned in Footnotes, and an Index.

6. Work of the Vatican Information Bureau

Volume 9, *Le Saint-Siège et les victimes de la guerre (The Holy See and the Victims of War, January–December 1943)* 1975, 689 pages, consists of a 61-page Introduction and includes 492 documents in English, French, German, Italian, and Latin, a List of 480 unpublished documents in abridged form or mentioned in Footnotes, and an Index.

7. War Refugee Board

Volume 10, *Le Saint-Siège et les victimes de la guerre (The Holy See and Victims of the War, January 1944–July 1945)* 1980, 684 pages, consists of a 62-page Introduction and includes 488 documents in English, French, German, Italian, and Latin, as well as a List of 791 unpublished documents in abridged form or mentioned in Footnotes, an Appendix, and an Index.

B. Documents

Volume 1
Le Saint-Siège et la guerre en Europe
(March 1939–August 1940)

No. 27, pp. 127–28

Great Britain's Minister [Francis] Osborne
to Monsignor [Domenico] Tardini
(A.E.S. 2386/39, original memo)   Rome, May 6, 1939
rec'd 6:30 P.M.

Britain's first response to Pius XII's peace conference proposal.

1. The preliminary reaction of Mr. Chamberlain and Lord Halifax is one of warm appreciation of the courage and faith displayed in the Pope's initiative.

2. It is understood that the purpose underlying the suggested conference is to afford an opportunity for discussion of the questions of Danzig and Franco-Italian relations. In these matters His Majesty's Government are not immediately concerned as principals, and would therefore desire, before returning an official reply to the Vatican, to have an opportunity of exchanging views with the French and Polish Governments. Lord Halifax would be glad to know whether these Governments have already been approached by the Vatican and whether His Majesty's Government are therefore at liberty to consult them.

3. He would also be interested to learn whether His Holiness had any ideas or suggestions as to where the suggested conference should meet, who would preside over it, and whether there were any question of its being held in Rome under Vatican auspices, i.e., presumably, in the Vatican City.

4. Lord Halifax also ventures to express the hope that His Holiness, when his project takes final shape, will have due regard to the position and the feelings of the President of the United States.

5. A principal difficulty foreseen by Lord Halifax lies in the possible reactions of those who might detect in the proposed conference an introduction to what they would fear would prove to be another Munich Conference, and he hopes that, when the project matures, His Holiness will have particular regard to this danger.[1]

---

[1]This memorandum essentially repeats the May 5 dispatch from Halifax to Osborne, D.B.F.B. Third Series, V; no. 380, pp. 435–36.

No. 44, p. 146

His Excellency Amleto Cicognani, Apostolic Delegate
to the Under-Secretary of the N.C.W.C., Monsignor [Howard J.] Carroll
Enclosed with report no. 366/39 (A.E.S. 4632/39, orig.)
Washington, May 15, 1939
The Pope wishes to inform President [Franklin D.] Roosevelt of the steps taken toward peace talks.

On May 3rd His Eminence Cardinal [Luigi] Maglione, Secretary of State of His Holiness, upon orders received from the Holy Father, directed the diplomatic representatives of the Holy See in France, Germany, England, Italy and Poland to consult with the heads of these governments in order to determine their intentions concerning peace, and to emphasize the opposition among all peoples to war, and if possible to bring about a realization that the present international difficulties could find their best solution in a conference of the nations concerned, rather than in wars and constant threats of war. The proposal of a conference was subordinated to the possibility, necessity or usefulness of such a meeting in the present uncertain political situation.

The steps taken by the Holy See to learn the sentiments of these governments, and to create a better international feeling have had a measure of success. In fact the Holy See is of the impression that the governments consulted are sufficiently well disposed for peace and reluctant to enter into war. There has also been a noticeable betterment of the general situation and a conference does not seem necessary at the present time. In the opinion of the Holy See the previous tense situation has somewhat subsided.

The Holy Father desires that the President of the United States be advised of these steps, through the offices of the Apostolic Delegate, and that he be further informed that His Holiness had intended to invoke his assistance and cooperation in the event that the European Powers had acceded to the suggestion of a Conference.

No. 89, pp. 207–9

His Excellency [Amleto] Cicognani in Washington
to Cardinal [Luigi] Maglione

Rome, July 11, 1939

The Apostolic Delegate communicates with Secretary of State Sumner Welles on the international situation.

The following excerpt is taken from the memorandum by Monsignor Ready, Secretary General of the National Catholic Welfare Conference, who was present.

Mr. Welles then spoke of the present serious preoccupation of the United States Government in the recurring crises in Europe and the Far East, which threatened the peace of the world. Mr. Welles said he spoke to His Excellency at the request of President Roosevelt and the President was particularly concerned that all the forces for peace should work cooperatively to gain for society a much desired reign of peace amongst all nations. Mr. Welles said he expressed the mind of the President in holding that the Holy Father's influence amongst the nations was a principal consideration for believing that a peaceful settlement might be brought to society in this troubled time.

Mr. Welles referred to the President's appeal to Hitler and Mussolini, April 14, 1939. In that appeal, the President hoped that through a conference all matters affecting the friendly relations of nations could be explored. Mr. Welles said that this Government's first concern was to avert war; that war could be averted only when nations agreed to settle the economic and territorial disputes which led to enmity amongst nations. Mr. Welles said the United States Government was prepared to take part in a conference of nations to adjust the present causes of world unrest. Such a conference could be successful only if the nations came to it in good faith and with a sincere desire for peace.

Mr. Welles said that the President believed the same moral law which kept the peace between individuals operated between nations; that a spirit of aggression by an individual against his neighbour upset the peace of a community. The same thing was true amongst nations. If world society was to be constantly fearful of aggression on the part of certain nations, then there could be no hope for peace nor for the solution of world and national problems which pressed heavily upon all governments.

Mr. Welles then spoke of the reports he had received about the Holy See's endeavors for peace in the last months and said that the action of the Holy See had given great encouragement to the Government of the United

States. Mr. Welles then repeated the earlier declaration that the President desired to work cooperatively with everyone and every government striving for peace; that the President believed a conference for the settlement of economic and territorial claims should be arranged in order to avert war.

His Excellency, the Apostolic Delegate replied that the President's communication of April 14 had been transmitted to the Holy See, as requested by the President through the United States Department of State; that the Holy See felt great difficulty in following up the message of April 14 because the governments addressed believed that they were unfairly singled out from amongst the nations....

No. 97, pp. 215–17

Memo by Monsignor Tardini

(A.E.S. 5414/39, autogr.)   Vatican, August 16, 1939

Consists of alleged Press information, sent by Great Britain's Minister. The Internuncio of Holland wired the same information.

Press Release

Two identical communications from the German and Italian Embassies to the Holy See respectively were consigned today to the Cardinal Secretary of State's Office in the Vatican.

After asserting their strong attachment to peace and expressing their deep sympathy with the efforts which the Holy See is continually making in the interests of a peace with justice and "even with certain sacrifices" (this is probably a reference to a remark in the Pope's recent letter to the French-Canadian Catholics, sent through Cardinal Maglione, the German and Italian Governments state that they wish once again to show their firm desire to solve peacefully the differences which today divide Europe. With this object in view they make known that, while being ready immediately to defend themselves against all attempts to impose arrogant decision upon them by force, they submit to the democratic powers the following "final proposals" for a settlement by agreement.

1. A 30-day truce, with a reciprocal promise not to take any steps on either side, in order to secure time to organise a conference of the Foreign Ministers of France, England, Italy, and Germany.

2. Since the British guarantee to Poland contemplates the fact that Poland is to be the judge whether the *casus belli* clause should function in case of a threat to her independence, Great Britain will transmit to Poland the solution of the Danzig question reached by mutual agreement between the four Foreign Ministers, asking her whether she considers her independence threatened

or not by that solution. A reply that this independence is not threatened would signify Poland's acceptance of the solution.

3. Once this question—considered today the most dangerous of all in consequence of the mechanism of the guarantee which is the sole one that leaves the nation guaranteed the arbiter of the *casus belli* is removed, the truce can be extended in order that the four Ministers may gradually examine the other questions in the order they may decide.

The two Axis Governments finally express the hope that the acceptance of their proposals may lead to a general slackening of tension, favourable to a gradual and pacific discussion of all outstanding questions, and manifest their confidence that the Holy See will give its moral support to the end that this "extreme and concrete contribution to peace may not remain unheard."

No. 130, p. 248

Great Britain's Minister Osborne to Monsignor Tardini
Br. Leg. no. 38/94/39 (A.E.S. 6819/39 orig.)

Rome, August 26, 1939

Great Britain's minister wishes to transmit personally to the Pope, Lord Halifax's thanks for the message of peace.

I have been instructed to convey personally to the Cardinal Secretary of State, or even directly to the Pope himself, a message of appreciation of His Holiness' broadcast appeal for peace.[1]

In view of these instructions, and since His Eminence is not available, do you think that His Holiness would be disposed to receive me in audience so that I may personally deliver Lord Halifax' message in accordance with his instructions? If so, the earlier I can be received the better. A telephone message to the Legation (80.846) will always reach me.

I enclose for your personal information a copy of the communication I have prepared for delivery.[2]

---

[1] Cf. Halifax's telegram to Osborne dated August 25 (no. 124, note 1).
[2] Document not found.

No. 134, p. 251

Great Britain's Minister Osborne to the Secretariat of State
Br. Leg. no. 38/96/39 (A.E.S. 6819 orig.)
Rome, August 26, 1939
From London, the following proposal was suggested: Make Danzig and
Corridor a free city, protected by the other Powers.

His Majesty's Minister to the Holy See has received the following
telegram addressed to him from London by Sir Ernest Graham-Little M.P.:
"Deeply moved by fatherly message from His Holiness. Humbly suggest following action in present crisis. Polish Corridor and adjacent territory to
become independent state like Monaco, Lichtenstein, Tangier, guaranteed or
administered by disinterested Powers, securing complete freedom for all
nationals and for trade. Poland might accept suggestion if His Holiness
deigned to propose it."
Mr. Osborne has replied that he has forwarded a copy of this telegram to
the Secretariat of State.

No. 246, pp. 372–73

President Roosevelt to Pope Pius XII
(A.S.S.11.863, 1940, autogr.) Edit. FRUS 1940, Vol. I, p. 125.
Wartime Correspondence, 31.
Washington, February 14, 1940
Roosevelt thanks the Pope for receiving Myron Taylor, serving as inter-
mediary to work toward peace and harmony among peoples.

In my letter of December 23, 1939, I had the honor to suggest that it
would give me great satisfaction to send to You my own representative in
order that our parallel endeavors for peace and the alleviation of suffering
might be assisted.
Your Holiness was good enough to reply that the choice of Mr. Myron C.
Taylor as my representative was acceptable and that You would receive him.
I am entrusting this special mission to Mr. Taylor who is a very old
friend of mine, and in whom I repose the utmost confidence. His humanitarian
efforts in behalf of those whom political disruption has rendered homeless are
well know to Your Holiness. I shall be happy to feel that he may be the channel
of communications for any views You and I may wish to exchange in the interest of concord among the peoples of the world.
I am asking Mr. Taylor to convey my cordial greetings to You, my old
and good friend and my sincere hope that the common ideals of religion and

humanity itself can have united expression for the re-establishment of a more permanent peace on the foundations of freedom and an assurance of life and integrity of all nations under God.

Volume 5
Le Saint-Siège et la guerre mondiale
(July 1941–October 1942)

No. 473, pp. 684–90

Ambassador Myron Taylor to Pope Pius XII
(A.E.S. 6699/42, orig.)   Vatican City, September 19, 1942
The United States will fight until total victory; the Pope must not be carried away by Axis propaganda in favor of a peace compromise.

To His Holiness Pope Pius XII.

A statement by Myron Taylor made September 19, 1942, as a basis on which the parallel efforts for a just and moral peace of His Holiness and President Roosevelt may rest.

It is of high importance that, at this juncture when the Allied Powers are passing to the offensive in the conduct of the War, the attitude of the United States Government with respect to the present world struggle be restated to the Holy See.

Before the war became general, President Roosevelt, in parallel effort with the Holy See, explored every possible avenue for the preservation of the peace. The experience of those days of fruitful cooperation, when the high moral prestige of the Holy See was buttressed by the civil power of the United States of America, is a precious memory. Although totalitarian aggression defeated those first efforts to prevent world war, the United States looks forward to further collaboration of this kind when the anti-Christian philosophies which have taken the sword shall have perished by the sword, and it will again be possible to organize world peace.

In the just war which they are now waging the people of the United States of America derive great spiritual strength and moral encouragement from a review of the utterances of His Holiness Pope Pius XII and of his venerated Predecessor. Americans, Catholic and non-Catholic, have been profoundly impressed by the searing condemnation of Nazi religious persecution pronounced by Pope Pius XI in his *Mit brennender Sorge;* by the elevated teaching on law and human dignity contained in the *Summi Pontificatus* of Pope Pius XII; by the famous Five Points laid down in 1939 by the same Pope as the essential postulates of a just peace; and by the forthright and heroic expressions of indignation made by Pope Pius XII when Germany invaded the Low Countries. Now that we are fighting against the very things which the Popes condemned, our conviction of complete victory is one with our confidence in the unwavering tenacity with which the Holy See will continue its magnificent moral leading.

Because we know we are in the right, and because we have supreme confidence in our strength, we are determined to carry through until we shall have won complete victory. The only thing that would make us lay down the arms taken up in defense of national security and world decency would be the complete and forthright acceptance of the Atlantic Charter and the Manifesto of the United Nations—the provisions of which, by the way, are in substantial agreement with the Holy Father's above-mentioned postulates for a just and lasting peace. Our cause is just. We fight, with conscience clear, for the moral rights of our nation, and for the liberties of our people; our victory will ensure those rights and liberties to the world. Even our enemies know that we seek no aggrandizement. Precisely for the reason that our moral position is impregnable, we are not open to the compromises usual to those who look for merely material gains, and who will bargain for half a loaf if they cannot have the whole. A peace-loving people, we exhausted every honorable means to remain at peace; in the midst of peace negotiations, we were foully attacked by Germany's partner in the Orient. Like Austria, Czechoslovakia, Poland and the rest, we were made the victims of Axis aggression at the very moment when their diplomats were talking peace. How then could we have confidence in the word of any Axis Power? In the conviction that anything less than complete victory would endanger the principles we fight for and our very existence as a nation, the United States of America will prosecute this war until the Axis collapses. We shall not again allow ourselves to be imperiled from behind while we are talking peace with criminal aggressors of the kind referred to in the *Summi Pontificatus* as men without faith to the plighted word.

Our confidence in final and complete victory is based upon the most objective foundations. There is nothing of emotional optimism or wishful thinking in it. We are prepared for a long war. We foresaw early reverses. But in the end, we know that no nation or combination of nations can stand against us in the field.

In the first place, we are a nation united as never before in our history. Axis propaganda had made itself felt in the United States as elsewhere before our entry into the war, and we know they are boasting of divisions among us. Let no one be deceived. Our very love of peace made it difficult for some of our people to see the world menace of Nazism. Pearl Harbor opened their eyes. The dishonorable attack of Japan at the very moment when her special ambassador was talking peace at Washington united overnight Americans of all shades of opinion. Among the architects of this unity are the foremost

Catholic leaders in our country, the bishops and the prominent laymen of all racial strains. Their public utterances and the editorial statements of Catholic papers after the aggression of Pearl Harbor can be summed up in these words: Prosecute the war to a victorious conclusion; and then bend every effort for a peace that will be just, charitable and lasting. Most notable of all Catholic pronouncements was that contained in the letter of the Catholic Hierarchy to the President of the United States pledging the whole-hearted cooperation of Catholics in the nation war effort. This letter, individually authorized by the Bishops of the United States, solemnly engaged "the lives, the treasure and the sacred honor" of American Catholics in the defense of their freedom against aggression. The response of the President was historic: "We shall win this war" wrote Mr. Roosevelt, "and in victory we shall seek not vengeance but the establishment of an international order in which the spirit of Christ shall rule the hearts of men and of nations."

The same unity based on high purpose pervades all the people of the United States. Contrary to Axis propaganda claims, the vast majority of our people are responsive to Christian inspiration, even though many may not be practical church-goers. The Axis charge that there are sixty million Atheists in the United States is sheer nonsense—a perversion of statistics on church membership and attendance by which the persecutors of religion are trying to use the church for their own sinister purposes....

There is reason to believe that our Axis enemies will attempt, through devious channels, to urge the Holy See to endorse in the near future proposals of peace without victory. In the present position of the belligerents, we can readily understand how strong a pressure the Axis powers may bring to bear upon the Vatican. We therefore feel it a duty to support the Holy See in resisting any undue pressure from this source. It is for this reason that we feel impelled to make known our views on the subject of peace, and to point out that the growing power of the United States is now being applied to reestablish those principles of international decency and justice which have been so well expounded by the Holy See. We are not so close geographically to the Vatican as some of our enemies, nor are we in a position to enjoy as many of the indirect day-to-day contacts as they. Nonetheless, we have the fullest confidence that due weight will be given to the considerations advanced by a nation which numbers among its citizens so many millions of devout Catholics, and whose government is in such close agreement with the principles enunciated by the Holy See on the issues of this war and the kind of peace which must follow it.

The people of the United States have a deep and sympathetic understanding of the Holy Father's desires for peace as he looks out upon a world convulsed with the harrowing spectacle of death and destruction on every side. The promotion of world peace, we know, is one of the great functions of the Holy See.

Though deferred, that peace will come—not a specious peace of strategy nor a short-lived peace of compromise. It will be the peace of "justice and charity" for which the Holy Father has so often prayed; it will be the peace "in which the spirit of Christ will rule the hearts of men and of nations" as promised by the President of the United States. The United States and its allies will win that peace. And in its consolidation, we should want nothing better than a continuation of those parallel efforts made by the Pope and the President before the war became general. In such a continuation, so devoutly to be hoped for, much can be accomplished to ensure that the peace will be lasting....

The war aims of the United States are peace aims. The world knows them. The Atlantic Charter lays down conditions which in our deepest conviction are irreducible. Any proposal under the plausible title of a "negotiated peace," which falls short of these aims, would only tend to confuse issues which we are determined to keep clear and to decide definitively.

No. 476, pp. 692–94

Pope Pius XII to Ambassador Myron Taylor
(A.E.S. 6795/42, orig. typed with Pius XII's autographed corrections)
Vatican, September 22, 1942
The Pope is not disposed toward a peace compromise that would consist of oppression of the rights and consciences of certain nations.

We have read your Memorandum very carefully,[1] and We have found it intensely interesting.[2] The issues are so clear-cut; of the definite, determined stand of the United States government it leaves no shadow of doubt.

It gave Us great satisfaction to know[a] from Your Excellency how united in this hour of national trial are all[b] the Catholics of the United States, under the enlightened leadership of the Bishops,[c] and that[d] between the Bishops and the President and his Government there exist[e] such sincere relations of mutual trust.

It has been a pleasure for Us to hear Your Excellency recall[f] President Roosevelt's aim and efforts to bring about a peace that will be worthy of man's personal dignity and of[g] his high destiny. This peace, as We have constantly repeated, must be based on justice and charity. It must take into consideration the vital needs of all nations; all must find it possible of fulfillment; it must bear within itself the seeds of longevity. Moreover, to Our mind, there is not the slightest chance of a peace being genuine and lasting, unless, to begin with, the mutual relations between governments and peoples, as well as those between individual governments and their own peoples, are based not on utilitarianism,[h] arbitrary decrees or brute force, but on fulfillment[i] of contracts made, on the sacred observance[j] of justice and law, tempered by Christian charity and brotherly love[m] on reverence for the dignity of the human person and respect for[n] religious convictions; and unless the worship of God again exercises its due influence in the individual and national life of all peoples.

For this reason, despite what any[o] propaganda may say to the contrary, We have never thought in terms of a peace by compromise at any cost. On certain principles of right and justice there can be no compromise. In our Christmas allocutions of 1939, 1940, and 1941 the world may read some of these essential principles expressed in unmistakable language, We think. They light the path along which We walk and will continue to walk unswervingly. It is deeply gratifying to Us to know that the peace aims of the United States have given full recognition to these basic principles of the moral order. The world need have no fear, nor hope either, that any pressure from without will ever make Us change Our direction or falter in Our clear path of duty. Geographic and other circumstances do make it possible for Us to have more frequent contact with some nations than with[p] others which are at war. And how deeply We feel this separation from so many of Our dear children, how it pains Our paternal heart, God alone knows. Hence,[q] the visit of Your Excellency has been[r] all the more welcome and pleasurable to Us. But the[s] principles guiding Our hopes and efforts for world peace have their foundation deep, and We shall never approve of, much less further a peace, that gives free rein to those who would undermine the foundations of Christianity and persecute Religion and the Church.

---

[1] Regarding Pius XII's decision to give a written reponse to Taylor, Monsignor Tardini wrote: "His Holiness wanted to give His Excellency Taylor a summary in writing of what he had told him during the audience of September 22. These notes were given to His Excellency Taylor by the Holy Father during the third, and last, audience of September 26."

[2] Cf. Nos. 372, 473

[a] *corr. pour* hear [b] *how...all ajouté pour* that [c] *are united rayé* [d] *there exist rayé* [e] *and his...exist ajouté* [f] *It...recall ajouté au lieu de* No one is more keenly aware than we of [g] *ajouté* [h] *corr. pour* utility [i] *corr. pour* the sacred observance [j] on observance *ajouté* [m] *tempered... love ajouté* [n] a man's *rayé* [o] *corr. pour* foreign [p] *ajouté* [q] *corr. pour* This makes [r] *has been ajouté* [s] *ajouté pour* The.

No. 477, pp. 694–95

Ambassador Myron Taylor to Pope Pius XII

(A.E.S. 6702/42, orig.) Vatican City, September 22, 1942

Collaboration with the British will introduce religious tolerance in Russia.

INFORMAL MEMORANDUM ON THE RUSSIAN POSTWAR POSITION[1]

Early in the Russian campaign distinction was made, to accord with Christian principles, between the rights and well-being of the Russian people, and those mistaken theories of Government and the practices of the Government then in power.

It was not sought to divorce the Russian people from the enlightened benefits of and salvation through religion and its observances, but rather to hold out to the Russian people the promise of a better life, with real religious freedom.

That government and people are giving their lives and all they possess to fight the Hitler peril to their freedom.

Who shall say that, as an ally in a Cause so just, even the Russian Government itself may not yield to the influence of an association with Christian Allies and the great moral force of their Cause and become a responsible and beneficent member of the family of peace-loving nations dedicated to the future prevention of war. Certainly, without Russian adherence to the United Nations Charter, and to those settlements which will be made at the end of hostilities, the future stability of Europe, and of the world, will be less certain of attainment.

It would seem logical, both from a moral as well as a practical standpoint, that the effort should be earnestly made to bring Russia more and more completely into a world family of nations, with identical aims and obligations.

The Russian Government's present intentions may be illustrated by its signature to the Atlantic Charter and its preamble, which, among other things, asserts adherence to the principle of Religious Freedom, and by its expressed attitude toward Poland, the Baltic and Balkan States, in the discussion of postwar settlements. We are led to believe that the field is open for collaboration— and generous compromise. This attitude, if encouraged and translated into reality, means much for the future security and welfare of the Baltic States, the Balkan States, and of Europe.

Great importance can likewise be attached to the value to Russia of a developed international organization to prevent Germany (Prussia particularly) from rearming and precipitating another war. This consideration is of very practical value, Russian economic self-containment considered. She is asked to surrender, in return for the advantage of security, only that she cease her ideological propaganda in other countries, and to make religion really free within her borders.[2]

---

[1] Submitted during the September 22 audience.

[2] On the same day Monsignor Tardini recorded his impressions regarding the document: "This memo on Russia demonstrates that the Americans believe it is possible for a Communist Government, once it wins the war, to enter the European family of nations like a meek lamb. This is far from the truth. If Stalin wins the war, he will be the lion that will devour all Europe. I told Taylor [cf. nr. 480] that neither Hitler nor Stalin will be able to remain quiet and tranquil in the European family of nations. I am surprised that such obvious matters are not understood by those who govern and by such high-ranking political personalities." (A.E.S. 6702/42)

No. 479, pp. 702–3

Ambassador Myron Taylor to Pope Pius XII

(A.E.S. 6702/42, orig.)   Vatican City, September 22, 1942

Deportation of Jews in France and the examination of measures to be taken to protect them.[1]

Since July 16th arrests and deportations of men, women, and children from France have proceeded with mounting fury and intensity spreading from the occupied zone, where 28,000 were arrested, to the unoccupied zone, from which 11,500 have already been deported. Men, women, and children of all ages have been included. The victims seem to be those refugees who entered France since 1933. Only those who have United States visas actually stamped in their passports are exempted. Women convalescing from operations and from childbirth, men who have fought in the French armies in the present war and children as young as two years of age have been included. In the early days of the deportations women were given the choice of leaving children as young as two years of age behind. Most mothers accepted this choice. Later cables indicate that all children as young as two years of age are now themselves under threat of deportation. They are being taken from homes and camps maintained by private organizations in unoccupied France, such as the OSE and the Swiss Red Cross.

Cables from churches, nonsectarian organizations, Jewish organizations, and offices of the J.D.C. in Geneva, Marseilles, and Lisbon report that 5,000 children are now being cared for in unoccupied France and that 1,000 to 3,500 of these are under immediate threat of deportation. The cables which are received almost hourly by all refugee organizations in New York beg urgently that immediate action be taken to rescue these children through emigration to the United States.

On August 13th, Messrs. McDonald, Baerwald, and Warren requested Honorable Sumner Welles to intervene with the Vichy Government to halt the deportations. On the same day a request was wired to Archbishop Rummel to consider the possibilities of requesting intervention by the Vatican. Later the Department of State reported that Mr. S. Pinkney Tuck, Chargé d'Affaires at Vichy, had been instructed to intervene vigorously to request that deportations be cancelled at least with respect to those whose emigration was in prospect. No report on the results of this action has been received from the State Department although it is noted that United States visa holders in the meantime have been exempted from deportation. Archbishop Rummel reported that he had conferred with the Apostolic Delegate immediately....

---

[1]Document dated September 9, 1942, when Taylor was leaving America. It was submitted during the papal audience of September 22.

No. 488, pp. 722–23

Pope Pius XII to Ambassador Myron Taylor[1]
(A.E.S. 7001/42, copy with corrections by Pius XII)

Vatican, September 26, 1942

Pope's intervention on behalf of civilians exposed to bombings.

The Holy See has always been and still is greatly preoccupied, out of a heart filled with constant[a] solicitude, with the fate of civil populations defenseless against the aggressions of war.

Since the outbreak of the present conflict no year has passed, that We have not appealed in Our public utterances to all the belligerents—men who also have human hearts moulded by a mother's love—to show some feeling of pity and charity for the sufferings of civilians, for helpless women and children, for the sick and aged, on whom a rain of terror, fire, destruction and havoc pours down out of a guiltless sky (November 1940, Easter 1941). Our appeal was little heeded, as the world knows, and tens of thousands know to their own personal grief.[b]

Now We have been asked to take occasion of this visit of Your Excellency to repeat Our appeal in a personal way, and to ask you to carry it to your esteemed President of the United States, of whom Your Excellency is so worthy and so valued a Representative. To refuse to comply with such a request would seem to bespeak little confidence in the noble sentiments of Christian brotherhood and generous sympathy for innocent victims of wrong, of which Your Excellency and the President have given conspicuous[c] proof.

We lay Our appeal, therefore, before you on behalf of countless human beings, children of our one, same Father in heaven; and if aerial bombardments must continue to form part of this harrowing war, let them with all possible care be directed only against objects of military value and spare the homes of non-combatants and the treasured shrines of art and religion.

----

[1] On September 26 Taylor was received by Pius XII for the third time before his departure for America. Monsignor Tardini arranged the documents in Taylor's file: "September 26, 1942. In this morning's audience His Holiness gave His Excellency Taylor the following documents: 1. Response to the President (cf. no. 485). 2. Summary of His Holiness' talk during the September 22nd audience (cf. no. 476). 3. Notes on the bombing of civilians (see above). 4. Memo on prisoners in the hands of the Russians (cf. no. 489). 5. Notes on the Information Service with the United States (cf. no. 490)."

[a] *corrigé pour* fatherly [b] *adjoint en marge* [c] *corrigé pour* splendid. *Une premiere correction, puis rayée* noble.

No. 489, pp. 724–25

Pope Pius XII to Ambassador Myron Taylor
(A.E.S. 7005/42, orig. autogr.)   Vatican, September 26, 1942
Regarding the condition of prisoners in Russia.

There is scarcely need to stress the fact, already well known, that the Holy Father has done all in His power to alleviate the suffering and misery caused by the war, and this particularly in the interest of prisoners and internees, striving very especially to procure for them and for their families the comfort of an exchange of news.

Receiving countless heart-rending appeals especially in recent months from Italy and Rumania for news of prisoners of war in the hands of the Russians, His Holiness has sought to give His attention also to these unfortunates, availing Himself, in this mission of mercy, of the good offices of the government of the United States of America very especially and of several others.

Because all these efforts have thus far failed and in view of the constant increase in the number of requests received from all quarters, official and non-official, for some news of these prisoners, His Holiness does not hesitate now to make an appeal directly to His Excellency President Roosevelt, whose influence can be inestimable and perhaps decisive, especially since at present the desires of the Holy See in this regard could be easily satisfied. It is only asked that, in accordance with the usual international regulations, some information, of a general and innocuous nature, regarding these prisoners be made available.

It is well to recall at this time that the Holy See has not ceased to interest itself in the Russian prisoners in the hands of their enemies, and is disposed to devote itself still more assiduously to this task if that were to meet with the pleasure of the Russian Authorities.

No. 490, p. 726

Pope Pius XII to Ambassador Taylor
(A.E.S. 7005/42, copy)   Vatican, September 26, 1942
Pope's appeal to provide information service to prisoners.

Impressed very forcefully by the increasingly numerous and insistent appeals directed to Him from all quarters for news of close relatives and intimate friends in the United States of America, His Holiness is desirous that, if at all possible, the information service of the Holy See, which is carried on in the interest of prisoners, refugees and civilians alike, now be extended to the United States. In expressing this desire His Holiness is deeply encouraged by the knowledge that this activity has already provided for countless thousands in many parts of the world a measure of tranquillity and peace of mind and by the assurance that the inestimable benefits of this merciful enterprise might easily be extended to the United States.

To this end, therefore, He would request that His Excellency the President of the United States seek to facilitate the arrangements necessary for the establishment of this service.

A very large number of requests for such information from the United States have already been received; that the number has not been multiplied many times is due solely to the fact that, unfortunately, the Holy See has been obliged to let it be known that, temporarily at least, it cannot accept such requests.

In the case of those few requests of an urgent nature which have been forwarded to the United States on the recommendation of Ecclesiastical Authorities, the obstacles and difficulties that have been encountered have been such as to counsel the complete cancellation of this very important service.

In the United States, as elsewhere, the Apostolic Delegate would be charged with the direction and control of this service. He would receive and forward the small, open forms on which it is permitted to write a message of not more than twenty-five words of a purely personal character, intended to relieve the anguish or preoccupation of a distant loved one. These messages are rigidly censored before being sent from Vatican City, but the Holy See is quite willing that they be submitted for censorship in the United States if this would facilitate the matter.

No. 492, pp. 727–29

Monsignor Tardini to Ambassador Myron Taylor

(A.E.S. 7007/42, copy)   Vatican, September 26, 1942
    Report on religion in Russia.

RELIGIOUS SITUATION IN RUSSIA

Strictly personal memorandum giving summary of consideration expressed by H. E. Mons. Tardini in conversation with H. E. Myron Taylor.[1]

1. There is no indication that any of the numerous churches closed to the faithful in past years have been reopened, nor that high taxes, imposed for the exercise of public worship on those few churches which have remained open, have been reduced. Father Leopold Braun, Rector of the only Catholic Church in Moscow writes: "There is talk of a reopening (of the churches) but I have no certain proof."

2. Nor is there any indication that any priest, who is a Russian citizen, has been freed from prison or from the sentence of deportation to which he had been previously condemned.

According to latest available statistics it would seem that there are still approximately one hundred Catholic priests of the Archdiocese of Mohilew detained in prison or in concentration camps.

3. For more than a year now there has been no news of His Excellency Mons. Edward Profittlich, Titular Archbishop of Andrianopoli and Apostolic Administrator of Estonia. Archbishop Profittlich, a citizen of Estonia, was arrested at Tallinn June 28, 1941 and deported to the Urals, probably in Kasan.[2]

4. Communists in Albania and Montenegro were recently found to be in possession of "instructions" from Moscow recommending that they "cultivate the division between the various religions and direct their attack particularly against Catholicism."

5. Father Braun has pointed out that the organization of the militant Russian atheists ceased some time ago to be active and that, furthermore, official antireligious publications are no longer printed but he noted that copies of some such publications are still on sale.

---

[1]With regard to this encounter, Monsignor Tardini noted: "September 27, 1942. 12 o'clock. His Excellency Taylor came to say good-bye. I gave him some notes about Russia. I added that, according to the information in our possession, the religious situation in Moscow is a little different than in other parts of the country. Stalin wants to show the diplomats that there is religious freedom in Russia and, therefore, in Moscow the churches are frequented freely and those who practice their religion are not disturbed. This is not so in other parts of Russia. Furthermore, a good number of Catholic priests, Russians, are either still in prison or in exile.

"Mr. Taylor told me that the United States is making every effort to insure religious freedom in Russia: Whenever Stalin asked for or asks for arms or when he asked for or asks for loans, the United States has insisted and insists on this matter.

"Mr. Taylor adds that it is necessary for Russia to become part of the family of nations. To which I answer that Stalin (him only?) will not be comfortable in any family."

On the genesis of the document, there is another note by Tardini: "Notes given today to Mr. Taylor. In the September 2 conversation, Taylor spoke about Russia and I observed that there was no proof that Stalin had changed the Communist program in religious matters. Mr. Taylor recalled the Notes I had given him last year [cf. nr. 82] and asked for another copy. And I promised to satisfy him" (A.E.S. 7007/42).

[2]Cf. nr. 94 #10; and *Actes*, Vol. 3, doc. 307, p. 460; doc. 487, p. 768.

Volume 6
Le Saint-Siège et les victimes de la guerre
(March 1939–December 1940)

No. 20, pp. 82–83

Chief Rabbi Herzog to Cardinal Maglione

No number (A.S.S. 1939 Varia 934, orig.)   Jerusalem, May 1, 1939

Request for Papal audience.

You have probably heard by now from Mr. Macaulay, the Irish Legate to the Holy See, of my desire for an audience with His Holiness, the Pope.[1] I wish to place before the Supreme Pontiff a matter of a religious nature, altogether non-political, which is of vital importance to Jewry. Kindly try to arrange that audience in principle and let me know, by wire, if possible.[2] I shall then suggest to His Holiness, through you, a range of alternative dates within the next few weeks. You will readily appreciate that a journey to Italy, particularly at the present time, is no small matter and the arrangements must therefore be planned well ahead. There is with the Supreme Pontiff a letter of recommendation from my dear friend Cardinal MacRory, Primate of all Ireland, addressed to the Pope long before His Election.[3]

Monsignor Montini's Notes:

Check in Archives. His Holiness cannot receive him. He will be able to speak with the Cardinal Secretary of State.

---

[1]See no. 15.

[2]Monsignor Montini responded to the Minister of Ireland asking him to inform Mr. Herzog; see no. 23.

[3]Unpublished.

No. 23, p. 86

Monsignor Montini to Macaulay, Minister of Ireland
to the Holy See

(A.S.S. 1813, draft)   Vatican, May 13, 1939

The Chief Rabbi will be received by the Cardinal Secretary of State.

Your Excellency,

With reference to Your Excellency's letter of April thirteenth regarding the desire of Dr. Isaac Herzog for an Audience of the Holy Father,[1] I have the honour to inform you that Dr. Herzog, if he comes to Rome, will be received by His

Eminence the Cardinal Secretary of State.[2] I am also to request Your Excellency to be good enough to have this answer communicated to Dr. Herzog.[3]

---

[1] See no. 15.

[2] In fact, Herzog only came to Rome toward the end of February 1940 and was received on February 28 by Cardinal Maglione (A.S.S. 11149).

[3] As the answer to his letter of May 1st (see no. 20).

No. 65, p. 143

Minister Osborne of Great Britain to Monsignor Tardini
W/18/30 (A.E.S. 8789/39, orig.)   Rome, September 13, 1939
News about the bombing of the Germans in Poland.

You told me yesterday that His Holiness the Pope might take an early opportunity of urging on the belligerent Powers the observance of the laws for humanising war which they have announced their intention of respecting.

In this connection it will be interesting to see whether the news which I have just heard over the radio is confirmed, namely, that the German General Staff has announced its decision to shell and bomb open cities and villages in Poland because the inhabitants, misled by their Government, have opposed the advance of the German troops into Poland.

It hardly sounds credible, but if it is, it might be worth bringing to His Holiness' attention.

No. 125, pp. 211–12

Cardinal Maglione to Bishop Sheil, Auxiliary Bishop of Chicago
Telegram without no. (A.E.S. 91/40)   Vatican, December 31, 1939
Thanks for the gift offered to the Pope by the American Jewish organizations.

Holy Father is pleased devoted homage paid glorious memory of His unforgettable Predecessor through conspicuous charitable offering.[1]

In the light of the doctrine and of the example of Christ who proclaimed and made men brothers in Himself and who taught them to discern His own Person in the poor and the suffering the August Pontiff feels deep satisfaction and gratitude for this munificent and beneficent act.

His Holiness charges Your Excellency to convey the expression of His sincere thanks to all the donors upon whom He implores from God the choicest gifts.

I shall later communicate to Your Excellency in what manner and through which committees you may provide for the distribution of the fund.[2]

---

[1]See no. 126.

[2]See no. 131. Bishop Sheil thanked the directors of the "United Jewish Appeal" in a letter of December 29: "Is it not bitter mockery, an odious hypocrisy, for any man who professes to believe in the Fatherhood of God and the Brotherhood of man to hate and to persecute his fellow men? Can any man truthfully say he loves God unless he loves his neighbor? The Evangelist, St. John, answers that question in powerful and graphic language. 'Let us therefore love God because God first hath loved us. If any man say, I love God and hateth his brother he is a liar. For he who loveth not his brother whom he seeth, how can he love God whom he seeth not. And this commandment we have from God that he who loveth God, love also his brother.' It must be evident therefore, that Catholics or Protestants who foment racial and religious hatred are traitors to the religion they profess.

My dear Jewish friends, this magnificent gift of yours in memory of the Great Pope Pius XI deserves and should receive the gratitude and admiration of every Catholic worthy of the name. It is further evidence of the traditional generosity of your people towards their neighbors and fellowmen. It should still forever the tongues of those who charge you so unjustly of narrow, exclusive racialism.

Be sure, dear friends, we Catholics can sympathize with you to the full in the suffering, the oppression and injustice to which your people have been so cruelly subjected. Like you, we also have our refugee problem, thousands of men, women and children who are the victims likewise of intolerance and tyranny. The refugee problem is not a problem of any one race or religion, but a problem which affects all humanity. It is a problem which can be solved only by men of good will standing together.

We will gladly join hands with you in striving to build a better world where men and women may live long in peace, harmony and security, as God Almighty intended them to live. We will labor eagerly with good men and women from which millions of human beings suffer so grievously. We are eternally grateful to you for the noble tribute of esteem and admiration you have paid to our great Pope, Pius XI, of blessed memory

No words I am able to command can adequately express my profound and abiding gratitude for your princely gift to our Holy Father, Pope Pius XII. I am sure that our Holy Father will be deeply moved by the noble spirit which prompted you to honor in this gracious and generous manner the memory of his predecessor, that truly great and godly man, Pope Pius XI of happy memory.

No man in our day or generation fought more vigorously or courageously the fanaticism of intolerant racialism than Pius XI. When cruel and tyrannical laws were enacted against your people, his fearless voice was raised in indignant protest. He denounced racial intolerance and hatred as contrary to the laws of God, to the dictates of right reason and to the welfare of civilization. Consequently, any man or group of men who fosters this ignorant and malignant spirit of racialism is the enemy of religion and of civilization. It seems beautifully appropriate therefore that you should honor the memory of this courageous champion of human rights by enabling his most worthy sucessor to bring some small measure of relief to the victims of this odious type of tyranny.

Although the Jewish people have suffered, more perhaps than any other people, from the excesses of malign racialism, yet the painful problems growing out of this inhuman, ungodly fanaticism, are by no means exclusively Jewish problems. They are of profound and vital concern to Catholics, to Protestants and to men of good will everywhere. Least of all can we Americans be indifferent to the victims of tyranny and oppression? Our traditions, our institutions, our national spirit and temperament, nurtured by and rooted in the soil of liberty, make tyranny in every form peculiarly odious to us."

No. 172, pp. 265–66

Cardinal Maglione to Bishop Boyle, Bishop of Pittsburgh
(A.S.S. 7324, draft)   Vatican, March 21, 1940
Thanks for the gift offered to Cardinal Hlond by the Americans and a request to continue the help.

I acknowledge receipt of a check in the amount of ten thousand dollars ($10,000.00) forwarded through His Excellency the Apostolic Delegate by the Bishops' Committee for Polish Relief for transmission to His Eminence Cardinal Hlond.[1] It gives me pleasure to assure Your Excellency that the said amount has been consigned to His Eminence in accordance with the desires expressed by your Committee.

At the same time, I am to tell you of the deep interest and appreciation with which the Holy Father is following the labors of your Committee in favor of prostrate Poland. Since the beginning of the war, the sad plight of this Christian people has been one of His heaviest preoccupations, and He has spared no efforts in providing alleviation for their sufferings. The burden has been greater than His resources, already strained by the numerous demands which the present untoward conditions in Europe have occasioned, would permit Him to expend; so that it was with heartfelt satisfaction that He welcomed the generous action of the American Bishops to raise funds for the relief of His beloved and sorely tried children in Poland. His Holiness wishes Your Excellency and your confreres in the Hierarchy to be assured that He reposes the greatest confidence in the assistance that you will furnish Him in carrying out this noble mission of charity, and that whatever moneys you may be able to collect for this purpose will be immediately put to use where the need is greatest. From a full heart, the Common Father sends His affectionate Apostolic Benediction to Your Excellency and to your brother Bishops as well as to all who contribute to this noble cause.

---

[1] See no. 139.

No. 196, pp. 296–98

The Secretariat of State to Ambassador Taylor
(A.S.S. 7515, draft)   Vatican, April 26, 1940
Information on the work of papal assistance to Poland.

The Secretariat of State to His Holiness has the honor to address this communication to the Personal Representation of the President of the United States of America to His Holiness the Pope for the purpose of making known the efforts which have been made and are being made by the Holy See to afford assistance to the stricken people of Poland.[1]

In carrying out their sacred mission of apostolic charity, the Sovereign Pontiffs have always been in the forefront of those who seek to alleviate the suffering which is the inevitable concomitant and consequent of war. Thus during the world war of 1914–1918, the then Sovereign Pontiff, Pope Benedict XV of venerated memory, marshalled the resources of the Holy See, in men and in treasure, for the relief of the civilian populations in war-torn countries and for the amelioration of the lot of military prisoners. It is well known also that this Pontifical work in favor of afflicted humanity was continued throughout the period of destitution which, notably in Germany, followed the cessation of hostilities.

The sad conditions ensuing upon the occupation of Poland in the autumn of last year made an instant appeal to the paternal compassion of the present Holy Father Who immediately sought by every means in His power to extend, in addition to spiritual comfort, that material help which was so sorely needed by the people of that country. Beginning in October 1939, official representations were made to the Government of the Reich with a view to securing passage into Poland of the relief at the disposition of the Holy See.[2] The replies of the German Government to these and to repeated subsequent representations were dilatory and evasive.[3] An endeavor was then made to send money to the distressed Poles on order that they might be in a position to help themselves, but the restrictions imposed and the unfavorable rate of exchange offered were such as to justify the fear that by this means only a small proportion of effective aid would ultimately reach its destination. When it finally became evident that it was not the purpose of the German Government to permit the Holy See, in its own name, to minister to the needs of these people in their tragic plight, there remained no recourse but to look elsewhere for means of arriving at the desired end.

Accordingly when information reached the Holy See that the German Government had agreed to allow the American "Commission for Polish Relief" to send supplies into Poland and to station representatives there for the purpose of supervising the distribution of these supplies to the civilian population, the Holy See saw in this permission a possible channel for communicating its own relief to the Poles. It is true that at the same time it was reported reliably from Berlin[4] that the German authorities, while authorizing the representatives of the "Commission for Polish Relief" to remain at Warsaw to receive the supplies shipped from America, would not permit them to exercise effective supervision over distribution. Nevertheless, in spite of this discrepancy in the information in its possession, the Holy See, in view of the urgent necessity of getting immediate aid to a people in desperate straits, has decided to avail itself of the good offices of the American "Commission for Polish Relief" as one of the agencies through [which] it will work in its efforts to succor the Poles. His Excellency the Apostolic Delegate at Washington, under instructions from this Secretariat of State,

Pius XII meets with Myron C. Taylor, President Roosevelt's personal representative to the Vatican. Except for a period of leave for illness, Taylor spent most of the wartime years in Rome.

A letter from Roosevelt to Pius XII announcing the appointment of Taylor. In it, Roosevelt expressed "the sincere hope that the common ideals of religion and of humanity itself can have united expression for the reestablishment of a more permanent peace...."

Refugees, mostly women and children, make a home in the papal apartments at Castelgandolfo, outside Rome, during the fighting in Italy.

Jewish refugees Giacomo Di Porto, left, and his wife, Eleanora, found refuge at the Convent of Notre Dame de Sion in Rome.

L'aiuto della Chiesa Cattolica agli ebrei durante la guerra

NEW YORK, 4.

Il Direttore americano del Comitato Soccorsi in Italia, Reuben Resnik, ha dichiarato che la Chiesa cattolica si è resa altamente benemerita per il prezioso aiuto dato agli ebrei perseguitati durante la guerra. Il Resnik, secondo quanto riferisce l'INS, ha detto che tutti i membri della gerarchia cattolica in Italia, dai Cardinali ai sacerdoti, hanno salvato la vita di migliaia d'ebrei, uomini, donne e bambini che furono ospitati e nascosti in conventi, chiese, istituti religiosi, case di cura per religiosi, ecc.

Riconoscimenti

Sul medesimo foglio americano leggiamo che durante la funzione di ringraziamento celebrata nel tempio israelitico a Roma e radiodiffusa, il cappellano israelita della quinta armata americana ha tenuto un discorso in cui tra l'altro ha detto: «Secoli fa Roma pagana festeggiava la morte apparente del popolo ebraico. Oggi in Roma cristiana la prima capitale dell'Europa non è più così.

Se non fosse stato per il soccorso veramente reale e sostanziale e l'aiuto, dato ad esso dal Vaticano e dalle autorità ecclesiastiche di Roma centinaia di rifugiati e migliaia di rifugiati ebraici sarebbero indubbiamente periti molto prima che Roma fosse liberata».

An article datelined New York, left, in January, 1946 relates how Reubin Resnik, Director of the American Committee to Help Jews in Italy, praised the efforts of the Catholic Church for Jews during the war. The INS story tells how the Catholic hierarchy saved the lives of thousands. Right: An American newspaper describes a service in a Rome synagogue after the liberation at which a Jewish chaplain notes the "substantial assistance of the Vatican and Rome's ecclesiastical authorities" in protecting Jews.

An article in a Geneva newspaper in September, 1942 tells how Pius XII protested the treatment of Jews in Vichy France. The Pétain government had instructed local church authorities to ignore the papal protest. Nevertheless, it was read in most churches.

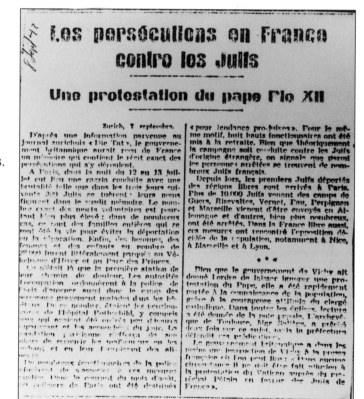

Les persécutions en France contre les Juifs

Une protestation du pape Pie XII

Zurich, 7 septembre.

D'après une information parvenue au journal zurichois « Die Tat », le gouvernement britannique aurait reçu de France un mémoire qui contient le récit exact des persécutions qui s'y déroulent.

À Paris, dans la nuit du 12 au 13 juillet eut lieu une razzia conduite avec une brutalité telle que dans les trois jours suivants 300 Juifs se tuèrent; leurs noms figurent dans le susdit mémoire. Le nombre exact des morts volontaires est pourtant bien plus élevé; dans de nombreux cas, ce sont des familles entières qui se sont ôté la vie pour éviter la déportation ou la séparation. Enfin, des hommes, des femmes et des enfants au nombre de 7000 furent littéralement parqués au Vélodrome d'Hiver et au Parc des Princes.

C'était là que la première station de leur chemin de douleur. Les autorités d'occupation ordonnèrent à la police de Paris d'amener aussi dans le camp des personnes gravement malades dans les hôpitaux. De ce nombre, étaient les pensionnaires de l'hôpital Rothschild, y compris ceux qui avaient été opérés peu d'heures auparavant et les accouchées du jour. La population parisienne s'efforça de son mieux de secourir les malheureux en les cachant et en leur fournissant des aliments.

De nombreux fonctionnaires de la police cherchèrent de s'associer à ces mesures cruelles. Pour le contrôle du mois d'août, 4 officiers de Paris ont été destitués

« pour tendance pro-juives ». Pour le même motif, huit hauts fonctionnaires ont été mis à la retraite. Bien que théoriquement la campagne soit conduite contre les Juifs d'origine étrangère, on signale que parmi les personnes arrêtées se trouvent de nombreux Juifs français.

Depuis lors, les premiers Juifs déportés des régions libres sont arrivés à Paris. Plus de 10.000 Juifs venant des camps de Gurs, Rivesaltes, Vernet, Pau, Perpignan et Marseille viennent d'être envoyés en Allemagne et d'autres, bien plus nombreux, ont été arrêtés. Dans la France libre aussi, ces mesures ont rencontré l'opposition décidée de la population, notamment à Nice, à Marseille et à Lyon.

* * *

Bien que le gouvernement de Vichy ait donné l'ordre de laisser ignorer une protestation du Pape, elle a été rapidement portée à la connaissance de la population, grâce à la courageuse attitude du clergé catholique. Dans toutes les églises, lecture a été donnée de la note papale. L'archevêque de Toulouse, Mgr Saliège, a prêché deux fois sur ce sujet, tout in la préfecture défendit ses prédications.

Le gouvernement britannique a dans les mains une instruction de Vichy à la presse française où l'on peut lire: « Dans aucune circonstance il ne doit être fait allusion à la protestation du Vatican auprès du maréchal Pétain en faveur des Juifs de France ».

Pius XII records his Christmas message for peace in 1943. Partly hidden by the Pope is Luigi Cardinal Maglioni, papal Secretary of State. Standing behind the Pope's chair is Giovanni Battista Montini, the future Paul VI.

25 GIU. 1944

TELEGRAMMA DI STATO

MOD. I-1944 3000

Indicazioni d'urgenza

Circuito sul quale vi deve fare l'inoltro del telegramma

Spedito il ___ 19 ___ ore ___ pel circuito N. ___ all'Ufficio di ___ Trasmittente ___

Qualifica | DESTINAZIONE | PROVENIENZA | Num. | Parole | DATA DELLA PRESENTAZIONE | VIA D'ISTRADAMENTO
| | CITTÀ DEL VATICANO | | | Giorno e mese — Ore e minuti | e indicazioni eventuali d'Ufficio

1571   Son Altesse Sérénissime l'Amiral Nicolas Horthy de Nagybanya

Régent du Royaume de Hongrie   BUDAPEST

plusieurs côtés on Nous supplie de tout mettre en oeuvre pour que dans cette noble et

valeresque Nation ne soient étendues et aggravées les souffrances, déjà si lourdes, en-

rées par un grand nombre de malheureux, a cause de leur nationalité ou de leur race.

tre coeur de Père ne pouvant demeurer insensible à ces instantes supplications en rai

n de Notre ministère de charité qui embrasse tous les hommes Nous Nous adressons pert

llement à Votre Altesse faisant appel à Ses nobles sentiments dans la pleine confian

l'Elle voudra bien faire tout ce qui est en Son pouvoir pour que soient épargnés à ta

e malheureux d'autres deuils et d'autres douleurs.   PIUS PP XII.

Indicazione e timbro della autorità mittente: SEGRETERIA DI STATO.

3983/44

Telegram in French from Pius XII to Hungary's Regent, Niklos Horthy, protesting the deportation of Jews. The Pope pleaded with Horthy to use his office so that "many unfortunate people may be spared further afflictions and sorrows."

has already turned over to the said Commission a considerable initial contribution, and other sums are on deposit in American banks for further contributions.[5]

The Holy See is convinced that the work of the "Commission for Polish Relief" will be greatly facilitated among the Polish people, most of whom are Catholics, if the widest possible publicity is given, both in America and in Poland, to the fact that the Holy See is contributing largely to the Commission's work of relief. To this end, it has been suggested that consideration might be given to the advantage which would derive in many ways from the presence in Poland as representatives of the Commission of two Catholic citizens of the United States.

The Secretariat of State, therefore, expresses the hope that the Personal Representation of the President of the United States to His Holiness the Pope may inform His Excellency the President of the motives which actuate the Holy See in its contributions to this noble charitable undertaking, and that His Excellency may find it possible to lend the high prestige of his support to the achievement of the two purposes set forth in the preceding paragraph.

Monsignor Montini's Notes:
Prepare Italian translation. Send copy to Berlin and to Washington.[6]
Approved and delivered to Mr. Taylor, April 26, 1940.

---

[1]See no. 192.
[2]See particularly nos. 104 and 107.
[3]See nos. 124 and 136.
[4]See no. 178.
[5]See no. 182.
[6]The content of this message was communicated to the two representatives on April 30 (A.S.S. 7515).

No. 201, p. 306

The Chief Rabbi to Cardinal [Joseph] MacRory
Telegram no. 223 (A.E.S. 4562/40, orig.)   Jerusalem, May 12, 1940
The Grand Rabbi asks the intervention of the Holy See for the Polish Jews in Lithuania.

Entreat you plead speedily for intervention Holy Father with Lithuanian Government behalf Polish Jewish refugees including many distinguished rabbis now at Vilna threatened forcible repatriation to German and Russian occupation zones. Jewish Relief Organisations ready provide their maintenance and arrange gradual emigration to Palestine and overseas.

Enclosure
Cardinal MacRory to Cardinal Maglione
No number (A.E.S. 4562/40 autogr.) Armagh, May 14, 1940
The Cardinal sends a telegram from Chief Rabbi Herzog.

I received yesterday the enclosed cable from Rabbi Herzog, Jerusalem, who is Chief Jewish Rabbi.[1] Before going to Palestine he spent many years as a Rabbi here in Ireland and he and I were good friends. I suppose that is the reason why he now appeals to me to plead for the intervention of the Holy Father.

I am sorry to add to your many cares, but I consider it my duty to bring this matter under Your Eminence's notice.[2]

---

[1] See nos. 15 and 20.
[2] Response to Cardinal MacRory on May 31, 1940 (A.E.S. 4562/40) that his recommendation would be given consideration.

No. 225, p. 328

The Secretariat of State to the Representation
of the President of the United States
(A.S.S. 76224, draft) Vatican, June 5, 1940
Request for information about the Poles arrested and deported by the Russians.

The Secretariat of State to His Holiness has the honor to make the following communication to the Representation of His Excellency the President of the United States to His Holiness the Pope.

Information has been received[1] to the effect that some twenty thousand Poles, of the more cultivated classes, were arrested at Lwów by the Soviet authorities on or about April 15, 1940, and deported to Western Siberia, particularly to Turkestan. The Secretariat of State will be very thankful for any news which the Representation of His Excellency the President of the United States may be able to obtain and to communicate in regard to this reported deportation and to the present fate of the deportees.[2]

---

[1] Probably by the Ambassador of Poland.
[2] See no. 332.

No. 257, pp. 364–65

The personal Representative of the President of the United States
Myron Taylor to Cardinal Maglione
No number (A.S.S. Guerra 1939, Polish-Civil-Pol. 10, orig.)

Rome, July 15, 1940

Recognition of the efforts of the Holy See in Poland.

The Personal Representative of the President of the United States to His Holiness, Pope Pius XII, presents his compliments to His Eminence the Cardinal Secretary of State and has the honor to advise that he has submitted to the President the *note verbale* N. 7515 of April 26, 1940[1] with reference to the unsuccessful efforts which the Holy See has been making to send relief to Poland and, at the request of the President, has the honor to submit the following with reference thereto.

Both the President and the people of the United States are deeply sensitive of the great efforts which His Holiness, the Pope, has made, not only to preserve but also to induce peace on the earth; and, as well, the great services which have been rendered by His Holiness in alleviating and seeking further to alleviate, the suffering that has been occasioned by war.

The Government of the United States is also deeply concerned and anxious that the maximum of relief should be extended to the civilian populations of war stricken areas in Europe.

There are a number of organizations, associations and private persons engaged in raising money for this purpose in the United States. The Government has no connection with any of these private organizations except that provided by the Neutrality Act,[2] and the government is not a participant in any of their respective activities. The Government has no function in connection with their administration and no control over their activities so long as they conform to the law.

The only agency for relief which is either official or quasi-official so far as the Government of the United States is concerned is the American Red Cross.

The Government is, of course, concerned that there should be coordination between these various agencies, so that there will be no conflict which would be prejudicial to the main purpose of relieving the destitution and suffering due to war conditions. It is also clear that these activities should be coordinated so that there should be no conflict as between them in connection either with the time which each sets for the raising of monies by public subscription or with the disbursement of this aid in such a way as to produce the maximum relief.

It is beyond the power of the President to name the members of the commission as suggested, as this power rests exclusively in the Commission for Polish Relief. The substance of the specific requests therefore has been transmitted to the Commission for Polish Relief, and doubtless that organization will communicate direct to the Holy See with reference thereto.

The Personal Representative of the President has been further requested to express the hope that the Secretary of State to His Holiness, the Pope, will inform His Holiness of the deep sympathy which the President has for the humanitarian purposes upon which he has been so effectively engaged.

---

[1] See no. 1996.
[2] November 4, 1939, see FRUS 1939, I, 680.

No. 332, pp. 431–32

Edward Reed[1] to Nuncio [Francesco] Borgongini Duca in Italy
No number (A.S.S. Guerra 1939, Polish-Civil-Pol. 10, orig.)

Rome, October 6, 1940

The United States can do nothing for the Poles residing in territory occupied by the Russians.

With reference to three communications, nos. 7623, 7624 and 7625, all dated June 5, 1940,[2] which were addressed to the Honorable Myron C. Taylor by the Secretariat of State of His Holiness concerning the whereabouts and welfare of certain Polish nationals, I have been directed by the Secretary of State of the United States to request Your Excellency to be good enough to inform the Secretariat of State of His Holiness that, according to information received by my Government from its Embassy in Moscow, the Soviet authorities have refused to undertake investigations on behalf of the Government of the United States for the purpose of ascertaining the whereabouts and welfare in the Soviet Union of persons who are not American citizens.[3]

It is the understanding of my Government that persons of Polish nationality now in Soviet occupied Poland are considered by the Soviet Government to be citizens of the U.S.S.R. and, as such, are not the appropriate subjects of an inquiry on the part of a foreign government. Although my Government is aware of the unfortunate plight in many instances of these Polish nationals, it regrets, however, that there would appear to be nothing which it, or its representatives in Moscow, might do on behalf of the individuals or groups named in the communications from the Secretariat of State of His Holiness.[4]

---

[1] Chargé d'Affaires of the United States in Italy.
[2] See no. 225; the two other Memos were not published.
[3] The United States had almost insurmountable difficulties to protect the North American citizens in Poland territory occupied by the Soviets (FRUS 1940, II, 177).
[4] The Nuncio sent Reed's letter to Cardinal Maglione on October 9 (report no. 8196).

Volume 7
Le Saint-Siège et la guerre mondiale
(November 1942–December 1943)

No. 251, pp. 430–31

President Roosevelt to Pope Pius XII
(A.E.S. 5495/43, orig. signature autogr.). Edit. *Wartime Corresp.*, pp. 91–93
FRUS 1943 Vol. 2 *Europe*, pp. 919–20

Washington, June 16, 1943
rec'd, July 13, 1943

Roosevelt appreciates Pius XII's efforts regarding Italy and promises that the air attacks will be limited to military objectives.

Your Holiness:[1]

The communication of May 19, 1943 from Your Holiness[2] setting forth in eloquent language the deep feelings of emotion with which Your Holiness views the devastating effects of war on Italy strikes a very responsive chord in my heart. No one appreciates more than I the ceaseless efforts of Your Holiness to prevent the outbreak of war in Europe in 1939 and subsequently to limit its contagion. Your Holiness is familiar with the repeated efforts which were made in 1940 by this Government, and by many elements within the United States to deter the Chief of the Italian Government from plunging his country and countrymen into a ruinous war whose outcome, I reminded him even at that time, could only prove disastrous.

The sympathetic response of Your Holiness to the many appeals of the Italian people on behalf of their country is understood and appreciated by me. May I say that Americans are among those who value most the religious shrines and the historical monuments of Italy. However, my countrymen are likewise united in their determination to win the war which has been thrust upon them and for which the present government of Italy must share its full responsibility. My countrymen and I deplore the loss of life on both sides which must result and the destruction of property and resources.

Attacks against Italy are limited, to the extent humanly possible, to military objectives. We have not and will not make warfare on civilians or against non-military objectives. In the event it should be found militarily necessary for Allied planes to operate over Rome our aviators are thoroughly informed as to the location of the Vatican and have been specifically instructed to prevent bombs from falling within the Vatican City. This may be an opportune time to warn Your Holiness that I have no reason to feel assured that Axis planes would not make an opportunity to bomb Vatican City with the purpose of charging Allied planes with the outrages they themselves had committed.

My country has no choice but to prosecute the war with all force against the enemy until every resistance has been overcome. Your Holiness will understand, I am confident, that in this struggle for human liberty no exception can be made to the full prosecution of the war against any legitimate military enemy objective. Any other course would only delay the fulfillment of that desire in which Your Holiness and the governments and people of the United Nations—and I believe the people of Italy likewise are joined—the return of peace on earth.

Believe me, with the assurances of my highest regard, Yours very sincerely,

---

[1]The letter was announced by a telegram from Cicognani, no. 1184, of June 17, 20 h. 51, received in the Vatican at 13 h. of the 18th. It was sent with Report 782/43 of the same day in the Department of State dispatch bag that arrived in the Vatican on July 13. In the telegram and the report Cicognani does not add anything with the transmission of Roosevelt's response.

[2]Cf. no. 200.

No. 272, pp. 458–59

President Roosevelt to Apostolic Delegate Cicognani in Washington
(A.E.S. 4087/43, copy)   Washington, June 29, 1943

The President promised that Italy would be able to choose its own government. Meanwhile the United States must continue the war, but had no intention of damaging Rome's artistic and cultural patrimony.

The Secretary of State has shown me your letter of June 15[1] containing a further communication from His Holiness concerning the position of Italy in the present unhappy conflict.[2]

His Holiness again expresses his concern over the fate of the Italian people. Unfortunately, the government of Italy for a period of twenty years has glorified the use of force and has used it ruthlessly against the Greeks, the Ethiopians, the Albanians—to mention only a few of the victims of Fascist aggression. The people of Italy have been made the instrument of this pagan policy. When the Italians are liberated from Fascist domination and are free once more to demonstrate their innate good judgment, they will be given an opportunity to choose the kind of government based on democratic principles that they may wish to establish. It is my intention, and in that I am joined by the people of the United States, that Italy will be restored to nationhood after the defeat of Fascism and will take her place as a respected member of the European family of nations.

I have noted the observations of His Holiness with respect to the possibility of the bombardment of Rome. As in the past careful consideration has been given to the expressions of opinion of His Holiness. I recently reassured His Holiness with respect to the bombing of Vatican City. I trust His Holiness will understand that should the conduct of the war require it, recognized military objectives in and around Rome cannot be ignored. There is no intention to attack or damage non-military objectives or the historic and art treasures of Rome.[3]

---

[1]Cf. nos. 250 and 249.

[2]FRUS 1943, Vol. 2, Europe, did not publish Roosevelt's letter to Cicognani, but reproduced the President's memo to Hull with his notes for a response to the Delegate (p. 923).

[3]Monsignor Cicognani thanks Roosevelt in another letter addressed to him on July 2, after having received Maglione's telegram of July 27 (no. 269).

No. 281, pp. 472–73

The Legation of Great Britain to the Secretariat of State

(A.E.S. 4099/43, orig.)   Vatican City, July 7, 1943

Prime Minister Eden rejects the idea to declare Rome an open city. The English will bomb the city if necessary.

Memorandum

Certain remarks made recently by an official of the British Air Ministry at a press conference on June 23rd were misinterpreted by some of the foreign press as an invitation to the Italian Government to initiate negotiations about making Rome an open city.[1]

As a result of this misunderstanding three Parliamentary Questions on June 27th asked the Secretary of State for Foreign Affairs to state whether His Majesty's Government had made, or would make representations to the Italian Government in this sentence.

Mr. Eden replied:[2]

"His Majesty's Government have made no approach of any kind to the Italian Government in regard to the bombing of Rome and we do not intend to make one. I repeat that we should not hesitate to bomb Rome to the best of our ability and as heavily as possible if the course of the war should render such action convenient and helpful."

In a Supplementary Question Mr. Eden was asked on what authority the above–mentioned statements in the foreign press had been made. He replied that there had been a misunderstanding of some remarks made unofficially and not for quotation at a press conference, but that the position of His Majesty's Government was as he had just stated.

In reply to a further Supplementary Question, asking whether the principle of having Rome declared an open city should not be considered as being in the interest of humanity, Mr. Eden replied that he thought that it would be in the interest of humanity if Mussolini were to realise that the best thing to do for his country was to accept the unconditional surrender terms of the Allies.

Monsignor Tardini's Memo:
7-7-43. Received from Minister Osborne and sent to His Excellency.

---

[1] The R.A.F. proposal was known to the Vatican from June 26 and June 28 through the Swiss press. The June 24 *Journal de Génève* contains this statement: "Only if Rome were declared an open city would the Allied Air Force be able to refuse to bomb it and be able to declare itself ready to publish a decree in this regard. But, if this would not happen, the military, industrial and defense objectives of Rome could be legitimately attacked by the R.A.F." (*Bollettino Stampa,* no. 145, anno 30, June 26, 1943).

[2] In the afternoon of June 30. Radio London spread Eden's response the evening of the same day, and in Italian during the night.

No. 303, pp. 502–4

Pope Pius XII to President Roosevelt
(A.E.S. 4102/43, draft, A.S.S. 69419, copy) Edit. *Wartime Corresp.,* pp. 95–96
FRUS 1943; *Europe,* Vol. 2, p. 131.

Vatican, July 20, 1943

Message following the bombing of Rome. As a neutral State, the Holy See wishes that the homes of the poor be spared. The Pope witnessed the destruction in Rome, and deplores the bombing of cities. He hopes Rome will be spared new attacks.

Our Secretary of State acknowledged at once by telegram the receipt of Your Excellency's message of the tenth instant, and[1] he expressed Our grateful appreciation of the assurances given that "neutral status of the Vatican City as well as of the Papal domains throughout Italy will be respected" during the military operations ahead.

The neutrality of the Holy See strikes its roots deep in the very nature of Our apostolic ministry, which places Us above any armed conflict between nations. Yet it is this same God-given mission to safeguard and defend the eternal, spiritual interests of all men redeemed by Christ that makes Us the more sensible of human pain and sorrow. The war continues to multiply these sufferings a hundredfold for so many millions of peace-loving, innocent men and women that Our paternal heart can find no rest except in constant, increasing efforts to dry the tears of aging mothers, of widows and orphaned children, and to hold back by every means at Our disposal the mounting flood that threatens to bury completely beneath its raging waters once fair lands of Europe and Asia.

Moved by this strong, insistent love for humankind We cannot but take this occasion of the message which Your Excellency has kindly[2] addressed to Us to repeat an appeal made by Us more than once in these past few years. It is a prayer that everywhere, as far as humanly possible, the civil populations be spared the horrors of war; that the homes of God's poor be not laid in ashes; that the little ones and youth, a nation's hope, be preserved from all harm—how Our heart bleeds when We hear of helpless children made victims of cruel war; that churches dedicated to the worship of God and monuments that enshrine the memory and masterpieces of human genius be protected from destruction. We repeat[3] this appeal unwilling to yield to any thought of its hopelessness, although almost daily we must continue to deplore the evils against which We pray. And now even in Rome, parent of western civilization and for well nigh two thousand years centre of the Catholic world, to which millions, one may risk the assertion, hundreds of millions of men throughout the world have recently been turning their anxious gaze. We have had to witness the harrowing scene of death leaping from the skies and stalking pitilessly through unsuspecting homes striking down women and children; and in person We have visited and with sorrow contemplated the gaping ruins of that ancient and priceless Papal basilica of St. Laurence, one of the most treasured and loved sanctuaries of Romans, especially close to the heart of all Supreme Pontiffs, and visited with devotion by pilgrims from all countries of the world.

God knows how much We have suffered from the first days of the war for the lot of all those cities that have been exposed to aerial bombardments, especially for those that have been bombed not for a day, but for weeks and months without respite.[4] But since divine Providence has placed Us head over the Catholic Church and bishop of this city so rich in sacred shrines and hallowed, immortal memories, We feel it Our duty to voice a particular prayer and hope that all may recognize that a city, whose every district, in some districts every street has its irreplaceable monuments of faith or art and Christian culture, cannot be attacked without inflicting an incomparable loss on the patrimony of Religion and Civilization.

Meanwhile the war proceeds at a quickened pace; and as the peoples of the world are being told to prepare themselves for increasingly destructive battles that will drain the lifeblood of many thousands of the armed forces and, to Our grief be it said, of civilians, Our own soul makes ready for a more grievous ordeal of sorrow and anxiety. But it is with no diminished hope and confidence that in this very hour We call on God, Our sole stay and comfort, to hasten the dawn of that day when His peace will erect the glorious temple built of living stones, the nations of the earth, wherein all members of the vast human family will find tranquillity, security in justice, and freedom and inspiration to worship their Creator and to love their fellow men. It is the day, as Your Excellency says, longed for by all men of good will. But not all realize that that temple will stand and endure only if set on the foundation of Christian, more than mere human charity, not alloyed with vindictive passion or any elements of hate. Such charity the divine Redeemer of mankind proclaimed as His commandment, illustrated by His example and sealed with His blood.

Through it men can once again be united as loved and loving children of their divine Father in Heaven.

We avail Ourselves of this occasion to renew Our good wishes, while we pray God to protect Your Person and the people of the United States.

---

¹Cf. no. 297. According to Monsignor Tardini's chronological notes, Pius XII decided to prepare a response immediately on July 15. The draft of the 11th prepared by Tardini, was continued by the American Jesuit Vincent McCormick, who presented his version the morning of the 19th, a little before the bombing, and corrected it on the 20th. The following day the Pope reviewed it, sent it on the 25th to Monsignor Montini, and signed it on the 26th with the date of July 20th. On the 27th, the letter was entrusted to Tittmann, who sent it, via Berne (A.E.S. 4102/43).

²This word was added by Pius XII in place of "with such thoughtful kindness has addressed."

³This part of the letter, as far as the following paragraph that ends with "Religion and Civilization," was added on the 20th after the bombing, and was corrected the following days.

⁴Phrase added between the 23rd and 24th of July.

No. 413, pp. 648–92

Enclosure
Archbishops Mooney, Spellman and Stritch
to President Roosevelt

(A.E.S. 1315/43, copy attached to report)

Washington, September 15, 1943

Disappointment created among American Catholics by the aerial bombardments of Rome, and the present difficult situation. Responsibility of the government; measures to be taken.

Mr. President:

We deem it our sacred duty as American Catholic Bishops to manifest the deep concern we feel for the moral prestige of our Country and for the security and freedom of the Holy See in view of recent war developments on the Italian mainland.

You know the grave fears we expressed on the moral risks our Country assumed in bombing Rome. Reliable information we have since received on the results of that action show how ineffective were the diligently planned precautions to restrict precision bombing to military objectives. Thousands of civilians were killed and a whole district of the city, including an ancient religious shrine and Rome's famed Campo Santo, was seriously damaged. America's best justification in the face of a grave moral responsibility that even the Nazis never took in regard to Athens or Cairo, was the failure of the Fascist Government to make Rome an open city. It was heartening to us when on the 23rd of July you told us that our Government used every argument and pleaded with the Axis powers to make Rome an open city, and that we did our best and still hoped that the Germans and the Fascists would make it an open city. The Fascist Government fell on July 25th and on July 31st the succeeding anti-fascist government of Italy enlisted the good offices of the Holy See in communicating its desire to declare Rome an open city and in asking for a statement of the essential conditions required for the acceptance of this declaration by the Allies. The failure of the Allies during more than a month to give an effective answer to this communication of the Holy See not only weakened the position of the Holy See as a strong force for peace but increased our responsibility for the events that followed.

In the meantime Rome was bombed again on August 13th with further serious loss of life in the civilian population and further damage to religious establishments. In addition, the fact that the Italian Armistice was signed and announced before an effective answer was given to the request regarding the declaration of Rome as an open city aggravates the imperilled position of the Sacred City now occupied by the Nazi troops, and makes us even more clearly share the moral responsibility for eventual disastrous consequences of the military occupation.

We still keep in mind, Mr. President, the assurance you gave to the Holy Father to safeguard the Papal domains, which include not only Vatican City but numerous extraterritorial establishments throughout Rome serving the Administrative Agencies of the Holy See in its worldwide spiritual mission. We express the concern of more than twenty million American Catholics and their anxious hope that their Government will not have to share further responsibility for even more disastrous developments that threaten the Holy See under the conditions now obtaining in Rome. With the City of the Popes in control of forces that hate Christianity and its outstanding spokesman in the world today and would welcome any pretext for wreaking destruction there, the plight of the Holy See and all that it stands for in Rome is, indeed, critical. Frankly, we feel that the United Nations, and particularly those who control the action of our own Government which is so powerful in their councils, have here a responsibility for which not only the judgment of history but the conscience of citizens today will hold them accountable.

We realize how difficult the situation is but we refuse to doubt that there is in the councils of the United Nations the wisdom, the restraint, and the military genius to dislodge the enemy from Italy without making Rome the theater of direct military operations. Millions throughout the world will acclaim every effort that is made to circumvent the ill will of those who now occupy Rome. Military measures which offend the religious sense of so many citizens in so many nations may have consequences fatally prejudicial to the interests we all have at heart in the making of the peace and to the national and international collaboration necessary to that blessed end.

In addressing you, Mr. President, in this important matter which troubles our people and tends to cloud the high purposes to which we have consecrated our war effort for the freedom of men and nations, we wish again to assure you that our Hierarchy, in deep patriotic devotion, places in you its confidence that it will be spared the news that our armies have joined battle on the sacred soil of Rome.

No. 457, pp. 691–92

Minister Osborne of Great Britain to Cardinal Maglione

s.n.r. (A.E.S. 6792/43, orig.)   Vatican City, November 7, 1943

The British government always promised that the Vatican would be carefully spared.

1. I have the honour to acknowledge the receipt of Your Eminence's Note No. 6520/43 of November 6th[1] on the subject of the dropping of four bombs on the territory of the Vatican City and to inform you that I have telegraphed to London your request that the competent British authorities should carry out an investigation in order to establish to whom responsibility for this most regrettable occurrence is to be attributed.

2. In this connection I would invite Your Eminence's attention to the personal message from Mr. Eden to His Holiness the Pope which I communicated to Your Eminence in my Urgent and Confidential letter of June 23rd last.[2] In this it was stated that, in the event of its becoming necessary for military reasons to bomb the City of Rome, Allied pilots would be specifically ordered to ensure that no bombs fell in the Vatican City. In the light of this assurance it is evident that no Allied plane would bomb the Vatican City itself.

3. Mr. Eden's message continued, however, that His Majesty's Government had no reason for confidence that Axis planes would not bomb the Vatican City for the purpose of charging the Allies with the outrage.

4. Your Eminence will also recall that I have on various occasions informed you that His Majesty's Government had reason to believe that British aircraft and British bombs, captured by the Axis Powers, were being expressly reserved for such a purpose.

---

[1] Cf. nr. 454.
[2] Cf. nr. 453, note 3.

No. 459, pp. 693

Tittmann, United States Chargé d'Affaires, to Cardinal Maglione
No number (A.E.S. 6793/43, orig.)   Vatican City, November 8, 1943
The American government will search for those responsible for the bombing of the Vatican.

I have the honor to acknowledge receipt of Note No. 6520/43 dated November 6, 1943, from the Secretariat of State of His Holiness,[1] on the subject of the bombing of the Vatican City, and to inform Your Eminence that a full translation thereof was sent by telegram to my Government on the same day. I have no doubt but that the request of the Holy See that the competent American authorities should carry out an investigation in order to fix the responsibility for this most regrettable deed will be immediately complied with by my Government.

In the meantime, may I remind Your Eminence of the repeated assurances given by President Roosevelt to the effect that throughout the period of war operations the neutral status of the Vatican City, as well as the Papal Domains throughout Italy would be respected. Permit me also to point out that, if I am correctly informed, President Roosevelt in a communication to His Excellency the Apostolic Delegate in Washington which was destined for the Holy Father, mentioned the possibility that Axis airplanes might bomb Vatican City with a view to blaming the Allies for the outrage.

---

[1] Cf. no. 455.

Volume 8
Le Saint-Siège et les victimes de la guerre (January 1941–December 1942)

No. 62, pp. 158–61

The Secretariat of State to British Minister Osborne
(A.S.S. 32 208, draft)   Vatican, March 31, 1941
Request to facilitate the work of the Information Service for Prisoners of War.

1. The Secretariat of State of His Holiness have had the honour of receiving the Note of March 10th (N. 1/13/41)[1] which His Excellency the Minister of His Britannic Majesty's Government so kindly sent them, in reply to the Note of December 13th 1940[2] in which His Britannic Majesty's Government was

requested to facilitate the charitable work being undertaken by Papal Representatives with a view to alleviating the sufferings caused by the present war.

2. The Secretariat of State thanks, first of all, the British Government for having acceded in some measure to the aforementioned request; and particularly for having agreed:

a) that individual requests for information may be addressed to the Home Office and to the corresponding Authorities in the Dominions and in India, regarding civilian internees, and to the Prisoners of War Information Bureau in London, regarding Prisoners of War.

b) that as regards arrangements for visits for pastoral purposes to camps where military prisoners of war are interned, so far as the United Kingdom and India are concerned, arrangements be reached between the local Vatican Representatives, the War Office in London and Army Headquarters in India, respectively. In this regard the Secretariat of State desire that the necessary instructions be given for the early conclusion of these arrangements, especially where there seems to be a greater need for them: for India, with the Apostolic Delegate, His Excellency the Most Rev. Leo Peter Kierkels, and for Kenya, with the Rev. Father John McCarthy, who is acting as *locum tenens* of the Apostolic Delegate at Mombasa.

c) that the general permit, already granted to the Apostolic Delegate in the United Kingdom, covering visits, for pastoral purposes, to civilian internment camps can be extended to the representatives of the Holy See in India and in the Colonies.

3. The Secretariat of State must, however, point out that in the existing war conditions the most urgent need is that of making possible the transmission of the personal information which serves to quiet the anxiety of distant friends and relatives. Nevertheless, the concessions described above would seem insufficient not only because of the steady increase in requests for information but also because the public, conscious of the charitable mission co-natural to the Holy See, obviously applies to it, particularly from Italy, with ever-increasing frequency.

The system of having recourse, in each individual case, to the Prisoners of War Information Bureau or to the Home Office in London, aside from not taking into account the special position of the Holy See, does not seem practical and cannot suffice: such a system, were it to be applied to the tremendous number of requests for information, would not only involve much additional labour for the above-mentioned offices, but would, as well, prolong considerably the transmission of information and, unfortunately, also the anguish of those who await it.

4. However, such is the sense of duty which motivates the Holy See, in conformity with the evangelical precept of Charity inspiring its every action, and such is also its confidence in the sympathetic understanding, on the part of

the English Government, of the highly humanitarian aspect of this activity, that the Secretariat of State confidently take the liberty to advance the following considerations:

5. In the first place, since His Majesty's Government laments that the Government of the Third Reich has declined to accede to similar requests of the Holy See, the Secretariat of State feel compelled to assure the English Government that every possibility has been exhausted in the effort to extend the work of Charity of the Holy See to prisoners, who are in the hands of the Germans, and to civilians in the occupied territories. The Holy See, however, cannot believe that the English Government would like, on its part, to allow the same thing to happen: such a policy would be too far removed from the declarations of those English statesmen who have so often and, indeed, with noble and binding assertions, become the outspoken heralds of humane and Christian values.

As regards the Italian Government, the Secretariat of State are in a position to affirm that they found the Italian Authorities better disposed: the latter have permitted the Apostolic Nuncio in Italy to visit the English prisoners and internees and have given assurances that they will furnish the lists of the same to the Holy See, and, from time to time, relevant information.

6. In the second place, the Secretariat of State take the liberty to point out that their request for lists of Italian prisoners of war should not involve much additional labour for the Authorities and Offices concerned.

In the event, when the Authorities and Offices, in places where prisoners and internees are located, were to receive an order to meet in every way possible the requests of the local Representatives of the Holy See, they would find in these Representatives auxiliaries ready to collaborate discreetly and effectively, so that any additional labour should not become a burden or a source of complication.

7. In the third place, it seems that the furnishing of the desired data cannot be said to be contrary to the norms of the existing International Convention.[3] Indeed, Art. 2, #3 of the Convention *(les mesures de représailles à leur égard sont interdites* [reprisal measures in their regard are forbidden]) would seem to advise against depriving prisoners, in the hands of one power, of the benefit of the assistance in question solely because those in the hands of the enemy power are deprived of it. Furthermore, the spirit of the entire Convention (Cf. Art. 8, Tit. III, Sect. IV, Tit. VI) does not in the least exclude the generous and humanitarian service which the Holy See is obliged to render in these contingencies. Nor can it be believed that the improvement brought about by this Convention should make the position of prisoners less favourable in this war than it was in the last war, during which the Holy See not only secured a wide sphere of beneficent action, but also enjoyed, in many instances, quite appreciable facilities from the belligerent powers.

8. The Secretariat of State, therefore, take the liberty to renew, and define more clearly, their request that, so far as military conditions permit, the lists of the prisoners of war taken by Great Britain be communicated to the Apostolic Delegates in Egypt, India and South Africa,[4] and to the Rev. Father John McCarthy, *locum tenens* of the Apostolic Delegate at Mombasa, and that their charitable efforts in the interest of prisoners of war and of civilian internees be authorized and favoured by His Britannic Majesty's Civil and Military Authorities.

9. The same Secretariat of State trust that this request will be graciously acceded to, not only because of its being far from implying any disadvantage to the English people, but also because it will be, to the same people, a source of deep satisfaction when, later on, the entire world will come to know what courteous deference the Government of His Britannic Majesty will have shown towards the work of Charity undertaken by the Holy See.[5]

---

[1] See no. 44.

[2] See *Actes* 6, no. 402, p. 508 ff.

[3] Geneva Convention of July 27, 1929 relating to the treatment of prisoners of war.

[4] Testa, Kierkels and Gijlswijk. In February the Delegate in London had already been asked to intervene: "Every day it is more urgent that the Apostolic Delegate in Egypt have a list of Italian prisoners for the Holy See to be able to respond to the innumerable requests. I ask Your Excellency to beg your Government to comply solicitously to promote this humanitarian work as best possible...." (telegram, no. 87, February 23, 1941).

[5] See the response, no. 83.

No. 71, pp. 168–69

British Minister Osborne to Cardinal Maglione

No. 7/8/41 (A.E.S. 3328/41, orig.)   Vatican City, April 23, 1941

The help asked for Belgium will only aid the Germans and prolong the war.

On April 4th you asked me[1] to forward to my Government a further appeal, based on humanitarian grounds, to allow foodstuffs to pass to Belgium; you added that your understanding was that the German authorities had agreed to the control of distribution by a neutral commission.[2]

In their reply to my telegram my Government instructed me to explain to Your Eminence that their attitude is based on the considerations set forth in my Personal letter to you No. 7/4/41 of March 6th.[3] This attitude they feel bound to maintain, because the import of overseas supplies into Belgium, or into any other country in German occupation, so far from bringing relief, would, by assisting the German war effort and so prolonging the war, only extend the period of suffering and oppression for the peoples of the occupied territories.

Humanitarian considerations might rather suggest an appeal to Germany to feed the people she has conquered and despoiled. It is the aim of His Majesty's Government to help these subjugated peoples by ending Nazi domination and they cannot believe that these peoples would desire to see the day of their liberation postponed by any measure that would be of assistance to Germany.[4]

---

[1]On the occasion of our conversation.

[2]We have not found any document concerning such an agreement.

[3]See no. 43; letter dated March 8.

[4]Probably at the same time, the British minister had transmitted the French translation of a letter by Cordell Hull, United States Secretary of State addressed to a correspondent to whom he defined the attitude of his government regarding the problem of assistance to the European countries occupied by the Germans. "...The responsibility and duty of assuring help is incumbent on the occupying authorities. Given that the German Government has the direct obligation to replace the supplies it took from occupied territories and to feed the people in these countries, it is extremely difficult to understand how no effort has been made to oblige them to fulfill this duty when it seizes the country in question by force...."

No. 83, p. 188

The British Legation and the Secretariat of State

No number (A.S.S. 37346, orig.)   Vatican City, May 12, 1941

The English Government will facilitate visits by papal representatives to prison camps.

His Britannic Majesty's Minister to the Holy See presents his compliments to the Secretariat of State and has the honour to state that he duly communicated to London a copy of the Secretariat's Note No. 32208 of March 31st,[1] on the subject of facilities for the charitable work of Papal Representatives in the alleviation of sufferings caused by the war.

Mr. Osborne has now received a reply to the following effect. Mr. Eden states that while he is unable to agree, in the light of his information, that there is need of a third channel for the communication of information about prisoners of war and interned civilians to their relatives, he is anxious that all possible facilities should be assured to Papal Representatives for visits to camps for pastoral purposes. In order to ensure the grant of such facilities he has requested that instructions be sent to the local British authorities to make arrangements for such visits in consultation with the local Catholic representatives, especially in India and Kenya. Further information in this connection will be available later.

As regards the request by the Vatican that they be furnished with lists of prisoners of war, Mr. Eden states that it would be a misapprehension to suppose that compliance with the request for extra copies of lists giving the names of over 200,000 Italian prisoners of war now in British hands would not entail a great deal of additional work. He has carefully investigated this matter and he is satisfied that in fact much extra labour would be required to meet the Vatican's request. And he adds that it will be realised that British G.H.Q. in the Middle East must have many calls on the manpower available for work of this nature.

Memo by Monsignor Montini:
Ex Aud. SS.mi 15-5-1941
This note is not very satisfactory.

―――――――
[1]See no. 62.

No. 87, pp. 196–97

The Secretariat of State to British Minister Osborne
(A.S.S. 37346, draft)   Vatican, May 19, 1941
Renewed efforts to obtain lists of prisoners of war.

The Secretariat of State have the honour to acknowledge receipt of the Note, of May 12th,[1] of His Britannic Majesty's Minister to the Holy See, on the subject of facilities, requested by the Secretariat of State in their Note No. 32268 of March 31st 1941,[2] for the charitable work of Papal Representatives in the alleviation of suffering caused by the war.

It has been noted with satisfaction 1) that the Secretary of State for Foreign Affairs is anxious that all possible facilities should be assured to Papal Representatives for visits to camps for pastoral purposes; and 2) that in order to ensure the grant of such facilities he has requested that instructions be sent to the local British Authorities to make arrangements for such visits in consultation with the local Catholic representatives, especially in India and Kenya.

On the other hand it appears that Mr. Eden is unable to agree that there is need of a third channel for the communication of information about prisoners of war and interned civilians to their relatives. He has arrived at this conclusion in the light of information at his disposal.

The Secretariat of State, therefore, take the liberty to inform him about the following facts:

1) The number of requests for information concerning victims of the war, far from diminishing, is constantly increasing perhaps because of the prolongation of the war, the complication of military operations and the restriction of the means of communication: all of which serve to show that the other channels are not sufficient.

2) The fact that so many requests are made to the Holy See is explained by the consciousness, throughout the Christian world, of the charitable mission

which is co-natural with the Catholic church. In fact, the exercise of Christian charity is not only one of the principal teachings of the Church, but is also an outstanding field for its activity and constitutes one of the most important pastoral duties of the Church.

3) The Secretary of State for Foreign Affairs will then not fail to understand that so great a duty must be carried out especially in time of war when the sufferings of peoples are not only of the physical order but also, and more especially, of the moral order and therefore in need of assuagement through the comfort which can come only from religious convictions.

With regard to the request of the Holy See that it be favoured by the British Authorities with the lists of prisoners of war, it is to be pointed out that, although what was asked was indeed the granting of a favour—a request which paid homage to the high sentiments of humanitarianism which the British Government wishes to be the constant inspiration of its action—it was, however, not the intention of the Holy See to request anything which would impose very grave burdens on the authorities concerned. But since the Secretary of State for Foreign Affairs is convinced that such would be the case were the lists of prisoners in British hands to be compiled, or rather recopied, the Secretariat of State venture to propose that the Holy See take it upon itself to have the required lists compiled or recopied by its own Representatives or by these persons whom the British Authorities will wish to authorise in each concentration camp.

With the hope that His Britannic Majesty's Government will be pleased to reconsider favourably, in the light of what has been said above, the point of view expressed in the before-mentioned Note of His Britannic Majesty's Minister and will grant to the Holy See the desired facilities, the Secretariat of State express in anticipation their grateful appreciation.

---

[1] See no. 83.
[2] See no. 62.

No. 159, p. 291

The Secretariat of State to Ambassador Taylor[1]
(A.S.S. 41477, draft) Vatican, September 25, 1941
Request for intervention in order to obtain information about prisoners of war in Russia.

In view of the fact that the Holy See is endeavoring to offer every possible spiritual and moral assistance to those who are suffering from the unfortunate consequences of this war, it would deeply appreciate any representations which might be made by the United States Commission now in Moscow to the competent Authorities there with a view to bringing about an understanding of this charitable mission and a helpful cooperation on the part of all con-cerned—especially to assure that prisoners in Russian hands will be afforded adequate religious and moral assistance.

The Information Bureau of the Vatican, which has enjoyed some suc-cess in securing comforting information of soldiers for their distressed fam-ilies, would likewise be most appreciative of any steps taken by the commission in Moscow to assure an active participation of the competent authorities in this most important work. A relaxation of present restrictions would be of inestimable assistance to the Holy See and would most cer-tainly serve to quiet the dreadful anxieties of thousands of families which await some news of fathers and sons. If Father Braun,[3] an American priest in charge of the Church of St. Louis in Moscow, were to be called upon in this regard, he would, no doubt, be of great assistance.

These charitable endeavors of the Holy See are prompted by a sincere desire to be of utmost assistance to men of all nations in these difficult and try-ing days of war and are not intended to interfere with or hamper in any way the undertakings of other organizations. Consequently steps have been taken to provide for Russian prisoners the same services which are now requested for prisoners in Russia.[4]

---

[1] See no. 125. Taylor is in Rome from September 9 to 22, 1941; see *Actes* 5, p. 190 ff.
[2] See Monsignor Tardini's Note on the religious in Russia, ibid. 241–44.
[3] Leopold Braun, Augustinian of the Assumption.
[4] See infra no. 242.

No. 160, p. 292

Cardinal Archbishop of Westminster Hinsley to Pope Pius XII
Telegram no. 163 (A.S.S. Guerra, Belg-Civ.-Belgium 17, orig.)

London, September 26, 1941, 15 h. 22
rec'd, September 27. 18 h. 30

Request for intervention in favor of Belgians condemned to death by the Germans.

The whole Hierarchy of England and of Wales implore Your Holiness to intervene to save the lives of twenty-five Belgian hostages, fathers of families threatened with death at Tournay.[1]

---

[1] Telegram sent to the Nuncio in Berlin on September 28 (no. 325) and the delegate in Lon-don was informed (telegram no. 135). Monsignor Orsenigo approached the under-secretary at the "Auswartiges Amt" on September 29; see the note of von Weizsäcker no. 651 of September 29, AA (Bonn) St. S. Vol. 3, ser. 535, p. 240071.

No. 164, pp. 294–95

The Secretariat of State to Ambassador Taylor

(A.S.S. 40894, draft)   Vatican, September 29, 1941

Assistance to Poles deported to Russia.

From information received by the Holy See it appears that the conditions, of the spiritual and material order, under which the Poles deported to Russia—and especially to Asiatic Russia—are living are extremely sad; and their number would seem to be considerable—the Committee set up in London to help them estimates it, according to the Polish Ambassador to the Holy See, at a million and a half.[1]

The Holy See, has tried by every possible way to come to the assistance of those unfortunates, but up to the present has found it impossible to satisfy this charitable desire; hence it seems that until now the American, English and Japanese Red Cross have likewise been unable to do anything in favor of these deported Poles.

Now, however, it is reported that organized assistance will, from now on, be sent to the Poles deported to Russia.[2]

The Holy See entertains the hope that recent developments may make it possible for it to carry on its work of charity among these poor people by way of material and spiritual assistance. In this regard, the Holy See places its confidence in the lofty humanitarianism of the American Government, with the hopeful expectation that an intervention on the part of that Government will meet with welcome success.

The same help is earnestly requested in favor of the Lithuanians who have been deported to Siberia and are said by the Lithuanian Red Cross as stated by the Lithuanian Minister[3] to the Holy See to number 200,000.[4]

Monsignor Montini's Memo:
To check cf. Minister's Memos[5]

---

[1] In his letter of September 18 (see no. 154).

[2] Cf. ibid.

[3] Stanislas Girdvainis.

[4] The Chargé d'Affaires Tittmann acknowledged receipt of the Memo, of which a copy was transmitted to the Delegate in Washington (A.S.S. 41477): "Would Your Excellency, with the tact that distinguishes you, follow this initiative to have the desired results." Tittmann wrote on November 8 that the two Memos of the Vatican to Taylor (see no. 159 and this memo) were received by the addressee and transmitted to the President of the United States.

[5] Unpublished.

No. 211, pp. 361–62

The Chargé d'Affaires Tittmann to the Secretariat of State
No number (A.S.S., 43845, orig.)   Rome, November 26, 1941
The United States cannot help the Poles and Lithuanians in Russia.

The Assistant to the Personal Representative of the President of the United States of America to His Holiness the Pope presents his compliments to the Secretariat of State of His Holiness and has the honor to refer to the latter's Memorandum dated September 29, 1941,[1] addressed to Mr. Myron Taylor, regarding the condition of the Poles and Lithuanians who have been deported to Russia. A reply in the following sense has now been received from the Department of State.

The Secretariat of State of His Holiness is informed that the Government of the United States shares the humanitarian interest in the welfare of refugees in the Soviet Union, including those from Poland and Lithuania, as expressed by the Holy See. No occasion, however, has thus far presented itself which would cause the Government of the United States to believe that the condition of these unfortunate persons would be alleviated by any intervention on its part with the Soviet Union. For the purpose of bringing about better conditions for these people who are in such deep distress the Government of the United States will not hesitate to take such steps as may seem appropriate in case such an occasion should arise.[2]

---

[1] See no. 164.
[2] See FRUS 1941, I, pp. 260–69.

No. 272, p. 427

The Secretariat of State to the Chargé d'Affaires Tittmann
(A.S.S. 45776, draft)   Vatican, January 30, 1942
Information on the prisoners of war in Russia.

The Secretariat of State has the honor to propose the following matter for the kind consideration of the Chargé d'Affaires of the United States of America near the Holy See.

It is well known that the Holy See has done everything in its power, since the outbreak of the present conflict, to alleviate the suffering and need which is resulting therefrom. Amongst the enterprises undertaken is that of relieving the anxieties of families awaiting some news of loved ones, who are fighting at the front. The Holy See is desirous, now, of obtaining and transmitting some news of prisoners captured on the Russian front, just as it has been doing on behalf of those taken on other fronts. To this end, the American Authorities are approached in the confident hope that they may be able to facilitate the obtaining of information in the hands of the Russians.[1]

A request has likewise been made to the German and Italian Authorities and the Holy See has good reason to hope that it will be favorably received.[2]

---

[1] See no. 257.
[2] See *infra* no. 288.

No. 275, pp. 430–31

British Minister Osborne to Cardinal Maglione
No. 28/2/42 (A.S.S. Guerra, Grec.-Civ.-Greece 1/4, orig.)

Vatican City, February 2, 1942

8,000 tons of grain will be transported to Greece, but this does not release the occupying Government of its responsibility.

With reference to the question of supplies of foodstuffs for Greece,[1] I have the honour to inform Your Eminence that I have received the following telegram from London:

"In view of the appalling food situation which has developed in Greece, His Majesty's Government decided that some action on their part to meet the emergency was necessary. The following statement was made in the House of Commons today by the Minister of Economic Warfare,[2] by agreement with the United States Government.

"As the House is aware, His Majesty's Government have always refused to allow foodstuffs to be shipped through the blockade and thus to relieve the enemy of his responsibilities for feeding the peoples he has enslaved. This general policy, which is also the policy of the United States Government, remains unchanged.

"Nevertheless the United Kingdom and United States Government have viewed with increasing dismay the appalling conditions obtaining in Greece. Despite their undoubted ability to do so, the German Government have done practically nothing to meet the situation created by the pillage and extortion of their armies in the spring of 1941. They have, indeed, shown themselves quite indifferent to the fate of the Greek population, no doubt because the resources of Greece are too small to be of any value to the German war machine.

"His Majesty's Government and the United States Government are accordingly prepared to authorise a single shipment of 8,000 tons of wheat or flour to Greece, to be applied under the auspices of the International Committee of the Red Cross, in relief of the present emergency. This is in addition to the existing relief scheme, namely shipments of foodstuffs from Turkey (which is inside the blockade area).

"The two Governments continue to maintain in the most categorical manner that it is incumbent upon the enemy to feed the countries occupied by him, and their policy in this respect remains unaffected by the exception which it has found necessary to make in the special circumstances obtaining in Greece.

"While we shall do our utmost to expedite the shipment I should warn the House that, besides arranging for the supply of wheat or flour, it may take some little time to arrange shipping and the necessary safe conduct from the enemy."[3]

---

[1]See nos. 258 and 269.

[2]Hugh Dalton, to the House of Commons, January 27, 1942.

[3]The same day, Monsignor Roncalli in Istanbul (no. 92) received a telegram and on February 10 the British Minister was thanked for his communication (A.S.S. 46196). Obviously, the decision of the London Government represented an about-face.

No. 288, pp. 441–42

The Chargé d'Affaires Tittman to the Secretariat of State
No. 2 (A.S.S. Guerra, Ital.-Mil.-Russia 12, orig.)

Vatican City, February 19, 1942

The United States did not obtain any information on the prisoners of war in Russia; general information on the organization of the central bureau of information in the United States.

The Chargé d'Affaires of the United States of America presents his compliments to the Secretariat of State of His Holiness and has the honor to acknowledge receipt of the latter's Note dated January 30, 1942,[1] expressing the desire of the Holy See to obtain and transmit some news of prisoners captured on the Russian front, and setting forth the hope that the American authorities may be able to facilitate the obtaining of information regarding prisoners in Russian hands.

The Chargé d'Affaires did not fail to inform his Government of the contents of the Note and he now has the honor to quote hereunder the reply thereto received from Washington, which is dated February 10, 1942:

"The warmest sympathy is felt by the Government of the United States for the motives inspiring the Holy See in its attempt to bring about some degree of alleviation of the sufferings resulting from the war. It regrets that, unhappily, the earnest and repeated attempts which it has heretofore made to obtain from the Soviet Union information of the nature that the Holy See desires were unsuccessful, and there seems to be no prospect that a favorable outcome would be likely to result from any further similar attempts.

"The United States Government has also been advised of the attempts that the Holy See is making to obtain and disseminate information regarding war prisoners, civilian internees and other persons in general in belligerent areas. The International Committee of the Red Cross, as the Holy See is aware, has set up, as provided for by Article 79 of the Geneva Prisoners of War Convention, the Official Central Information Agency for Prisoners of War. The Agency organized by the International Red Cross is expected also to function as the official central information bureau for civilian internees in so far as the provisions of the Convention of Geneva are applied to them. In the office of the Provost Marshal General of the United States War Department there has been established the official American information bureau contemplated by Article 77 of the Convention; also set up there is a similar information bureau to concern itself with the civilian internees. The aforementioned bureaus cooperate with the American Red Cross, with the International Committee of the Red Cross and, through the latter and the representatives of the protecting powers, with the official information bureaus established in enemy countries. Therefore, it is suggested that the Holy See may be desirous of taking up with the International Committee and of coordinating the activities of the Information Bureau of the Vatican with those of the official Central Information Agency which the Convention provides for.

"Instructions have been given to the American Chargé d'Affaires at Berne, should he be approached by representatives of the Holy See, to interest himself in the matter and to cooperate in any discussions between the Holy See and the International Red Cross on the subject."

---

[1] See no. 272.

No. 311, p. 464

British Minister Osborne to Cardinal Maglione
No. 4/34/42 (A.S.S. Guerra, Pol.-Mil.-Spain 200, orig.)

Vatican City, March 18, 1942

Urgent request to intervene for Poles interned in Spain.

1. In my Memo No. 339/13/31 of October 15th[1] I invited Your Eminence's attention, on the instructions of my Government, to the situation of certain Poles interned in Spain and suggested that the question of their

being permitted to proceed to neutral countries might well form the subject of a charitable appeal by the Holy See to the Spanish Government.

2. It has now been reported that the situation of some 800 Allied Prisoners of War in Spain is becoming very serious owing to increased German pressure for their return to German Occupied Territory. In addition to about 450 Poles, there are some 35 Yugoslavs, 20 Czechoslovaks and 7 Greeks. The Nuncio at Madrid has already interested himself on behalf of these Prisoners and has done all he can for them, but the need of further assistance is urgent.

3. I am therefore instructed to suggest to Your Eminence that His Holiness might be willing to appeal to the Spanish Government on humanitarian grounds for permission for the Prisoners to leave Spain, if not for belligerent, then for neutral destinations. It is considered that a strong appeal by His Holiness to General Franco offers the only possibility of saving them.[2]

Monsignor Montini's Memo:
Mention what has been done.

---

[1] See no. 172, note 4.
[2] See no. 309.

No. 327, p. 479

British Minister Osborne to Cardinal Maglione
No. 4/42/42 (A.S.S. 47979, orig.)   Vatican City, March 25, 1942
For the exchange of wounded prisoners of war, the good offices of the Holy See are no longer needed.

1. With reference to Your Eminence's Note No. 46964 of March 3rd[1] on the subject of the negotiations between the British and Italian Governments for the exchange of sick and wounded Prisoners of War, I have learnt from His Majesty's Minister at Berne[2] that the message transmitted to him through the Nuncio,[3] for urgent communication to London, was duly dispatched. I have since heard from Berne that His Majesty's Government have now replied to the Italian Government that they agree to the repatriation of 344 sick and severely wounded Italian Prisoners so far passed by the Mixed Medical Commission, together with 575 Italian medical and sanitary personnel who are surplus to requirements in the Middle East.[4] His Majesty's Government intend, subject to reciprocity, to comply with Article 68 of the Convention and they will repatriate in due course all Italian Prisoners of War

who are recommended by Mixed Medical Commissions and also any other surplus protecting personnel.

2. No repatriation of chaplains is contemplated in the present operation. In dealing with chaplains His Majesty's Government will, as they are military officers, have to have regard to the views of the Italian Government, if it is found that any are superfluous.

3. Since the negotiations now appear to be proceeding satisfactorily, it does not at the moment appear necessary further to invoke the good offices of the Holy See since these good offices, which are highly appreciated, have had the effect desired in expediting the reply of the Italian Government.[5]

---

[1]Unpublished; see no. 293, for it seems that the date of the original was changed at the last moment since the draft has March 2.

[2]David Victor Kelly.

[3]Monsignor Bernardini.

[4] See no. 313.

[5]The London Delegate informed the Vatican on April 2: "There is talk about the exchange of Italian-English prisoners. I ask your instructions if, when it becomes public, we should divulge the humanitarian collaboration of the Holy See. In my opinion it would benefit present circumstances." (telegram, no. 142, A.E.S. 3220/42); see *infra* no. 339, note 2.

No. 351, p. 509

British Minister Osborne to Cardinal Maglione
No number (A.S.S. Guerra, Holland.-Civ.-Spain 1, orig.)

Vatican City, April 15, 1942

Request to intervene for Dutch interned in Spain.

1. With reference to my Note no. 4/34/42 of March 18th[1] and to Your Eminence's reply no. 47340 of March 26th[2] on the subject of the situation of the Polish and other Allied Prisoners of War in Spain, I have the honour to inform Your Eminence, by instruction of my Government, that the Netherlands Government in London would be grateful if the Holy See would be so good as to extend their representations to the Spanish Government to cover forty Dutch Prisoners who find themselves in similar conditions in Spain.[3]

2. I should be glad to learn what effect these representations have had and whether it has yet been found desirable that His Holiness should address a personal appeal to General Franco on the subject.[4]

---

[1]See no. 311.

[2]Unpublished; see no. 330, note 4.

[3]Telegraphed to Nuncio in Madrid on April 17 (no. 355).

[4]See *infra*, no. 401.

No. 361, pp. 520–21

British Minister Osborne to Cardinal Maglione
No. 4/60/42 (A.S.S. Guerra, Ital.-Gen.-Milit., 108, orig.)
Vatican City, April 27, 1942
Regarding assistance to prisoners of war given by the English Government.

1. With reference to Your Eminence's Note no. 47457 of March 14th[1] regarding the work of the Vatican Information Bureau in ensuring communication between Prisoners of War and their families, I am glad to say that I have now been informed that, as has already been notified to the Apostolic Delegate in London, His Majesty's Government are able to agree to the system of family messages between Prisoners and their relatives. I assume therefore that the difficulties in regard to the transmission of the message-forms ("moduli") to which Your Eminence referred in your Note, will no longer be encountered.

2. The following are the facilities, in some cases already granted, which His Majesty's Government are prepared to allow to Apostolic Delegates or, in their absence, to their accredited representatives, in so far as concerns Prisoners of War throughout the British Empire for whom His Majesty's Government in the United Kingdom are responsible, viz.:

1. Apostolic Delegates, or their representatives, subject to the approval of the local military authorities, whose consent will not be withheld except on security grounds, shall on application be permitted freely to visit for pastoral purposes camps or other places where Prisoners of War, of whatever nationality, are interned;

2. In so far as Italian Prisoners of War are concerned, Apostolic Delegates, or their representatives, shall be permitted to arrange for the exchange of messages between Prisoners of War and their families, provided that no responsibility for the transmission of such messages falls upon any British authorities, and provided also that the delivery to and collection from Apostolic Delegates of messages sent by Prisoners of War to their families, and of messages to Prisoners of War from their families, shall be effected through Camp Commandants only and subject to such limitations by local authorities as the latter may consider necessary.

3. These facilities do not necessarily apply to Canada or South Africa, whose Governments have not yet notified their assent to them, but I trust that it may only be a question of time before they too agree.

4. His Majesty's Government regret that, for reasons which I have already communicated to Your Eminence,[2] they remain unable to agree to general arrangements for the supply of lists of Italian Prisoners of War to Apostolic Delegates or other Vatican Representatives for communication to the Vatican Bureau.

These lists are already being supplied to the Protecting Power and the International Red Cross Committee.

5. Lastly His Majesty's Government state that they deeply appreciate the services rendered by the Vatican authorities to British Prisoners of War in Italy and their families. But, as there are also large numbers of British Prisoners in German hands, His Majesty's Government would urge that further efforts should be made to obtain from the German Government, in favour of Vatican Representatives in Germany and German-occupied territories, facilities similar to those which have been granted by the Italian Government.

If such facilities were granted by the German Government His Majesty's Government would at once reciprocate in regard to German Prisoners in their hands.[3]

---

[1] Unpublished.
[2] See no. 44.
[3] The contents of this Memo were communicated to the Papal Representatives on English territory.

No. 394, pp. 556–57

United States Chargé d'Affaires Tittmann to Monsignor Montini
No number (A.E.S. 4331/42, orig.)   Vatican City, June 10, 1942
Request to intervene for Roman Jews condemned to forced labor.

May I venture to bring to your attention, in the most personal and informal manner, a subject which has been causing me much concern and regarding which I have already spoken to you?

There is enclosed a photograph entitled, "Jews at Work Along the Banks of the Tiber," which appeared in the Rome newspaper, *Il Messaggero* of June 7, 1942.

I cannot begin to tell you how degrading I consider the situation which this photograph represents. It seems all the more appalling to me that it could exist within the shadow of St. Peter's, the fountain of Christian charity.

I feel certain that the Holy See must have already approached the appropriate authorities with a view to eliminating this shameful persecution, if not from Italy, at least from the precincts of the sacred Eternal City. In this connection I note that Article I, Paragraph 2 of the Concordat between the Holy See and Italy states:

"In considerazione del carattere sacro della Città Eterna, sede vescovile del Sommo Pontefice, centro del mondo cattolico e meta di pellegrinaggi, il Governo italiano avrà cura di impedire in Roma tutto ciò che possa essere in contrasto col detto carattere." [Because of the sacred character of the Eternal City, seat of the Pontiff as bishop and center of the Catholic world and pilgrimages, the Italian government will forbid all that is in contrast with this mission.]

I have no idea, of course, whether the foregoing paragraph is pertinent or not, but it sounds as though it might be.

Monsignor Montini's Memo:
    Ex Aud. SS.mi June 10, 1942
    Show this to His Eminence the Cardinal Secretary: he should decide if mention should be made to the Ambassador.

Cardinal Maglione's Memo:
    June 11, 1942
    I begged the Ambassador to intercede for these poor Jews. He promised me he would.[1]

---

[1] See *infra* no. 399.

No. 401, p. 562

Cardinal Maglione to British Minister Osborne
(A.S.S. 51345, draft)   Vatican City, June 19, 1942
    Information on the Holy See's efforts for Polish internees and others in Spain.

In reference to my Memo, No. 47340, of March 26, 1942,[1] I now have the honour of assuring the British Legation that the Holy See has continued to interest itself unceasingly in the fate of all the internees at Miranda del Ebro in Spain.

Hence, I have recently given further instructions to His Excellency the Apostolic Nuncio at Madrid[2] to intensify his representations to the Spanish Government in favour of the Polish internees, with a view to obtaining authorization for the latter to proceed to other neutral countries, especially to Argentina and Chile.

In reply, His Excellency has informed me[3] that he has been continuing his conversations with the Minister of Foreign Affairs, with the Ambassadors of Argentina and Great Britain and with the Polish Minister, regarding the situation of the Polish, Czech, Dutch and Yugoslav citizens interned at Miranda.

The Apostolic Nuncio assured me, furthermore, that he has been striving very solicitously to obtain the desired permission in favour of the Polish internees and that he is hopeful that it may be possible to provide for the transfer to Argentina of two-thirds of the four hundred Poles who are classed as incapable of military service.

As soon as I receive further information in this regard I shall transmit it to Your Excellency without delay.[4]

---

[1] See no. 330, note 4.

[2] Monsignor Gaetano Cicognani. See no. 337, note 2 and no. 351, note 3.

[3] With his telegram no. 374 of June 21 (A.E.S. 4510/42).

[4] On June 29 Cardinal Maglione informed the Polish Ambassador that he had spoken with the Spanish Minister for Foreign Affairs on the occasion of his visit to the Vatican on June 23, 1942.

No. 451, pp. 623–24

The British Legation to the Secretariat of State
No. 4/120/42 (A.S.S. Guerra, Pol.-Mil.-Spain 200, orig.)

Vatican City, August 19, 1942

Request to intervene for Polish internees in Spain.

His Britannic Majesty's Minister to the Holy See has the honour to refer to the Note addressed to him by the Cardinal Secretary of State No. 51345 of June 19th[1] on the subject of the Polish and other internees at Miranda del Ebro in Spain.

Mr. Osborne has been informed that it is now most important to expedite the negotiations with the Argentine Government and he has been instructed to express the hope that the Holy See may be willing to use their influence for this charitable purpose by further and urgent representations at Buenos Aires.[2]

---

[1] See no. 401.

[2] Telegraphed to Nuncio in Madrid on August 25 (no. 278, A.E.S. 6531/42), and communication given to the British Legation on August 26. The following day the Polish Ambassador insisted again on the critical atmosphere that reigned in the camp, making one fear that "a riot could have serious consequences..." (no. 122/SA/ 190). Again telegraphed to Nuncio in Madrid: "Awaiting news beg you to inform me about condition of Miranda Ebro internees and steps to be taken" (Telegram no. 279, A.E.S. 6532/42). See *infra* no. 464.

No. 455, pp. 627–28

British Minister Osborne to Monsignor Montini
No. 4/126/42 (A.S.S. Pol.-Mil.-Spain 200, orig.)

Vatican City, August 27, 1942

Renewed insistence for liberation of Polish internees in Spain.

1. As I mentioned to you yesterday on the telephone, Montgomery,[1] when he was in Madrid, had a conversation with our Ambassador there, Sir Samuel Hoare.

2. Sir Samuel thinks it essential that the release of the Poles at Miranda del Ebro[2] should be effected as quickly as possible. Great discontent prevails in the camp where conditions are most trying. There has already been one abortive attempt at escape and the Ambassador fears some sort of outbreak by the prisoners which might result in many of them being shot by the Spanish guards.

3. Negotiations are proceeding with the Argentine Government for the reception of these Poles in Argentina and, although definite consent has not yet been given, there is good reason to believe that it will be forthcoming. In my Memorandum No. 4/12/42 Urgent of August 19th,[3] I expressed the hope, on instructions from London, that the Holy See might be willing to use their influence for this charitable purpose by making further urgent representations to the Argentine Government on the subject. Sir Samuel Hoare suggests that the good offices of the Cardinal Archbishop of Buenos Aires[4] might also be invoked for this purpose.

4. His Eminence the Cardinal Secretary of State told me that he had appealed to Señor Serrano Suner on behalf of these men on the occasion of the latter's visit to the Vatican and that Señor Suner had promised to do what he could in the matter.[5] Nothing has, however, been done since then. Sir Samuel thinks that the only hope of ensuring early action lies in a personal appeal by the Pope to Señor Suner for the release of the internees. Would you be so kind as to inform His Holiness and to express the hope that he may see his way to making this appeal? As you are probably aware there is considerable discontent among the Poles in Great Britain in respect of what they regard as the undue reticence of the Vatican on the subject of German atrocities in Poland. The release of these Polish prisoners through Vatican intervention might do something to allay this feeling.

5. While this letter deals only with the Polish internees, you will remember that in my Note to the Cardinal Secretary of State No. 4/34/42 of March 18th[6] I suggested that His Holiness might be willing to appeal to the Spanish Government for permission for a number of other Allied prisoners of war to leave Spain.

[1] Hugh Montgomery, chief secretary of the British Legation.
[2] See no. 451. note 2.
[3] See no. 451.
[4] Jaime Luis Copello.
[5] See no. 404, note 3.
[6] See no. 311.

No. 498, pp. 671–72

Memo of the British Legation

No number (A.E.S. 7186/42, orig.)   Vatican City, October 3, 1942

News on the famine in Greece; severe warning to the Italians who are responsible for the destiny of the population.

Reliable information has reached London and has been published by the BBC to the effect that the Axis authorities in Greece are robbing the starving population of the entire harvest of corn, grapes, olives and currants; even vegetables, fish, milk and butter are being seized.

During the week of September 9th to 15th there was a strike in the Athens and Piraeus district as a protest against the seizure of the harvest. As a result there were a number of executions, 800 arrests and 380 deportations, largely among mine workers.

It is estimated that last winter about 500,000 Greeks died of starvation. Regular shipments of wheat are now being brought from Canada in Swedish ships to relieve the desperate conditions prevailing. But with the seizure by the Axis of this year's harvest and of all kinds of food products, the situation is likely to be equally desperate during the coming winter and, as a result of the weakness of the population after a year of starvation, mortality even higher.

But it may be that the Axis Powers welcome the decimation of the Greek people on the grounds that it will provide living space for their own nationals.

Italy is the Occupying Power and Italy is responsible for the proper feeding of the Greek people. The death of half a million Greeks last winter, out of a pre-war population of about seven million, is the best comment on the fulfillment of this duty and responsibility.

After the war the story of Greece will be an indelible blot on the good name of Italy, at any rate of Fascist Italy. First the perfidiously planned and executed aggression; its failure in the face of the heroic Greek defense; the rescue by the German armies after the loss of thousands of young Italian lives owing to the culpable negligence and incompetence of the Italian military authorities; the joint occupation of Greece in the name, and on the responsibility, of Italy; the denuding of the country by the Germans by a system of mixed extortion and pillage; the ensuing famine and death of half a million Greeks;

the exploitation of the black market and the capitalisation of starvation by Axis officials and officers; and now the seizure of this year's harvest, with the resulting almost certain condemnation to death by starvation of many hundreds of thousands more Greeks.

The fate of Greece is also a striking illustration and warning of the Nazi New Order in Europe for which Italians are fighting and from which they themselves are suffering.

Monsignor Tardini's Memo:
    October 3, 1942
    Perhaps information could be asked through the Berne Nunciature.[1]
Even His Excellency Monsignor Roncalli in Istanbul might know something.[2]
(We cannot telegraph to Athens.)

---

[1] We have not found such a request addressed to Monsignor Bernardini.
[2] See *infra* no. 504.

No. 499, pp. 672–73

British Minister Osborne to Monsignor Montini
No number (A.S.S. 1942 Varia 99, orig.)

Vatican City, October 5, 1942

Internment of British prisoner who fled from an Italian camp and took refuge in the Vatican.

I write to confirm what I said to you this afternoon.[1]

A British prisoner of war, escaped from a camp in the neighbourhood of Viterbo, entered the Vatican City this morning and came to my apartment, where he now is. His belief was that on reaching the neutral territory of the Vatican City he would be able to claim the protection of the Holy See and to remain at liberty, within the limits of the Vatican City.

His name is Albert Edward Penny
Petty Officer, -P/JX 125054
Late H.M.S. Submarine Oswald

He has been a prisoner of war in Italy since August 1940. He is a Catholic.

When I saw you this afternoon my purpose was to inform you of Petty Officer Penny's arrival (of which, of course, I had no prior knowledge), to place him under the protection of the Holy See and to recommend him to the charity of His Holiness. You suggested that it might be possible to arrange that he be exchanged for an Italian prisoner of war in British hands of equal rank and you said that you would instruct the Apostolic Delegate in London by telegram to propose this to His Majesty's Government.

I should be grateful if you would at the same time ask Archbishop Godfrey to inform His Majesty's Government that I hope that this solution may be found acceptable, but that, if it is not, I should be glad if they would inform me urgently of their view on the question and of the attitude that they would wish me to adopt.

---

[1]We publish the first of a long series of documents; negotiations finally ended after three months for the exchange of British prisoners with the Italian prisoners; see *Actes* 6, p. 9, note 1 and *Actes* 7, p. 174, note 3.

No. 535, pp. 707–8

M. Sargent to Godfrey, the Apostolic Delegate in London
No. 2/82 (London, Archdiocesan Delegation)

London, November 6, 1942

Request to stop reprisals against prisoners of war.

In your letter of the 16th October[1] you were so good as to make known to the Secretary of State that His Holiness the Pope had learned with great sorrow of the reprisals against prisoners of war whose welfare he has so much at heart, and that he had charged you to urge His Majesty's Government, in his name, to repudiate the use of such reprisals.

Mr. Eden desires me to inform you that His Majesty's Government in the United Kingdom, who highly appreciate the action taken by His Holiness in this matter, have already made their position clear. On the 13th October they invited the Protecting Power[2] to lay before the German Government their solemn protest against the breach of the Geneva Convention committed by that government in chaining British prisoners of war and to urge them to desist from it, and have said that in that case the counter measures of a similar character which His Majesty's Government felt themselves forced to take in order to protect their prisoners of war in enemy hands would immediately be withdrawn. No reply to this communication has yet been received.[3]

---

[1]Unpublished, addressed to the British Minister of Foreign Affairs. See nos. 513 and 515.
[2]That is, Switzerland, Cf. E. Bonjour, Geschichte der schweizerischen Neutralitat VI, 136.
[3]The Delegate transmitted the communication by telegram no. 222 of November 11 (A.E.S. 8968/42).

No. 575, 756–57

Chief Rabbi Hertz to Pope Pius XII
Telegram, No. 424 (A.E.S. 9248/42)

London, December 23, 1942, 18 h. 45
rec'd, December 24, 19 h. 15
Request to intervene for Jews in Eastern Europe threatened with annihilation.

In the name of worldwide religious Jewry respectfully beseech intervention your Holiness to save annihilation of Israel Eastern Europe. We invoke the fatherhood of God and the brotherhood of Man to save one suffering people.

At this momentous hour—Agudas Israel World Organisation of Orthodox Jews.[1]

---

[1] We have found similar telegrams from Jews residing in Colombia, of December 2 (A.E.S. 8914/42), sent by the Archbishop of Bogota, Monsignor Ismael Perdomo (1872–1950); from the Jewish Community of Costa Rica, of December 2 (A.E.S. 8913/42); from the Jewish Community of Bolivia of December 3 (A.E.S. 8912/42); from Jews residing in the Diocese of Manizales (Colombia) of December 4, sent by Bishop Luis Concha (1891; Cardinal 1961) (A.E.S. 8911/42); from the Rotary Club of Managua (Nicaragua), of December 9 (A.E.S. 8783/42); from the Women's International Organization of Zionists in Egypt, of December 12 (A.E.S. 8836/42), sent by the Chargé d'Affaires in Cairo, Father Hughes; from the Jewish Community in Mexico, of December 15 (A.E.S. 8780/42), sent by the Archbishop of Mexico, Monsignor Luis Martinez (1881–1956); from the Jewish Community in Potosi (Bolivia), of December 22 (A.E.S. 9034/42); from the Union of Orthodox Rabbis of the United States and of Canada, of December 23 (A.E.S. 9276/42).

No. 578, p. 758

British Minister Osborne to the Secretariat of State
No number (A.E.S. 9156/42, orig.)   Vatican City, December 29, 1942
Joint Declaration of the Allies regarding the persecution of the Jews by the Germans.

His Britannic Majesty's Minister to the Holy See has the honour to communicate to the Secretariat of State of His Holiness a copy of the Joint Declaration regarding the German persecution of the Jews, which was issued on behalf of the United Nations in London, Washington and Moscow on December 17th.[1]

It has been suggested that His Holiness the Pope might endorse the Declaration in a public statement. Failing this, His Majesty's Government would strongly urge His Holiness to use his influence, either by means of a public statement or by action through the German Bishops, to encourage German

Christians, and particularly German Catholics, to do all in their power to restrain these excesses.

---

¹Text in FRUS 1942, I, 68–70 and Tittmann's telegram ibid., 70 ff.

Volume 9
Le Saint-Siège et les victimes de la guerre (January–December 1943)

No. 7, p. 70

Cardinal Maglione to [Monsignor William] Godfrey,
Apostolic Delegate in London
(A.E.S. 75/43, draft)   Vatican, January 7, 1943
The Holy See and Poland (partial translation).

I wish to acknowledge receipt of your esteemed report No. 895/42, dated October 10, 1942¹ in which Your Excellency sent the text of a declaration of the "Executive Committee of the League of Nations"—relating to the Occupation of Poland—that Lord Lytton² sent you for the Holy See....

---

¹Unpublished. The Delegate wrote: "...Your Eminence already knows that every one feels the greatest compassion for the sufferings of the Polish people. At meetings and in the press, Poland is the main topic. Among Catholics, and generally, the question of Poland is the key to the position of the "United Nations" and the attitude of Great Britain toward Poland is proof of the good faith of the English...."

²Neville Stephen Lytton, third Lord Lytton (1879–1951), artist and painter. The undated Resolution states: "The Executive Committee of the League of Nations Union has received with indignation the recent reports on the campaign of annihilation carried on in cold blood, and as matter of policy, by the German Army Commanders and the Nazi officials in the countries occupied by them, and more particularly in Poland. It is of the utmost importance that those who can speak for all nations whose moral conscience is not dead should express their horror at this relapse into barbarism."

No. 8, p. 71

The British Legation to the Secretariat of State

No. 11/2/43 (A.E.S. 283/43, orig.)　　　　Vatican City, January 7, 1943

New request for the Holy See's intervention in favor of the persecuted Jews.

His Britannic Majesty's Minister to the Holy See has the honour to invite the attention of the Secretariat of State to the Memorandum on the subject of the German persecution of the Jews, which he handed to His Holiness on December 29th.[1]

It has been suggested that His Holiness might also be able to use his influence in countries such as Italy, France and Hungary, where the Jewish persecution has not so far shown itself in a marked degree, to prevent any deterioration of the local situation and to strengthen local resistance to possible German pressure for increased anti-Semitic measures.

Mr. Osborne would be grateful if the above suggestion might be submitted to His Holiness for careful consideration in connection with the suggestions previously laid before him.[2]

---

[1] See *Actes* 8, no. 578. After the audience, the Minister wrote to the Foreign Office on December 31 (58/3/42): "...It is clear that the Pope regards his broadcast as having satisfied all demands for stigmatization of Nazi crimes in the Occupied Countries. The reaction of some at least of my colleagues was anything but enthusiastic. To me he claimed that he had condemned the Jewish persecution. I could not dissent from this, though the condemnation is inferential and not specific, and comes at the end of a long dissertation on social problems....As a matter of fact his criticism of the totalitarian systems were unmistakable, and, given his temperament, I think he deserves credit for much of what he said" (F.O. 371/37538)...(See FRUS 1943, II, p. 912). Osborne repeated his impressions on January 5, 1943: "...He [Pius XII] promised that he would do whatever was possible on behalf of the Jews. I doubt if there will be any public statement, particularly since passage in his Christmas broadcast clearly applied to Jewish persecution (my telegram No. 284). I impressed upon him that Hitler's policy of extermination was a crime without precedent in history" (F.O. 371/37538).

[2] We did not find the written response.

No. 54, pp. 129–30

The Secretariat of State to Tittmann, United States Chargé d'Affaires

(A.S.S. 61441, draft)　　　　Vatican, February 15, 1943

Request to facilitate the work of the Vatican Information Service, particularly in Northern Africa.

The Secretariat of State to His Holiness has the honour to inform the Chargé d'Affaires of the United States of America to the Holy See that, with a view to overcoming the difficulties which seem to be in the way of the Vatican information service, it has been deemed opportune to solicit also the good offices of His Excellency Archbishop Spellman and of His Excellency Mr. Myron C. Taylor.[1] To this end the attention of their Excellencies has been drawn to the moral obligation of the Holy Father of helping so many of His suffering and anxious children who have recourse to Him in order to obtain news of their dear ones.

Archbishop Spellman and Mr. Taylor have been requested to initiate, if possible and expedient, new negotiations with the President of the United States, and to explain that this service is not intended as an opposition to any other similar organization, but would rather prove advantageous to the United States by enhancing its reputation for charitable sentiments and also by facilitating the reciprocity of the service on behalf of American internees and prisoners of war.

As regards the information service for prisoners of war and civilians in French North Africa, the following proposal has been made in order to meet the difficulties of the American Government: that the Holy See would nominate as its correspondent in French North Africa a White Father of Maison Carreé, to be designated by the Superior General of the Society. The correspondent thus selected should organize the service in a manner similar to that already in operation elsewhere by the other representatives of the Holy See, and arrange for the compilation of the messages in conformity with the requirements of the local military authorities. Such messages would be duly submitted for censorship and would be forwarded to the Vatican by the fastest route. Messages from the Vatican would be transmitted in the same way and would be subject to the same conditions of censorship.[2]

In conveying this information to the Chargé d'Affaires of the United States of America to the Holy See, the Secretariat of State avails of the occasion....

Monsignor Montini's Memo:

This memo was prepared following a conversation of the Substitute with Mr. Tittmann,[3] who was grateful for the information that our Office gave him....

---

[1] See no. 42.

[2] See *infra* no. 229.

[3] During the meeting Tittmann presented a Memo which he had transmitted via Berne on February 10; see FRUS 1943 II, p. 954 ff.

No. 68, pp. 144–159

Memoranda of the Secretariat of State
No number (A.S.S. Information Office, Vatican, draft)[1]

Vatican, March 1, 1943

Vatican assistance to war victims in Greece. Assistance to the Poles. Vatican activities on behalf of refugees, especially Jews. Memorandum on Vatican efforts to promote the exchange of sick and maimed prisoners. Solicitude for prisoners of war and internees. Activities on behalf of prisoners in Russia and Russian prisoners elsewhere. Difficulties met by the Information Service. Statistics of activities. Information on prisoners of war transported to the United States.

I

Assistance Rendered to War Victims in Greece[2]

Immediately after the occupation of Greece by Axis forces, the Holy Father hastened to go to the aid of the Greek people, and the Apostolic Delegate in Greece, His Excellency Monsignor Roncalli, was invited to furnish information regarding the local situation, and to indicate the particular needs to be met and the best means of doing so.

The work was begun in August 1941, when the Papal Nunciature at Berne was commissioned to send powdered and condensed milk to the Greek children.[3] Further supplies followed this first one, so that to the present a total of 15 tons of the same foodstuffs have been sent from Switzerland. Through the same Nunciature several tons of vegetables and medicines have been dispatched to Greece.

Through the Papal Nunciature in Budapest the Holy See sent to Greece several tons of flour, in 1942 as well as in 1943. Medicines and vitamins have also been sent from Hungary.

Medicines have also been sent from Italy, especially quinine and other remedies for malarial fevers.

Negotiations were opened in Turkey, Bulgaria and Rumania for the supply of vegetables for Greece, but without result. This year it is hoped to be able to obtain some wagon-loads of vegetables from the Rumanian Government.

Moreover the Holy Father kindly placed at the disposition of the Apostolic Delegate to Greece several sums of money for the same charitable purpose.

In September 1941, at the request of some important citizens of Greece, the Holy See asked the British Government, through diplomatic channels,[4] to forego the confiscation of 350,000 tons of grain already purchased by the Greek Government. Unfortunately the negotiations were not successful in spite of the insistence with which they were urged, perhaps for this reason or because it was generally hoped that free passage would be open to ships which would eventually carry grain to Greece. The Diplomatic Representative of the President of the United States of America to the Holy See[5] was also informed of these negotiations. The Holy Father, after a second and a third refusal from the British Government, was even disposed to approach His Britannic Majesty, provided that would not cause displeasure to the Government.[6]

The idea was also entertained of sending Greek children to Switzerland on the initiative of the Holy See. The Papal Nuncio at Berne dealt with the question, but the proposal was unsuccessful.

In November 1941, a supply of medicines was requested from the United States of America, but it was not possible to obtain them.[7]

Through the initiative of the Apostolic Delegate in Athens, kitchens for the people have been opened in various parts of Greece, where food is distributed to the poor free of charge or at a nominal price. These kitchens, called "Foyers de la divine Providence" were founded in December 1941, on the arrival of the grain obtained by the Holy Father in Hungary. In less than a year they have served more than half a million meals, costing nearly 8,000,000 drams. At present, nearly 12,000 meals are distributed daily.[8]

For the sick, dispensaries have also been erected, where the bulk of the medicines used are those sent through the work of the Holy See.

The Apostolic Delegation in Greece has opened an Information Office similar to that of the Secretariat of State to His Holiness, and nearly 50,000 requests and messages have been dealt with in less than a year.

II

Activities of the Holy See on Behalf of the Poles[9]

The work of charity which the Holy See has been carrying out on behalf of the Poles since the beginning of the war has been the object of the following generous contributions of the American hierarchy:

1940	His Excellency Monsignor Spellman	800,000 lire
1940	His Excellency Monsignor Spellman to His Eminence Cardinal Hlond	$ 10,000.00
1940	Bishops' Committee for Polish Relief	$ 146,324.31
1940	Bishops' Committee for Polish Relief	$ 216,000.00
1941	Collection made by the Bishops' Committee	$ 47,000.00
1941	Collection made by the Bishops' Committee	$ 15,000.00
	Total	800,000 lire + $ 434,324.31

The Holy Father graciously deigned to distribute this sum as follows:

$50,000.00 were placed at the disposal of the Commission for Polish relief;

$10,000.00 were placed at the disposal of the Bishops' Committee for Polish refugees in America;

$10,000.00 were placed at the disposal of His Excellency the Apostolic Delegate for eventual subsidies for Poles deported to the U.S.S.R.

The distribution of the relief money was generally entrusted to the Papal Representatives, who, with due consideration of varying conditions and necessities, had recourse also to local associations and charitable organizations chiefly Polish, so that the subsidies of the Holy See might be delivered in money or in kind to the persons in need.

Subsidies were given, in a greater or lesser degree, in the various nations which offered hospitality to the Polish refugees. The subsidies were devoted to the payment of lodging expenses, clothing, doctors' fees and medicine bills, boarding houses for students, Homes for ladies and girls, journeys to Poland, journeys from one country to another and to America. They were also used for the organization and maintenance of hostels, shelters, and orphanages, for the establishment of a hospital (England), for assisting needy priests and religious, for arranging for preaching and religious assistance especially at Easter, for the printing of healthy reading material and books of devotion and religious instruction, for the acquisition and delivery of textbooks in the ecclesiastical sciences to Seminaries and certain religious congregations in Poland, for the periodical furnishing of abundant supplies of food, for the purchase and supply of Altar wine and oil for liturgical use, for funerals and prayers for the dead, for visits carried out under the orders and in the name of His Holiness to Polish internees and refugees—visits in which the consoling words of the Common Father were accompanied by gifts of money, food and clothing etc. Besides the above-mentioned offerings of the American Hierarchy, other offerings received by the Holy See were also used with a view to making those subsidies more adequate: offerings of Peter's Pence were devoted to the relief of the Poles, as were, especially, several large sums of money which the Holy Father, in His paternal and especial benevolence for Poland, deigned to place at the disposal of the Relief commission on behalf of the afflicted Poles.

Of the offerings received from the American Hierarchy, some ten thousand dollars still remain. This sum is obviously insufficient to provide for the necessities which present themselves continually, for the maintenance of those works of charity which require periodical assistance and especially for meeting the very grave demands for relief which, as can be foreseen, will inevitably follow in the wake of this terrible war.

III
Activity of the Holy See on behalf of Refugees especially Non-Arians[10]

Certain charitable persons in the United States of America made an offering to the Holy Father of $125,000.00, destined by the donors themselves for "the victims of the persecution without distinction of race or religion."

Of this sum:

$50,000 were handed over by the Holy Father to the American Committee,

$75,000 were forwarded to the Holy See.

These $75,000 were thus subdivided:

$30,000 were placed at the disposal of Raphaelsverein of Hamburg;

$ 3,000 were placed at the disposal of Caritasverband of Lucerne;

$ 7,000 were placed at the disposal of the Dutch Catholic Committee;

$35,000 were placed at the disposal of the Secretariat of State to His Holiness.

This last sum was used in bestowing small subsidies but was chiefly employed in financing the journeys of emigrants who were 99% non-Arian.

This fund at present consists of $ 20,316.41.[11]

IV
Memorandum

In their visits to the various concentration Camps of Prisoners of War, the Papal Representatives have found, unfortunately, many prisoners maimed, wounded, or suffering from tuberculosis, whose sad state they immediately reported to the Holy See as worthy objects of the charity of the Holy Father.

The paternal heart of His Holiness was moved to compassion by the sad plight of His beloved children and by the sorrow thus caused to their desolate families, and He gave orders for arrangements, if possible, for the repatriation of these invalids through a reciprocal exchange between Italy and England.[12]

His Eminence the Cardinal Secretary of State obtained from the Italian Government assurance that they were willing to repatriate, according to the provisions of the conventions, these British prisoners forming part of the categories determined by the same Conventions, provided that the British Government were willing to make a similar concession in favour of invalid Italian prisoners.

The Holy See sent a note to the British Minister informing him of the assurance obtained from the Italian Government and requested him to intimate as soon as possible whether the English Government was, in turn, disposed to grant a speedy exchange of invalid Italian prisoners in their hands.

It is to be hoped that the British Government will soon announce its willingness to cooperate with this work of charity of the Holy See.[13]

V
Solicitude of the Holy See for Prisoners of War and Civilian Internees

His Excellency Monsignor Spellman is requested to:

a) interview the Papal Representatives, find out their needs and the difficulties which they have to overcome and render them every possible assistance.

b) send accounts (accompanied by reports of the local ecclesiastical authorities and by photographs, etc.) of the spiritual assistance being rendered and of the general condition of the prisoners of war and civilian internees.

VI
Activities of the Holy See on Behalf of Prisoners in Russian hands and on behalf of Russian Prisoners[14]

Finding it impossible to render any other assistance to prisoners of war in Russian hands, the Holy See concentrated its efforts in seeking to obtain lists of these prisoners and in trying to establish a news service between them and their respective families. To this end special representations were made to the Governments of the United States of America, of Great Britain and of Sweden, and the Apostolic Delegates of London, Washington, Teheran and Istanbul were also requested to use their influence for the same purpose.

1) In September 1941 the Secretariat of State availed itself of the presence in Rome of His Excellency Mr. Myron C. Taylor, Representative of the President of the United States of America, to request that Government to obtain, through the services of an American commission then in Russia, an active cooperation of the Russian authorities with the relief work of the Holy See on behalf of the prisoners of war. At the same time the Apostolic Delegate in Washington was instructed to lend his support to this proposal of the Holy See.

Towards the end of December 1941, the Apostolic Delegate informed the Secretariat of State of a declaration of the American Government that all its efforts in this regard had been futile.

A little more than a month had elapsed when the Holy See deemed it opportune to solicit once again the good offices of the American Government, and in a Note to Mr. Tittmann, the Chargé d'Affaires of the United States, it expressed the hope that the American authorities would be able to facilitate the exchange of news of prisoners in Russian hands.

On February 19, 1942, the Chargé d'Affaires of the United States, while expressing the admiration of his Government for the Secretariat of State [declared] that he regretted that all efforts in this regard had been so far unsuccessful, and that no hope could be entertained of a more favourable response to similar representations in the future. This was confirmed two months later by a communication from the Apostolic Delegate to the effect that the Russian Government had absolutely refused to consider any such proposal. The Apostolic Delegate added that the American Government would renew its efforts and that the matter might possibly be simplified by the communication of a definite plan on the part of the Holy See. This plan was immediately forwarded to the Apostolic Delegate.

In the beginning of July the Apostolic Delegate reported that in a long conversation with Mr. Welles[15] he had learned that towards the end of June the American Government had insisted once again with the Soviet authorities and had presented the plan outlined by the Holy See. Unfortunately the reply was absolutely in the negative: the Russians would not agree to any exchange of lists or to any communication of news.

2) On July 11, 1942, the Cardinal Secretary of State presented an Aide-Memoire to the British Minister[16] informing him of the activities of the Holy See in this connection and calling his attention to the determined opposition of the Soviet Government with regard to giving news of the prisoners they had captured.

The British Minister communicated with his Government, but so far he has not been able to give any reply on the subject of the above-mentioned Aide-Memoire.

3) On April 20, the Italian Embassy to the Holy See presented the Secretariat of State with a copy of a protest sent to the Soviet Government, through the medium of Sweden, on the treatment meted out to Italian prisoners of war. Following this, the Papal Nuncio to Italy was requested to approach the Swedish Minister and to inform him of the ardent desire of the Holy See to assist in transmitting news of the prisoners taken on the Eastern front. The Nuncio was also to assure the Swedish Minister of the support of the Holy See with a view to obtaining humane treatment for prisoners in Russian hands.

On May 29, 1942, the Papal Nuncio to Italy communicated that in connection with these matters a Note had been sent to the Government at Stockholm seeking to bring new pressure to bear on the Soviet authorities. This was done in a Note of the Swedish Government to the Russian Minister in Stockholm on June 29, 1942, but on September 21, the Swedish Minister in Rome informed the Nuncio that no reply had so far been received from the Soviet Government.

With a view to facilitating some concession in this matter on the part of the Russian Government, the Papal Nuncio in Italy has been instructed recently to ask the Swedish Minister to suggest that for the moment the Holy See would be satisfied with the communication of the names of prisoners and the addresses of their families, without, however, abandoning the hope of further concessions in the future.

4) As soon as the Holy See heard of the intention of the Polish Government in London of sending His Excellency Monsignor Gawlina, the Polish Military Ordinary, to Russia, the Secretariat of State hastened to instruct the Apostolic Delegate in London to consult with Monsignor Gawlina as to the best means of sending news of prisoners of war in Russia, especially their names and family addresses. The Apostolic Delegate in London reported that Monsignor Gawlina was already en route, and that everything would be forwarded to him by diplomatic channels. The Secretariat of State then requested the Apostolic Delegate of Teheran to remind Monsignor Gawlina of the Holy See's earnest desire to obtain news of prisoners in Russia, and the Delegate was asked to intervene himself for the same purpose.

Following on the announcement of Monsignor Gawlina's arrival at Teheran, further representations were made to the Apostolic Delegate. He then reported that he sought in every possible way to realise the activity desired, but from information received, it was evident to him that it was not possible to do anything in favour of prisoners and internees in Russian hands.

To date no information has been received here from His Excellency Monsignor Gawlina.

5) The Holy See had already advised the Apostolic Delegate in Turkey that information regarding prisoners in Russian hands would be welcomed and the Apostolic Delegate replied that he would endeavour to treat the matter through the Russian representative in Ankara, taking the question up personally on the occasion of his forthcoming visit to that city, but he foresaw many serious difficulties. In fact this effort produced no results.

6) Although numerous representations had already been made by the Holy See to the Government of the United States, on the occasion of the recent visit to the Vatican of His Excellency Mr. Myron C. Taylor, the Holy Father addressed directly to the Head of the American Nation a Memorandum asking him to use his powerful influence to obtain from the Russian Government the desired news concerning prisoners of war in Russian hands.

So far no reply has been received to this move.

7) The Rumanian Government recently commissioned the Representative of the Rumanian Red Cross, His Excellency M. Petrescu Comnene, to contact the Holy See with a view to obtaining news of prisoners in Russian hands. During his conversations with the Secretariat of State, he revealed in strict confidence that the Russian Government bases its relations with its ene-

mies on the Fourth Convention of the Hague (1907), which provides for the exchange of information, but not for visits to camps. On the other hand, supporting the desire of the International Red Cross (as expressed by his Excellency M. Petrescu Comnene) to quote the Holy See's activities in particular regarding the question of prisoners of war in Russian hands, the Secretariat of State was glad to inform him that there was no objection to the International Red Cross mentioning in its declarations that the Holy See had frequently intervened as stated.

2.

Apart from its efforts for prisoners taken on the Russian front, the Holy See has not failed to direct its attention to the Russian prisoners of war.

In a dispatch of August 18, 1941, His Eminence the Cardinal Secretary of State approached the Nuncios in Budapest and Bucharest with a view to obtaining the lists of Russian prisoners.

On August 30, 1941, the Papal Nuncio in Bucharest, in a communication dated December 7, 1941, reported that the Government had granted him permission to visit the above-mentioned prisoners, although not all of them had yet been assembled in concentration camps.

The Holy See took this occasion to renew to the Papal Nuncio its request to do everything possible to obtain the lists of prisoners, in view of the proposed visit.

To the request made by the Papal Nuncio on April 8, 1942, for permission to visit the Russian prisoners in German hands, a reply was sent giving the authorization to ask such a permission.

On May 10, 1942, the above-mentioned Papal Nuncio forwarded a detailed report of the visit paid to Russian prisoners in Rumanian hands.

The Holy See had also prepared a small religious picture for the Russian prisoners and sent it to the Papal Nuncio for distribution on July 8, 1942.

The Papal Nuncio to Hungary, after a first communication that he had not succeeded in obtaining any information about Russian prisoners in Hungary (September 28, 1941), informed the Secretariat of State on October 10, 1941, that there were only 4 Russian prisoners in Hungarian hands and that these were in a hospital.

VII
Difficulties met with by the Information Service for Prisoners of War, especially in Kenya

From the outbreak of the present war, the Holy Father, mindful of His universal mission of charity, could not ignore the numberless appeals addressed to Him on all sides from relatives anxiously seeking news of their dear ones missing from the various battle fronts. To cope with these requests He established an Information Office for prisoners of war and civil internees, with this twofold object:

1) to give immediate notification of the fate of their dear ones involved in operations of war—imprisonment, transfer, etc.

2) to facilitate as speedily as possible the exchange of personal communications in the form of short messages (of 25 words), sent by ordinary post or by radio broadcasts received by the Papal Representatives, and sent, duly passed by local censorship, to the addressees.

Though at first the English Government did not seem unfavourable towards this charitable work of the Holy See, subsequently they failed to give it any official recognition. That is, until April 27, 1942, when the British Minister to the Holy See wrote in his Note 4/60/42:[17]

"The following are the facilities, in some cases already granted, which His Majesty's Government are prepared to allow to Apostolic Delegates, or, in their absence, to their accredited representatives, in so far as concerns prisoners of war throughout the British Empire for whom His Majesty's Government in the United Kingdom are responsible, viz:

1) Apostolic Delegates, or their representatives, subject to the approval of the local military authorities, whose consent will not be withheld except on security grounds, shall on application be permitted freely to visit for pastoral purposes camps or other places where Prisoners of War of whatever nationality are interned;

2) In so far as Italian Prisoners of War are concerned, Apostolic Delegates, or their representatives shall be permitted to arrange for the exchange of messages between Prisoners of War and their families, provided that no responsibility for the transmission of such message falls upon any British authorities, and provided also that the delivery to and collection from Apostolic Delegates of messages sent by Prisoners of War from their families shall be effected through Camp Commandants only and be subject to such limitations by local authorities as the latter may consider necessary."

These concessions allowed the realization of object No. 2 mentioned above, regarding correspondence between Prisoners of War and their dear ones.

3. As for object No. 1 proposed by the Holy See as above, the British Minister stated:

4. "His Majesty's Government regret that, for reasons which I have already communicated to Your Eminence, they remain unable to agree to general arrangements for the supply of lists of Italian Prisoners of War to Apostolic Delegates or other Vatican Representatives for communication to the Vatican Bureau. These lists are already being supplied to the protecting power and the International Red Cross Committee."

1.

The divergent attitude of the British Government to the above-mentioned objects of the activity of the Holy See seems to have been prompted by the position arising from the Convention of Geneva 1929, in regard to the International Red Cross. In fact, by this Convention re the publication of lists of prisoners and the forwarding of the corresponding information, Articles 77–80 lay down definite obligations to the International Red Cross on the part of the signing Powers.

This does not prohibit, however, the same service to an institution such as the Holy See which considers as its natural mission the alleviation and abbreviation of all kinds of suffering. The request seems all the more legitimate considering the ease with which the captor nation could supply an extra copy of the communications which it must make by force of the above-mentioned convention.

Other Governments have recognised the suitability of this request, and in fact conform to it by supplying the lists of prisoners under their control, together with information concerning them.

2.

Regarding Prisoner's correspondence, the convention quoted does not impose on the signing Powers any obligations to the International Red Cross (see Articles 35–41).

Article 36 was drawn up through special agreement between the English and Italian Governments; it allows Prisoners of both Nations to write weekly one letter and one postcard. The letters must not exceed 24 lines.

The above-mentioned concessions for messages (see Note of the English Minister quoted above 4/60/42 2) involve no limitations other than this: "subject to such limitations by local authorities as the latter may consider necessary."

Unfortunately, these concessions have been absolutely ineffectual in Kenya,[18] until last November when some slight improvement was made. The application of the concessions was modified and fixed as from December 1, 1942 (see the enclosed instructions[19] given by the authorities in Kenya).

In effect:

1) Radio messages (even when subject to censorship) are prohibited;

2) Written messages can be sent by post only when considered "essential" for humanitarian reasons, for [example:] when news has not been received for a considerable period;

3) If the prisoner uses the Vatican message service, each message (that is, of 225 words) is counted as a letter (of 24 lines);

4) In replying to messages received, the prisoners can use only certain short formulae printed on the message form;

5) If the number of messages becomes too great, the whole question will be reconsidered.

The Information Office of the Holy See can furnish documentary proof of the deficiencies of the news service to and from the prisoners in Kenya, both from letters of persons who complain of the lack of news over many months (for some the period exceeds two years), and from a list of prisoners of a certain camp who have implored the intervention of the Holy See to obtain news of their families.

On the other hand, attention is drawn to the arrangements made by the Holy See in favour of Prisoners of War in Italian hands.

1) Full use is made of Radio and Telegraph to send messages to and from the prisoners.

2) No limitation is imposed on the dispatch of messages written by the prisoners, nor of those addressed to them.

The Holy See cannot remain insensible to the numerous appeals addressed to it in such a spirit of faith. On the other hand, uneasy lest the Italian authorities curtail the concessions, in view of the lack of reciprocity, to the sole disadvantage of British prisoners, it hopes that the central authorities responsible may take the necessary steps to ensure a regular news service also for the Prisoners of War in Kenya.

The Holy See trusts that its service will not be considered superfluous, nor an encroachment nor a challenge to services already protected by International Convention, but as an indispensable complement redounding to the honour and advantage of the authorities who sanction and favour it.

VIII
Statistics of the Requests and of the Replies[20]

	Requests	Replies to Request	Percentage of Replies
June 1940	36,191	15,788	42.45%
1941	462,071	203,856	47.84%
1942	538,042	249,675	46.46%
January–February 1943	112,315	48,315	43%
Totals	1,123,615	517,634	46%

IX
Sections for English-Speaking Prisoners

June 1941–February 1943:
    Names Broadcast......................n. 57,952
    Messages Broadcast..................n. 24,558

January 1942–February 1943 (I):
    Requests.................................n. 16,389
    Messages to Prisoners..................n. 25,398
    Messages to Families (by courier)...n. 100,642

(I) As regards requests, messages to prisoners and messages to families forwarded by courier, the period June 1941–January 1942 has been omitted, the Section's activity in this direction having really started on January 1st 1942.

X
Information Service for the United States of America

It has been learned that many prisoners are being transferred from India and from England to the United States of America.

It would be very convenient if the Apostolic Delegate in Washington could obtain from the competent authorities concessions and authorisation similar to those guaranteed elsewhere to the Papal Representatives with regard to prisoners of war and civilian internees.

In particular it would be necessary to obtain:

    a) lists of the names of prisoners of war and civilian internees and an indication of the state of their health.

b)   authorisation for the Papal Representatives to act as a medium for the transmission of news to and from the prisoners of war and civilian internees in the form of short messages of a family character, not exceeding 25 words and written on forms prepared for that purpose.

c)   permission for periodic visits to the Concentration Camps for the purpose of spiritual and moral assistance.

These concessions are all the more urgent and more necessary in view of the fact that the Italian authorities have already made arrangements facilitating the information service and other works of assistance being rendered by the Holy See to North American prisoners of war. Thus, for example, during the past few months the Vatican Information Office has been able to telegraph 230 names of American prisoners in camps in Italy. It would seem that this news was the first to reach the United States and its communication evoked expressions of profound satisfaction and gratitude from the families concerned.

In the same period, lists of these prisoners were handed to the Chargé d'Affaires of the United States to the Holy See, together with lists of 21 prisoners in hospitals and 223 in camps in the Philippine Islands. (See accompanying report on the section of the Information Office devoted to English-speaking prisoners.)

In order that the information obtained may satisfy in some way the desires and anxieties of the distant families, it is necessary that it be transmitted to the Vatican in the fastest possible manner.

The Vatican Radio, which already broadcasts to 15 countries and has reciprocal contacts with some of them, permits of the transmission of news concerning prisoners of war and would prove a rapid means for the efficient operation of this service with the United States of America.

It is important, therefore, that the steps already taken for the establishment of the telegraphic contact with Washington should be brought to a successful conclusion.

To this end the Apostolic Delegate has been requested to study the possibility of an agreement with an American Station, and preferably with Mackay Radio, which is already in relation with Vatican Radio (Enclosure n. 7).[21]

At the moment the question may be viewed in more favourable light owing to the Radio contact recently inaugurated with the Apostolic Delegation in Tokyo, which has obtained lists of prisoners of war and permission to transmit the names by Radio or by courier.

---

[1]These notes and summaries were prepared and given to Archbishop Spellman of New York, who was in the Vatican. On April 2, copies were sent to New York (A.S.S. Guerra Varia 120): "In accordance with your suggestion I am forwarding to you the enclosed copies of the Memoranda, dealing principally with the activity of the Holy See on behalf of refugees and prisoners of war. The originals were given to Your Excellency before your departure from Vatican City." Cf. *Actes* 7, p. 232, note 1.

[2]See A. Martini, *La fame in Grecia nel 1941 nella testimonianza dei documenti vaticani inediti.*

[3]See *Actes* 8, no. 126, note 14, p. 244.

[4]See *Actes* 8, no. 145, annex, p. 270 ff.

[5]Myron Taylor; see *Actes* 8, no. 157, note 1, p. 288.

[6]See *Actes* 8, no. 180, p. 323.

[7]See *Actes* 8, no. 193, p. 337 ff.

[8]A memorandum of February 6, 1943 of the State Department gives detailed information on the assistance given by the Swiss and Swedish Red Cross on behalf of the Greeks; see FRUS 1943 IV, 171–73.

[9]See *Actes* 6 and 8, particularly the Introductions.

[10]See *Actes* 6 and 9 passim.

[11]See *Actes* 6, nos. 125 and 126, pp. 211–14.

[12]See *Actes* 8, no. 293, pp. 447–49.

[13]See nos. 41 and 58.

[14]See *Actes* 8, no. 480, pp. 647–55, to find the citations.

[15]Under-Secretary of State.

[16]Mr. d'Arcy Osborne.

[17]See *Actes* 8, no. 361, p. 520 ff.

[18]See *infra* nos. 177 and 285.

[19]Unpublished.

[20]See *La Chiesa e la guerra* where one finds details of the activities of the Information Office. See the proceedings of March 2, 1943....This service for the Prisoners of War was established by His Holiness, Pope Pius XII in August 1940 in the Secretariat of State....

[21]The statistics for 1940 give 5,252 names and 2,509 minutes of transmissions, for 1941, 103,162 names and 56,478 minutes, for 1942, 226,755 names and 132,154 minutes of transmission.

No. 292, pp. 428–30

Apostolic Delegate Cicognani to Under-Secretary of State Welles

No number (Arch. Deleg., draft)   Washington, August 13, 1943

Request to facilitate the work of the Vatican Information Service.

In a letter of July 1, 1943,[1] His Excellency, the Apostolic Delegate, presented for the consideration of the State Department a proposal emanating from the Vatican Secretariat of State with reference to a possible acceleration of the preparation and transmission of lists of prisoners of war, in order that the families of the prisoners might be notified sooner. In a reply dated July 17, 1943, Mr. G. Howland Shaw[2] informed the Apostolic Delegate that the United States government had already taken steps to arrange for the compilation of these lists in the field of military operations wherever feasible.

The Apostolic Delegate was subsequently informed by Mr. Myron C. Taylor that the plan was under consideration, and was later advised that it would surely be adopted, and that official notification to this effect would be forthcoming. In view of the fact that under the system of preparing the lists after arrival of the prisoners in the United States camp rosters were made available to the Apostolic Delegation, it was felt that the preparation of the lists in the theaters of operations would not interfere with this service, but that the lists would be put at the disposal of the Vatican representative in the particular territory for eventual transmission to the Cardinal Secretary of State. This appeared to be contained in the information furnished [to] the Apostolic Delegate by Mr. Taylor, and on the strength of this assurance, the Apostolic Delegate so advised the Cardinal Secretary of State on July 28th,[3] while pointing out that official notification to this effect was as yet wanting.

Subsequently to this magnanimous gesture on the part of the American government, and to the official authorization for the extension of the Vatican Information Service to North Africa for the use of civilians (as contained in a letter from Mr. Welles on June 12, 1943),[4] the Vatican Secretariat of State, with the proper approval of the United States authorities, dispatched to Algeria the Very Reverend Monsignor Walter Carroll in order to supervise the inauguration and organization of the Information Service.[5]

In carrying out the duties entailed by this work, Monsignor Carroll has had occasion likewise to come in contact with the compilation of the lists of prisoners. According to information reaching the Apostolic Delegate from the Cardinal Secretary of State, Monsignor Carroll has advised His Eminence that several lists of prisoners are already prepared and ready for transmission. It would appear, however, that the American Authorities in North Africa have not yet received instructions allowing them to permit Monsignor Carroll to forward these lists to Vatican City. Monsignor Carroll has informed Cardinal Maglione that the local authorities are favorable to the transmission of these lists, but that they are unwilling to take upon themselves the responsibility of approving such action without explicit directions from Washington.[6]

In the light of the foregoing, the Apostolic Delegate respectfully requests that whatever action is possible be taken to facilitate this humanitarian and charitable activity of the Holy See. It is a fact of experience that the families of soldiers are oftentimes made to suffer more by uncertainty as to the fate of their loved ones than by the actual news that they have been wounded or even killed. The Holy See had this in mind when it undertook to transmit to the United States through its own radio facilities, several hundreds of lists of American soldiers who were prisoners of war in Italy. Charity, mercy, and any possible kind of relief belong to the mission of the Vatican throughout the world. In addition, the geographical location of the Vatican, particularly with regard to Italian prisoners of war, and the means of communication at its immediate disposal as well as its direct contacts with local bishops, would appear to place it in a very advantageous position for the performance of this eminently human and charitable work. The good results in the field of charity, and the excellent influence which such action would inevitably have in elevating still higher the already great prestige of the United States would seem to abundantly counterbalance anything which might indicate duplication of work in other quarters. Experience has shown in countless cases that there is really no duplication involved.

Hence the Apostolic Delegate requests that the United States government authorize making available to Vatican representatives the lists of prisoners of war which are compiled in the various theaters of operation.[7]

----

[1] Unpublished; see no. 245, note 4.
[2] Assistant Secretary of State.
[3] See no. 277.
[4] Unpublished; see no. 229, note 1.
[5] See no. 256.
[6] See no. 283, note 5.
[7] See infra nos. 306 and 354

No. 425, pp. 556–58

Monsignor Carroll to Monsignor Montini
No number (A.S.S. Guerra Varia 190, orig.)
Maison-Carreé (Algiers), November 13, 1943
Report on activities of the Information Service established in Algiers, and on the situation in general.

As you will have learned from a telegram[1] which I sent through Washington last week, I arrived here November 5th from America. Since my return we have been able to accomplish much, despite local difficulties, restrictions, etc. The Information Bureau here is now functioning quite smoothly and the courier service between Algiers and Sicily is in operation. I am anxious to get over to Palermo to speak with the Archbishop,[2] in order to coordinate the services, but I am at present engaged in discussions which, I hope, will soon lead to the establishment of direct radio communication with Vatican City. The American Authorities have given their approval for this radio service and we are now working out the details. There remains always, however, the possibility of a strong British or French veto to this proposed service.

As soon as this radio communication with Vatican City has been definitely established, I shall visit Sicily, and possibly Naples, to organize and extend the Vatican services to those areas. The Allied authorities have already assured me that I shall have no difficulty in getting there.

The principal obstacle which we encounter here is bureaucracy. Each point that we raise must be proposed to the three Powers and there must be approval not only by each of the Powers, but also by all of the numerous governmental agencies directly or indirectly concerned. Naturally, this means considerable delay.

I am planning to visit the various prisoner-of-war camps in the North African area at the Christmas Season. It will be practically impossible to purchase gifts for the men, but we are printing small prayer books, in Italian and German, on the frontispiece of which we should like to print a brief message from the Holy Father, together with His Apostolic Blessing.

As Your Excellency knows, the Vatican Information Bureau here is being staffed by the White Fathers, under the direction of Mons. Birraux.[3] They have undertaken the work with great zeal and enthusiasm and are proving very efficient. Mons. Birraux has been most helpful and has placed all his facilities at the disposition of the Holy See. We have likewise enlisted the assistance of several Communities of Sisters. Thus far there has been only one bureau—at Maison Carreé—but now that the Service has been officially authorized we expect to open within the next week a small office in the center of the city, where the public may be received.

Within the next few days I shall prepare a short article on the North African Information Bureau which might be useful to the editors of "Ecclesia."[4] I shall endeavor likewise to obtain some interesting photographs.

During my stay here, Your Excellency, I have made many very valuable contacts. However, in conformity with the instructions which I received before leaving Vatican City, I have remained aloof from the political situation here. I have, nevertheless, been observant of the scene about me and I should like, if I may, to offer a few observations. First of all, Algiers, politically, is in a state of constant confusion and instability. There is neither agreement nor unity here. Self-interest seems to reign supreme. There is no united popular support of any of the various groups here; in fact, the people seem to look to France and hope that an eventual Allied invasion there may produce a Government more in line with the desires of the people. At the same time there is widespread criticism of the Catholic Hierarchy, especially in Catholic circles, for its alleged failure to provide counsel and direction in this period of general confusion. There is no desire, as far as I can see, on the part of these sincere critics, to have the Bishops take sides politically. But it is felt that they might well insist, time and time again, on general Christian principles, on the importance of laying a Christian foundation for any future Government of France and on the danger of all materialistic tendencies. Likewise, it is noteworthy, I feel, that some of the bishops are privately, and even publicly, defending their support of Vichy and Marshal Pétain with the rather dangerous assertion that Catholics are obliged to support that Government near which the Holy Father retains His Nuncio.[5]

[1]Unpublished; see no. 354, note 5.

[2]Cardinal Lavitrano.

[3]Superior General of the White Fathers, see no. 42, note 4.

[4]A brief report on the activities in Northern Africa was published: 2 (1943) December, p. 57. See no. 28, note 2.

[5]On November 19, Monsignor Carroll sent another report, addressed to Cardinal Maglione: "...I hope to leave tomorrow for Gibraltar. I shall bring the lists of about 50,000 names of prisoners of war: if possible I'll give them to the Americans in Gibraltar, otherwise I'll continue the trip to Madrid, and give them to His Excellency the Apostolic Nuncio. It is my intention to visit the prison camps in Northern Africa at Christmas, and to distribute the prayer manuals...." (See A.S.S. Guerra, Varia 199 and no. 575, 190.)

No. 466, pp. 600–603

Monsignor Carroll to Monsignor Montini
No number (A.S.S. Guerra Varia 190, orig.)

Madrid, December 14, 1943

Report on activities, on communications with Sicily and Southern Italy, on the Information Service for prisoners of war, and on visits to prison camps.

I take the liberty to write you this hurried note in English in order to inform Your Excellency of the more recent developments in the Algerian situation.[1]

I left Algiers the afternoon of December twelfth and arrived here at noon today. I expect to leave Madrid Wednesday, December 16th, and shall probably be in Algiers Thursday afternoon.[2] I had two reasons for making this trip: 1) to bring lists of approximately 125,000 prisoners of war; and 2) to try to obtain some information regarding the projected radio service between Algiers and the Vatican. Although I cabled for technical information from Algiers November 11th, I had still received no reply December 12th. I now learn that the cables to and from the Vatican were delayed several days in the code room of the American Embassy here. I was very pleased on my arrival here to find the desired information, for I feel certain now that a very satisfactory service can be arranged. The American and British Authorities have given their full approval and have been awaiting only this technical information before initiating the service.

As soon as telegraphic communications between Algiers and the Vatican have been established, I shall go to Sicily and Southern Italy in order to establish closer contact with the Archbishops and Bishops there and to coordinate the communications of the entire area with the Holy See.[3] The American Authorities have granted permission for the establishment of direct radio-telegraphic communication between Algiers and the Ecclesiastical Authorities of Sicily, Southern Italy and Sardinia as soon as the Algiers-Vatican circuit is functioning. The courier service between Sicily and Algiers is already functioning. When I go to Sicily and Southern Italy in the near future, I shall try to have the Archbishops and Bishops prepare reports on general conditions, their needs, etc., and shall forward them through Madrid by the fastest and safest courier.

The American Authorities have been most anxious to be of assistance and in recent days were becoming very impatient regarding the opening of the telegraphic communications with Vatican City, especially in view of a cabled complaint received from the State Department demanding an explanation for the failure to get this service started. These authorities have, likewise, been most helpful in facilitating any travelling that I have to do; they provide me with a high priority and rapid transportation, gratis at any time that I need to travel.

The Vatican Information Bureau at Algiers is now functioning very smoothly. Unfortunately, the American and British Authorities have thus far had only one copy of their lists of prisoners-of-war available, necessitating our making copies of those lists. It is equally unfortunate that the American lists of German prisoners do not all give the family address of the prisoners. Both of these defects are now being corrected and it is hoped very shortly to receive copies of complete lists from the American Authorities. I might mention here, also, that the "delay" stipulated in the Washington authorization has now been set at two weeks. We are obtaining lists (for copying) from the French on a very delayed basis, chiefly because the French are only now compiling their lists. In all this work the White Fathers are showing remarkable adeptness and enthusiasm. His Excellency, Mons. Birraux,[4] who is keenly interested in the project, has placed ten priests at the disposition of the Bureau; these are ably assisted by several religious communities and Catholic Action groups in Algiers. A new office is to be opened in downtown Algiers December 15th to care for requests for information on the part of civilians; this has now been authorized and will be advertised by radio and newspaper. Undoubtedly there will be thousands of such requests to handle and it is to be hoped that the radio service may soon be operating to care for this service, too.

I should be very grateful to Your Excellency if you would find occasion to express to His Holiness my great personal gratitude, as well as that of all the collaborators in the Vatican Bureau at Algiers, for the magnificent message of consolation and encouragement, which He has so kindly sent, together with His Apostolic Blessing to the prisoners-of-war in North Africa.[5] I know that this renewed evidence of paternal and affectionate interest on the part of the Common Father will be received with great joy by the prisoners-of-war, whose devoted attachment to the Vicar of Christ is a source of edification and comfort to all who come in contact with them.

The visits to the camps have already begun. I have been able to visit many of the smaller groups in Algeria and hope to have an opportunity later to go to the more distant camps. Meanwhile, two of the White Fathers are preparing to leave for a tour of Tunisia and Morocco. It is our hope that most, if not all, of the camps will be visited during the Christmas season. Naturally, we should have liked to prepare parcels for each prisoner, but there is an incredible lack of goods and supplies on the Algerian market. Recently we succeeded in obtaining 63,000 packages of cigarettes, but there is no hope of finding clothing or edibles. It has been decided, therefore, to leave a sum of money with the chaplain at each camp, in order that he might provide a "treat" for his men or obtain, locally, something needed by the group or by individuals. It is still not certain, in view of the great scarcity of paper, whether we shall be able to print the little prayer books for the prisoners, but we are praying and hoping that this may yet be possible.

Regarding the morale of the prisoners, I can only repeat what I told Your Excellency in an earlier letter;[6] namely, that the prisoners in the hands of the Americans and British are, generally, very well treated and are quite happy; those in the hands of the French, however, are poorly clad, underfed and, in general, rather badly treated; reports from all sectors verify this statement. This is due, in large part, no doubt, to the fact that the French Authorities are not in a position to provide food and clothing equivalent to that offered by the Americans and British; but it seems equally true that the spirit animating the directors of the French camps is one of animosity and revenge.

I avail myself of this occasion, Your Excellency, to offer my cordial good wishes to you for the coming Christmas season and to assure you of my constant prayerful remembrance of you, that the Infant of Bethlehem may bestow upon you at that time His special blessing and a very generous share of heavenly guidance and assistance.[7]

---

[1] See no. 425.

[2] The Nuncio in Madrid telegraphed on December 20: "Monday 13 current Monsignor Carroll arrived and has now left for Algiers...stating that he would leave for Sicily and Southern Italy from Algiers and arrange for radio contact with Naples, Bari and Salerno and establish courier service" (telegram no. 603, A.S.S. Guerra Varia 190).

[3] Receipt acknowledged December 30 (telegram no. 475).

[4] See no. 42, note 4.

[5] See nos. 464 and 425, note 5.

[6] See no. 308.

[7] In another report of January 4, 1944, Carroll gives final information. "...It will doubtless be of interest...to learn that no mention was made in the Algerian newspaper of the Holy Father's Christmas message...."

Volume 10
Le Saint-Siège et les victimes de la guerre
(January 1944–December 1945)

No. 67, p. 140

M. Perlzweig[1] to the Apostolic Delegate Cicognani in Washington
Acknowledgment to the Pope for his interventions on behalf of the persecuted Jews in Europe.

I beg you to accept my warmest thanks for your very kind letter of February 11th which I have just seen on my return to New York.[2]

It is scarcely necessary for me to assure Your Excellency that the repeated interventions of the Holy Father on behalf of Jewish communities in Europe has evoked the profoundest sentiments of appreciation and gratitude from Jews throughout the world. These acts of courage and consecrated statesmanship on the part of His Holiness will always remain a precious memory in the life of the Jewish people.

I should like to take this opportunity also of expressing my personal sense of appreciation for the kindness with which I was recently received by Monsignor Carboni,[3] who heard what I had to say with so much patient courtesy and human insight.

---

[1] Maurice L. Perlzweig, World Jewish Congress representative.
[2] Unpublished.
[3] Monsignor Romolo Carboni, auditor, Apostolic Delegation in Washington.

No. 132, p. 205

The British Legation to the Secretariat of State
No number (A.E.S. 1839/44, orig.)   Vatican City, April 1, 1944
Request for intervention on behalf of Hungarian Jews.

It is hoped that the Holy See, in accordance with the principle of universal charity, will exercise such influence as they can to protect Jewish refugees in Hungary from being handed over to the German authorities.[1] It is understood that the influence of His Holiness has in the past been very effective in this matter, but it is appreciated that in changing circumstances action may be more difficult. In any case any action in this sense that it may be found feasible to take will be highly appreciated.[2]

[1]Chief Rabbi Hertz in London had written to the Delegate, Monsignor Godfrey, on March 22 (Arch. Deleg. London): "The very serious turn of events in Hungary renders the plight of the Jews in that country perilous in the extreme, and only the urgent intervention of His Holiness the Pope can save hundreds of thousands of human lives from the horrors that befell them in Rumania and Poland. As Chief Rabbi, I earnestly appeal for such intervention. The lay leaders of my community, as well as the Executive of the National Committee for Rescue from the Nazi Terror, wholeheartedly associate themselves in this appeal through you to His Holiness." Godfrey transmitted the request to the Vatican on March 30 (telegram no. 410, A.E.S. 1945/44): "The Holy See has been concerned about the fate of the Jewish residents in Hungary and has already appealed in this regard to the Apostolic Nuncio in Budapest even though one does not have too much hope." The Delegate informed the Chief Rabbi of Maglione's response (letter of April 4; Archiv. Delegat. of London). Hertz immediately thanked him (letter of April 10, ibid.).

[2]The Secretariat of State responded to the Legation on April 5 (A.E.S. 1839/44): "...The Holy See has renewed its earnest request with regard to the fate of the Jewish residents in Hungary through the Apostolic Nuncio in Budapest." The "Agudas Israel World Organisation" branch in London was informed by Monsignor Godfrey of the efforts by the Holy See on behalf of the Jews in Hungary. They thanked the Delegate on April 13.

No. 230, pp. 316–18

The Apostolic Delegate Cicognani to Cardinal Maglione
Telegram, no. 176 (A.E.S. 3195/44)

Washington, June 13, 1944, 18 h. 05
rec'd, June 14

Solidarity of North American Bishops with Bishops of France; they insist that the authorities protect religious monuments and works of art.

The following message is sent at the request of the Administrative Board of the National Catholic Welfare Conference. To His Eminence Cardinal Maglione. Your Eminence, it is reported that bishops of France have appealed to the bishops of the United States to intervene with responsible authorities in order that the civilian population and monuments of religion and art of France and Europe be spared the horrors of bombing. The bishops of the United States respectfully request Your Eminence to assure their brethren in France of their common and profound concern for the suffering of their defenseless flocks.

They concur in the attitude of their brother bishops of all countries in condemning indiscriminate bombing or similar methods of warfare which injure the innocent and helpless without the justification of military necessity. They ask however that all these be reminded that the bishops of this country since the outbreak of this frightful conflict have repeatedly urged that every precaution be taken to avoid unjustifiable destruction of life and property and have expressed deepest sympathy for the innocent victims of such warfare whether on the British and the Continent of Europe or Africa or Asia or among the afflicted islanders of the South Pacific. They have received assurance from their civil and military leaders that every precaution is being taken to confine the war within legitimate military objectives. The killing of innocent civilians and the destruction of property which is not being devoted to the war effort is indeed deplorable and they hope that any such things which have occurred have been the results of accidents and miscalculations. It is gratifying that our authorities have shown their desire to save from damage and destruction monuments of culture and history in the war area by setting up the American commission for the protection and salvage of artistic and historic monuments in Europe[1] which cooperates closely with the military authorities. The bishops of the United States beg Your Eminence to assure their distressed brethren in France that their tragic plight and that of their flocks does not cease to be the object of the United States. In union with the Vicar of Christ they beseech Almighty God to lighten the burden of all suffering humanity and speedily to restore to all mankind the inestimable blessing of a peace of justice and charity. Signed Archbishops Mooney, Stritch, Spellman, McNicholas, Murray, Mitty, Rummel, Bishops Noll, Alter, Ryan.[2]

---

[1]"American Commission for the Protection and Salvage of Artistic and Historic Monuments in Europe" (later "in War Areas"), the creation of which was announced on August 20, 1943.

[2]Edward Mooney (1882–1958), Archbishop of Detroit from 1937; Samuel Stritch, Archbishop of Chicago from 1939; Francis Spellman (1889–1967), Archbishop of New York from 1939; John McNicholas (1871–1950), Archbishop of Cincinnati from 1925; John Murray (1877–1956) Archbishop of St. Paul, Minnesota, from 1931; John Mitty (1887–1961), Archbishop of San Francisco from 1935; Joseph Rummel (1876–1947), Archbishop of New Orleans from 1935; John Noll (1875–1956), Bishop of Fort Wayne from 1925; Karl Alter (1885–1977), Bishop of Toledo from 1931; James Ryan (1886–1947), Bishop of Omaha from 1935. The Secretariat of State sent a telegram to the Nuncio in Vichy (no. 571/A.E.S. 3193/44 on June 20) affirming that the American Episcopacy deplored the indiscriminate bombing in France.

No. 241, pp. 326–27

Chargé d'Affaires Tittmann to Cardinal Maglione
(A.E.S. 3980/44, orig.)   Vatican, June 24, 1944

The "War Refugee Board" reports on the imminent massacre of Jews in Hungary, and requests the intervention of the Holy Father.

I have been instructed by my Government in a telegram dated June 13, 1944 to deliver the following message to Your Eminence from the War Refugee Board, Washington:

"We know His Holiness has been sorely grieved by the wave of hate which has engulfed Europe and the consequent mass enslavement, persecution, deportation and slaughter of helpless men, women and children. His

Holiness, we also know, has labored unceasingly to reinculcate a decent regard for the dignity of man activated by great compassion for the sufferings of a large portion of mankind. The tireless efforts of His Holiness to alleviate the lot of the persecuted, the hunted and the outcast are also known to us. We are certain His Holiness is aware of the deep feeling of abhorrence aroused in the American people by the mass deportations, persecutions, enslavement and slaughter in the Balkans, Czechoslovakia, France, Germany, Norway, Poland and elsewhere. We are confident that His Holiness is also aware of the deep concern of the Government of the United States relative to these reversions to usages of ancient barbarism and of the constant effort to prevent their recurrence which it has made.

We believe it is appropriate, because of the common concern of the Holy See and the Government and people of the United States with such matters, to call to the Holy See's attention the apparently authentic reports that the present authorities in Hungary have undertaken to persecute the 800,000 Jews in Hungary and are planning their mass slaughter both in Hungary and after deportation to Poland merely because they are Jews. The authorities and people of Hungary have been warned by the Government of the United States of the material consequences that the perpetration of such inhuman acts of barbarism will entail. It is both timely and fitting we believe that the moral values involved and the spiritual consequences that must flow from indulgence in the persecutions and mass murder of helpless men, women and children be brought to the attention of the Hungarian authorities and people. We earnestly hope, therefore, that His Holiness may find it appropriate to express Himself on this subject to the authorities and people of Hungary, great numbers of whom profess spiritual adherence to the Holy See personally by radio through the Nuncio and clergy in Hungary as well as through a representative of the Holy See who might for that purpose be specially dispatched to Hungary."[1]

Monsignor Tardini's Memo: 25-6-44.
Seen by the Holy Father.

---

[1] See FRUS 1944, I, pp. 1068–69. Arthur D. Morse, in *While Six Million Died,* gives another version of this communication, under another date. This, according to him, was not forwarded.

No. 253, p. 341

Archbishop Griffin of Westminster to Cardinal Maglione

Telegram no. 548 (A.E.S. 4376/44)   London, July 3, 1944, 11 h. 48
rec'd, July 10, 13 h.
Request for intervention on behalf of Hungarian Jews.

Have been requested by World Jewish Congress[1] to support their appeal to Holy Father to intervene on behalf of Hungarian Jews.[2]

---

[1]See no. 249.

[2]Answered on July 14 by telegram no. 179 (A.E.S. 4376/44), assuring that the "Holy See even through Papal Nunciature Budapest has left nothing undone and is still doing everything possible to alleviate sorrowful plight all those who are suffering on account nationality or race."

No. 272, pp. 358–59

The National Jewish Welfare Board to Pope Pius XII

No number (A.E.S. 6512/44, orig.)   New York, July 21, 1944
Acknowledgment of Pope's efforts on behalf of Italian Jews.

As freedom is being won back for the oppressed peoples of Europe, word comes to us from our army chaplains in Italy telling of the aid and protection given to so many Italian Jews by the Vatican and by priests and institutions of the Church during the Nazi occupation of the land. We are deeply moved by these stirring stories of Christian love, the more so as we know full well to what dangers many of those exposed themselves who gave shelter and aid to the Jews hunted by the Gestapo.

From the bottom of our heart we send to you, Holy Father of the Church, the assurance of our unforgetting gratitude for this noble expression of religious brotherhood and love. We glory in this bloodless victory over the forces of evil that are bent on uprooting religion's eternal teachings of the sacredness of life and the oneness of humanity under God. It is our fervent prayer that your example, your influence and your intervention may yet save some of the remnant of the Jews in other lands who are marked down by the Germans for murder and extinction, and we pray that just as liberty has been restored to the Eternal City, so may freedom very soon be restored to all mankind. Then, with all men rescued from human tyranny, they may once more serve their fellow men and the God of all mankind in love, in freedom and in enduring peace.

No. 273, p. 359

The World Jewish Congress to Cardinal Maglione
Telegram, no number (A.E.S. 4955/44)   London, July 21, 1944
                                                          rec'd July 24
Thanking the Holy See for its intervention in Hungary, a final appeal to Regent Horthy is requested.

World Jewish Congress gratefully conscious His Holiness aid behalf sorely afflicted and menaced Jews Hungary which has been followed by offer of Regent of Hungary secure release certain categories of Jews particularly children. His Holiness' efforts bring us new hope at eleventh hour of saving from death surviving remnants of decimated European Jewry and gives solace our persecuted brethren at moment of their present extinction. In expressing gratitude for Holy Father's noble humanitarian work we would respectfully and earnestly request his continued aid in urging Regent of Hungary speedily and practically carry out his offer by arranging quickest release greatest number of Jewish children and adults for whom sanctuary will be prepared and found.[1]

---

[1] See No. 281.

No. 291, pp. 374–75

The Secretariat of State to British Minister Osborne
(A.E.S. 4970/44, draft)   Vatican, August 7, 1944
Intervention on behalf of civilian internees in Egypt.

The Secretariat of State of His Holiness presents its compliments to His Excellency the British Minister to the Holy See and begs to call to his attention the situation of the civilian internees in Egypt. There are still about three thousand men interned in Egypt the vast majority of whom are of Italian nationality.[1]

Internment has lasted many years and has resulted in very grave financial, social and moral difficulties amongst the families resident in Egypt. Active hostilities between Great Britain and Italy have long ago ceased. At the present stage of the war it is therefore suggested that the changed conditions are such as to make possible a general act of clemency which might not some months ago have recommended itself to the authorities responsible for military security.[2]

His Excellency will understand that the Holy See is actuated in making such a request by motives of a humanitarian and religious order. Wherever it is possible, no matter what the race or the religion of those suffering from the consequences of the war, it has been and is the Christian policy of the Holy See to intervene in the sense of mercy and clemency.

It is confidently felt that His Majesty's Government will welcome this opportunity of restoring to complete liberty these three thousand men still interned in Egypt. They are practically all of them men capable of working and living as useful members of the community. In fact the Holy See is aware of what His Majesty's Government has already done for the useful employment of several thousands of ex-prisoners and ex-internees. For moral, social and financial reasons it is particularly the civilian internee who needs honourable employment in order to reestablish his family after the long sufferings of the War.

It is felt by the Holy See that the intervention of His Majesty's Government would be sufficient to enable them to obtain release from internment and employment in accordance with their aptitudes.

Whilst realizing the wartime preoccupations of His Majesty's Government, the Secretariat of State nourishes the firm certainty that its urgent request for an act of clemency towards these internees will meet a favourable response from His Majesty's Government.[3]

---

[1] The Italian Ambassador thanked the Secretariat of State, Memo No. 269 of August 6, for the care given the Italian internees in Egypt (A.E.S. 4960/44).

[2] In a memo of August 7, the Secretariat of State requested the liberation of Italian priests and religious interned in Egypt (A.E.S. 49979/44).

[3] The response, dated August 13 (77/10/44; A.E.S. 5809/10/44) assures that "internment policy in Egypt has been dictated by the behaviour of the internees and by consideration of security. It has never been more harsh than these factors demanded; it has been constantly under review, and it has been relaxed greatly in conformity with changes in the situation."

No. 298, p. 380

The Archbishop of New York Spellman to Pope Pius XII
No number (A.S.S. 1944 Varia 1246 autogr.)

Rome, August 12, 1944

Recommendation of the Under-Secretary to the Minister of War Patterson and suggestions for an audience.

Judge Patterson[1] who will have the honor of an audience with Your Holiness tomorrow morning has been in charge of all the war production program of the American Government. He is Under-Secretary of State for war and his assistant, General Somervell,[2] will also accompany him to the audience. Judge Patterson is a very quiet type of man, of few words, but he is very close to President Roosevelt. Therefore I would, in all humility, suggest that Your Holiness speak most frankly with the Judge, explaining the needs of the Italians and the hopes of saving them for the family of nations, of the dangers and tragedies if the Italians do not get work with which to gain honestly their daily bread. Italy has been conquered but it can be saved and sincerely won to the Allied cause with justice, with understanding and with reasonable help or it can be lost to anarchy and chaos if she does not have help to help herself. I would suggest talking to Judge Patterson exactly as if talking with the President, and I would ask the Judge to bring Your Holiness's message to the President.

Monsignor Montini's Memo:
Received in audience 13-8-44.

---

[1] Robert P. Patterson, Under-Secretary of War.
[2] Brehon B. Somervell.

No. 305, pp. 389–94

Roncalli, the Apostolic Delegate in Istanbul, to Hirschmann,
Attaché of the United States Embassy
No. 4627 (Arch. Delegation, draft)   Istanbul, August 18, 1944
Information on the charitable work of the Delegation on behalf of Jews.

I hope you will not regard my delay in answering your letter and questionnaire[1] of August 1, as an indication of my lack of interest in your humanitarian work. The many requests for the charitable intervention of the Apostolic Delegation in connection with the recent political events in Turkey[2] have prevented an earlier reply.

I trust you will find the enclosed answers[3] satisfactory and I repeat that I am always ready to help you in your charitable work as far as in my power and as far as circumstances permit.

Enclosure
Reply to the Questionnaire
Presented to the Apostolic Delegation
by Mr. Ira A. Hirschmann on August 1, 1944

1. Because of the purely religious character of its mission and of the lack of official contact with the Diplomatic Corps, the Apostolic Delegation in Istanbul has no information regarding the present situation of the Jewish people in Hungary apart from that received from the Jewish Agency for Palestine and from the daily newspapers. The enclosed copy[4] of the recent legislation of the Hungarian Government on this matter was the only communication received from the Hungarian Legation in Ankara on this subject.

2. a) At the request of the Jewish Agency for Palestine and of Chief Rabbi Herzog, the Apostolic Delegation urged the Papal Secretariat

of State to do all in its power to save the Jews in Hungary. The Secretariat of State replied that this was already being done and that the Apostolic Nuncio in Budapest was actively engaged in the same work.[5]

b) The Apostolic Delegation has forwarded by diplomatic courier several thousands of "Immigration Certificates" destined for Jews in Hungary. These were delivered to the persons concerned by the good offices of the Apostolic Nunciature in Budapest and the same Apostolic Nuncio later informed that those certificates had enabled their owners to escape transportation and to obtain the necessary permissions for Emigration.[6]

3. The telegrams of July 6th[7] were merely further representations to the Papal Secretariat of State to intervene on behalf of the Jews in Hungary and Rumania. The actual text of these telegrams may not be revealed without the special permission of the Vatican authorities.

4–5. It is not the intention of the Apostolic Delegation to make any further representations on behalf of the Jewish people in Hungary: the only means of doing so is through the Papal Secretariat of State and it seems certain the Vatican has done and is doing its best, both directly and through the Apostolic Nuncio in Budapest, to ameliorate the conditions of the oppressed peoples. The Apostolic Delegation in Istanbul is always willing to recommend particular documents which may be useful. It is also willing to recommend particular cases to the special care of the Apostolic Nuncio, as has been done for example, in the case of Rabbi Salomon Halberstan.[8]

6. There is no evidence that the Vatican has been instrumental in procuring special treatment for persons who are Jewish by definition but Christians by faith. The dispositions, however, promulgated by the Hungarian Government on July 8th (see copy enclosed) do distinguish between Jews in religion and converted Jews.[9]

7. In years past, the Holy See, in agreement with the respective Governments, was able to obtain Immigration visas for some of the South American countries for limited numbers of Italian and German Jews.[10] The Apostolic Delegation is unable to state whether any such projects are now in prospect.

8. In the present circumstances it would seem that the only assistance which the Apostolic Delegation can render in facilitating the emigration of Jews is in forwarding by courier the Immigration Certificates.

9. The Apostolic Delegation has already made the desired inquiry and shall communicate immediately the reply of the Apostolic Nuncio in the matter.[11]

10. Owing to the political nature of the accusations brought against the persons mentioned in the lists, the Apostolic Delegation feels that it is not in a position to take any action in the matter. Such representations would be better made directly to the Governments concerned through the

medium of the American Embassy at the Vatican and the Papal Secretariat of State.[12]

---

[1] Archives of the Apostolic Delegation in Istanbul, no. 4627.

[2] On August 2nd, Turkey broke diplomatic relations with Germany.

[3] See Enclosure I.

[4] Unpublished.

[5] See no. 249, note 1.

[6] In his book, *Caution to the Winds* (New York, 1962, pp. 179–85), M. Hirschmann, refers to the same communication of August 18, making the Apostolic Delegate Monsignor Roncalli speak about the "baptismal certificates." Rather, as one can see, these were "immigration certificates," of the Jewish Agency for Palestine, represented by Chaim Barlas in Istanbul. Especially in Budapest, these became a kind of Jewish Habeas Corpus. On August 16, Roncalli sent these certificates to Nuncio Rotta (Delegation Archives, no. 4626), stating: "Since the package of 'Immigration Certificates' sent in May contributed towards saving the Jews for whom they were designated, I also accepted from the 'Jewish Agency for Palestine' these three packages of certificates, which I am forwarding to you, asking you to give them to the addressee, that is, Mr. Milkos (sic) Krausz [Moshe Kraus, secretary in Budapest for the Jewish Agency]." This mistake was used by Arthur D. Morse in *While Six Million Died*, cit., pp. 365–66.

[7] Unidentified.

[8] Unpublished.

[9] See no. 265, note 6. Here is an excerpt: "...the following was agreed upon for Jews:

1. Sending baptized Jews to work abroad has ceased.

2. a) Special administration of baptized Jews was given to a "Council of Baptized Jews," constituted on July 6, 1944; b) Up until August 1st, baptized Jews will remain in the country, but it is ordered that they be separated from non-Jews; c) They will have every possibility to practice their religion.

3. a) The facilities ordered for domiciled Jews in Budapest will be extended to baptized Jews abroad; b) a revision about baptized Jews serving in the work force in Germany is envisioned.

4. As soon as possible, who is to be considered a converted Jew will be settled, not only for ages 16 to 60, but for Jews of all ages.

5. Jews who are not converted serving in work companies in Hungary will be replaced by baptized Jews.

6. Converted Jews will be authorized to quit working on Sundays and feast days at an hour that will permit them to satisfy their religious obligations.

7. Exempted from wearing the Jewish star are: a) members of priests' families of Christian sects (parents, brothers and sisters, spouses and infants of Protestant pastors); b) those wearing ecclesiastical-papal decorations); c) members of the Order of the Holy Sepulcher."

[10] See *Actes* 6, no. 419, p. 524; *Actes* 9, no. 492, p. 637.

[11] The investigation requested, in no. 9: "Would Your Excellency feel free to inquire of the Apostolic Delegate in Budapest whether, by his presence as an observer of events, he might ascertain that the Hungarian government abides by the representations it has made in its recent announcement through the International Red Cross of its intention to initiate certain ameliorating conditions in its treatment of Jewish people in Hungary?"

[12] Hirschmann had sent a list of persons in Rumania and Hungary who were concerned for political reasons.

No. 323, pp. 417–18

The Secretariat of State to M. Amery
(A.E.S. 5836/44, draft)   Vatican, September 15, 1944
Request for information on prisoners of war and internees.[1]

1. There is no news about the transfer of many Italian prisoners of war to Australia. The exact number and addresses of these is unknown. It would be very useful to secure a list of these Prisoners of War.

2. With reference to such a transfer, it is requested that the prisoners of war who are still in India be sent to camps where the conditions of climate, milieu and hygiene are more suited to needs of these prisoners.

3. Many missionaries of Italian and German nationality were interned at the beginning of the war. It is requested that at least the Italian missionaries be left free in their residences. As to the Germans, it would be necessary to secure for them a way of living in keeping with their priestly and religious status.

----

[1] These were the points mentioned by the Pope to Minister Leopold C. Amery, of India, during an audience on this day. The text was sent by the Secretariat of State. A second memo (unpublished), prepared by the Congregation for the Propagation of the Faith on ecclesiastical students of India and Ceylon in Rome, desiring to return to their country. In the response of November 28 addressed to "India Office, Whitehall, London," M. Amery explained the dispositions taken by the authorities in India (A.E.S. 5836/44, unpublished).

No. 337, pp. 429–30

Pope Pius XII to United States Ambassador Taylor
(A.E.S. 7853/44, draft)   Vatican, October 4, 1944
The Pope supports and encourages the North American Agency for the help given to the Italians.

It was with real pleasure that We read Your Excellency's letter of September 18th,[1] in which on behalf of President Roosevelt and American Relief for Italy Inc., Your Excellency very kindly expressed appreciation of Our encouragement of the "National Agency for the Distribution of Relief Supplies for Italy."[2]

Constantly animated as We are by the resolve to avail Ourselves of every occasion to alleviate the sad consequences of a conflict which, alas, We were unable to prevent, We are most happy to give Our fullest support to an organization that has been set up with the object of bringing help to one of the peoples most severely tried by the war; all the more so because the elements constituting this National Agency give every reason for confidence in its lofty ideals and thorough efficiency. Indeed information already reaching Us affords gratifying proof of the earnestness of its generous, zealous leaders. This confidence has now been increased by the assurance Your Excellency gives that American Relief for Italy Inc., has accomplished much and we express the hope that, under the able and enlightened leadership of Your Excellency, other governmental and benevolent organizations will lend their hearty cooperation to further the most praiseworthy aims of this National Agency.

While then We implore the most plentiful blessings of God on the united efforts of all concerned with these noble enterprises, We voice the prayer that the work already begun may develop and grow apace and that it may serve to offer suffering peoples an unmistakable testimony of the active presence in the world of that Christian charity without which justice would be inadequate to ensure for mankind the inestimable gift of peace.

We are happy on this occasion to renew the expression of Our sincere good wishes to Your Excellency.

---

[1] See no. 326, note 3.
[2] See no. 326, note 4.

No. 355, p. 444

The Secretary of the Jewish World Congress Easterman to Pope Pius XII
Telegram. no. 996 (A.E.S. 6915/44)

London, October 14, 1944, 16 h. 35
rec'd October 16, 11 h. 30

Request for intervention on behalf of Hungarian Jews.

Desperate appeals reaching us save surviving Jews in Hungary.[1] Germans now preparing carry out plans deporting three hundred thousand men, women, children. Your Holiness intervention by public call in name of humanity may avert this appalling tragedy. We are sure our ill-fated innocent people will not appeal in vain for utmost and urgent last hour efforts save them from doom.[2]

---

[1] See no. 321, notes.
[2] See no. 362.

No. 357, p. 446

Memo by Monsignor Tardini
(A.E.S. 6915/44, autogr.)   Vatican, October 18, 1944
The Holy See's efforts on behalf of the Jews.

Today Mr. Taylor[1] was accompanied to the audience by a U.S. Representative[2] who asked His Holiness many questions (Can you imagine how much a woman who belongs to Parliament speaks!). Mr. Taylor gave the Holy Father copy of a telegram from London about the Jews.[3]

The responses of the Holy See must be complete and heartfelt. To say simply "we will do all that is possible" seems like bureaucratic coldness. Even though little may be obtained, the Holy See must demonstrate its interest.[4]

---

[1]Roosevelt's personal representative.

[2]Mrs. Edith Nourse Rogers, Republican Congressional representative from Massachusetts.

[3]From the World Jewish Congress, no. 355.

[4]On October 31 Taylor transmitted the weekly report to the director of the Committee for Refugees in Washington. It read: "I also want to pay tribute to many non-Jewish groups and individuals who have shown a true Christian spirit in their quick and friendly reaction in support of the helpless of Europe. This help has come from both Protestant and Catholic organizations. The American Friends Service Committee and the Unitarian Service Committee have made important contributions, as have other Protestant groups. The record of the Catholic Church in this regard has been inspiring. All over Europe, Catholic priests have furnished hiding places and protection to the persecuted. His Holiness, Pope Pius XII, has interceded on many occasions on behalf of refugees in danger. In this country, too, we have received help from Catholic leaders. At a most critical point in the Hungarian situation, Archbishop Spellman wrote a truly impressive supplication to the Catholics of that country to protect and help the Jews. This moving statement was broadcast in Hungarian, and reprints of it were dropped over Hungary" (A.E.S. 7125/44). See the same testimony, a year later, in the "Final Summary Report" of the War Refugee Board of September 15, 1945. See no. 117.

No. 396, p. 484

United States Ambassador Taylor to the Secretariat of State
Memo no. 267 (A.E.S. 7627/44)   Rome, November 15, 1944
Intervention for foreign Jews in Slovakia.

The Personal Representative of the President of the United States of America to His Holiness the Pope presents his compliments to the Secretariat of State of His Holiness and has the honor to transmit herewith the substance of an urgent telegram received from the Department of State at Washington, concerning the welfare of Jews in Slovakia who claim nationality of the United States and of other Republics of America:

"November 11, 1944. The State Department has received information that German authorities in Slovakia have begun evacuation from a camp at Marianka of Jews who claim nationality of the United States[1] and of other Republics of America. It is reported that Auschwitz is the destination of the persons being removed. Will you please request the Swiss to inform the German Government that the Government of the United States urgently expects to obtain assurances that no action has been taken by the German authorities in Slovakia which deprived claimants of citizenship in the United States of any rights to which they are entitled. If the rights have been deprived any of the claimants of citizenship in the United States or if they have been removed from Slovakia to other areas under German control, the names of the persons concerned and information concerning their whereabouts and welfare should be provided by the German Government. Please telegraph developments."

In transmitting the foregoing information to the Secretariat of State of His Holiness it is suggested that the Holy See may wish to request its Apostolic Nunciature at Bratislava to give this information to the local authorities and express expectation that the persons released to them by the German authorities will be given humane treatment.[2]

---

[1] See no. 345.
[2] See no. 402. Answered on November 26 (no. 406).

No. 398, pp. 485–86

The Secretariat of State to Ambassador Taylor
(A.S.S. 87033/S, draft)   Vatican, November 17, 1944
Request on behalf of Italian prisoners interned by the Allies in Italy.[1]

It has been reported that there are at present time about 10,000 Italian Prisoners of War who are rendering service to various units of the Allied Armed Forces.

The special interest of the Holy See has been requested on behalf of these prisoners in view of the fact that they are in the position of being prisoners within the confines of their own national territory which has, moreover, now been declared free and subject to Italian national authority.

It would be an act of real generosity if a free status were to be given to these prisoners who could then still continue to render service even after they had been granted this freedom.

Monsignor Montini's Memo:
14-12-44. Entrusted to Monsignor McGeough[2] for Ambassador M. Taylor.

[1]Request made after an appeal by General Pietro Gazzera, High Commissioner for prisoners of war, sent on November 7. On January 15, 1945, Monsignor Montini was able to communicate, after information from Taylor, that Washington was still waiting for a counter-proposition from the Italians.

[2]Monsignor Joseph McGeough, of the Archdiocese of New York (1903–70), in the service of the Secretariat of State; later, Representative of the Holy See in Ethiopia and in South Africa. Since 1960, Titular Bishop of Emesa.

No. 418, pp. 512–13

Monsignor Tardini to Cicognani, Apostolic Delegate in Washington
Telegram no. 2045 (A.E.S. 8100/44)   Vatican, December 14, 1944
The Holy See's efforts on behalf of Slovak Jews.

Apostolic Nunciature Berlin solicitously interested on behalf of Jews relating to Your Excellency's telegram 2466,[1] dated sixth of month[2] stating German Government responded that since these Jews are citizens of South American Republics they have their own powerful protection.

Regarding Slovak Jews, the Holy See has repeatedly and in many ways tried to help them both directly and through the Apostolic Nunciature Bratislava, inviting the Slovak Episcopate to develop more intense activity.[3] Then, recently, once again this Slovak Legation expressed its vivid regrets about the measures adopted and, in particular, for the transfer of Jews from the territory of the Republic, contrary to assurances given.[4]

The above-mentioned Legation, with memo of the fifth of the month,[5] answered that the Slovak Government protested, however in vain, with the German authorities against such transfer and that the German authorities should have informed the Slovak Government that Jews having American passports could be exchanged with United States citizens and that until they arrive in Germany, those Jews would remain on German territory and would be (according to the memo) treated in a suitable manner.[6]

[1]November 17, 1944 (A.E.S. 7694/44) concerning assistance to Jews deported to Germany.

[2]This is telegram no. 367, December 5 (A.E.S. 8100/44). See no. 375, note 3.

[3]See no. 382, no. 402, no. 406.

[4]See no. 403.

[5]See no. 403, note 4.

[6]Cicognani communicated this information to Stettinius on December 16 (581/42), who responded on December 26, 1944: "The continuing efforts of the Holy See and the Apostolic Nuncio in Berlin and Bratislava on behalf of persecuted Jews are most gratifying to the agencies of this government concerned with this difficult problem and I desire to express the appreciation of the Department of State to the Holy See and to you for these persistent humanitarian activities" (Arch. Delegat. Washington). In return, the Chief Rabbi Hertz wrote to Godfrey, on 5-1-45: "All the deeper is our

appreciation of the sympathy that His Holiness the Pope, and all those associated in the leadership of the Vatican, have shown in the fate of our doomed brethren. The whole House of Israel will be ever mindful of the many and persistent efforts that have been made by Roman Catholic authorities to rescue Jews threatened with barbarous murder. I should be deeply grateful if you would kindly convey to His Holiness our warmest expressions of lasting gratitude" (Archives Apost. Deleg. London).

No. 443, p. 535

Ambassador Taylor to Monsignor Tardini
No number (A.E.S. 484/45, orig.) Rome, February 1, 1945
Request for Pope's intervention on behalf of Jews.

We have received the enclosed telegram from London[1] having relation to the reported annihilation of Jewish people remaining in German occupied territories.

The Marchioness of Reading,[2] President of the British Section World Jewish Congress, requests that His Holiness through channels which He may find available use His influence to prevent further cruel and inhuman treatment of the Jewish people. We also urge this intervention and bespeak a more Christian and humane attitude toward this unfortunate race.[3]

Monsignor Tardini's Memo:
2-2-45. To review...To suggest...
Monsignor Dell'Acqua's Memo:
February 2, 1945. It is well known that little can be obtained from the German government for the Jews.

------

[1] This telegram, dated January 26, 1945 (A.E.S. 484/45), also announced that a similar request had been made of the International Red Cross for application of the 1929 Geneva Convention and of the 1934 Tokyo project.

[2] Wife of the Marquis Gerald Rufus Isaac, President of the English Section of the Jewish World Congress (cf. *Lexikon des Judentums,* col. 652).

[3] Response to Taylor of February 7, 1945 (A.E.S. 484/45), that the Holy See had asked the Nunciature in Berlin to intervene in this regard with the German government.

No. 460, p. 551

The Secretariat of State and the British Legation
(A.S.S. 90430/SA, draft) Vatican, March 2, 1945
Return of Italian civilians from Albania.

The Secretariat of State of His Holiness presents its compliments to His Britannic Majesty's Legation and takes the liberty to recommend the following matter to the latter's kind attention and consideration.

The Secretariat of State has been reliably informed that efforts are being exerted, with some considerable hope of success, to effect the repatriation of all Italian women, children and sick persons from Albania.[1]

With a view to furthering this very worthy cause, the Secretariat of State warmly recommends it to the good offices of His Majesty's Legation in the confident hope that the charitable project may soon be realized.[2]

----

[1] An office memo of January 19 (A.S.S. 90430) concerning about 50 persons of the National Bank of Albania in Tirana, states: "Spoke to an important person of the Italian Foreign Ministry, who had already been informed about matters. What now remains is: a) inform the interested party; b) study if steps should be taken for all Italians in Albania (cf. Report of Monsignor Nigris); and, for this particular case appeal to the Allies."

And Montini added: "Inform the Bank of our interest. Arrange for entry of all women and children."

[2] A similar memo was addressed to Taylor.

No. 461, p. 551

Notes of the Secretariat of State

(A.S.S. 90445, SA, orig.)　　　　　　　　　　　　　　　Vatican, March 3, 1945

The Holy See's attitude regarding the postwar situation.

I received Mr. Conway's[1] telephone call at the Allied Communications Center, via 23 Aprile, Saturday, March 3, at 5:15 P.M. Mr. Conway had prepared eight questions (approved by the American censors) on which he was anxious that the Holy Father offer some comment. He asked if he might not be put into direct contact with His Holiness. When he realized that this would not be possible, he asked if I might offer some comment. I replied that, if he wished, he could read the questions to me and that if there were any comment to be made I would let him know later by cable. Then he posed the following questions:

1. Whether His Holiness has any ideas regarding greater cooperation between the United States and the Vatican for postwar organization and postwar peace.

2. How are conditions in Italy and what might the United States do to ameliorate conditions there?

3. Has the Holy Father any comment to make on the Yalta results so far announced by Roosevelt and Churchill?[2]

I expressed appreciation of this thoughtfulness in making this transatlantic call (the second call made since the resumption of service) and added that if there were any comment to be made on his questions I would inform him of it by cable.

Perhaps it would be well to send the attached cablegram.[3]

[1]Mr. Robert Conway, of the *New York Daily News*. These memos were received through Carroll.

[2]The Yalta Conference with Churchill, Roosevelt, and Stalin on February 11, 1945.

[3]A telegram to Conway signed by Carroll (A.S.S. 90445) stated: "No comment here at present regarding matters proposed in interesting telephone conversation. Kindest personal regards." But the text approved by Tardini and sent on March 7 (no number) is as follows: "Offer following comment on question proposed in interesting telephone conversation: 1) Vatican willing and anxious all times afford fullest cooperation any undertaking aimed at establishing just and enduring peace and at advancing the welfare of human society. Question 2)Vatican, deeply concerned over tragic fate of poor unfortunate victims of war everywhere, would view with particular satisfaction and appreciation any efforts expended towards improving their lot and towards providing them with possibility of decent livelihood. Question 3) No comment."

No. 466, pp. 557–59

The Apostolic Delegate Cicognani to Monsignor Tardini

Rap. no. 718/45 (A.E.S. 2712/45, orig.)   Washington, March 9, 1945

Report on the conditions of Poland occupied by the Russians.

Yesterday Mr. Waclaw Bitner, Esq. (Attorney, Director of the Polish Catholic Press Agency, 2 East 65th Street, New York, 21, N.Y.), came to the Delegation to present the attached document.[1]

Miss Bytniewska Ir., who prepared it, was part of a secret Polish organization ("Polish Underground"), succeeded in fleeing from Poland and is now in New York. Before leaving the country, she was able to see His Excellency, Archbishop Sapieha, of Cracow.[2] Unable to write in that difficult moment, he confided his appeal to the bishops of the United States verbally to her. She has recorded his words and his thought with great accuracy. Because Russian troops now occupy Cracow,[3] she requests that you do not mention the Archbishop's name.

I have already used and will continue to use this document in my conversations with bishops.

Monsignor Tardini's Note:

31-3-45, V[isto] S[anto] P[adre]. [Seen by the Holy Father.]

Enclosure
Archbishop Sapieha's Appeal to American Bishops and to the Bishops and Clergy of the Catholic World

Unable to send this appeal by mail or wire, and being cut off from the Apostolic See and the world, I am entrusting it to a lieutenant of the Polish

Underground Army to be communicated to the Bishops and Catholic Clergy of America, to Catholic Poles abroad and to Catholics the world over.

In the name of God the Lord and His Church, in the name of justice and humanity I implore you to appeal to all Catholics of your country and to your competent government authorities—to defend the Christians and the whole population of Poland against acts of violence, deportations and executions as practiced actually in Poland by the Soviet occupants.

I emphasize it quite particularly that this Bolshevik tide is endangering the entire Christian world, and that contrary to promises and to information from Soviet sources, the Church and Christianity in Poland are being utterly and cynically exterminated by the Bolsheviks.

In order of giving you a picture of what is actually going on in Poland, I give you herewith a few facts and figures concerning the events which occurred in December and in the first half of January:

1.   417 priests from the Lublin district have been deported into the interior of Russia. The Lublin Theological Seminary has been liquidated.

2.   Twelve priests, professors of the Lublin University, have been executed by the Bolsheviks.

3.   The monastery of the Capuchin Fathers in Lublin has been liquidated.

4.   It is being reported in the Tarnow district that the Bolsheviks are closing churches and parochial schools. The teaching of religion in public schools has been forbidden.

5.   Children of school age are being deported into the interior of Russia. From the vicinity of the city of Tarnow alone, eight hundred children have thus been deported.[4]

Having no possibility of communicating with the Vatican in the name of all tortured Poles, I appeal to the American Bishops to exert all their efforts in behalf of Poland, the victim of unspeakable wrongs and persecution and to communicate the contents of this appeal of mine to the Holy Father. I appeal simultaneously to the Catholic Poles and to Americans of Polish origin to do their utmost in supporting our President and our Government in London, and to devote their best efforts to maintain Catholic institutions abroad and in Poland. I have no certitude whatever as to the possibility of maintaining in the future mutual communications with the rest of the world, and of informing you of further developments in Poland.

---

[1] See Enclosure.

[2] Adam S. Sapieha (1867–1951), Archbishop of Cracow from 1925.

[3] The city of Cracow was occupied by the Russian army on January 19. See no. 436, n. 3.

[4] A note by the Polish Ambassador reveals statistics of Polish children deported to the URSS, statistics established by the Ministry of Foreign Affairs that gave these figures: Evacuated to Iran, 15,000; deceased in URSS, 40,000; remaining in URSS (according to the registers),

77,834; remaining in URSS (but not registered), 7,000. Total 139,834. (Note of 7–9–44, A.S.S. 83636).

No. 478, p. 569

Monsignor Montini to Reverend Landi[1]

(A.S.S. 92641/SA, draft)   Vatican, April 16, 1945

Assistance offered to the Pope by American Catholics to support his charitable works.

Amongst the countless appeals made to the Holy Father for His charitable assistance in cases of dire need, there are to be noted, especially, numerous requests for clothing and shoes addressed directly to the Common Father by persons who have been deprived of even these basic needs by the tragic events of recent years.

His Holiness is making every effort to come to the assistance of these poor unfortunates, but, naturally, there are limitations imposed on Him by the fact that the material resources available can satisfy only a portion of the demand. In view of these limitations, I am taking the liberty to forward to you the enclosed specimens of the requests that are addressed to the Holy Father, daily, in great numbers. It is interesting to note in this regard that scores of these heart-rending pleas for help have already been received from one diocese alone.

The magnificent assistance of the American Catholics to the people of Italy has been a source of inspiration and consolation to all who have at heart the welfare of the human race. It is with a grateful remembrance of that assistance that I am forwarding the enclosed letters to you in the hope that it may be found possible, through your good offices, and generous efforts, to obtain, perhaps from the same sources, a measure of collaboration in this charity which is so near and dear to the paternal heart of the Common Father.

Monsignor Montini's Memo:
Seen by the Holy Father, April 17, 1945.

---

[1] The Reverend Andrew Landi (from Brooklyn), representing the "War Relief Services" of the United States Episcopacy.

No. 481, p. 572

The Secretariat of State to the British Legation

(A.S.S. 90478/SA, draft)   Vatican, April 19, 1945

Request on behalf of the Italian internees in Germany.

The Secretariat of State of His Holiness has been requested[1] to call to the attention of the competent Allied authorities the unfortunate situation of Italian military personnel interned in Germany by the authorities of that country.

It has been learned that the Allied authorities have accorded to Italian soldiers captured while fighting under the Allied Command and successively liberated by the advancing armies the status of recovered United Nations prisoners of war. For the other categories of Italians, whether military or civilian, liberated from German prisons or internment camps, instructions have been issued that they shall be considered as displaced persons and treated as such. It is urged that a general category of prisoners of war, as in the first classification, would be an efficacious means towards the alleviation of their present anomalous position with the accompanying uncertainty and preoccupation for the future fate of these soldiers on the part of their families.[2]

---

[1] By the Commissioner for Prisoners of War, General Pietro Cazzera.

[2] Osborne responded on April 21 (no. 85/2/45. A.S.S. 90478/SA) that "since the question appears to be one concerning primarily the Italian Government, a copy of the Note is being communicated to His Britannic Majesty's Ambassador for such action as he may deem desirable." The same Memo was addressed to Taylor, who responded on April 30 (no. 410, A.S.S. 90478/SA).

No. 482, p. 573

Pope Pius XII to Archbishop Cushing of Boston[1]
(A.S.S. 91186, draft)   Vatican, April 23, 1945
The Pope acknowledges the offering from the Diocese of Boston for war victims.

It has been for Us a source of intimate pleasure and consolation to receive from you, Venerable Brother, your kind greetings for the Feast of Our Lord's Nativity and the assurance of the prayerful intercession of the Clergy and Faithful of Boston being offered for Our intentions and inspired by your pastoral example and guidance.

The burden of heavy sorrow which it has been our lot to bear during the years of Our Pontificate in sharing the trials of Our countless children suffering everywhere would indeed be insupportable were it not for the sustaining heavenly graces bestowed upon Us by Divine Providence through the devout prayer of Our Catholic people throughout the world. May it be a comfort to Our beloved sons and daughters of your Archdiocese to know how greatly We appreciate their prayers, as well as an encouragement for them to continue their spiritual support in the increasing difficulties of this critical hour.

It is likewise with particular gratitude that We note the extraordinary testimony of your generosity and desire to share Our efforts to lighten, at least in some small part, the present widespread suffering as evidenced by the munificent donation which you have forwarded to Us.[2] The fact that this amount, destined by you for the Vicar of Christ, has come from the spontaneous tribute offered by the loyal Clergy and Faithful of Boston to their new Archbishop,[3] has brought us an added joy and consolation, and deserves a special expression of Our appreciation to those who contributed. It is Our wish, Venerable Brother, that you convey Our sentiments of gratitude, in pledge of which We cordially impart to them and to their Beloved Pastor, Our affectionate and paternal Apostolic Benediction.

---

[1] Monsignor Richard Cushing (1895–1970), Archbishop of Boston from 1944.

[2] On January 3, 1945, Monsignor Cushing sent the Holy Father the sum of $100,000. This arrived on March 12. A note of Montini states: "Ex Aud. SS.mi 18-3-45. Hold for the Pope's Soup Kitchens" (prot. 91.186).

[3] Monsignor Cushing succeeded Cardinal William O'Connell on September 25, 1944.

No. 487, p. 576

Monsignor Montini to Archbishop Mooney of Detroit[1]
(A.S.S. 90194/SA, draft)   Vatican, May 3, 1945
Acknowledgment of the Pope for assistance given by the Catholics of the United States.

His Holiness Pope Pius XII, who has followed with the greatest interest the noble initiative which the Bishops of the United States, through their auxiliary Organization, the "War Relief Services" of the National Catholic Welfare Conference, have so successfully undertaken to assist the suffering throughout the world, has graciously given to me the very pleasant duty of conveying to you, to Archbishops Stritch[2] and Spellman[3] and the other members of the Administrative Board this expression of His paternal appreciation.

The Holy Father has noted the vast extent of these activities embracing, as they do, so many of those countries which have been devastated by the war and left prone by the innumerable phases of human suffering produced in the course of the mighty cataclysm presently afflicting mankind. That this opportunity for giving concrete expression to the promptings of Christian charity should have been availed of so promptly and effectively manifests yet once again the practical and truly universal character of the spirit of Catholic Action in the United States and the unstinting generosity of your faithful people.

With particular satisfaction the Supreme Pontiff has learned of the charitable activity in favor of the multitudes of Polish people scattered over three continents in their enforced exile from their homeland as a result of the war. This is indeed a magnificent work and is, in very fact, a fulfillment of Our

Divine Lord's admonition to His followers to spend themselves in the works of mercy. That it is done in His name is evident to all; and that it will redound to the honor and glory of your noble country in bountiful blessings upon the Nation and upon those who have made possible the achievement of such great good, has for its guarantee the divine promise of Our Savior.

Here in Italy especially His Holiness has been afforded the opportunity of evaluating your munificent gesture of Christian charity in coming to the aid of a people so gravely afflicted by a conflict which has affected the greater part of its territory and brought in its wake misery to the most remote hamlets. The clothing collected in such large quantities together with the foodstuffs and other supplies already sent or to be shipped, has been and will be a saving boon to innumerable innocent victims; and the knowledge that these generous donations have come from the Catholics of America has been a source of profound consolation and solace to the Common Father and to the clergy and Catholic populations of Italy for it has been an unmistakable manifestation of the fraternal charity and compassion of their brethren in the United States.

As an earnest expression of His particular affection and gratitude for all that has been accomplished and for the great good which your charitable program of relief so nobly envisions for future accomplishment, His Holiness imparts from His heart to Your Excellency and your fellow Bishops of the American Hierarchy, as well as to your zealous co-laborers on the staff of the National Catholic Welfare Conference and its "War Relief Services" His paternal Apostolic Benediction.

------

[1] Monsignor Edward Mooney.
[2] Archbishop of Chicago.
[3] Archbishop of New York.

Part VI
Notes
Index

PART I

A. OVERVIEW: JUDGING PIUS XII

1. Michael Schwartz, *The Persistent Prejudice: Anti-Catholicism in America* (Bloomington, Ind.: Our Sunday Visitor, 1984), p. 246.

2. Washington, D.C.: The Catholic University of America Press, 1961.

3. New York-Toronto, 1964.

4. New York: *America*, July 18, 1964, pp. 70–73.

5. Pope John Paul II's statement during a meeting with Jewish leaders at the start of his 1987 visit to the United States.

6. Winnipeg: *Jewish Post*, November 6, 1958.

7. *Time,* December 23, 1940, pp. 38–40.

8. January 30, 1989, in a speech at the Bethesda Regional Library, Washington, D.C.

9. *30 Days*, 1998, No. 4, p. 38.

10. San Francisco: Ignatius Press, 1985.

11. Joseph L. Lichen, *A Question of Judgment: Pius XII and the Jews,* Washington, D.C.: National Catholic Welfare Conference, 1963; reprinted in *Pius XII and the Holocaust*, Milwaukee, Wisconsin: Catholic League for Religious and Civil Rights, 1988.

12. S. Hamerow, *On the Road to the Wolf's Lair: German Resistance to Hitler,* Boston: Harvard University Press, 1997, pp. 304–5.

13. London: Ruskin House, 1958.

14. Washington, D.C.: The Catholic University of America Press, 1961.

15. Edward Flannery, "A Response to Rosemary Ruether," in *Auschwitz: Beginning of an Era?,* New York: KTAV, 1977, p. 104.

16. Paulist Press, 1965; revised, 1985.

17. Nazi leaders had violated the Code of Canon Law then in force (Canons 2332 and 2343).

18. New York: KTAV, 1980, p. 209.

19. *Long Island Catholic*, August 14, 1980.

20. New York: *Jewish Forward,* March 20, 1998.

21. New York: *Catholic New York*, April 23, 1998.

22. New York: Hawthorn Books, 1967.

23. New York, October 20, 1958; reprinted in *Texas Catholic*, November 8, 1958.

24. Philadelphia: Jewish Publication Society, p. 292.

25. New Hope, Ky.: St. Joseph Canonical Foundation, 1990.

26. Rome: *Inside the Vatican*, May 1998, pp. 52–57.

27. New York: Basic Books, 1997, p. 29.

28. Washington, D.C.: St. Maximilian Kolbe Foundation, 1988.
29. April 22, 1998.
30. New York: New York University Press, 1992.
31. Rocklin, Ca.: Prima Publishing, 1997.
32. New York: William Morrow and Company, 1988, p. 11.

PART I
B. THE HISTORICAL RECORD

1. HarperCollins, 1997, Vol. 1, p. 149.
2. *Mit brennender Sorge.*
3. *The Tablet* (London), December 30, 1939, p. 748. Cf. Pius XII, *Selected Encyclicals and Addresses*. New York, Roman Catholic Books.
4. Ibid., May 18, 1940.
5. *New York Times*, December 25, 1941.
6. Ibid., "War News Summarized," August 6, 1942.
7. New Haven: Yale University Press, 1997, p. 264.
8. *Inside the Vatican*, October 1998, p. 19.
9. A.S.S. Guerra, Varia 153, orig.
10. January 5, 1943.
11. July 19, 1943.
12. In his book, *The Last Three Popes and the Jews* (New York: Hawthorn Books, 1967), Lapide points out that at least on six occasions Pius XII pleaded loudly for human brotherhood and for an end to bloodshed. The Pope mentioned Jews specifically, referring to them in unmistakable terms.
13. *Civiltà Cattolica,* 1972, Vol. 1, pp. 319–27 and pp. 454–61.
14. *30 Days,* July/August 1989.
15. *L'Osservatore Romano*, September 8, 1945.
16. Ibid., April 5, 1946.
17. Ibid., July 30, 1944.
18. March 30, 1998.
19. "A Medieval and a Modern Pope," *Washington Post*, April 1, 1998.
20. October 30, 1983.
21. San Francisco: Ignatius Press, 1996, p. 7.
22. Michael O'Carroll, *Pius XII: Greatness Dishonoured* (Dublin: Laetare Press), 1980, p. 45.
23. *Life,* November 1, 1943.
24. *Crossing the Threshold of Hope* (New York: Knopf, 1994), p. 97.
25. *Inside the Vatican*, May 1998.
26. The Catholic press in Nazi Germany and Austria was destroyed by brute force, beginning with the "Law Concerning Editors" in December 1933, and with the Amann Regulation of April 1935. By 1940, although some old

names remained, they were altered, and the substance of these once valuable Catholic publications was gone. They were no longer of use to the Church in the relentless warfare waged against her by the Nazis. Contrary to the 1933 Concordat, for example, in covering the "Immorality Trials," which were used to vilify the Church, a Catholic editor was forced to act against his conscience on pain of job loss or worse. Additional Nazi regulations appeared in February 1936 on restrictions to religious content; in October 1937 on restrictions in the purchase and distribution of periodicals; and in December 1937 on curtailing advertisements. Diocesan gazettes were subjected to Gestapo censorship and seizure. *The Tablet* of London gives the names of thirty-seven Catholic papers closed down by the Nazis (August 10, 1940, pp. 107–8). It lists thirty diocesan papers and magazines prohibited in Germany, plus all diocesan magazines in Austria, many taken over by the Nazis to serve the Party. Thus they were unreliable regarding the state of affairs in German church life (August 17, 1940, pp. 126–8; November 30, 1940, pp. 430–31). If not seized, a publication acquired a Nazi censor, appointed to insure conformity. Also listed as closed down were twenty-five other mission publications, educational journals, and youth papers. Books, calendars, defensive and apologetic works, pamphlets, leaflets, placards, spiritual works, many identified by name, were forbidden or confiscated. The attack encompassed publishing houses, such as the printers of *Mit brennender Sorge*, Pope Pius XI's anti-Nazi encyclical. Catholic libraries were closed for not having Nazi works, or for having books that were not "purged." *Klerusblatt,* the organ of diocesan associations of Bavaria, on August 28, 1937, was forbidden to publish until further notice and suppressed again in March 1940.

PART II
D. TRIBUTES TO PIUS XII'S HUMANITARIAN WORK

1. 1881–1956.
2. *Before the Dawn*, Sheed and Ward, 1954. Reprinted as *Why I Became a Catholic* (Fort Collins, Colo.: Roman Catholic Books, 1999).
3. January 5, 1964.
4. New York: Harper Perennial, 1933, p. 209.
5. New Hope, Ky.: St. Joseph Canonical Foundation, 1990, p. 9. Quote from *Figaro,* January 4, 1964.
6. San Francisco: Ignatius Press, 1990.
7. January 28, 1965.

PART II
E. EPILOGUE

1. New York: Hawthorn Books, 1967, p. 214.
2. Englewood Cliffs, N.J.: Prentice-Hall, Inc., 1976.
3. Radio Broadcast, August 24, 1939.
4. Pehle was Executive Director of the United States War Refugee Board.
5. *Washington Post*, October 14, 1998.
6. "A Debate Over Honoring Poland's Jews," December 23, 1998.
7. Ridgefield, Conn.: *Sursum Corda!*, Summer 1998, p. 49.

PART III
C. CHURCH, SHOAH, AND ANTI-SEMITISM
GENERAL NOTES

1. *Actes et documents du Saint-Siège relatifs à la Seconde Guerre Mondiale,* Libreria Editrice Vaticana, Città del Vaticano, 12 Volumes, 1965–1981. Hereinafter designated *ADSS*. Volumes 6, 8, 9, and 10 treat of the humanitarian interventions for Jews and other victims of the war years.

2. The close and trusting relations of the Jewish local leaders with the papal representative and the Holy See were particularly in evidence in Rumania, Hungary, Yugoslavia, and Slovakia. Of the international Jewish organizations engaged in rescue operations we can cite some of those most active in appealing for the interventions of the Holy See at critical moments. A partial list:

World Jewish Congress (London and New York)
American Jewish Congress
American Jewish Committee
War Refugee Board
Jewish Agency for Palestine
Union of Orthodox Rabbis of the United States and Canada
Emergency Committee to Save the Jews of Europe
Delasem (Italy)
Agudas Israel World Organization
Hijefs (Switzerland)

Joseph Hertz, Chief Rabbi of the British Empire, and Isaac Herzog, Chief Rabbi in Palestine, were also spokesmen for their own communities at this period. One reads from time to time the surprising and uninformed assertion that Pius XII was concerned "only for baptized Jews." This is a cruel misrepresentation of the universal humanitarian efforts of the Pope for all the victims of the war, without distinction of nationality, religion, or race. The organizations listed above which so readily had recourse to Pius XII and to his representatives everywhere, are the best witnesses to the contrary.

3. *ADSS* 8, p. 453; ibid., 543.

4. *ADSS* 8, pp. 443–5; ibid., 295–7; 333–4.

5. *ADSS* 9, pp. 505–6.

6. *ADSS* 9, pp. 371–72.

7. *ADSS* 10, p. 328. In some postwar writings this telegram is reduced to a simple "letter" as if not reflecting the urgency of the situation. Such an error is possible only in total ignorance of the record. In addition, the papal message was the first to arrive in Budapest in protest. Other world leaders, such as the King of Sweden, came afterwards with their admonitions.

8. *ADSS* 10, p. 462.

9. *ADSS* 9, p. 635.

10. *ADSS* 3, pp. 85–6; 1, p. 234–5.

11. *ADSS* 5, p. 672.

12. *ADSS* 5, pp. 673–5; 675–7.

13. *ADSS* 9, p. 71.

14. *ADSS* 5, p. 705.

15. Ennio di Nolfo, *Vaticano e Stati Uniti. 1939–1952.* Milano: Franco Angeli Editore, 1978, p. 193.

16. *ADSS* 8, pp. 665, 669. Cf. *Foreign Relations of the United States,* 1942, p. 775.

17. *ADSS* 6, pp. 665–6; 669–70.

18. *ADSS* 9, p. 71; *ADSS* 8, p. 758.

19. *ADSS* 9, p. 71. Cf. *Foreign Relations of the United States,* 1943, p. 912.

20. *ADSS* 7, pp. 179–80, 235–6, 237. The diplomatic papers of the Polish ambassador to the Holy See in wartime are held, in copy, by the Hoover Institution on War, Revolution and Peace, Palo Alto, California. Papée's account of his audience with the Pope on January 21, 1943, here cited in translation, is identified as 1222/SA/6, of January 23, 1943.

21. International Christian Press and Information Service (Geneva), no. 3, January 1940. "The 'Silence' of the Oecumenical Movement."

22. "Oecumenical Committee for Refugees," of which Dr. W. A. Visser't Hooft was a member.

23. *ADSS* 8, p. 597; 9, pp. 132–4.

24. Arieh Ben-Tov, *Facing the Holocaust in Budapest. The International Committee of the Red Cross and the Jews in Hungary, 1943–1945.* Dordrecht: Martinus Nijhoff Publishers, 1988, p. 136.

25. Ibid., p. 80. For the scriptural-theological meditations of Dr. Max Huber, president of the International Committee of the Red Cross, on this

moral dilemma, Cf. his short essay "The Good Samaritan" (London: Gollancz, 1945).

PART III
D. THE MYTH IN THE LIGHT OF THE ARCHIVES

1. *L'Osservatore Romano*, October 9, 1958.

2. *Actes et documents du Saint-Siège relatifs à la Seconde Guerre Mondiale*, edited by P. Blet, A. Martini, R. A. Graham, B. Schneider. Città del Vaticano: Libreria Edizioni Vaticana, 12 Volumes, 1965–1981.

3. P. Blet, *Pie XII et la Seconde Guerre Mondiale d'après les archives du Vatican*. Paris: Perrin, 1997; Mahwah, N. J.: Paulist Press, 1999 (translation).

4. R. A. Graham, "Il vaticanista falsario. L'incredibile successo di Virgilio Scattolini," in *Civiltà Cattolica*, 1973, III, 467–78.

5. Cf. *Actes et Documents*, Vol. 9, pp. 491 and 494.

6. Pius XII, "Allocuzione concistoriale" (June 2, 1945), in *AAS* 37 (1945) 159–168.

7. Thus, when we prepared the first volume, we did not know who had drafted the appeal of Pius XII for peace issued on August 24, 1939, duly corrected and approved by the Pope himself. Only further research enabled us to discover that the original author had been Monsignor Montini [B. Schneider, *Der Friedensappell Papst Pius XII. vom 24. August 1939*, in *Archivum Historiae Pontificiae 6* (1968) 415–24], though it is difficult to know which of the two authors wrote any particular part.

8. Cf. O. Chadwick, *Britain and the Vatican during the Second World War.* Cambridge: Cambridge University Press, 1986.

Index